Some Comments From Readers of
LOSERS ARE PIRATES: A CLOSE LOOK AT THE
PBS SERIES "VIETNAM: A TELEVISION HISTORY":

"The PBS series 'Vietnam: A Television History', along with some
valuable and informative materials, unfortunately includes much that
is highly tendentious and misleading. Several of us who served as
consultants to the series pointed out these serious flaws, but our
advice was largely ignored. Seen as a whole, the series will therefore
contribute very little to an accurate assessment of America's most
unpopular war. Many of the omissions, misinterpretations and
instances of bias in the PBS series are pointed out by
James Banerian in his book LOSERS ARE PIRATES, a brief
but valuable effort to try to set the record straight."

> – Guenter Lewy
> author, AMERICA IN VIETNAM
> *consultant to the PBS series*

"(LOSERS ARE PIRATES is) an interesting and useful contribution
to bring truth back to the historical record of the Vietnamese war."

> – Nguyen Ngoc Huy
> political scientist
> *consultant to the PBS series*

"The work is a vital corrective to the PBS series. The series should
not be viewed without constant reference to LOSERS ARE PIRATES.
The PBS series perpetuates misguided stereotypes of French
intellectuals regarding Communism in Vietnam.
LOSERS ARE PIRATES tells us more about the Vietnamese
and their war than the series does."

> – Stephen B. Young
> Dean, Hamline University
> School of Law
> *consultant to the PBS series*

"LOSERS ARE PIRATES is an important historical account
of the Vietnam War and the events that followed the
American involvement. It is must reading for anyone who
is a serious student of the Vietnam War."

> – Al Santoli
> Vietnam veteran
> *author,* EVERYTHING WE HAD

Losers
Are Pirates

A Close Look at the PBS Series
"Vietnam: A Television History"

Edited by James Banerian

Sponsored by
Vietnamese Community Action Committee

LOSERS ARE PIRATES:
A CLOSE LOOK AT THE PBS SERIES
"VIETNAM: A TELEVISION HISTORY"

Acknowledgement:
Excerpt from *"Little Girl in the Yellow Rain"*
by Al Santoli, Copyright 1984 by Al Santoli

Library of Congress Catalog Card Number: 85-61423

ISBN: 0-932729-01-0

Sphinx Publishing, Inc.,
4234 East University
Phoenix, Arizona 85034
(602) 437-0207

CONTENTS

PREFACE TO
THE REVISED EDITION

When Part 1 of *Vietnam: A Television History* aired on October 4, 1983, my initial reaction was simply shock. For nearly one hour that evening, my friends and I witnessed the first of a string of shows about the recent conflict in Southeast Asia produced supposedly as an "educational" series by Public Television. And yet the program contained enough misinformation to make us wonder what kind of education the viewers were supposed to be getting. Perhaps most unsettling was the experience of watching Communist Vietnamese leaders and cadres appearing on the screen along with propaganda movies being used as "historical data" without any question or debate as to their veracity. Meanwhile, countless non-Communist individuals who might have had a different view of the "Roots of War" were never heard from. It did not take us long, then, to conclude that the program was grievously biased.

In my outrage, I shot off a letter of protest to PBS and followed it up the next day with another letter after watching Part 2 of the series. This personal protest continued each week until the final episode as I attempted to point out to the producers some of the inadequacies of the series through details of each program. I was helped in this by my Vietnamese friends who were also disturbed by the series and supported my efforts to, in their words, "defend the honor of those who died for freedom."

As time went on, it became clear that many viewers were troubled by the series. These included Vietnam scholars, former American soldiers who had served in Vietnam, government officials, political commentators, and others. Scholars of the war have cited historical inaccuracies and omissions, biased presentations, and distorted interpretations that crop up throughout the production. The program seemed to be an irregular mixture of cliches and one-sided memories, causing consultant Douglas Pike to conclude: "Whatever this thing is, it is not history."

i

Vietnam veterans objected to the image they were given by a decidedly antiwar and anti-military production staff. One interviewee on the show, former prisoner of war Robinson Risner, complained that the producers had promised to let him preview his segment before the broadcast, but he never heard from them again. Looking at the way the series treats Risner, it is no wonder the producers suddenly disappeared.

Vietnamese refugees found fault with the series' content at numerous points. They felt their people were being presented in a distorted light–the South Vietnamese are shown as thieves and whores, their soldiers are described as "puppets" and mercenaries. The history of Vietnam certainly becomes skewed as Ho Chi Minh is elevated to universal heroism and the Communists monopolize all the virtue in the entire nation.

Persons who defend U.S. involvement in Vietnam get very little attention in the program, while critics are portrayed so generously that one can almost see haloes shimmering over their heads.

Some critics responded to the PBS series in articles and commentaries, not all of which are given as wide a circulation as the favorable reviews, if only because it is still fashionable to criticize, not clarify, the war. With friends' advice, I decided to go ahead and produce a book reviewing the series, presenting our ideas and relevant information that is either ignored or depreciated in the 13-hour documentary.

The information in this book comes from many sources. Among these are materials written by persons who were allegedly consultants for the series, but whose works seem to have been neglected by the producers for philosophical reasons. As well, I have relied on oral testimony from refugees and veterans with regards to their personal experiences during the war. Refugees were helpful in clarifying some aspects of Vietnamese history and culture as they pertain to this study. This book also contains excerpts from materials written in Vietnamese which also were not perused by the production crew and their supposedly objective translator. Translations which appear in this book are my own.

A segment of a story by Al Santoli, "Little Girl in the Yellow Rain", printed in *Reader's Digest,* can be found after Part 9 as one of the supplemental readings. It is being reprinted here with the author's permission. My thanks go to Mr. Santoli for his cooperation in allowing the use of his material.

Production of this book was made possible by donations from various individuals and groups within the Vietnamese refugee community living in the United States. Of particular note are the Vietnamese Community Action Committee in San Diego and a larger ad hoc committee which formed during the early months of 1984 to raise funds for this venture. I would like to thank all the sponsors in San Diego, Orange County, Los Angeles, San Francisco, San Jose, and other points in California; friends and supporters in Utah, Texas, Tennessee, Kansas, Washington State, Virginia, South Dakota, Arizona, Wisconsin, Michigan, the District of Columbia area and Canada.

During the second half of 1984, a group in Southern California calling itself the Vietnamese Studies Group contributed its valuable support to the publication and distribution of this book. This group held a formal reception to mark the introduction of the book in October of that year. Through the efforts of the Studies Group and their companions in California, the first printing of *Losers Are Pirates* received considerable distribution and future printing was made possible. Much of the credit for this success must go to Bui Binh Ban, whose energetic support helped stimulate the refugee community in Orange County to constructive action in countering the PBS film.

My work was encouraged by a large number of support letters from refugees across the country. I should note that in all the time since the PBS series first aired I have not met or even heard of a single refugee from Vietnam who defends the program. Meanwhile, many refugees have protested the broadcast of the show in San Diego, Orange County, Washington, D.C., Houston, Milwaukee, and San Jose. In an interview with the San Diego *Union* in 1983, Executive Producer Richard Ellison discounted the protests of refugees over the program, claiming they represent a "fragmented group of diverse viewpoints." I would like to take this opportunity to thank my fragmented supporters for their diverse viewpoints, which, once brought together, make a helluva lot more sense than what we saw on television for three months.

Certain individuals were particularly helpful in the production of this book, and I wish to acknowledge their assistance here.

In San Diego, my consultants included: Kieu Phong, Ha Thuc Sinh, Duong Phuc, Tran Van Luu, Vu Thanh Thuy, Le Van Khoa, and Tran Huyen Tran. Trang Kien graciously allowed us to use his facilities for the initial production of this book.

In Orange County, my advisers included: Nhat Tien, Pham Kim Vinh, and the officers and members of the ad hoc committee to support the book; Nguyen Cong Huan, editor of *Vietnam Ngay Nay*, and Do Ngoc Yen, for *Nguoi Viet* news; the Association of Former Vietnamese Educators Overseas; Do Tien Duc, Tran Thanh Truc, General Tran Van Nhut, Mai Cong, and other members of the Vietnamese Studies Group; and all other sponsors, too numerous to name.

Thanks go, as well, to Giao Chi in San Jose for his consultation, and the staff of *Dan Toc* magazine for their support.

The staff of the Complete Print Shop in Phoenix, Arizona, helped put together the final layout and printing of this edition. I must thank Bui Quang Lam and his crew for their patience and untiring efforts to make this book presentable for the public.

Several Vietnam veterans living in San Diego offered their opinions about the PBS series and gave a considerable boost to the protest of the film. I wish to express my special gratitude to them here. These individuals include: Robert Baker, Robert Bielke, Art Watson, and Robert Van Keuren. Others who gave helpful information were Dave Hill, and a group meeting in the San Diego Vet Center.

I realize that this book cannot do justice to the American Vietnam veterans I have become acquainted with during my research. This writing was done largely from the viewpoint of the Vietnamese, and from the study of readily available documents. Still, I do hope that I have reflected accurately the thoughts and feelings of the veterans I talked to. As well, I hope this book will be a challenge to some of them, namely those who find it convenient to blame the Vietnamese for their personal hurt because they have not had an opportunity to see the war from the Vietnamese perspective.

Other persons deserve thanks. Connie Bahner did much of the typing for the first edition of this book and located materials for me in the library of the University of California at San Diego. Stephen

Denney and the Indochina Project at Berkeley University provided a number of worthwhile articles concerning the series which I was able to use. Reporter Barbara Moran of the San Diego *Union* made noteworthy efforts to bridge the communication gap between Vietnam veterans and the refugees; Ms. Moran is a good example of journalism put to constructive use in the community.

While many persons have contributed to the book in one form or another, I alone accept full responsibility as editor and writer for its content and views. Individual opinions are indicated as such; general views or comments are mine and should not be attributed to any other person. I have tried to ensure the accuracy of the data presented here, spending many hours personally going through resources and checking many leads. A lot of information was rejected; a lot more might have been included. I have tried to make my presentation responsible and clear. However, I am sure that at times my feelings on this emotional topic have come out, and for this I beg the reader's indulgence.

In the months following the first broadcast of the PBS film, I received a quite limited response to my protest from the series' producers. One PBS official in Washington, D.C., suggested that my opinions are too fixed. He chided me for using "loaded language" in my letters, such as the term "Communist" which I applied to certain characters in the war. This type of language, he wrote, has "perjorative implications" that did not promote rational understanding of the issues. From this person's comments, I gather that avowed Marxist-Leninist Ho Chi Minh, who taught his people that Stalin was a hero for all humankind, should be referred to as simply a "guy" or an "individual" without any further elaboration. Readers who are uncomfortable with my loaded language should feel free to substitute for "Communist" any word they please.

Peter McGhee, the Program Manager for National Productions at WGBH in Boston, answered my letters with confessed reluctance and echoed the sentiments of his colleague noted above. He did promise to give my report of the series "the same careful consideration and expert review" used in making the documentary. Mr.

McGhee and his producers have been sent copies of my book and have yet to respond, even to acknowledge receipt of the material. Needless to say, WGBH has declined to answer any of the many arguments against the series included in this book.

Lawrence Grossman, former president of PBS and now the head of NBC, did acknowledge receiving my book, but promised he would not read it for a very long time, when he should have the "leisure" to do so. In any case, he feels that James Banerian has some "strong opinions" about the war, whereas he, Stanley Karnow, and Richard Ellison are as innocent as babes. So much for objective reasoning.

In the meantime, Reed Irvine and his organization, Accuracy In Media–a self-styled "watchdog" of the media–received a small grant from the series' biggest sponsor, the National Endowment for the Humanities, to produce a brief "rebuttal" to the 13-hour documentary. A number of articles criticizing the series have been written by scholars, commentators, veterans and other observers, dampening the image of "universal acclaim" touted by the people at PBS.

Forced to respond to their critics, WGBH has resorted to evasive tactics aimed at protecting the program's image without actually justifying what the program says. These maneuvers include making repeated statements regarding the show's self-proclaimed greatness, sending "thank you" notes to people who never supported their production, and explaining all objéctions to the film as being nothing more than the emotional outbursts of a few disgruntled expatriot Vietnamese.

As the reader will see, there is much more to the criticism than what the producers would have us believe. This book hopes to present some of the discontent expressed by persons who watched the film with a knowledgeable eye and did not like what they saw. Some of the series' consultants have spoken in support of my effort. One of them, Nguyen Ngoc Huy, a political scientist and negotiator for South Vietnam at the Paris Peace Talks, is currently engaged in translating *Losers Are Pirates* into Vietnamese and French for the edification of a larger audience.

All this is meant to suggest that there is good reason for criticizing the PBS *Television History*. Yet, in the final analysis, the readers must decide if the information being presented here is honest and worthwhile to their view of the war. I hope that in these pages I have contributed something positive to the study of Vietnam, Cambodia and Laos through the unfortunate medium of a critical review of a major history lesson.

                              – James Banerian
                                January 1985

INTRODUCTION:
REVIEWING THE WAR
IN
SOUTHEAST ASIA

1975 was a fateful year for the countries of Vietnam, Laos and Cambodia. On April 17th, the Communist Khmer Rouge took control of Phnom Penh, the capital of Cambodia as the Republican Government finally collapsed after years of fighting. Two weeks later, on April 30, the Saigon government of South Vietnam formally surrendered to the Communist forces led by Hanoi and a second country had fallen. In December of the same year, a new government was formed in Laos which gave power to the Communist Pathet Lao.

Many observers around the world viewed with relief the apparent end to the fighting in Southeast Asia. The war had lasted decades; countless lives had been lost, and the countries formerly of French Indochina suffered greatly in their introduction to the modern world. The political conflict and the military actions taken in Southeast Asia had troubled the minds and hearts of people all over the world. It seemed the time had come for peace and rebuilding.

But the killing and suffering did not stop. Millions of Cambodians were executed, tortured or starved to death by the Khmer Rouge in four years of savage "revolution". The Hmong tribespeople of Laos have become victims of an extermination campaign directed by the Vietnamese Communists utilizing chemical warfare and military attacks. Some tens of thousands of Lao have been arrested and sent to "seminar" camps where many are starved, tortured and mistreated. Vietnamese soldiers, government officials, artists, clergy and others have been confined in concentration camps scattered across Vietnam. Thousands more have been forced to live on farm labor camps and plantations in unproductive areas of their country. Hanoi has contracted with the Soviet Union to deliver laborers to Siberia to work on the Soviet oil pipeline in repayment of the war debt. The people and cultures of Cambodia and Laos are being gradually eliminated by means of a "Vietnamization" campaign involving the military occupation of the two countries, the forced migration of Lao and Cambodians from the cities which are then occupied by Vietnamese, forced intermarriage with Vietnamese, obligatory education in the Vietnamese language, the renaming of streets, villages and, in time, entire provinces with Vietnamese titles ... All three countries have been thrown into extreme poverty and oppression. Meanwhile, the fighting and subversive activities of the Vietnamese Communists have extended into Thailand.

Hordes of Southeast Asians have fled their homes as refugees since 1975. The most famous of these are the Vietnamese "boat-people", whose risky flight across the sea was given little attention by the news media until 1979 when Malaysia threatened to drive any more refugees out to sea unless the world did something about the growing number coming to her shores. The International Red Cross estimates that 300,000 boatpeople have perished on the sea, victims of rough waters, lack of provisions and attacks by pirates. Land refugees from Laos, Cambodia and Vietnam face security patrols of Vietnamese Communist and their allies, as well as bands of robbers in the unguarded areas along the Thai borders. Stories of rape, murder, robbery, detainment and torture are common among all refugee groups. And, too, life in the refugee camps offers more problems: inadequate housing, improper sanitation, food shortages, ill treatment by camp workers and guards, and the despair of never knowing when one might be accepted for settlement in another country ...   Instead of things getting better for the Southeast Asians, they are getting worse.

Here in America the war has not ended either. The dilemmas, the questions, and the uncertainty remain in the minds of those who cared about our country's involvement in that difficult war. We are concerned about the nation's strength and honor, its position in the world and directions for the future. We are troubled by our government's decisions and our military's actions and their implications in our lives now. Our anger and frustration have been bottled up inside us for nine years, ever since our historic defeat in Vietnam. We still have not learned how to deal with this reality and place it in perspective.

This is certainly true for the Vietnam veterans. For the young men and women who served during the war, the experience was perhaps the most profound one of their lives, and at the same time the one most difficult to face. Many had felt they were not receiving the support of the folks back home; when they returned to the States, they were often met with coldness or hostility. A decade or more later, they are still left with questions about themselves and the society they live in.

The war has left a bad taste in the mouths of many Americans. Few people are interested in talking about it. One can almost visualize a cloud of perplexity and shame hanging over people's heads when the subject comes up. A sinister image has been laid on us, an image of horrible mistakes, of senseless destruction, of blood on our hands. Yet, at the same time, there is a recognition of the Communist heritage in Indochina and a suggestion that claims of America's supposedly reprehensible behavior in that "immoral war" do not make sense in the context of Communist brutality. There are doubts – and perhaps, as well, the desire to finally know what really happened.

So at some time or other America must look back at the war in Southeast Asia and across the waters of the Pacific to see what is happening now in order to learn, to understand and to find some personal answers. The situation in Southeast Asia is not, and has never been, a simple matter. Southeast Asia cannot be looked at with old, fixed attitudes and idle speculation about what might have been. Instead, it must be approached with an open mind, with no intellectual restraints, otherwise it will never make sense and we will never overcome our confusion and guilt. The war and its legacy must be looked at boldly and with a critical eye neglecting no facet of its complicated form. No shallow or superficial review will satisfy our deep-seated hunger to know the truth and regain our self-esteem.

Interest in the war was beginning to reawaken in late October 1982 when a week-long series ran on a Los Angeles television station. The series was called *Vietnam: The Ten Thousand Day War* (sic) and aired two hours each night. The program was characterized by its uninhibited use of Communist propaganda film footage; dull, repetitive and uninspired production; and a rather amateurish analysis of its subject. Vietnamese residents of Southern California protested the series to the station, all to no avail as it was shown for a second time in mid-1983.

In early February 1983, a four-day conference was held at the University of Southern California with the name "Vietnam Reconsidered: Lessons From A War". The conference covered 13 topics and included films, presentations and panel discussions. The slate of panelists numbered more than 50, with a large proportion of journalists (the conference was co-sponsored by the USC School of Journalism). Only four Vietnamese were originally invited to participate as speakers; no Cambodians, Lao, or Hmong sat on the panels. American Vietnam war veterans also were not represented, although many came to make statements from the floor (after paying an admission charge). Floor discussions were heated at times, and dissatisfaction was expressed by the veterans, refugees and others. The direction the conference was intended to take might be seen in the fact that its proceedings were recorded by Harrison Salisbury, the New York *Times* associate editor who distinguished himself for sending dispatches from Hanoi based on propaganda material, not fact. It is not certain that many lessons were learned in those four days at USC, but it did become clear that eight years later the war remained an emotionally charged issue.

The PBS series, *Vietnam: A Television History*, was greeted with greater expectations. Beginning in October 1983, the program was to run for thirteen parts until the end of the year. It was to cover the so-called "American war" in Southeast Asia from its roots to its "legacy". The reputation of PBS and the fact that it is a national educational network had a lot to do with viewer expectations. Viewers anticipate more objectivity from public television than from a private television corporation and greater sensitivity to differing opinions. Futhermore, the PBS series was presented as an educational documentary, with instructional guides, audio materials and production manuals accompanying the films. The producers boasted a staff of over 50 researchers as well as materials from archival films, 300 personal interviews, and television news stories from U.S. and foreign networks. With several years of production and a multi-million dollar budget, the producers apparently felt quite confident that they were offering a significant contribution to the history of the war.

Early press reviews of the series reflected some of this confidence. One example is the article by Fox Butterfield written for the New York *Times*. Butterfield called the program "a meticulously researched and carefully balanced ... documentary that may broaden many Americans' understanding of Vietnam, if not change their opinions about the war...", adding that the series "has something to offend, and please, both hawks and doves". Similar comments were made by other reviewers and the program's alleged objectivity and balance were often noted, along with commendations for the producers who brought to the air a number of rare and curious historical documents.

Later reviews were more critical. In January, 1984, an *Accuracy In Media* (AIM) report panned the series as "The Flawed History of Vietnam". Editor Reed Irvine disputed the program's claim to balance, declaring that "the balance all too often seemed to come out balanced on the left". The AIM report focused on a few specific points, such as the series' contention that Ho Chi Minh was primarily a nationalist, the role of the American media in bringing about the fall of Ngo Dinh Diem, the incompetence of reporting during the Tet Offensive, and the series' failure to put the war into post-war perspective. Irvine was especially critical of the use of public funds in sponsoring the program.

Based on the reviews seen by this writer, approval for the series seems to come from two groups: those who opposed America's involvement in the war and others who have limited background in the history of Southeast Asia and the war. Persons in the first group find that the series confirms many of their perceptions and prejudices, thereby justifying their past anti-war attitude. If they have any complaint, it is that the series does not criticize the U.S. harshly enough. Persons in the latter group are simply not in a position to judge the overall balance and accuracy of the program. They are satisfied, since the series reflects what they learned largely through the media – a matter of the blind leading the blind.

On the other hand, the program is criticized by Vietnam scholars, government officials, military officers, Vietnam veterans, and Vietnamese refugees, who consider it a biased and inaccurate representation of the war. According to these critics, the series does not contain a balance of opinions on some essential topics nor does it necessarily give a true or complete picture of the war and what was actually happening on the field. One common complaint of refugees is the way the program uses propaganda information from Communist sources which is often inaccurate and always biased. Throughout the program Communist officials, soldiers and political cadres are interviewed without an opportunity being given to non-Communist sources to provide a balance. Serious gaps and omissions in information are noted throughout the series by Americans and Southeast Asians who were themselves personally involved in the matters being described. And, too, the overall presentation of the series gives the strong impression of a biased and non-objective attitude on the part of the producers which, these critics fear, will lead to harmful conclusions on the part of the American viewers.

More than a few Vietnamese critics of the PBS presentation have suggested the producers were politically motivated in making the series. They have theorized the producers are trying to influence public opinion in order to see that diplomatic relations are established between the U.S. and the Communist Vietnamese government and that war reparations be made to the Hanoi regime to compensate for all the damage done to the country by the U.S. during the war. Or, they say, the producers hope to convince the American public that the U.S. should not intervene in conflicts in the Middle East or Latin America in order to avoid a "second Vietnam". Some Vietnamese have even accused the series of – deliberate or not – aiding the KGB in a campaign of misinformation aimed at influencing the course of U.S. foreign policy. In any event, the series has angered and upset a lot of people and it would seem that this is not without good cause.

This book will cover separately each of the 13 parts of the series, highlighting various points of content or presentation. One or more supplementary readings follows each chapter to provide examples of the many ideas not expressed in the series which are, we feel, essential to an understanding of the war. There are two introductory chapters: a general overview of the problems in the series and an essay on journalism. Conclusions will be found at the end of the book. Also, a brief appendix comprised of some comments on the

PBS series by Vietnamese is included. Because Stanley Karnow's companion book is an important element of the Vietnam TV project, select criticisms of his *History* are included throughout the book. Karnow's bulky volume is too large for a complete review here. However, this writer feels the items chosen for criticism will suffice to indicate the overall weakness of Karnow's work.

Before we begin looking at the series in detail, it may be helpful to the reader if we point out exactly what this book is not intended to be and what its intended purpose is.

First of all, the book is *not* intended to give a comprehensive history of Vietnam or the war in Southeast Asia over the past 50 years. Our resources are limited; we do not have a multimillion-dollar budget to work with nor the time in which to respond adequately with such a massive task. We don't pretend to tell everything.

We do not defend the U.S. policy in all its shapes and forms as it coursed through the war for over thirty years. We do not deny that mistakes were made by the American government in its understanding and handling of the war. In many cases, contributors to this book have been among the first to criticize specific actions of the American government or individuals connected with it.

We do not deny that American military actions caused extensive damage to parts of Vietnam, Cambodia and Laos or that wartime violence sometimes resulted in tragic incidents or atrocities.

It is not our intention to defend the South Vietnamese government in all its actions or individuals within the government for personal actions they might have committed while they were in power. Every government in the world has its problems and South Vietnam, too, had its share. These must be looked at in context.

We do not deny that the *Television History* contains some truth in parts of its presentation. We are not interested in quibbling over details or nitpicking in order to sound off our complaints. It is only because we believe that there are major and serious errors in the program that we endeavor to bring our complaints to the public.

This critique does have a number of substantive and positive aims. These are:

— to provide some major points of argument with the producers

of the series regarding information and opinions expressed
during the course of the thirteen parts;
— to indicate places where we feel information has been mis-
represented or omitted, thus giving the viewers an inaccurate
picture of the war from its roots to its legacies;
— to provide a context for certain parts of the war's history which
we feel are superficially treated by the producers;
— to dispute the opinion that the program is objective and
balanced;
— to dispute the opinion that the program is adequately
researched and accurate;
— to express our views of one aspect of the war which is not dealt
with in the series, namely: the role of the U.S. news media in
affecting understanding of the war;
— to better inform the producers and the sponsors of the series,
as well as educators and the general public, of the realities of
the war in Southeast Asia as we see them.

A document as small as this book cannot pretend to be conclusive.
Nonetheless, it can provide a viewpoint different from that given by
the series and a forum for those who, for one reason or another, were
not permitted to speak on the television series.
We have a very special concern regarding this television series.
Even before it was shown in the United States, the program was
broadcast in Europe and other parts of the world. Marketing of the
films, videotapes and accompanying materials had already begun.
The series is intended to be used as educational material for adult-
level classes with an instructor's guide, viewers' guide, and other
accessories. Our concern is that this program is being used as a
historical document despite its serious flaws and inaccuracies.
Some Vietnamese have lamented that in a few years the program
may be shown to their children in schools, giving the children a poor
impression of their parents' role in the war and their reasons for
being in the United States. These refugees are afraid that in the
future there will be no one to dispute the information presented in
the series, that its influence will extend beyond 1983, when it was
first shown, and continue to trouble them in the future. We feel this
concern is valid and so make public our complaint about the series
and the intentions of the producers.

We, the editor and sponsors of this book, will readily admit to our own personal bias. We share the pain and anguish of those who suffer under Communism, a system which promotes the destruction of cultures and societies with a policy that expresses disregard for human rights. While millions of people live under conditions of brutal oppression, facing imprisonment, torture, exile, or other forms of abuse by Communist governments, and while citizens of Communist countries are denied the essential freedoms that are the right of all human beings, we cannot sit still, though we should enjoy the freedom they long for. Stanley Karnow and Richard Ellison may consider the Communist Vietnamese to be heroes. We do not. No doubt this attitude will be reflected in the following pages.

Now, let us look at *Vietnam: A Television History.*

BEHIND THE SCENES

Recounting history is not an easy task. If that history revolves around a war, the job is no simpler. The many events, issues and characters involved in a war are complex and often controversial. Rarely can one map out a clear transition from one point to another. Essential background information may be lacking or clouded by secrecy or the absence of crucial records. Argument and debate may cause one issue to be interpreted in several different ways. In the end, the historian is left to his or her own sense of rational judgment while sifting through data about the past to form impressions and make interpretations.

Retelling the modern history of Vietnam, Cambodia and Laos is a challenge to historians, even those who have observed the region for years or decades. An enormous amount of information has been written, filmed or taped concerning the Southeast Asian conflict, making it by far the most recorded episode in the history of humankind. However, this huge store of information may be more of a detriment to understanding the war than an aid, unless it is used with a critical eye and a fair knowledge of the fundamental issues. Careless use of such resource material can result (and already has resulted) in misinterpretation and misunderstanding of the war. Research and study are further hampered by the current nature of the two wars, which have generated strong emotions that influence viewpoints and inhibit fair judgment. The historian must take pains to avoid the traps laid by personal biases and presumptions. Caution and prudence must precede any investigation and dominate the historian's final presentation.

Despite the difficulties, one might yet hope to see a documentary or historical account of the Indochina Wars that presents the people and the issues of the wars in a fair and balanced manner. By "fair and balanced" we mean that all responsible viewpoints would be reviewed with an attitude of respectful consideration and objectivity by persons more interested in offering the facts than in proving theories. Put another way, one might hope to find a history that does not tell its audience what to think but, instead, provides the substance for intelligent reflection so that individuals may form their own opinions and draw their own conclusions. Post-war histories, while not without their disadvantages, do have the added benefit of hindsight, which, when properly applied, can enable us to see the events and outcome of the war in a clearer perspective. "Lessons" from a war may not emerge until the dust has settled, or at least until such time as we can stand back and re-examine the events without feeling the burden of immediate involvement.

It is unfortunate – if not tragic – that the PBS series *Vietnam: A Television History* neither meets the basic goals of fairness and balance nor takes advantage of post-war realities to help enlighten its audience. Like the television camera which gives the series its visual cues, the *Television History* looks at the war with a very narrow focus, pointing at specific targets while avoiding the immense environment that surrounds them. In this way, the broad perspective is missed and what the viewer sees is not necessarily a faithful reproduction of the way it was. In fact, the *Television History* strays so far off course that many Vietnamese refugees watching the program gave up in disgust after only two or three episodes.

In order to understand why the series failed so badly, it is necessary to look at the producers and examine their perspectives as they approached the history of the war.

The Beginning

According to Executive Producer Richard Ellison, the series was conceived by himself and journalist Stanley Karnow along with communications professor Lawrence Litchy. All three agreed that "the United States stood in need of a full-scale television history" covering Vietnamese culture and tradition, colonial domination and war and the period of U.S. involvement, "officially" known as the "Vietnam era". Station WGBH in Boston had just such a program in mind and the two teams "joined forces". But they needed money. (1)

One review of the series describes the process that developed: "The orientation of the original production team (actually three teams, one American, one British and one French) was decidedly left-leaning and it seemed certain that the product was doomed to be nothing more than an unabashed ideological statement on the war." However, this approach did not attract sponsors, so "the script was revised and made less doctrinaire. The fear of total dishonesty held by many – 'made in Hanoi' as one early critic predicted – was not realized." The producers "labored mightily" to allow objective journalism (albeit "American-style") to prevail and "in doing so have trampled on both the sacred cows of the left and the shibboleths of the far right". (2)

If objectivity was not the original intent of the series, did the program truly convert to honesty in the end? This writer feels that it did not and that, aside from scattered token references to "opposing views", there is a basic message that comes out of the series. That is what this book is about.

Chief Correspondent

The principal researcher for the so-called "Vietnam Project" is Stanley Karnow, referred to as its "Chief Correspondent". Karnow's credentials as a journalist are often cited as evidence of his qualifications for the task. He served as a correspondent for *Time* and *Life* in Paris and Southeast Asia, and later for the *Saturday Evening Post*, the *Washington Post*, and NBC news. He was associate editor for the liberal *New Republic* and contributed to a number of publications, including the *New York Times Magazine* and the *Atlantic*. Among Karnow's book credits are an account of the Chinese Cultural Revolution entitled *Mao and China: From Revolution to Revolution* and the *Southeast Asia* volume for the *Time/Life* series. His new work is the "companion book" for the television series called *Vietnam: A History*, subtitled *The First Complete Account of Vietnam at War* (1983, Viking Press).

A Harvard graduate, Karnow also studied political science in Paris, an experience which he believes gives him a unique advantage in reviewing American foreign policy. In essence, Karnow feels his perspective is more detached and impersonal than that of other observers and his knowledge of the French language has enabled him to get closer to the Vietnamese Communist leaders, some of whom received their education at French schools. (3)

Karnow has been described as a "dove" on Vietnam and criticized for writing for the leftist *National Guardian* in his early years as a journalist. (4) But these points are not as important as the fact that Karnow is neither a historian nor a qualified researcher, as his *History* clearly shows. He has tried to create a popular account of the war while at the same time providing enough information to make the reading educational, so much as Karnow would like to educate. For style he relies on his journalistic skills. The language is colorful, action shifts from scene to scene, mundane details are skimmed over or omitted, and analysis is light. The result is a mishmash of history (as journalists see history), generalization, hasty investigation, speculation, interpretation, observations borrowed from other sources (who are not given specific credit), personal narrative, anecdotes, and a profusion of quotable quotes (bandied about without reference to their original contexts). All this is done without footnotes, an apparent concession to the goal of avoiding too academic a style (however, making it difficult to cross-check his story).

In keeping with the tone set by the intimate designation "companion", the author feels free to interject the first person into his history whenever he sees fit. The reader learns, for instance, that Karnow first worked with photographer Larry Burrows for *Life* magazine in 1950. The reader may never have cared, but the reader was never asked. At the same time, we discover that Karnow's landlord in France in the 1950s was "the son of a prominent socialist of the 1920s and great-grandson of Karl Marx", a fact which might reveal something about the Chief Correspondent's political influences at the time.

Karnow is not shy to publicize his personal opinions in his "historical" account. In an objective history, frank statements of personal notion are annoying and an imposition on the reader who wishes to make up his or her own mind on some particular issue. Like Karnow, the reader may not be particularly fond of Richard Nixon; but what does the author hope to prove by referring to something he calls "pugnacious paranoia" on the part of the former president (p. 609) or by saying that "... determined to demonstrate his power, (Nixon) plunged into a crazy sequence of events in Cambodia"? (p. 603) Karnow, who has never held responsibility for public office and whose major decisions in life include choosing which color socks to put on each morning, is hardly in a position to speak so brazenly of a U.S. president, especially when his own insight is so often shallow and unconvincing. Yet this he does with the assistance of public funds and in the name of "education."

Another example of the way Karnow's commentary may interfere with the reader's assessment of an issue can be found in his description of South Vietnam's strategic hamlet program. The author informs us that Ngo Dinh Nhu was an "unleavened intellectual", the Saigon regime's earlier agroville program was a "scheme" and a "botch", and the strategic hamlets failed so miserably that peasants actually "rallied" to the Viet Cong. (pp. 255-7) The real questions about the program (what were its goals, how was it carried out, what problems did it encounter, and so on) are lost in these and other negative judgments made by the author. The reader must go elsewhere for objective information.

The *History* also suffers whenever Karnow indulges in fanciful romanticism. This he does often, especially when talking about the Communists, whose "nationalist zeal" makes his head spin. One can almost see the stars in his eyes as he recounts the travels of Nguyen Ai Quoc (Ho Chi Minh), shares a tear with Pham Van Dong, or follows Col. Bui Tin on the perilous journey to the South through the "web of trails" in Laos and Cambodia. The fact that as associate editor of the Communist army newspaper Bui Tin is an experienced propagandist and story-teller is lost on the Chief Correspondent as he brings his book to a close in classic style: After decades of war, South Vietnam finally rests in the hands of the Communists. Col. Bui Tin of the victorious army reassures all "patriots" that they have nothing to fear; this should be a time of joy for all! Thirty years in the Viet Minh and North Vietnamese Army, a veteran of Dien Bien Phu, a trooper of the Ho Chi Minh Trail, and now surviving a tank skirmish on a Saigon bridge, the colonel strolls into the park behind the presidential palace, stretches out on the grass and gazes up at the sky, "exalted!" (pp. 669-70)

One can only read this and shudder – has history come to this?

Karnow compares the effort involved in writing his book to "an elephant getting pregnant. It takes a long time before you're ready to give birth." (5) Apparently it was a troubled birth, since one can find in the book some awkward statements that are not given the attention they deserve. For example, in recounting the disorder in Vietnam during the 1930s, the author writes: "In Ho's native Nghe An province, they even set up a 'soviet.'" (p. 124) According to the text, "they" refers to "hungry peasants", although it should be the Communist revolutionaries. Karnow does not mention the Communists until *after* this remark, and then never connects them to the soviets in Nghe An and Ha Tinh provinces, thereby giving the impression that illiterate starving peasants spontaneously engineered uprisings with Communist intent. The reader may conclude that this was a careless error on the author's part, but that is not certain, given Karnow's inability to distinguish between a poor farmer and a trained revolutionary. The error further serves to reinforce Karnow's theory that Vietnam was ripe for an "agrarian revolution" that had deep historical roots among the ordinary peasants. As well, the author fails to note that the soviets were a disaster and that as a result the Communists were nearly crushed by the French.

If Karnow's *History* is notable for what it says, it is also revealing for what it does not say. Although the author pursued interviews with top Communist officials, he shows surprisingly little interest in the atrocities they directed. One of many examples is the Land Reform Program in North Vietnam in the 1950s. This program – which witnessed the deaths of perhaps a hundred thousand Vietnamese from execution, torture, imprisonment, exile and starvation, and turned many former supporters of the Viet Minh into enemies of the regime – is one of the most significant events in Vietnamese Communist history. Yet in Karnow's book, it occupies less than two pages from purpose to aftermath and is described in vague, general terms. (pp. 225-6) The only index reference to it is "Agricultural Reform Tribunals", which can only be found by extra effort. (Meanwhile, the index includes such staples of Vietnamese history as Joe Namath, Gregory Peck and Ulysses S. Grant.) The scanty account of the Land Reform is followed by ten pages of Ngo Dinh Diem's "cruelty" and failure to gather the support of the people. Karnow calls his history "the first complete account of Vietnam at War"; it would appear that some parts of history are not as complete as others.

Despite Karnow's obvious biases and opinions, the Chief Correspondent has managed to convince some reviewers that he took on this task with an open and objective mind. He strives, for instance, to dispel any suggestion that he is out to whitewash the Communists by beginning his story at the end, with a description of post-war Vietnam, which he visited in 1981. All is not well in that sad country, moans Karnow in his chapter "The War Nobody Won". Poverty, hunger, corruption and repression rule the day! He talked with one woman, "a distinguished lady, formerly a dissident member of parliament" in South Vietnam who now regrets having opposed the Saigon regime because "with all its faults, it was preferable to Communism." (p. 36) Karnow distrusted her lament at first, but became convinced after meeting with people who had fought with the Viet Cong and now were dissatisfied with the Hanoi regime. It is a sign of Karnow's nearsightedness that he refused to believe what was patently clear and had been predicted for many years prior to the fall of Saigon: that Communism is a brutal system that would demoralize and oppress the people of the South just as it did the North. For his own reasons, the Chief Correspondent would not believe there were troubles in Vietnam until the Communists themselves told him so. Even then his eyes were not opened, since in the rest of his book Karnow persists in portraying the Communists as heroes of a bold "nationalist" struggle resisting the foreign interference of the United States. Did he justify this to his distinguished dissident lady friend? He does not say.

At the conclusion of his massive work, Karnow expresses his gratitude to all the people who helped him write his "first complete history of Vietnam." This incredible list includes everyone he talked to, from high officials in the U.S. government to Viet Cong terrorists, making no distinction whatsoever with regards to their individual or comparative integrity and honesty. The same man who thanks Tom Dooley and Henry Cabot Lodge also is grateful to Premier Pham Van Dong and NLF spokeswoman Nguyen Thi Dinh! The matter of which ones Karnow preferred talking to is another story.

Karnow's writing forms the textual basis for the *Television History*. However, each of the 13 parts was written and produced by others. Some critics of the series maintain that the book is stronger than the series in that it contains more detail. (6) Both productions share the same basic viewpoints and this writer is not aware of any complaints from Karnow about the series, even when its "facts" do not match those recorded in his book.

Such is the written history of the "Vietnam war" of Stanley Karnow. Perhaps the saddest thing about this book is that it has enjoyed a place on the national best-seller list for months.

The Production

Executive Producer Richard Ellison is a freelance producer with experience in current affairs and popular science programs. He has worked for CBS, Time/Life Films, and served as director of current affairs programming for PBS for one year before becoming an independent agent.

A number of reviewers of the *Television History* have commended Ellison for trying to make the Vietnam series as balanced and objective as possible. Even Stephen Morris, who blasted the series in an article for the *Wall Street Journal*, credits Ellison with pursuing a "spirit of fair-mindedness." (7) Another writer describes the producer's attitude as a "painstaking search for balance." (8)

Remarks made by Ellison suggest broad-minded goals: "We will not find all the answers, but our goal will be reached if we can help viewers form the questions and invite them to draw their own conclusions." (9) "We tried hard not to load it in any particular direction. In all faith, we tried to do a responsible job that will enlighten, not obfuscate." (10)

All this sounds nice, but it does not obscure the fact that Ellison and his crew entered upon their project armed with a number of doubtful assumptions about the war and how it should be presented.

One misguided assumption is the idea that balance and honesty could be assured by calling on consultants from every corner of the intellectual globe. The series approached, so we are told, "more than sixty eminent scholars" in different fields. The series' *Guide* names 55 "consultants", not all of whom are either eminent or scholars.

To be sure, there are some responsible individuals among those listed, including: Guenter Lewy, who hoped his book *America in Vietnam* would dispel some of the myths about the war; Douglas Pike, Director of the Indochina Studies Project at UC-Berkeley and authority on the Viet Cong; Gerald Hickey, anthropologist, author of *Village in Vietnam* and two volumes on the highland people of Vietnam; and Peter Braestrup, whose important study of media distortion of the Tet Offensive is not mentioned in the series' credits.

Producer Ellison talks about the importance of "teamwork" in his production and mentions that some "intense" seminars were held to develop the series. But Coach Ellison must have forgotten to tell his whole "team" about his gameplan. Guenter Lewy called the consultant list a "sham" and said he had seldom been consulted by the producers. Stephen Young, Dean of the Hamline School of Law and another "consultant", said he was interviewed for a day and a half in 1978 and his advice was ignored. (11) Douglas Pike participated in a two-day conference criticizing the series conducted by Accuracy in Media. Other consultants have noted inaccuracies and omissions in the program. The reader may well wonder what happened in Ellison's seminars.

There are other, more controversial members of the consultant team. Tran Van Dinh, for example, a former supporter of Ngo Dinh Diem, later turned apologist for the Communists. Frances Fitzgerald, whose limited knowledge of Vietnamese culture and history was sufficient to condemn South Vietnam and America's place in the war. George Kahin, who asserted that the formation of the National Liberation Front was the result of spontaneous insurrection in South Vietnam without any connection to Hanoi; his theory has been disproven time and again by various observers (including Stanley Karnow), yet it still managed to sway the producers of the PBS series. And Gareth Porter, shameless supporter of the Communist revolutions in Southeast Asia who in 1976 declared that Cambodia was turning toward prosperity under the Khmer Rouge.

Another consultant for the series was Wilfred Burchett. Like jolly Saint Nick, Burchett traveled far and wide spreading good cheer (in his case it was the cheer of Communism) until he passed away in 1983. Observers generously described him as "pro-Communist" and he was exiled from his home continent of Australia. Burchett was involved in anti-American propaganda during the Korean war and he returned to harass the U.S. again during the

"Vietnam era." Some American POWs met him when he came to interview them for his television show; to the POWs, Wilfred Burchett was known as "Well-fed Bullshit." Burchett's name does not appear on the credits for the PBS series, perhaps because he was eventually identified as a paid stooge for the KGB. (12)

For this important project, Producer Ellison needed a skilled translator, someone both competent as a linguist and sensitive to the Vietnamese, to act as a contact and communications link (actually, he probably needed two or three for the job). He had many people to choose from. There are several hundred thousand Vietnamese living in the United States, some of them professors, teachers, former government officials, information specialists, professional linguists and other qualified persons who might be counted on to provide reliable translation. But nearly all of these were disregarded because they are refugees, and therefore suspected of bias against the Communists, whom the series needed to cooperate with. And so, for this grand production, the producers turned to Stanley Karnow's alma mater and selected Ngo Vinh Long.

Professor Long is not a refugee (some refugees would add cynically that he is not Vietnamese), but came to this country in 1964 as a student. He graduated from Harvard and became involved in Southeast Asian studies in the 1960s. Long participated in the antiwar movement and currently supports the Hanoi regime. Many refugees regard him as a Communist. The very mention of his name sets tempers flaring and once an irate refugee threw a Molotov cocktail at him. When Long and Don Luce (another notorious spokesperson for Hanoi) appeared at the USC "Vietnam" conference in 1983, security was tightened to avoid any untoward incidents. One newspaper asked Richard Ellison about the choice of Ngo Vinh Long as translator and the producer replied, "We were not aware of his reputation in the refugee community." (13) Indeed.

Harvard University seems to have generated a considerable degree of the inspiration for this project. The reader should be aware that the head of that university's history department, John Womack, has publicly admitted that he is a Communist, and he is proud of this fact. (14) It was also a Harvard biochemist named

Mathew Meselson who announced that the controversial "yellow rain" that has killed tens of thousands of people in Indochina and Afghanistan is nothing other than natural fungus residue in bee droppings! Interesting things are certainly being taught behind those ivy-covered walls.

The American television station behind the PBS series is WGBH of Boston. The AIM report on the series notes that WGBH "has produced such gems as the 'World' series which included programs that cast communist North Korea in a favorable light and examined race problems in Great Britain through Marxist eyes." (15) *Human Events* was concerned that the station "has developed what it calls 'close working relations' with the National Council of Churches in an effort to distribute 'instructional materials' on the series." Says the reviewer, "The NCC provided nearly a half million dollars to the communist Vietnamese regime, some of which has been given for concentration camps in 'new economic zones'." In 1977, NCC president James Armstrong signed a statement declaring that Hanoi "should be hailed for its moderation and for its extraordinary efforts to achieve reconciliation among all its people." (16)

In case there is any doubt which personalities the producers wish to be identified with, one need only look at their publicity photographs. In the series *Guide* Stanley Karnow is pictured standing with Communist Premier Pham Van Dong. In Fox Butterfield's favorable *New York Times* review, there is a shot of Producer Ellison smiling behind Premier Pham Van Dong. Not an American veteran. Not Henry Kissinger or Dean Rusk. Not General Westmoreland or William Colby. Not Nguyen Cao Ky or a refugee. Not even Clark Clifford or Daniel Ellsberg. They will only be seen with Ho Chi Minh's old comrade, a symbol (in their eyes) of the resistance and strength of the Vietnamese people.

This is not to suggest that Karnow and Ellison are Communist agitators, deliberately intent on subverting the nation through their TV series. But their effort to associate themselves with Communist leaders in Vietnam is undeniable. It comes about for two reasons. First, the producers wish to associate themselves with "winners", not "losers", and America and South Vietnam are clearly losers as far as they are concerned.

But the second reason is more important. The producers do not view themselves merely as journalists developing a documentary about a war. They also seek to be ambassadors of peace and reconciliation, reaching out to the Vietnamese whom they see as victims of America's mistakes. Their *Television History* is not simply an educational tool for understanding the war, but part of a sacred mission to act as a bridge between the allegedly sensitive and sympathetic elements of the United States and the "innocent victims" of brutal American foreign policy. More than just report history, the producers seek to mediate it and bring about a new era of friendship and cooperation between Americans and Vietnamese. These lofty goals are evident throughout their production as well as through efforts to promote the series by the American Friends Committee, a pro-Hanoi Quaker organization.

So narrow is their vision, however, that the producers cannot distinguish between the common people of Vietnam, Cambodia and Laos, who suffered in the war and the brutal Communist leaders who still repress and terrorize those poor people.

Lawrence Litchy, the program's Director of Media Research, is a communications professor for the University of Maryland. Litchy has studied how U.S. TV networks have broadcast the war and "screened all of the major networks' news and documentary coverage of Vietnam from 1965 to 1975." (17) His research findings have been included in several publications and he contributed to Peter Braestrup's two-volume edition of *Big Story*.

Any serious effort to investigate media coverage of the war is commendable. However, the *Television History* is a different type of production and neither Litchy nor anyone else connected with the series has explained how brief clips of TV news films (already edited, spliced, rewoven, and otherwise processed for consumption on the evening news) can be used as primary source material (as happens in the series) along with films from a number of "archives" (including personal files, U.S. military libraries and Communist propaganda organizations), mixed with private interviews conducted many years later and tossed into one uneven jumble that can easily confuse the viewer, who may well wonder where each film came from and what its original form was. The producers apparently see no reason to qualify their production or caution the viewers; they are content to reassure the audience that what we are seeing is exactly what the producers tell us it is. Unfortunately, the series does not always tell us what is being shown, or it tells only a part of the story and leaves the rest to our imagination.

Presumably because of funding problems, WGBH arranged with two foreign TV stations to produce several parts of the series. Central Independent Television of Britain produced four parts and Antenne-2 of France another two. In all, there are seven different producers for the 13 episodes, a fact which accounts for some of the unevenness of the series as a whole. (Some reviewers say that some parts of the series are better than others; the more pessimistic remark that others are worse than some.) WGBH and PBS have boasted of the "nearly universal acclaim" received by the series, which they feel confident is as balanced and objective as is humanly possible. It is therefore surprising to learn that the British and French stations have been permitted to produce their own versions of this series, so that there are at least three different *Television History*'s, each of which, we can rest assured, is as perfectly balanced and objective as the others!

Preconclusions

According to the series' *Guide*, the producers prepared a list of "key questions" to ask interviewees, questions designed to "illuminate" the events of the war. Some of the questions are striking, reflecting, as they do, the preconceived notions of the producers. Perhaps the most astonishing is the one that begins: "What enabled Communism to 'work' in Vietnam . . . ?"

The contention that Communism "worked" in Vietnam should come as a surprise to the hundreds of thousands of refugees who have fled that "success" over the years, not to mention the tragic souls wearing away in concentration camps, prisons, and other Communist institutions which are currently "working" quite well. Disregarding these realities, the producers insist that Communism attracted a "mass following" while other forms of "nationalism" or democracy did not. The "key question" does not allow for dissenting opinions.

This and several other conclusions reached by the producers are based on gross generalization, oversimplification and an unhealthy measure of misunderstanding about the war and the people of

Southeast Asia. A clear example of how poorly the producers express themselves can be seen in Stanley Karnow's summary conclusion about the Communist victory. Karnow writes: "The Vietnamese Communists struggled stubbornly for a generation, defeating France and later the United States, to unify Vietnam under their control. Their achievement, attained through immense human sacrifice, was a triumph of will over power. But the fruits of victory have been bitter." (18)

This statement is both simplistic and misleading. Among its inaccuracies are these: 1) It gives the Communists sole credit for defeating the French, overlooking the vast majority of the Vietnamese who supported the resistance yet were not Communists; the statement also ignores the crucial aid given the Viet Minh by China. 2) It pits the Communists against the Americans in the second war, implying that there was no South Vietnamese opposition to the Communist effort. 3) It gives complete credit for the 1975 victory to the Communists, again disregarding the many who supported the fight without being Communist, the thousands who lost their lives for reasons other than Marxism, and the countless who were betrayed by the Communists once the war was over. 4) The "immense human sacrifice" is more a reflection of the Communists' disregard for human life than evidence of some alleged fervor among the people. 5) By explaining the victory as that of "will over power", the author fails to grasp the numerous factors that entered into the Communist "triumph", including America's international and domestic political situation, considerable aid from China and the Soviet bloc, South Vietnam's defensive position, the confusion of the peasants, and so on. As for "will power", Karnow might have acknowledged that the Communists were willing to use terrorism, treachery, deceit, hatred and self-interest in order to pursue their goals; such enthusiasm is not necessarily laudible. 6) Finally, the "bitter fruits of victory", which include poverty, oppression and corruption, are largely due to inane socialist policies and not necessarily the war.

Through these statements as well as through their television series, the producers have made it clear that there are some matters which are axiomatic and cannot be debated. These include the following:

- The U.S. was mistaken for getting involved in Southeast Asia.
- The U.S. was mistaken in the way it handled the war.
- The U.S. was mistaken in getting out of the war, leaving behind the Saigon regime, which it created. (In short, the U.S. was damned if it got in, damned if it got out.)
- The Communists were nationalists with a justifiable cause.
- The Communist cause was apparent to the Vietnamese people and had strong popular support.
- Since the Communist cause was justified, the methods they used (terrorism, deception, manipulation, etc.) were justified.
- The South Vietnamese had no will to oppose Communism; their army did not want to fight for America's war; their government had no will to win.

To prove these and other ideas, the series employs shallow images, stereotypes, tokenism, cliches and narrow themes. Examples of these will be given in later chapters.

Exceptionalism vs. Communism

Central to the series' portrayal of the war and Stanley Karnow's *History* is the notion of America's "exceptionalism", which Karnow borrows from Prof. Daniel Bell, also of Harvard (one begins to wonder if there are no other institutions of higher learning in the world). The theory is summarized in Karnow's book in the chapter "The War Nobody Won", pp. 11-15. In brief, this idea contends that American involvement in Vietnam was rooted in this country's history and concept of America's uniqueness, or exceptionalism. America has been viewed as a land of opportunity, the hope of the future, and a model for the world. The American people were inspired by dreams of manifest destiny, "which signified belief in their obligation to export their benefits to less privileged civilizations abroad." Territorial expansion during the 19th century was coupled with idealistic yearnings to spread America's graces to the world. Later, although acquiring new territories, America did not seek to dominate them. And while some businesses did exploit the people of underdeveloped nations, the "more prevalent strain in America's expansionism was evangelical – as if the United States, fulfilling some sacred responsibility, had been singled out by the divinity for the salvation of the planet." America promised the world democracy, liberty, justice, prosperity and peace. Some commentators urged America to take the lead in the 20th century, to accept America's "duty to preserve global order." This concept "acquired fresh urgency after World War II, as the spector of monolithic Communism haunted the United States." Presidents began speaking in "cosmic language" representing the U.S. as the world's hope. And playing that role, America became involved in Vietnam.

The theory of America's "exceptionalism" as expounded by Stanley Karnow has its weaknesses, not the least of which is its narrow focus. In suggesting that America's history is one steady stream facing outward with idealism and arrogance, this facile theory conveniently ignores contrary elements of America's history: notable waves of popular isolationism that strongly influenced foreign policy, historic American efforts such as Wilsonian diplomacy and the respect for the integrity of nations, the characteristic unpreparedness of America's military for the wars it has faced, and so on. In place of these facts, Karnow's readers are treated to passages from Walt Whitman and Henry Luce, who supposedly typify America's spirit over the two centuries.

What is true is that America is a major power in a world that has seen many serious conflicts with repercussions that extend far beyond the borders of individual countries. If Americans see their country as a symbol for ideals such as freedom and democracy, then they certainly are not alone. Millions of people around the world look to the U.S. for hope and guidance on behalf of those ideals – many of these hopeful admirers are citizens of countries ruled by Communist governments. Perhaps the image is not entirely arrogant bombast, as Karnow proposes.

Furthermore, the threat of Communist expansionism following World War II was not simply a shadowy "spector", but a frightful reality for many people. From the day Lenin and his Bolsheviks seized control of the Russian government, the Soviets have advocated, supported, and, whenever possible, directed "revolutionary" movements in other countries. Every leader after Lenin has reiterated the goals of world revolution, aiding and abetting its manifestations in "struggles" in Europe, Asia, Africa, and the

Americas. To scoff at this reality is to wear one's ignorance on one's sleeve.

And here is one of the most serious deficiencies of the PBS *Television History:* its failure to look at what Communism is and how it has grown over the years.

Russia, too, had its own brand of singularity, nurtured by the idealistic intellectualism of the 19th century. Ironically, this Russian self-image once revealed itself as an evangelical movement based on faith in the Russian Church. Some of Russia's great thinkers, including Tolstoi, believed in the superiority of Mother Church and were confident that she would be the salvation of the entire world. At the same time, the czarist government was engaged in actions aimed at expanding Russia's already massive borders. The Russian Communists inherited this zeal for growth and hoped to inject it into the Soviet citizens, replacing the religion of Russian Christianity with the pseudo-religion of Marxism.

The spread of Communism was facilitated by European colonialism, whose impressive force threatened peoples and cultures around the world. Colonialism brought education and opportunity to some, but it exploited many others and challenged the governments and societies of colonized countries. Western values offered new alternatives to those dissatisfied with the traditional systems, which had proven incapable of countering the West. In short, colonialism encouraged discontent and planted seeds of its own destruction.

Meanwhile, the Communists recognized this state of affairs and adjusted their methods to take advantage of it. Put another way, "Russian Communists did not create the 'revolutionary situation' in Asia and Africa", but they "were quick to exploit it and 'to push what was falling'." (19) By themselves, indigenous nationalist groups were weak and their prospects for victory uncertain. Lenin decided to seize the initiative and support the nationalists abroad, using their efforts to bring down the "Western empire." This strategy of subversion of the colonial world has been called "Lenin's greatest legacy to the Russian Communists." (20)

Bolshevik leaders met with Asian nationalists at Baku in 1920 and there resolved to back the colonial revolutions. Initially, the program emphasized ideology, but this tactic floundered on the realities of the time. The Communists changed course and promoted the "nationalist" face of revolution.

After Stalin came to power, he concentrated his efforts on strengthening the home base of the revolution – Russia. Communists outside Russia received limited aid and often had to rely on their own devices in order to survive. Stalin did support the long-range goals of the revolution by training native cadres for more opportune times, but he would not risk losing his or Russia's power on their behalf.

After World War II, Stalin's mode was more sophisticated as he tried to protect Soviet strength in Eastern Europe. U.S. foreign policy was designed to contain what it saw as Soviet expansionism by bolstering Western Europe. By the 1950s, the U.S. had devised a new deterrent strategy that promised to meet with force any effort to alter the status quo. The Soviet Union responded by taking a different course for its "struggle." De-Stalinization included a broadening of the ideological base to attract more nationalist leaders in small countries, suggesting to the West that the creation of neutral Communist states might be an acceptable alternative. From this came the notion of "national communism", a concept which in fact contradicts the theory and goals of Communism. The Soviet Union was settling down to a prolonged conflict with the West.

Ho Chi Minh encountered Communism in the 1920s and liked what he found. Unlike conventional nationalist methods, the Communist system offered the organization, discipline, ideological base and material support needed to conduct a revolution. Just as importantly, Communist trainers accepted Ho, who had earlier rejected or been rejected by Vietnamese nationalists outside his country. Marxism offered a quasi-philosophy that suited Ho's shallow intellectual skills and Lenin's global doctrine provided a cause that satisfied Ho's bloated ego and desire for power. Ho Chi Minh envisioned himself as Marxism's apostle to Southeast Asia. He devoted himself to the world revolution until the day he died.

Characteristically, the *Television History* ignores most of the historical processes at work during this time and plays upon America's "exceptionalism." As far as the producers are concerned, the U.S., through its arrogant idealism, attempted to impose the democratic system on the Vietnamese, whom it wished to save from Communism, and that, they conclude, went against the wishes of the people.

From the Horse's Mouth

In his essay "Vietnam as Television History", Richard Ellison writes: "For our series to deal adequately with (the events of the war), it was in our view essential that Vietnamese viewpoints and experiences be included." Such Vietnamese views and experiences as are included in the series tend to come from the Communist side, although a handful of South Vietnamese are permitted to provide token responses to certain "key questions". Most of the "illuminating", it would seem, must come from the Communists.

By any standards, Communist Vietnam is a closed society. Visitors to the country are screened before being allowed to enter. Average citizens cannot talk freely with foreigners. People can be arrested for the things they say, not only in public, but in private, as well. Movement is restricted and fear of the security policy pervasive. Moreover, Communist leaders have a reputation for making false or self-serving statements to foreign journalists and for showing only those sights in Vietnam that have been properly arranged for the occasion.

The producers of the *Television History* seem to recognize this. Stanley Karnow remarks that talking to a person in Vietnam "is not like interviewing the man on the street in Oshkosh." (21) That's putting it mildly. Yet, during the series' 13 parts the viewer is never informed that the Communists demanded that interview questions be submitted to them beforehand for review. And the clipped film segments of those interviews give little indication of what Prod. Ellison admitted to one critic, that "many of their answers seemed virtually memorized." (22) Upon the producers' return from Vietnam, rather than complain about restrictions on free speech in that country, they actually complimented the Communists on their "candidness" and courage in agreeing to cooperate with foreign journalists.

The viewers may be rather confused by the fact that virtually all of these Communist officers and cadres are complete strangers to them. Who are Hoang Quoc Viet, Tran Duy Hung and Ton That Tung? What did they do during the war? The series does not say, beyond giving an obtuse rank or title. The viewers find themselves unable to identify these figures with any specific deed or policy

connected with the war. The interviewees become added parts of
the amorphous entity known only as the "Vietnamese". Their
credibility may be established by the program itself. Dr. Ton That
Tung, for example, is fixed in our minds as a mild, sensitive physician
who cares deeply about the suffering of his people. Why should the
viewers doubt him when he declares that no one in the North ever
complained during the war? It might make a difference if the series
were to say that dear Dr. Tung has "treated" political dissidents in
his office by administering lethal doses of "therapeutic" drugs.
Complaints? No, his patients never complain.

This attitude toward the Communists reflects a basic trust in
them as informants. As "nationalist heroes", the Communists are
given respectability. Their just cause imbues them with honesty.
And their suffering at the hands of the indiscriminately powerful
Americans blesses them with sincerity. What would Prod. Ellison
or Chief Correspondent Stanley Karnow say if they realized that the
Communist Vietnamese are solid racists who consider white people
inferior and American whites strong in technology but basically
stupid?

Victims of the Communists are naturally disturbed by what they
see in the program. To them, Communist officials are symbols of
brutal oppression. As one former POW said, those men with
epaulets on their arms are not boy scouts – they are the ones who did
the torturing and killing. Refugees, too, are dismayed to see
Northern officers and Viet Cong cadres boasting of the revolution's
"achievements" without a word of criticism for the Hanoi regime.
The very act of placing the Communists on American television is
insulting to them.

The series proceeds to depict the Communists as fantasy figures–
one American veteran aptly describes them as "Disneyland characters". Far from reflecting human feelings, the Communists in the
series transcend earthly emotions, maintaining intact what a
reviewer calls "the wartime legend of imperturbable Vietnamese
heroism." (23) While American leaders stumble about in confusion
and disarray and Saigon is replete with political chaos, the Communist leadership glides smoothly along its glorious course, borne
on by the sanctity of its purpose. And as an American soldier
"agonizes over killing an old woman", a Communist official

"proudly recites the martyrology of elderly fighters." (24)

Some refugees have complained that statements made by the Communists are inaccurately translated or modified in such a way as to favor the Communists. (25) One can find instances of this: A Viet Cong cadre complains of the "terrorism" of "America – Diem"; this comes out on the series as "Diem's repression". Mme. Nguyen Thi Dinh of the NLF relates how her brother was arrested by the French for putting up a flag with the hammer and sickle; the translation says he was only putting up "some red banners". Communist terminology is phased out of some quotations: "Comrade" Nguyen Ai Quoc becomes "Mr. Nguyen Ai Quoc"; "Chairman Ho Chi Minh" is said to be "President Ho Chi Minh" (suggesting that democratic rules placed him in power); and many derogatory references to Americans (such as "pirate") are dropped altogether. Sentences are paraphrased or summarized rather than literally translated. The smooth and simple translations that result stand in stark contrast to the statements of English-speakers, where every slip of the tongue, repeated word, twang and grunt is carefully recorded for posterity. How does one compare a scene of Pres. Kennedy stammering during a live press conference to staged films of Ho Chi Minh reading a speech to his compatriots? Or the slang of black Pvt. Jack Hill to the slick remarks of cadre Nguyen Bay in their contradictory testimony regarding an alleged massacre of civilians? The series dares make this comparison, apparently with a purpose.

A final word about Communist testimony: Over the years, the Vietnamese Communists have become experts in a tactic that might be called "atrocity diversion". By this strategy, the Communists emphasize some alleged atrocity committed by another party in order to divert attention away from their own brutal activities. In Hanoi, for instance, there is a war crimes museum created to "educate" visitors about the crimes committed by the "American imperialists" during the war. The museum includes photographs of napalm and fragmentation bomb victims, pieces of bombs and other macabre memorabilia aimed at proving the barbarity of the American war effort. Meanwhile the Commmunists say nothing of their own atrocities and visitors are too overcome with horror and shame to ask. Likewise in Cambodia, Vietnamese cadres guide visitors through museums depicting the atrocities of the Khmer Rouge; at the same time, the Vietnamese continue to mistreat and kill Cambodians without making a public scene of it. The *Television History* has provided another forum. Communist leaders will talk about America's use of Agent Orange, for example, but neglect to explain their application of "yellow rain" on civilian areas of Laos. The producers shy away from pointing out hypocracies such as these, while they join in the chorus denouncing the U.S.

From the Other Side

Even as the Communists are taken without qualification as reliable witnesses to the war, certain other groups are not so easily accepted. For instance, Vietnamese refugees are afforded little opportunity to speak from their point of view, and when they are, it is in relation to "key" areas of concern: the "debacle" at Quang Tri in 1972 (not the heroism at An Loc), prostitution and black market-eering in South Vietnam (not the general way of life of the people), America's betrayal at the end of the war (not how Communism had terrorized and impoverished the North after 1954), and so on. Revealing an incredible lack of insight, the producers believed that the refugees would be convinced of the overall "balance" of the program if the boat people were given a few minutes to talk about concentration camps at the tail end of the series.

This attitude toward the refugees is not surprising. Firmly convinced that the war was solely "America's war", the producers wish to reassure themselves that the South Vietnamese were of little significance in and of themselves, other than being victims of rash U.S. policies. Furthermore, the image must be fixed that the South Vietnamese were losers with no will to win; consequently one sees them in that context at every possible turn in the series, although the refugees would dispute the image.

The belittling of refugee testimony is based on a traditional rule of research which says that people fleeing a country are biased against that country and so their views about it are naturally colored. Stanley Karnow put it in his own words in the introduction to his account of life in Communist China, *Bitter Seeds: A Farmer's Story of Revolution in China*, when he said: "... I was aware of a multitude of pitfalls involved in using refugee accounts. Many a refugee's story must be taken with a healthy measure of scepticism. People naturally tend to embellish their narratives in order to enhance their own importance. Moreover, the person who may have risked his life to flee is not likely to be entirely objective about the country he has forsaken. Often, too, there is a desire to please the interviewer by telling him a 'good story'." (26)

This statement would be easier to swallow if similar considerations were declared regarding the value of testimony from the Communists these refugees were trying so hard to escape. In effect, it infers that people who flee brutality and oppression are more likely to lie than those who cause brutality and oppression. This same thinking is apparent in the *Television History*, which, as we will see, often accepts inaccurate or dubious information from Communist sources without confronting a refugee for a second opinion.

Furthermore, the above statement fails to acknowledge the substantial difference between bias and stupidity. People do not risk their lives for trivial reasons. The sheer numbers and mixed composition of the refugees from Vietnam, Cambodia and Laos should startle even the most stubborn observers. Does M. Karnow suggest that these many hundreds of thousands of people all have overly vivid imaginations and slipped through the jungles or over the waters simply so they could tell American journalists a "good story" and make themselves appear important? After working with refugees for several years, this writer feels confident in saying that as a whole, refugees are no more or less reliable than the average American, who has never fled an oppressive government. Refugees offer virtually the only source of intimate details concerning real life in Communist society and a variety of viewpoints which one could never find among official Communist informants. Their remarks about Communism, whether positive or negative, are certainly of greater value than those made by cadres given the official stamp of approval by the government and rehearsed prior to recitation before the cameras. And despite their alleged biases, refugees often prove to be quite sensitive and penetrating, especially as they recount their own personal experiences. Some individuals will exaggerate or prove untrustworthy at times. In this, refugees are no different from other people.

Despite complaints from some refugees during the airing of the series, Richard Ellison maintained his confidence in the program. In a newspaper interview, he wondered aloud what the refugees would think of the series after watching all 13 parts. (27) The answer seems to be: they don't like it.

The American veterans are also poorly treated in the series. Like the Vietnamese, the veterans are subjected to stereotyped themes, the worst of which is the "war crimes" theme. Taking for granted that Americans committed war crimes, the producers sought, and of course found, atrocities of different kinds: shooting old women, burning huts, bombing civilian areas indiscriminately, and even an alleged "My Lai"-style massacre in 1967 (see Part 5). As if horrors have never before occurred in war, the *Television History* features these from one side, giving the impression that death and destruction are a part of America's heritage in Vietnam. The tragedy is enhanced by the apparently "senseless" nature of the conflict.

At the same time, the producers strive to express sympathy for the individual soldier. Although the Americans were killers, there were mitigating factors (heat and humidity, watching one's buddies die, putting up with the "cowardice" of the South Vietnamese soldiers, etc.). Television's two-dimensional nature gives these factors little substance and at times they are dispensed with altogether. The viewer is left with the feeling that America's war was dirty, while the Viet Cong fought "clean ".

Besides being shown killing elderly women and burning huts, the American soldiers are depicted as stumblebums, foreign goons sweeping paths for mines while innocent villagers bicycle past. The image, too, is grossly stereotyped. This writer has met a number of veterans whose opinions about the war as a whole differ, but who affirm that as soldiers they acted professionally and did their jobs well. They object to the television image they have received and emphasize that what people see on television is not necessarily what the soldiers experienced.

The series' feeble attempt to express sympathy and honor to the veterans reveals the inability of the producers to come to grips with .the contradictions in their work. As elements of the antiwar movement, they wish to show what they see as the ugliness of the way American soldiers acted during the war; at the same time, they try to absolve the soldiers of guilt. The result is a clumsy combin-

ation: with one hand the program pats the veterans sympathetic-
ally on the back, while with the other it thumbs its nose.

Finally, the series all but neglects the people of Laos and Cambodia
who have suffered so much in the war. Only one hour is given to the
two countries, and that hour is incomplete and stops abruptly
without reminding the viewers that both those nations are currently
being oppressed by the Vietnamese Communists. Their experience
in the war and its "legacy" is just another shadow in the distance.

The American Ogre

Following the death of Stalin, the face of international Communism changed in several significant ways. New leaders arose in
the Soviet Union and policies took on new directions. The bitter
rivalry between Mao Zedong and his Russian comrades finally
erupted into a so-called "split" in the Communist bloc. Both China
and the Soviet Union faced serious economic problems. Revolts in
Eastern Europe troubled the Soviet Union. China experienced a
"cultural revolution." During the 1970s both powers sought accommodation with the U.S.

Despite their conflicts in some matters, Russia and China shared
some goals in Southeast Asia. Neither really gave a damn about the
fate of Vietnam itself, except as it suited their own needs. However,
neither wanted to see the U.S. deeply committed in South Vietnam. Both were stunned by America's use of power and were
forced to cooperate in order to combat it. Neither wanted Vietnam
to fall under the influence of the other, and an uneasy joint venture
developed to defend the North and carry on the war in the South
(such cooperation among rivals is not unusual; politics engenders
its own rationalism). And neither Russia nor China believed the
war would last so long.

As the war dragged on, antiwar sentiment in the U.S. spread.
Radicals became more vocal in their condemnation of American
involvement in Vietnam and later they accused the U.S. of
"expanding" the war into Cambodia and Laos.

In their eyes, America bore complete responsibility for the killing
and destruction of the war while the Communists were often depicted
as innocent victims of aggressive foreign policy. Charges of war
crimes became popular, leading even moderates to question

America's conduct in the war. Arguments became more emotional and a shift in public opinion occurred. Whereas during the 1950s the popular ogre had been Communism, in the 1960s it became America.

After the war, when the extent of Communist repression in Southeast Asia became apparent and refugees continued to flee their homelands, critics of the war took different positions. Some changed their attitude and admitted they had been mistaken about the Communists. Others surrounded themselves in silence and declined to discuss the issue. Defenders of the myth of the American ogre either discounted reports of Communist cruelty as propaganda or declared that Communist repression was the result of U.S. intervention in the war. The idea that Communism is inherently brutal is not even considered.

In the PBS history of the war, viewers are presented with American policies, American weapons, and American destruction. The motives, policies, and conduct of the Communists are overlooked. A reviewer writes: "One predictable result of this imbalance is the suggestion that the U.S. bears the prime, if not sole, responsibility for the war's more horrifying tragedies." For example, the episode "Cambodia and Laos" shows American officials, bombing, covert activities and deception. Prosperous Cambodia falls into a nightmare. Meanwhile, "on the screen, no (Viet Cong) official debates the fine points of Cambodian neutrality. No Northern Politburo members reflect on the decision to arm Pol Pot. No insiders candidly recount Hanoi's intentions for postwar Indochina." And though the program gives us its version of the Nixon Doctrine, "what doctrine Le Duan and Le Duc Tho might have been following, one can only guess." (28)

The PBS series has been described as a "dual-vision history" and a "one-eyed account." Through its limited and deficient presentation, it joins those who brazenly denounce the American ogre, whose awful legacy remains in Southeast Asia. Stanley Karnow and Richard Ellison recognize the problems of Communism, but not where they come from. They will discuss Communist brutality and repression only after the cloud of America has been lifted from the scene. By then, the image has been sealed: America's war. America's mistake. America's responsibility.

That is the principal message of the *Television History*.

Anthology and Guide

The *Television History* is intended for use in college-level and adult education. Accompanying the series is an *Anthology and Guide*, edited by Steven Cohen. (1983, Alfred A. Knopf) As stated in the preface "How To Use This Guide", the series and *Anthology* are to help the student "to search for meanings in the experience and to participate in the struggle to arrive at conclusions." The book covers each of the 13 parts in the series with a brief "Historical Summary" to set the scene, followed by a "Chronology" timeline, "Points to Emphasize" in discussion, a "Glossary of Names and Terms" related to each segment, selected readings called "Documents", a series of questions under the title "Critical Issues for Discussion", and finally a list of "Suggestions for Further Reading".

Despite the book's organization and ambition, it fails to provide a comprehensive and objective background for learning about the war. In fact, it may confuse students further with its pronounced antiwar tendency and the editor's apparent lack of knowledge of the issues he wishes to elucidate.

The *Anthology and Guide* elaborates on many of the misconceptions of the television series, such as the alleged popularity of the National Liberation Front. As Stanley Karnow himself admits, the NLF was created and controlled by the Politburo in Hanoi and as such was not a spontaneous outgrowth of hostility to Ngo Dinh Diem in the South. Politically the Front was not popular and it consistently failed to attract non-Communist dissidents to its cause. Cohen's *Anthology*, however, claims that "much of the opposition to Diem crystalized" with the formation of the Front, which convinced Hanoi to "back" it. It further claims the NLF had "wide-ranging appeal" and was the strongest of Diem's opponents. (p. 58, *Anthology*) The Front's Chairman, Nguyen Huu Tho, is called a "moderate", then quoted using rather immoderate language against the U.S., which he described as "the extremely ferocious and dangerous ringleader of imperialism." (p. 185, *Anthology*) Throughout the book, the writers trample on historical facts and bask in erroneous generalizations while ignoring post-war perspective.

The "Documents" are a mixed bag. Besides their rather dubious selection, the readings suffer from a severe lack of historical and environmental context. For example, the *Anthology* reprints Anthony Lewis' denunciation of the 1972 December bombing of Hanoi, which he described as a terrorist action. (p. 331, *Anthology*) The book provides no follow-up to note that Lewis' portrayal of the bombing proved to be unsupportable and highly exaggerated (see Part 10). The result is that Nixon comes out looking like a murderous madman.

Like the series, the book's "Critical Issues for Discussion" expresses "key" ideas as defined by the editor's arbitrary whims. The questions asked are often written to guide discussion to preconceived conclusions (no "struggle" is required). The "Follow-up" to Part 6, for example, quotes Mao's "fish in water" analogy for guerilla fighters and the people, then asks: Did this apply to Vietnam? How did Diem try to stop it? And why did he fail? – Doesn't leave much room for discussion, does it?

According to Cohen in his "Acknowledgements", the reading suggestions after each segment "provide the only current, selective reading list on the history of Vietnam for a college-level audience." In fact, not only are the lists incomplete, but the editor's blind trust in propaganda and leftist sources make one skeptical of Cohen's appreciation for the task he has taken on. Official Communist pronouncements and stories are given the same credibility as scholarly and professional work. Thus, Nguyen Khac Vien, General Editor of the Hanoi series *Vietnam Studies* (parts of which are written in the Soviet Union) is rated alongside Douglas Pike and Jeffery Race. Just how carefully the selection was done is seen in a comparison of Parts 3 and 6: Following Part 3, the *Anthology* recommends Chapters 12-17 of Bernard Fall's *The Two Vietnams*, for the author's "meticulous analysis of developments in the South" which is "highly critical of the Diem regime and of U.S. policy generally." (*Anthology* p. 86) When finishing Part 6, however, the reader searches in vain for a suggestion to read Fall's critical analysis of North Vietnam in the same book.

The *Anthology*, then, can be viewed as a written version of the television series. It is biased, inaccurate and poorly researched; as such, it is an inappropriate aid for education. The book's reflection on the series is clear: the editor gives special thanks to Ellison, Karnow and Litchy for spending many hours "making sure that (the *Anthology*) reflected the goals of the series."

Footnotes

1. Richard Ellison, "Vietnam as Television History", *Guide to Vietnam: A Television History*

2. Review of the series in *Indochina Chronology*, Vol. II, No. 3. July-September 1983

3. Robert Wells, "New Book Puts Vietnam in Perspective", book review for the *Milwaukee Journal*, October 1983

4. See "Brace Yourselves for PBS' 'Vietnam War' ", *Human Events*, August 6, 1983

5. Robert Wells, Note 3 above

6. For example, see Doan Van Toai and David Chanoff, "Stanley Karnow's Vietnam", *American Spectator*, January 1984

7. Stephen J. Morris, " 'Vietnam', A Dual-Vision History", *Wall Street Journal*, December 20, 1983

8. Toai and Chanoff, Note 6 above

9. Quoted in the series' *Guide*, note 1 above

10. Toai and Chanoff, Note 6 above

11. Reed Irvine, "Flawed History of Vietnam", *Accuracy in Media*, January-B 1984

12. Burchett was identified as a KGB agent in Congressional hearings by Soviet defector George Karlin. See *Indochina Chronology*, Vol. II, No. 3, p. 28

13. Harriet Swift, "PBS Series on Vietnam Angers Refugees", Oakland *Tribune*, November 9, 1983

14. William F. Buckley, Jr., "Learning History at Harvard", San Diego *Union*, August 7, 1984

15. AIM, Note 11 above

16. *Human Events*, note 4 above

17. Quoted from the series' official biographical information, dated August 1983

18. Stanley Karnow, "Vietnam Today: The Problems of Peace", printed in the series' *Guide*

19. Robert Strausz-Hupe, et al., *Protracted Conflict*, p. 11

20. Ibid., p. 12

21. Robert Wells, Note 3 above
22. Toai and Chanoff, Note 6 above
23. Ibid.
24. Ibid.
25. Harriet Swift, Note 13 above
26. Stanley Karnow, *Bitter Seeds: A Farmer's Story of Revolution in China*, Dragonfly Books, Hong Kong, 1964; from the 'Introduction'
27. Greg Gross, "Refugees Ired Over PBS TV Series on War", San Diego *Union*, November 7, 1983
28. Toai and Chanoff, Note 6 above

JOHNNY GOT HIS PEN:
JOURNALISM GOES TO WAR

One of the many controversies generated by the war in Southeast Asia is the argument concerning the role of the news media in influencing the outcome of the war. On one side of the conflict are the critics, who accuse the media of everything from bias and incompetence to high treason. Several of these critics have blamed the media for the ultimate loss of Indochina to the Communists. Below are some examples:

"For the first time in modern history, the outcome of a war was determined not on a battlefield, but on the printed page and, above all, on the television screen." – Robert Elegant, Correspondent

"The Vietnam war was lost on the television screens of the United States." – Sir Robert Thompson, Counterinsurgency Expert

"The American press corps made an indispensible contribution to destroying the morale of the American people and bringing about the defeat of the U.S." – Patrick J. Buchanan, Commentator

On the other side of the controversy are the defenders, who argue that news stories gave the only accurate picture of what was going on during the war, a necessary counter to the starry-eyed optimism that seemed to characterize official sources in Saigon and Washington. According to these observers, the accounts and interpretations coming out of the military and government diplomatic offices bore no resemblence to reality and it was the duty of the media to make the public fully aware of what was happening. Furthermore, the war itself, the deaths of hundreds of Americans every week and the general effects of the fighting, were news and the public had a right to be informed.

The debate rages. The enormity of media coverage of the war provides a vast battleground for confrontation. No other war has been so written about, filmed, commented on, editorialized and documented for the public.ᐟ TV networks spent millions of dollars to

bring the war into the homes of America, giving rise to the concept of
the "living room war." Over the course of two decades, hundreds of
reporters, cameramen and news teams visited Vietnam; some of
them lost their lives covering the war. A number of journalists
would go on to write books detailing their perspectives of the conflict.
Some war veterans turned to journalism after their tours and wrote
about their experiences.

Yet, despite all the attention gained, the war in Indochina remains
perhaps the most misunderstood war in modern history. This is due
in part to the nature of the conflict, with its complex factors, multitude of characters, and historical changes which occurred over
time.

It is also due to the way in which information about the war was
presented to the public, because it was based on this information
that Americans formed their opinions and made their decisions
about America's place in the conflict. It is in this respect that the
issue of media coverage became significant.

The "media" (which includes wire services, newspapers, news
magazines, television and radio broadcasting, and so on) is more
than simply an agent of the news. It is a major industry, a multi-
billion-dollar business with world-wide extensions. It is showbusiness, commercial entertainment with special features, colors,
styles and "big name" correspondents. And the media is educational, for as Americans find themselves bombarded with reports
about a shrinking world, they tend to rely more and more on the
media to explain and interpret events for them.

The responsibilities involved in handling the news are colossal.
The profession has grown and expanded, nurturing among its
members a sense of its unique function in society. Because of the
intricacies of the profession, many media specialists seem to
perceive themselves (consciously or subconsciously) as experts
who "know best" what is news and how it should be presented.
Some of these individuals have shown themselves to be extremely
sensitive to the gravity of their task. One "sex symbol" television
anchorman takes himself so seriously that he does not blink his
eyes when he delivers the news.

Newspeople, too, may be oversensitive to criticism of "lay"
persons, much like the self-confident physician who pales when a

patient dares to disagree with a diagnosis. They may become defensive when confronted with challenges to their right to record the news as they see fit – as they did in 1983 when Pres. Reagan banned press coverage during the initial stages of the Grenada "invasion." At that time, several well-known newspersons and commentators would be charging the Reagan administration with "censorship" and "repression", just as their comrades did in 1969 when they were attacked by Spiro Agnew.

After the Grenada outcry, *Time* Magazine published an article suggesting that the journalistic profession was being threatened by a "growing perception of arrogance." (1) Formal and informal surveys showed that public confidence in the media was declining and that people were disturbed by the media's response to Pres. Reagan. Some questioned the patriotism of the media representatives and perhaps felt that the press wanted to get into Grenada "not to witness the invasion on behalf of the people, but to sabotage it." (2)

Similar claims had been made regarding media intentions during the Indochina war, but these are neglected in the *Time* article. In fact, conspicuously absent from the article is any analysis of the war's coverage. It should be a ripe topic, too, for the PBS *Television History* of the war, but the producers avoid the controversy – which is easy to understand, since they violate a number of the alleged "crimes" of Vietnam war reporting. In Part 11, the series does a soft-shoe around the issue by quoting Spiro Agnew and some suspiciously self-serving comments by NBC's John Chancellor. There is also a hint that something was wrong with Tet coverage when presidential counsel Harry McPherson describes the "awful contradictions" between the optimistic cables from Saigon and the "different sight" he was getting from television. To this day, Dean Rusk remains puzzled at how a military defeat for the Communists should have become "a brilliant propaganda victory for them here in the United States." Laments AIM editor Reed Irvine, "This cries out for an explanation." (3) Alas, no explanation is forthcoming and the question is left hanging like a dead weight.

The Reporters

Many factors contributed to the way the war was reported to the people in the States. It is important to understand something about the correspondents who wrote the stories that eventually appeared in newspapers and on television (sometimes in contorted form). They are covered briefly in the early part of Peter Braestrup's study of Tet reporting, *Big Story*, and by Robert Elegant in his critical article "How To Lose A War" (*Encounter*, August 1981).

Vietnam journalists were often young and inexperienced in war reporting. They had little or no background in history, Marxism, world politics, or Asian affairs, and yet were expected to report on the complicated war in a foreign country. Likewise, they had limited knowledge of the military. Writes Peter Braestrup: "Few, for example, understood the differences between, say, a mortar and a howitzer, brigades and divisions, logistics and tactics, or between overall U.S. personnel strength in Vietnam (approaching 500,000 in January 1968) and the relatively small number of men actually firing weapons at the enemy (perhaps 100,000 . . .)." (4)

Robert Elegant suggests that, being unfamiliar with the war, young correspondents were moved by the war's brutality, destructiveness and waste. "Many confused the beastliness of all wars with the particular war in Indochina, which they unthinkingly concluded was unique in human history because it was new to them."

Like the American soldiers, news reporters received no training in Vietnamese culture, politics, or language. Although they used English-speaking Vietnamese informants, communication with the Vietnamese was limited and difficult. Frequently, the viewpoint of the Vietnamese was lost or forgotten as the dealine for a story came around. Unable to identify with or talk to the Vietnamese, reporters tended to focus on what Braestrup terms the "Western experience" in the war. The Americans were more visible, accessible and familiar; consequently, they received more first-hand coverage by the American press. In one survey, analyst Lawrence Litchy found that of 187 war subjects covered on weekly television during one period, only 28 were related to the South Vietnamese; the majority of the others presented the U.S. troops. (5) Commenting on this problem, Gen. William Westmoreland remarked that "people at home were left with the false impression that American soldiers were doing practically all of the fighting." (6)   In the living rooms of the U.S., it was all America's war.

Reporters had to answer the demands of their trade. There were short deadlines to meet and this meant that often there was no time to verify stories or information. Competition provided further pressures. There was no central bureau of all U.S. news agencies to coordinate reports and develop comprehensive stories. The networks, wire services, newspapers, and magazines fought to report the same stories, leading to much duplication of subject, but variation of description and theme. Despite the large number of correspondents in Vietnam, the actual scope of their reporting was quite limited.

The quest for sensationalism was all too apparent. Stories sold if they were exciting; reporters·tried to please their editors. Gen. Westmoreland was to complain that for correspondents drama usually took precedence over reality; reporters in Vietnam searched for action, violence or scandal, while ignoring the "pacification, civic action, medical assistance, the way life went on in a generally normal way for most of the people much of the time." (7)

Whatever information was gathered in the field eventually made its way to the editor's desk. There, stories were revised, clipped, rewritten or ignored, as determined by persons in charge. Reporters were sometimes frustrated to learn that the "news" that finally went to print or on the air was not always the "news" they had originally reported.

Another important factor in war reporting was the heavy turnover of correspondents. Many newspeople were in Vietnam for only a few months before being reassigned; others were there perhaps a year or 18 months. There were few incentives to stay behind. The war was a good special assignment for aspiring young journalists, but it offered little benefit to experienced reporters who might have remained in the field longer. Braestrup notes that from 1966-1968, TV personnel kept the shortest "tours", ranging from one to six months for reporters and one year for bureau chiefs. (8)   There was not much time for correspondents to learn about everything that was happening. As Gen. Westmoreland describes the situation, "Providing the press with background and perspective was like trying to paint a moving train." (9)

In Vietnam, the reporters were misfits. They found themselves
on temporary assignment in a foreign land with no tools for com-
municating with the locals. They could not identify with the
Vietnamese, who looked, acted and spoke differently. Nor did they
fit into the military or government "establishment", with which
they were often at odds. The result, says Robert Elegant, is that
correspondents retreated into their own world, the "brotherhood",
as Michael Herr called it. Journalists shared a common occupation, values, and ideals. Therefore, it was natural that they
"turned to each other for professional sustenance and emotional
comfort." There, reporters wrote primarily for the approbation of
their peers, to confirm their ideas about the war and justify
themselves and their purpose as journalists in a war zone. This
atmosphere of mutual support, coupled with the hostility that grew
between the media and official sources, segregated reporters from
the realities of the war they were describing. Few reporters lived
with the troops in order to view the whole process of the fighting
from a unit's perspective. A story might be made up of the
immediate results of a battle or operation, but not the conditions,
the atmosphere, the reasons for the operation and its long-term
consequences. The audience at home would see even less, the little
that managed to become public news. One example of this
limitation of the media was that the South Vietnamese could come
across looking like "a bunch of pimps, whores, war profiteers,
corrupt generals, or at least outright reactionaries." This isolation
of the media from the rest of Vietnam contributed to the distorted
picture of the war that emerged from news reports and stories.

The Hostilities

As America first became involved in Indochina, the news media
endorsed Kennedy and the policy of containing Communism in
Asia. Problems arose when reporters refused to accept the optimistic pronouncements that overflowed from U.S. officials in Saigon.
Gen. Westmoreland defends the "establishment." U.S. officials, he
says, "were in Vietnam to execute national policy and poor-
mouthing the Vietnamese was no way to do it." (10) By their
training and position as guests in a foreign nation, they were

expected to accent the positive, rather than point out all the negatives. In any event, the glowing optimism did not agree with what reporters were seeing, a situation which was exaccerbated by the Buddhist crisis. News reports reflected the different perspectives and the "credibility gap" began to creak open.

It was during the later years of the Diem regime that relations between the government and the press began to break down. Three correspondents were to find distinction through their criticisms of Pres. Diem. Two of them – David Halberstam (New York *Times*) and Malcolm Browne (AP) – shared a Pulitzer Prize for their reporting. The third, Neil Sheehan (UPI) had been in the running, as well. These writers set the trend for Vietnam reporting in the years to come as their articles and books became part of the small, select reading list, the "inner landscape" for war reporters in the 1960s. (11)

However, a number of observers began to criticize these reporters for trying to influence the war and politics of Vietnam. Gen. Westmoreland claims David Halberstam had a personal "vendetta" against Gen. Harkins, the U.S. military commander at the time. (12) Kennedy's press secretary, Pierre Salinger, accused Halberstam, Sheehan and Browne of harboring "a dedication to bringing down the Diem government." (13)   Time and time again the news media in general, or individuals within the media, would be accused of interfering in political affairs – trying to create the news rather than report it. The "adversary relationship" between the media and official circles turned to hostility.

One might call the situation a contest of professions. The diplomatic and military teams conducted their activites as officers of the American government while the media pursued its inherent goals of seeking out the news and presenting it to the public. Reporters were disturbed by contradictions between what they were being briefed on by the "establishment" and what they saw (or thought they were seeing) with their own eyes, as well as by the seemingly never-ending chain of predictions that the war would soon come to an end. The experiences of their predecessors had cautioned them to view official sources with distrust. Meanwhile, officials were disturbed by media inaccuracies and editorializing. Gen. Westmoreland says he "resented" the time he and his staff spent clarifying or correcting erroneous news reports for their superiors. (14)

As goals and values clashed, hostilities between the two sides tended to feed on each other. Robert Elegant suggests that newly arrived reporters often expected complete candor from official informants and were frustrated by anything less than that. Official reports, says Elegant, oscillated between "excessive candor and bald falsification." Incompetent journalism only made matters worse. Yet, even as American reporters complained of official evasion, reporters from other nations were "astonished" by the "openness with which the foolish Americans conducted their war."

Both the military and the press were further frustrated by the problems of trying to describe an unconventional war in conventional terms. The war in Vietnam could not be followed along lines of ground gained or lost, clear victories or defeats. It was a different type of conflict and new measures were demanded; pacification, weapons seized, body counts, infiltration rates, popularlity, and so on. These obscure terms were not always satisfactory in explaining the progress of the war and led to further misunderstanding as well as complaints of deception and over-optimism on the part of U.S. officials.

Beyond such mechanical notions, however, was the more important attitude change that took place in the 1960s. Robert Elegant feels that the media became politicized, and was bound to take sides, rather than recount the news. This partisanship was "inspired by the *engage* 'investigative reporting' that burgeoned in the U.S. in those impassioned years." The media turned against the government, "and, at least reflexively, for Saigon's enemies."

It became popular to criticize the war and the U.S. government. And in this the news media enjoyed an impressive degree of freedom. In what other war could a prestigious American newspaper allow an associate editor to visit the capital city of the enemy and then publish reports from that editor, fully aware that they were based on propaganda material supplied by the enemy? Where else but in Vietnam could reporters be given access to military transportation to all points of operation, and still find reporters complaining that the military was hiding things from them? At what other time in American history did a decisive defeat for the enemy appear to be a defeat for the Allies?

These things were not accidents. Too many reporters were looking for too many failures by the American government, and, lo and behold, they found them, even when these failures did not exist. Some journalists considered it their duty to uphold the honor of their comrades who had predicted doom for South Vietnam. These extremists (a minority, to be sure, but influential nonetheless) were committed to proving that the government was wrong. This was the observation of correspondent Marguerite Higgins, who had distinguished herself for reporting during the Korean conflict. Ms. Higgins concluded that "reporters here would like to see us lose the war to prove they are right." (15)

One of the fashions that arose during the war was the brilliant idea to provide the North Vietnamese with an opportunity to "tell their side of the story." In normal times, such an idea would have been considered ill-advised, if not downright treasonous. But the Vietnam War era was not normal times and many members of the antiwar movement (including their friends in the media) were so firmly convinced of America's immorality and deception that they adopted a faulty syllogism, here defined by Robert Elegant: "Washington was lying constantly; Hanoi contradicted Washington; therefore Hanoi was telling the truth."

In reality, there was little basis for such blind faith in the words of Communist leaders. However, during the war, the focus was on America's role, America's actions, America's problems, America's allies, and America's goals. The atrocities and deception of the Communists were conveniently shoved into a corner and quickly forgotten. There was certainly justification for looking carefully at the "American" side of the war – our actions are our responsibility. Yet the fact remains there was no Seymour Hersh pouncing on the story of mass executions by the Communists during Tet, despite almost immediate knowledge of the event. There was no editorial outcry when the Communists slaughtered thousands in Quang Tri in 1972, but newspapers blasted the December bombing of Hanoi, basing their attacks on exaggerated and misleading information. Such distortion would not have been possible if there had not already developed a generally tolerant attitude toward the Communists and a critical one toward the U.S. The hostilities had gotten out of hand.

Frankenstein

Journalists were by no means simply innocent bystanders of the war. They have not only recorded the war; they have also interpreted it for their audience. These interpretations have not always been historically sound and they have contributed greatly to the general misunderstandings about the war. While blame for the war and its outcome are quickly dished out to the several American presidents, their Secretaries of State, the South Vietnamese, and others, journalists would do well to keep in mind their own errors in perpetuating myth and erroneous notions and for dabbling in areas for which they have not been sufficiently prepared.

One strident critic of the media is former Nixon advisor Patrick J. Buchanan. In his criticism of media "arrogance" following the Grenada news blackout, Buchanan recalled the Vietnam conflict and the media's role there.

"But we are the free press, comes the retort. We are the watchdogs of democracy who keep government honest. We performed the great national service of exposing the official lies of the Vietnam War.

"But the greatest falsehoods told the American people in those war years were that the Viet Cong were simple peasants and patriots, that Ho Chi Minh was a nationalist, that this was a civil war in which we had no business, that the people of South Vietnam and Southeast Asia would be better off if the Americans packed up and went home, that our war effort was wrong-headed, if not downright wicked and immoral. That pack of lies did not come from Pentagon East." (16)

The war is "over", but the problem persists, as the recorded views of journalists remain to haunt scholars of the war even today. The war, alas, has spawned a new monster: the journalist-as-a-historian. While no one can say with all certainty that journalists "lost" the war for the Allies, a problem remains as journalist-historians, more interested in creating a popular story than in well-grounded research, continue to reinforce the cliches and misunderstandings promoted by their colleagues during the war.

The latest effort of the new wave of "Vietnam War" histories is the multi-volume Time/Life series entitled *The Vietnam Experience.*

Admittedly, this writer has not yet seen the work, but the advertising delivered in the mail is ominous. The "Dear Reader" letter opens by pointing out how official statements about the war in 1967 were overly optimistic (and consequently wrong) while the New York *Times* was more reserved (and therefore right). As one reads on, the letter explains how the Time/Life series is "the most comprehensive account of the war yet published", with "a clear and encyclopedic overview" that all will find "accurate down to the last detail." *The Vietnam Experience* covers "*all* facets of the war" presented from "*every* side." (sic) "At last", says the letter, "you can . . . satisfy your desire for the truth . . ."

This self-proclaimed Bible of the war covers the viewpoints of "veterans as well as politicians and journalists, . . . grunts as well as officers, . . . hawks as well as doves." (Note the absence of the South Vietnamese, Cambodians, and Lao.) Like the prophetic book of Ezekiel, this history transcends reality to show the war "as it appeared through the eyes of Ho Chi Minh and military mastermind Vo Nguyen Giap" – as if either of those comrades has ever been honest and objective in his pronouncements about the war. One wonders, too, what standards were used to qualify Gen. Giap – whose idea of military strategy is to see how many teenage boys he can throw into the line of fire – as a "mastermind."

The publishers are not stingy with praise for themselves.

"At last the whole story . . . Fully balanced perspective . . . No effort has been spared to make this the definitive work on the Vietnam War . . . Extraordinary."

Humility is no virtue in the offices of Time/Life.

Lacking an American victory to glorify, this history focuses on the "experience" of the war. The set of books is dedicated to the Americans who served and died in Vietnam, and accounts for their "acts of heroism and courage that got too little recognition" in the past.

This is incredible. For years the media has been presenting the Vietnam vets as killers, drug addicts and psychotics. Now, over 10 years after the Americans left Vietnam, Time/Life has brushed off its old files and discovered pictures and stories that show a different side of the vet: caring, courageous, honorable. Where have these pictures been for so many years and why have people waited until now to show them?

Who dares answer the question? Certainly not Time/Life.

A Television Travesty

The PBS series *Vietnam: A Television History* is perhaps the ultimate example of bad journalism. The program violates most of the informal rules of objectivity and fairness, and furthermore, fails to achieve even the standards created for it by its producers.

The program's benefactors in Washington, D.C., and Boston boast that the series has received "almost universal acclaim." Upon inspection, this claim proves to be far-fetched. There are a number of reviews solidly critical of the series, the better among these including articles by veteran Richard K. Kolb, in *Human Events* (June 16, 1984); Stephen Morris, in the *Wall Street Journal* (Dec. 20, 1983); Reed Irvine, in *Accuracy In Media* (Jan. B, 1984); David Chanoff and Doan Van Toai, in *The American Spectator* (Jan. 1984). On the other hand, one of the most complimentary reviews of the series was published in the Communist Vietnamese Army newspaper, *Quan Doi Nhan Dan* (see Appendix).

If the producers have difficulty grasping the concept of universality, they also fail to understand the meaning of "balance." Although assuring their viewers of a balanced and impartial historical account, the producers fail time and time again to present crucial facts or responsible viewpoints regarding critical issues, including: veterans viewpoints, the history of Vietnam, unrehearsed opinions of Ho Chi Minh and the Communists, and the thoughts of individuals who feel America's involvement in the war was justified. In place of an in-depth and informative history, viewers find a collage of images based on popular themes, not all of which are verifiable. To achieve "objectivity", the program presents what one reviewer calls a "collection of memories" for veteran observers, "moving steadily through the years at the lowest common denominator of fact, trafficking, as they must, in stereotype, oversimplification and visual cliche." (17)

This is not the only time the series fails to pass inspection. In the series' *Guide*, Executive Producer Richard Ellison describes the project's approach to presenting history for television. Writes Ellison: "That style is best described as 'plain'. No fancy intercut editing, no emotive music, no omniscient narrator. Plainness is in the interests of the philosophical objectivity, which is to manipulate the viewer as little as possible. The archival film is what it purports to be; sources are identified when necessary; contradictory viewpoints are clearly articulated; conclusions and value judgments are expressed by the participants and interview subjects, not by the program makers."

So says the executive producer. But, is that the way the show really is? Perhaps we should look carefully at each point of Ellison's "style." (18)

"No fancy intercut editing." – Scene in Part 4: President Lyndon Johnson delivers a speech on the White House lawn. He cries with apparent feeling, "Oh why, oh why don't people concern themselves with a country that's trying to maintain her independence from aggression?" But even as Johnson declares, "We are trying to do the reasonable thing, to say that power and brute force and aggression will not prevail", the picture moves to an incident allegedly taking place at exactly the same time: a unit of Marines enters a village near Danang; they proceed to rough-house the peasants, hold women and children at bay with their rifles, blow out a VC tunnel, pull mud-caked corpses from the mess and finally, the coup de gras, burn down the peasants' homes.

Part 8: William Colby defends the Phoenix Program against charges of abuse. Colby, who tries to defend the pacification program as a whole, is twice interrupted by Sidney Towle, who describes individual instances of abuse. This is followed immediately by movies of South Vietnamese jails.

Part 10: The narrator informs us that Richard Nixon was unconcerned about criticism of the December 1972 bombing of Hanoi. The picture we see is of a woman resident of Hanoi digging through the ruins of her home.

"No emotive music." – Since music is emotive by nature, we must assume Ellison means to say "there is no music at all", which is, of course, not true. George Ball speaks kindly of Pres. Johnson as a sympathetic melody plays in the background. A woman wails a plaintive tune over a grave. LBJ is buried to the sound of the "Battle Hymn of the Republic". No emotion here.

"No omniscient narrator." – The narrator serves to link together the fractured images of the series. His remarks (expressed in a dull,

hypnotic monotone, presumably also not emotive) often reflect
insight or understanding that goes beyond the mere introduction of
scenes. Examples: "It was a war with deep roots, deeper than
most Americans knew." "The consternation was indeed maximum."
"To Thieu, like his predecessors, the election was a means to control
the population and placate the Americans." "America had viewed
Vietnam as a crusade, as a challange, and finally, as a burden."
Statements like these can only be made by omniscient narrators and
Madam Sabrina, who reads crystal balls in the sideshow.

"Archival film is what it purports to be." – Most of the film in the
series does not purport to be anything of itself, but depends on the
context given it by the producers. Sometimes even this is lacking.
Example, opening scene in Part 8: A helicopter buzzes around a
field following "four guys with bushes on them"; as the chopper
descends, a terrified farmer comes out of the reeds with a child in his
arms, bowing fearfully to the American soldiers. What does this
scene purport to be? It looks to this writer like a commentary on
the war.

Most of the combat filmage used in the series comes from network
news archives. The film had already been edited before it reached
the hands of the series' producers, and then it was edited again. The
original context has long disappeared. Each scene becomes what
the producers want to make it.

All materials provided by North Vietnam and other Communist
countries are, naturally, propaganda materials and not historical
record. These films were staged, edited and fabricated for an ideological purpose, although the series never pauses to explain this.
Instead, they are used as historical documents of the same caliber as
films supplied by ABC News. Typical scenes shown in the PBS
series include the remake of the battle of Dien Bien Phu; Ho Chi
Minh speaking before cheering crowds, talking with peasants or
handing out cigarettes to the boys at the front (the untiring Uncle
Ho always at work for his people); grim, determined Vietnamese
warriors firing away at pirate American planes; a convoy of small
river boats weaving through the reeds as American bombs fall and
explode around them; porters on the Ho Chi Minh Trail toting sacks
of rice with the USAID symbol on them . . .

At times throughout the series, newsreel and propaganda films from the U.S. and South Vietnam are presented along with their original soundtracks. The films come across as hackneyed political statements; the viewers can choose to accept them or not. However, Communist films are removed from context and stripped of their propaganda purpose to serve ends other than those for which they were originally intended. They are given new narration and new context in order to suit the needs of the television producers. Viewers are given no preparation for the changes and are expected to swallow the films as factual and accurate. Meanwhile, Vietnamese who had been in concentration camps after 1975 recognized these films as the same ones they had been shown during "re-education."

Rather than promote an understanding of the war, the films offer some of the most ridiculous scenes in cinematic history: a pretty, young female cadre gingerly drops her arm to signal the firing of anti-aircraft artillery; ditchdiggers at Dien Bien Phu swing their shovels at machine-like speed and never duck as bombs explode around their heads; Uncle Ho passes out Dien Bien Phu brand cigarettes when the only kind he smoked were the imperialist Philip Morris; VC infiltrators fire their guns level to the ground to shoot down American planes flying overhead . . . As one Vietnamese commentator put it, these films are more appropriate for a documentary on the incompetence of Communist filmmakers than for historical lessons.

"Sources are identified when necessary." – Apparently it was rarely "necessary" to do this in the series, although this writer would like to know where some of those black-and-white movies came from and what was their original context. A number of films that presumably came from North Vietnam are not identified (suggesting they are historical records), for instance, the scenes of Communist troops at Ia Drang. Even when the source is told, the effect is filtered by gimmicks. Scenes of the battle of Dien Bien Phu are not identified as coming from the Russians until *after* they have been shown and used as historical documentary with appropriate narration dubbed in. The film of river boats dodging American bombs (which have the explosive force of small hand grenades) is identified as coming from East Germany, but the narrator continues with sincerity, "But its message is true" – that is, the bombing of Communist infiltration routes was not working. (If the bombs being dropped were truly like those in the film, it's no wonder the missions failed.)

Likewise, a number of persons interviewed for the series are not identified by anything but their names. When does Richard Ellison tell his viewers that Col. Bui Tin is a Communist newspaper editor or that Hoang Phu Ngoc Tuong had been a leader in the temporary government in Hue during the Tet Offensive? According to Ellison, it just wasn't necessary to do so.

"Contradictory views are clearly articulated." – In Part 1, Communist informants describe the rise of the Viet Minh as a popular movement supported by all the people, who revered Ho Chi Minh the Patriot. The non-communist version of this period is never given, although it is quite different. The result is that the Communists' long and bloody rise to power during the 1930s and 1940s comes across looking like a Girl Scout cookie sale.

Later in the series, Capt. Tran Van Ngo boasts that he "contributed to the liberation of the South" by killing three Americans with his bayonet. One American veteran in San Diego was angered by this statement; he claims the only way Capt. Ngo could have killed anyone with a knife is if the victims had been prisoners or wounded. The series does not pursue this angle and prefers to make the North Vietnamese soldier into a hero.

The series presents Ngo Dinh Diem as a tyrant, American policy as cruel and insensitive, American GIs as senseless killers, and the Communist leaders as cool and rational. No person is interviewed to express a contradictory viewpoint to any of these opinions.

"The program makers express no conclusions or value judgments." – Assuming that the narrator speaks for the program makers, we may wonder about such "valueless" comments as these: South Vietnamese president Khanh "continued to intrigue as head of the armed forces." Ngo Dinh Diem "shunted peasants into fortified villages." "Paid with American aid, armed with American weapons, South Vietnamese soldiers on patrol in 1969." These remarks are clearly loaded and reflect the double standard applied by the producers. We never hear that Gen. Giap "intrigued" as leader of the Communist forces in the North, or that North Vietnamese peasants were "shunted" to the mines or farms, or that Ho Chi Minh's government would have collapsed in a day if it had not been for massive Soviet and Chinese aid.

The reader can see that Richard Ellison has proven unable to deliver on a single one of his statements regarding his approach to television history. What can be the purpose of such statements, then, except to lull students into a state of complacency, wherein they trust that they are indeed viewing an open and balanced program, the result of scrupulous labor and research, a hallmark in television documentary production?

The Last Crusade

Before going on to look at the individual parts of the *Televison History*, it would be helpful to remember one important point about the production. That is the producers' sense of mission.

The producers knew they were developing a big story – the biggest, they believed, in all television history. They were aware of the topic's controversy, its capacity to generate strong emotions, its magnitude. They were overwhelmed by the awesome nature of their task, as of the war itself, and strove to apply the accumulation of their journalistic talents into creating the greatest documentary ever.

Unfortunately, they lacked the basic tools to do the job adequately. Being neither historians nor educators, they presumed to present history as an educational experience. With an insufficient background in the politics and history of Vietnam, they tried to interpret and explain these for us. Lacking a basic knowledge of the war on which to compare the relative merits of their various consultants, they hoped to be arbiters in the great debate. In their eagerness to do justice to the suffering caused by the war, they saw all Vietnamese as victims of U.S. aggression, including the Communists. They involved themselves personally with the Communist leaders, even publishing pictures of themselves with them, as if some great reconciliation were taking place. They were, they believed, the agents of a new wave of understanding, communicators of the true story of Vietnam, and ambassadors of justice.

Had they realized that they were, after all, only journalists working within a specialized profession, perhaps the series would have been much different.

In the final analysis, one may conclude that journalism and history are not always compatible. By profession, journalists must produce stories that are concise, timely, appealing and appropriate to a specific audience. Meanwhile, historians must deal with broader events, complex influences, the mundane as well as the spectacular, the concrete and the abstract, long-range matters and short-range, and countless indeterminate facts. Journalists are trained to look for that which will attract attention, yet history is not always shaped by attractive events. Journalists seek to encapsulate events, while historians must cover broad and vacillating ground. In values, objectives, skills and perceptions, the two professions are distinct and separate. This was admitted by Henri de Turenne, producer of the French version of the *Television History*. When his program was attacked by the French and Vietnamese viewers, de Turenne admitted the errors in his production, declaring in his defense, "I made a mistake, I regret it. I am not a historian. I am a journalist." (19)

The same may be said of Stanley Karnow and Richard Ellison.

Footnotes

1. William A. Henry III, Assoc. Ed., "Journalism Under Fire", *Time*, December 12, 1983
2. Ibid., quoting Editor Max Frankel
3. Reed Irvine, "Flawed History of Vietnam", AIM, January-B, 1984
4. Peter Braestrup, *Big Story* (Abridged), p. 12
5. Noted in Braestrup, Ibid., p. 37
6. William Westmoreland, *A Soldier Reports*, p. 306
7. Ibid., p 511
8. Braestrup, Note 4 above, p. 12
9. Westmoreland, Note 6 above, p. 510
10. Ibid., p 79
11. Braestrup, Note 4 above, p. 6
12. Westmoreland, Note 6 above, p. 79
13. Quoted in AIM, Note 3 above
14. Westmoreland, Note 6 above, p. 511
15. Quoted in Robert Elegant, "How To Lose a War", *Encounter*, August 1981

16. Patrick J. Buchanan, "It's Security vs. the Press",
    Tribune Co. Syndicate
17. *Indochina Chronology*, Vol. II, No. 3, July-September 1983
18. The editor expresses appreciation to the "Caveat Spectator"
    for this idea.
19. Quoted in *Southeast Asia Review*, No. 4, March 1984

PART 1: ROOTS OF A WAR

There is a brief review of Vietnamese history from earliest times to the French colonial period. The emphasis is on Vietnam's history of struggle against foreign invaders and sense of national unity. The effects of colonialism on Vietnam are described as well as the rise of Ho Chi Minh as a model "nationalist." The arrival of the Japanese in 1939 further inspires nationalist feelings and the Viet Minh is formed. The country suffers from economic ruin and there is a severe famine in 1945. After World War II, the Viet Minh take over Hanoi, the Allies allow France to return to the southern half of Vietnam while the Chinese occupy the North. Col. Peter Dewey is the first American to die in Vietnam.

The Antiwar Overture

As a prelude to the PBS history of the war, the viewers are taken on a brief tour of the program through a sequence of images representing important themes in the series. These scenes are noteworthy for their selection, as well as for the interesting narration that accompanies them.

To begin with, we see four American presidents explaining the domino theory in their own words. Then the narrator speaks:

"First a handful of advisers. Then the Marines. Finally, an army of half a million. That was the Vietnam war."

As one can see, the war is here described entirely from the perspective of the Americans.

"It was an undeclared war. A war without front lines or clear objectives. A war against an elusive enemy."

Now the narrator has taken us a step further. It was America's war, a senseless war brought on by America's fear of Communism. Right away the program suggests that there was something not quite right about it all.

"A war."

The narration concludes with this profound statement as a boy from Seattle lies bleeding, waiting to be evacuated. A veteran tells how the American army accomplished nothing but winning a "box on the map" that was eventually abandoned. Meanwhile, a Vietnamese villager complains that "wherever the Americans went they burned and destroyed and killed!" We are told that even little children wanted to kill the Americans. The war's "deep roots" are emphasized by the narrator's audacious assertion that it was "Ho Chi Minh and his followers" alone who fought against the French and later "the Americans and their South Vietnamese ally."

In this way, more curious ideas are suggested to the viewers. It was America's war. Americans died and killed for nothing. The Vietnamese did not want them, just as they had not wanted the French. It was Ho Chi Minh who led a popular struggle for his people.

The intrinsic evil of America's involvement in the war is shown in the way the war "turned South Vietnam inside out" and GIs were all turned into potheads. Fortunately, "uncensored" news reports brought the truth of the war home and Americans opposed the war "in huge numbers, openly and passionately." Then it all ended with the Communist victory, leaving unanswered questions and unresolved issues.

In the remaining 13 hours of the series, the producers hope to change all that. If the narrator's lifeless drone has not already put the viewers to sleep, they will find many answers to some carefully prepared questions that are suggested by the film. Whether they are true or not is another matter.

Vietnamese Tradition

The PBS history of Vietnam opens with a description of Vietnam's supposed tradition of warring and fervent nationalism. "The Vietnamese have known war a long time – more than 2,000 years," says the narrator. They fought off "China, their giant neighbor to the north" and honor the Trung Sisters, whose unsuccessful rebellion marked them as heroines, "part of a long line of Vietnamese who fought foreign domination." Communist Premier Pham Van Dong connects Ho Chi Minh to the early heroes of Vietnam, thus identifying the Communist Chairman with Vietnam's "historical nationalism." After fighting for a thousand years, the Vietnamese finally "evicted" the Chinese, then pushed south, "expanding rapidly" to their present borders, conquering "all who stood in their path."

Unfortunately for PBS television, reality is not so sensational. The "thousand years of struggle" against the Chinese was not a period of constant war between patriotic peasants and their foreign rulers, but ten centuries of relatively undisturbed domination by China marred here and there by sporadic rebellions of Vietnamese nobles against their overlords. Linking Ho Chi Minh to Vietnam's early kings is simply ludicrous; Ho was an internationalist and a revolutionary who rejected Vietnamese tradition and past to agitate for the socialist brotherhood of the whole world. Vietnam's "rapid expansion" actually took another thousand years and was more successful when it gradually absorbed other peoples rather than conquered them. The Vietnamese did not all grow up to be warriors any more than Americans did in their rapid expansion across an entire continent in less than 200 years.

Thus from the very beginning, the viewers become aware of the limitations involved in using television as a medium for presenting history. Restricted by time and technological scope, television simply cannot give an in-depth review of a country's development and the foundations of a culture that covers centuries and involves a multitude of factors, such as religion, society, and philosophy, many of which cannot be shown in visual images. In the case of the *Television History*, by stressing only a sensational "history of nationalism" the producers ignore the other 99 percent of Vietnamese history that has nothing to do with nationalism or warring but which has molded the characters of the people and culture of that land.

(Stanley Karnow's *History* is little better. Some 2,000 years of recorded Vietnamese history up to the French time are covered in barely eight pages and described in vague, general terms. "Merchants and missionaries (from China and India) converged on the (Indochinese) peninsula." "Chronic turmoil plagued the area." "Vietnamese communities ... developed a strong collective spirit" and the people "evolved into a breed of warriors." (pp. 98-99)

These dramatic exclamations are highly exaggerated and not backed up by documentation in the book. Karnow uses them to set the stage for what happens in the rest of his story as he links Vietnam's history to Ho Chi Minh, who is introduced in the preceding pages. The reader interested in early Vietnamese history will get no help from Karnow.)

In the TV series, the viewer is given no overview of traditional Vietnamese culture and society. Such a review is essential to an understanding of modern Vietnamese history, both to identify who the Vietnamese people are and also to show how twentieth century Communism has no roots in Vietnamese tradition. The producers would like to prove that Ho Chi Minh's "nationalist" movement was a natural outgrowth of history, an indigenous revolution, not a matter of Communist expansionism. In fact, the connection between Vietnamese tradition and Communism is one which is promoted only in Vietnamese Communist literature (see the "Suggestions for Further Reading" in Cohen's *Anthology and Guide*, p. 29). In order for the reader to see some of the weaknesses of this theory, a few comparisons of Vietnamese tradition and Communism may be helpful:

SOCIETY:

Tradition – The primary social unit in traditional Vietnam is the family, extended to include not only the parents and children, but also grandparents, aunts, uncles, cousins and so on. The family is the hub of most activities, and the source of most emotions, loyalties, ceremonies and expressions. The Vietnamese venerate their ancestors; every home, no matter how poor, has an ancestral altar and family graves are visited regularly. In their language, the Vietnamese refer to persons outside the family by relationship terms such as uncle, aunt, brother, sister, grandmother, grandfather, etc.

Communism – In the Communist system, the primary social and political unit is the Party. All activities, feelings and loyalties belong to the Party and its representatives. Family property and even family members should be voluntarily sacrificed for the goals of the Party. Relationships are broken down and children are encouraged to report on the daily activities of their parents, leading to distrust and a loss of respect between parents and their children.

During the Land Reform Campaign in North Vietnam, First Party Secretary Truong Chinh had his father denounced and executed. Such action is typical of a Communist devotee and one which Confucius would never have approved. All social ranks in Communist society are leveled; everyone is referred to as "comrade."

POLITICS:
Tradition – The primary political unit in traditional Vietnam is the village, or its subdivision the hamlet. Poor communications as well as an inclination of farming communities to keep to themselves has led to isolation of villages from one another. Official posts are held by village elders and other persons respected for their education or wealth. Few people have contact with province officials or the imperial court. A folk saying reflecting the prominence of the village says, "The king's law stops at the village gate."
Communism – Communism is a centrally-run state operation with power in the hands of a few leaders in the Party Politburo. The government strives to control the entire population under a uniform system of organized "cells" following common directives which are implemented by Party cadres. Local leaders are installed through mock elections; the people are given no choice as to who will lead them. Communist leaders distrust intellectuals and profess to give power to the uneducated "proletarians" and peasants. Many village cadres can neither read nor write adequately to conduct daily business.

ECONOMY:
Tradition – Vietnam's economy has always been based on agriculture. Some of the farmers own the land they work; others are tenant farmers. A section of "communal land" is usually set aside to help support village activities and feed the poor. Some coastal villages specialize in fishing and a number of other localities have craft specialties. Trading is rather small scale and there is little industry; consequently there are few persons who qualify as "bourgeoisie" or "proletarian" by any standard. The village economy aims at self-sufficiency, based on the family's needs.
Communism – Communism proposes "equal distribution of land to the poor" but only as a temporary stage leading to the total collec-

tivisation of land and property. Everything is state-owned and individuals have no rights regarding the use of property. Farmers and laborers produce for the state, which in turn provides them with rations of food and other essentials. Proletariat labor is seen as the foundation of the socialist economy. Merchants are exploiters and farmers not sufficiently progressive to take full part in the revolution.

CULTURE:
Tradition – Vietnamese culture is a blend of Confucianism, Buddhism, Taoism and other beliefs, including animism and spiritualism. The Vietnamese value family privacy, personal dignity, respect for elders and social harmony. The traditional hierarchy of respect in this society starts with the scholars on top, then farmers, laborers, and finally merchants. Buddhism has taught the value of human life in a constantly flowing sea of suffering. One's ultimate personal goal is the achievement of harmony with nature in tranquility and peace.
Communism – Communist "culture" is an artificial system imposed on the people by a strong government. It stresses loyalty to the Party, sacrifice for the state and the elimination of the "enemies of the people." The Communists honor soldiers as the protectors of the state and youth as the vanguard of the revolution. Intellectuals are either repressed or manipulated, thus art forms are restricted and lack creativity and imagination. Life has value only in relation to the revolution and each person should be proud to give his/her life for the "cause."

It is very clear from the above examples that Communism is fundamentally quite different from traditional Vietnamese culture. The Communist revolution in Vietnam (as in any Communist country) never had the widespread support of the people. While at times the peasants may have suffered in poverty or been oppressed by mandarins, it is debatable whether this would lead naturally to a "revolution" involving the destruction of society as they knew it and a leveling of all classes to a uniform state of poverty. It would be more reasonable to say that rather than destroy this traditional society, most people would be satisfied to get a better share of its benefits. It is presumptuous to suggest that the Vietnamese peasants yearned for justice, freedom, and democracy as they are known to Western society or to the rule of the proletariat as described by Marxism.

The point we wish to make here is that Communism is not grounded in Vietnamese tradition, is foreign to all of Southeast Asia and was brought into the area from the Soviet Union and China by specially trained cadres, including Tran Phu, Le Hong Phong, Nguyen Van Cu, Tran Van Giau and Ho Chi Minh. The Communists only gained support and came to power by exploiting popular slogans and the history of poverty and hardship endured by the peasants. And instead of improving the situation, the Communists have only made it worse.

The Anti-Colonial Resistance

The French took control of Indochina in the late 19th and early 20th centuries. The period of colonialism that ensued brought Vietnam, Cambodia and Laos into the "modern" world and stimulated a new sense of national and ethnic identity. Many Indochinese committed themselves to helping their respective nations progress in order to compete honorably in their new, broader world. Some believed that to do this it was necessary to throw out the French.

If the *Television History* is correct, Vietnam did not have a single anti-French resistance group worth talking about besides the Communist-controlled Viet Minh (full name Viet Nam Doc Lap Dong Minh Hoi, or Vietnamese Independence League), or a single nationalist leader other than Nguyen Ai Quoc (Ho Chi Minh). In fact, on this series Ho Chi Minh is given credit for inspiring, if not actually directing, virtually the entire anti-colonialist movement prior to 1945, including the Yen Bay uprising in 1930. We are told that the sole Vietnamese political opponent of Ho was the emperor Bao Dai, who is characterized as a puppet of the French and a playboy.

The *Television History* is not correct. There were many prominent nationalist groups and leaders remembered by the Vietnamese even today as heroes of the resistance. One group was the Vietnam Nationalist Party, whose leader, Nguyen Thai Hoc, was the person responsible for the Yen Bay rebellion and who was guillotined by the French along with a dozen of his followers because of it. The Nationalist Party was one of the stronger nationalist organizations during the pre-World War II era and was much better known at the time than the Communist groups.

According to the series, Vietnamese nationalist spirit was further awakened by the arrival of the Japanese in 1940. In fact, Vietnamese nationalist leaders had been inspired by Japan for several decades prior to that time. Another nationalist not mentioned in the program was Phan Boi Chau, who sought direction and assistance from Asian countries including Japan and China. He began his travels in 1905 and established what was known as the "Eastward Movement", encouraging young people and students to study abroad and learn from progressive nations in Asia. The patriot Chau was joined in this by Prince Cuong De, who eventually died in Tokyo in 1951. The two leaders formed the Vietnamese Modern Movement. In 1913, Chau was implicated in a bombing incident in Hanoi and sentenced to death in abstencia by the French (around this time, Ho Chi Minh was still washing dishes in a London hotel). Chau spent time in prison in China and in 1925 was picked up by French agents in Shanghai. Public outcry and a new colonial governor kept him from being executed, but Chau was confined to his home until he died in 1940.

There were other patriots, too, such as Phan Chu Trinh, the leader of the Private Schools Movement, whose death in 1926 sparked mass demonstrations and student strikes.

Another was the editor and writer Pham Quynh, who was murdered by the Viet Minh in 1945.

A political party of the 1930s and 1940s that achieved some prominence was the Dai Viet Quoc Dan Dang (Greater Vietnamese Nationalist Party) which looked to Japan for inspiration. Its leader, Truong Tu Anh, a fervent anti-Communist, was assassinated by the Viet Minh.

There was the Trotskyite leader Ta Thu Thau, a tough anti-colonialist who was arrested numerous times by the French as he carried out his violent political activities. Thau was killed by the Viet Minh in Quang Ngai province after World War II.

Two important politico-religious sects in the southern part of

Vietnam were involved in anti-French resistance in the 1930s and 1940s. These were the Cao Dai and the Hoa Hao. In 1947 the founder of the Hoa Hao, Huynh Phu So, was murdered by the Communists.

Among the intellectuals involved in the struggle against the French was Phan Khoi. This scholar was involved in the Private Schools Movement and wrote for the movement's magazine, which was summarily closed down by the French. Despite being thrown in jail, he continued his anti-French writing and also engaged in a literary debate with the Communist writer Hai Trieu. In the North after the Viet Minh declared war on the French, "Elder Phan" criticized Communist cadres and the old man would have been arrested had it not been for the intervention of his son, a high ranking official with the Viet Minh. He later was arrested by the Communists when he went to visit a famed nationalist author, Khai Hung. Ho Chi Minh sent the scholar up to the northern regions to cool off during the First Indochina War. When he returned to Hanoi he went back to criticizing the Party and their literary association, sparking a movement of protest among intellectuals in the North. The old man (by now in his seventies) was denounced and slandered as a traitor, a Trotskyite, an opium-smoker and a womanizer. Only his prestige among the people kept him from being executed outright by the Communists.

And there was Bui Quang Chieu of the Constitutionalist Party, who was assassinated by the Viet Minh. And Huynh Thuc Khang, Le Van Huan, Nguyen An Ninh, Dao Duy Anh – all of whom played a part in the early years of the resistance and none of whom is mentioned in the television series. Instead, only Ho Chi Minh and the Viet Minh are given credit for any "nationalist sentiment" and, as we shall see, that credit is misplaced.

(Karnow's *History* alludes to a few of the nationalists besides his hero Ho Chi Minh, but only briefly and with little recognition for their achievements. Karnow apparently hopes to discredit the Nationalist Party by stating incorrectly that it was created by the Chinese Nationalists of Chiang Kai Shek (p. 124). Although their names are similar, the Vietnamese Nationalist Party (Quoc Dan Dang) was not the offspring of the Chinese Kuomintang. It was formed in 1927 out of a group calling itself the Nam Dong

Publishing House, which admired Sun Yat Sen's Chinese revolution and published works reflecting Sun's "Three Principles." The Nationalist Party was created in November 1927 under the leadership of Nguyen Thai Hoc and Nguyen Khac Nhu. It copied from the Chinese nationalists in form and ideas, but this is hardly the same thing as saying the Vietnamese group was created by followers of Chiang Kai Shek. Karnow does not describe the hostility between the Communists and nationalist groups before 1945 nor the tactics used by the Communists to divide and weaken other groups. With regards to Phan Boi Chau's arrest in 1925, Karnow notes in passing that: "According to some accounts, (Chau) was betrayed by Communist rivals." (p. 112) The chief correspondent neglects to mention that by "Communist rivals" he means a certain Ly Thuy, later to be known as Ho Chi Minh. It seems Karnow's attempts to paint Ho as a saintly figure have blinded him to the more mundane realities of staging a revolution. His ignorance of Vietnamese history reaches a rather amusing point when he tries to show a "remarkable exception" to the claim of a French governor that the Vietnamese could neither read nor write their language. Instead of citing Nhat Linh or Khai Hung— famous writers of the first part of this century and founders of the *Tu Luc Van Doan*, the first modern literary group in Vietnam— or any of the noted Vietnamese scholars, authors, poets, newspaper editors and writers, Karnow selects . . . Gen. Vo Nguyen Giap! (p. 115)

(The reader should also note on page 92 of the *History* an item in the corner which Karnow dubs a "nationalist cartoon." The author tells us, "The peasants are shouting, 'Wipe out the gang of imperialists, mandarins, capitalists and big landlords!' " Karnow only gives us half the message. The entire caption reads: "Follow the example of the Nghe-Tinh (soviets)! Workers, Farmers, Soldiers! Wipe out the imperialists, mandarins, capitalists and big landlords!" The cartoon is clearly signed "The Communist Party.")

Ho Chi Minh the "Nationalist" and The Rise of the Viet Minh

Central to Karnow's theories and the flow of the television series is the rather ill-founded idea that the Communist movement in Vietnam was no more than a nationalist movement seeking to end French rule and later to reunite the North and South into one nation. To "prove" this, the series makes free use of propaganda films provided by the Communists as well as interviews with high-ranking Communist officials (whose places in the Communist leadership, incidentally, are not identified for the viewer in Parts 1 and 2). The crux of the argument is that Ho Chi Minh was a nationalist first and a Communist second.

The television series treats Ho Chi Minh's background rather lightly. We are shown curious scenes of Ho's life as a student, speaking at meetings, walking down the steps into the loving embrace of his "nephews and nieces," and so on. Through the magic of television a couple of his not-too-imaginative cartoons are drawn before our very eyes and his eyeballs roll teasingly in an old photograph. These clever images almost make us forget that Ho's hero was Josef Stalin and that his policies are responsible for the deaths of millions of people all over Indochina. In the series, every move and gesture Ho makes is portrayed as promoting the cause of nationalism. To seal Ho's status, former Asian Affairs Adviser Abbott Low Moffat tells us that everyone who met Ho in those days agreed he was "first a nationalist, second a Communist" and he repeats for emphasis, "He was a nationalist first and foremost." Former OSS officer Archimedes Patti informs us that we had Ho "on a silver platter" and the Viet Minh was "in our hands" right after World War II.

The producers apparently felt that their point was made since they did not quote any of the many scholars and observers who hold a different opinion about Ho Chi Minh's motives. One person not interviewed is Hoang Van Chi, an emigrant from Vietnam who wrote about the Viet Minh period in a book entitled *From Colonialism to Communism*. In this account, the author tells how Ho was first introduced to leftist ideas and then "devoted himself to the cause of international communism." (1) Chi admires Ho's many talents – his facility in several languages, his cleverness as a tactician, his worldly experience and cunning. At the same time, he has no illusions about Ho's ultimate loyalty, describing the revolutionary as a "professional agitator who (could) expertly play the nationalists' game." (2) He also quotes Ho's own statement in an

essay entitled "The Path that led me to Leninism," where Ho
wrote: "In the beginning, it was patriotism and not communism
which induced me to believe in Lenin and the Third International.
But little by little, progressing step by step in the course of the
struggle and combining theoretical studies of Marxism-Leninism
with practical activities, I came to realize that socialism and communism alone are capable of emancipating workers and down-
trodden people all over the world." (3)

Austrian-born Bernard Fall, a scholar of the two Indochina wars,
holds a similar view of Ho Chi Minh. In *The Two Vietnams*, Fall
briefly reminds the reader of Ho's background with the Communist
movement– as a founding member of the French Communist Party,
an agent of the Communist International, his assignments in
Russia, China, Europe and Southeast Asia – and remarks that
"(Ho's) careers as an international agent of Communism... and as
a Vietnamese 'nationalist' were to be so completely intertwined as
to fool all but the most penetrating of observers. In much of Asia
and among many American specialists . . . Ho was considered a
Nationalist first and a Communist second... In actual fact, he has
always been a dedicated Communist with Vietnamese reactions...
Thus, all his life, Ho has used nationalist catchphrases, the references to traditional heroes and values . . . but without ever losing
sight of his Party's goals... His career as a Communist has been on
record since 1920." (4)

The producers of the *Television History* obviously disagree with
this assessment. Had they been making an objective program, they
might have included both arguments and allowed viewers to decide
for themselves.

(Stanley Karnow's biography of Ho Chi Minh reads more like a
romantic novel than history. It begins with the dizzy idealist
wandering through the streets of Paris with Shakespeare in hand,
"earnest yet gentle, reserved but not timid" – one envisions a
modern-day St. Francis of Assisi. Karnow dismisses any evidence
of Ho's involvement with the Communist International. Karnow
tries to stress Ho's alleged "nationalist" tendencies by quoting
only half a line from Ho's essay: "It was patriotism and not communism that originally inspired me" without completing the
sentence "to Lenin and the Third International," and then reading

further. (p. 122) Thus, using only partial truths and ignoring any derogatory references to Ho's life, Karnow paints a convincing portrait of a heroic nationalist. It just happens to be misleading.)

The *Television History* neglects to detail Ho Chi Minh's activities during the 1920s, '30s and '40s in Vietnam. This is a serious omission, for such a history would give the viewers a much different view of the Communists and the man the series portrays as a nationalist hero. For the reader's benefit, we give below an outline of Ho Chi Minh's political activities and the history of the Vietnamese Communists up to 1945, compiled primarily from the following sources: Hoang Van Chi, *From Colonialism to Communism*; I. Milton Sacks, Assoc. Professor of Politics at Brandeis University, "The Indigenous Roots of Vietnamese Nationalism," reprinted in *Vietnam: Anatomy of a Conflict*; and Douglas Pike, former Foreign Service Officer and Director of the Indochina Project at Berkeley University, *History of Vietnamese Communism: 1925-1976.*

Ho was introduced to prominent Socialist figures in France and he joined the Socialist Party, writing for its newspaper *Le Populaire.* At Tours in 1920, Ho voted for the formation of the French Communist Party, throwing his lot in with the Third Communist International, which advocated world revolution as opposed to nationalist Communist struggle. Ho attended the Fourth Comintern Congress in Moscow in 1922 and there the Southeast Asian section of the Comintern (Communist International) was created. It was at the Second such Congress that Lenin had given the go-ahead to Communists around the world to join in temporary alliance with nationalist movements while maintaining the independence of the Communist movement. Learning from this and Comintern agent Borodin's strategy for manipulating the Chinese Kuomintang, Ho was able to devise a movement intended to follow through the expected stages of the revolution: first, the "bourgeois democratic revolution" bringing about independence through an anti-colonialist alliance and secondly, the "proletariat revolution" whereby the country would become part of the World Soviet Federation. In 1923 Ho attended the Peasant's International Conference and the next year he was a student at the Eastern Toilers University where he learned Marxism-Leninism and Bolshevik tactics. In order to get to Moscow, Ho had to pose as a Chinese nationalist on his way back to his "homeland."

The reader should keep in mind that Lenin and his Bolsheviks were considered extremists, even among the Socialists of their day. The creation of the Third International, which pushed for "revolution now!", was an act of deliberate rejection of the moderate Socialist aims being promoted by many Europeans at that time. When Ho Chi Minh joined the Third International, he was accepting a radical Communist position and acknowledging Russia as the home of the world revolution. It is, therefore, inconsistent for observers to describe Chairman Ho as a "moderate" or an "Asian Tito." He was, in fact, a radical Communist of the Lenin-Stalin school.

In 1925 Ho was assigned to the supervision of Mikhail Borodin in Canton. There, he founded the Revolutionary Youth League. With this group's newspaper, Ho tried to capture the attention of the expatriot Vietnamese in China and provide fundamental instruction in Marxism. In the May 1926 issue, Ho was ready to pronounce that "only a Communist Party can insure the well-being of Annam (Vietnam)."

While in China, Ho used various pseudonyms, especially Lee Suei (Ly Thuy) and Vuong Son Nhi, pretending to be a Chinese when he was with the authorities and a Vietnamese to his compatriots. Ho collaborated with other groups at times, and competed with them at other times. New recruits to the nationalist movement who refused to join Ho's Youth League were often betrayed to the French security police for cash and sent to jail. (Phan Boi Chau was similarly sold out to the French, according to some, by Ho himself. In this version, Ho's accomplice in that caper was Lam Duc Thu, whom Ho later ordered murdered by having him stuffed in a basket and thrown in a river.) The Youth League met with opposition from the Vietnamese nationalists. For one thing, the League engaged in illegal and unethical activities to raise money, including robbery and the sell-out of rivals. Then the betrayal of the famous patriot Phan Boi Chau made nationalists suspicious of the Marxist group and inclined them against cooperation. Finally, Chiang Kai Shek broke away from his alliance with the Chinese Communists and Borodin and his agents (including Ho Chi Minh) were forced to return to Moscow.

Ho attended a Pan-Pacific Trade Union Conference in May 1927. The conference supported a phony trade union agency which was in fact a front for the international Communist movement. For a while after that, Ho was agitating among Vietnamese residents in Siam (Thailand), creating the Annamite Fraternity of Siam.

Meanwhile, there developed divisions within the Vietnamese Communist movement based on regional, ideological and personal differences. By 1929 there were as many as three different Communist parties under Vietnamese control, namely the Indochinese Communist Party, the Annamese Communist Party and the Indochinese Communist Union. (It should be remembered that Ho Chi Minh was neither the only Vietnamese Communist trained in Moscow nor the undisputed head of the Communist effort in Indochina at the time.) The Communists were having serious difficulties as the anti-colonial groups suffered under French repression.

Finally, Stalin called Ho back to China to try to facilitate resolution of the differences among the Communist factions. At a conference in Hong Kong in early 1930, the Vietnamese Communist Party was formed amid mutual suspicion and the recognition of a need for cooperation in order to survive. The Party was headed by Tran Phu, the author of its platform. The Vietnamese Communist Party was administratively subordinate to the Comintern Far Eastern Bureau in Shanghai. It was also connected to the Pan Pacific Trade Union, which belonged to the Red International Labor Unions in Moscow and the Unitaire Confederation Generale du Travail headquartered in Paris (part of the French Communist Party). Thus, the Vietnamese Communist Party's international connections are quite clear. In 1931, the Party was renamed the Indochinese Communist Party (IPC). Strict discipline among Party members was essential. Activities were conducted in secret. Members took blood oaths and could be killed for serious breeches of conduct.

Following the lead of the nationalist groups (for example, the Yen Bay uprising directed by the Nationalist Party), the Communists began a program of violence aimed at causing political unrest throughout Indochina, including Cambodia and Laos, in order to divide the French colonies. In 1931, the Party tried to establish

soviets in Nghe An and Ha Tinh provinces, replacing local adminis-
trators with Communist cadres. This program failed and resulted
in the deaths of many landlords and village officials. The French
reacted with a heavy hand and the Communists suffered for their
rashness. (Karnow gets his chronology mixed up at this point. He
places a Nghe An soviet before Ho's return to China and does not
mention its failure. The author also makes the union of the rival
Communist factions Ho's idea, not orders from Stalin.) (p. 124) Ho
was arrested in China and not heard from again for nearly ten
years.

At that time, the Party decided that for survival's sake it would
have to fall back on the ruse of a united nationalist front and
cooperate with the Vietnamese nationalist organizations. Overt
terrorist and extremist tactics ceased while its underground movement continued to function. Nonetheless, the Party was troubled
by lack of financial support and a divided and thinned out leadership.
Tran Van Giau came to the southern part of Vietnam from Moscow
and revitalized the Party there, along with Le Hong Phong, among
others. The Communists needed to rely on nationalist fervor among
the Vietnamese populace to regain a foothold in the struggle for
power. From 1935-1939 the Comintern advocated the "united front"
approach to deal with fascist aggression in Europe and Asia. In
Vietnam, this meant the ICP had to collaborate, not with other
groups to oust the French, but with the French to fight the Axis
powers.

Meanwhile, the Trotskyite movement gained strength in Cochin
China. In the municipal elections of 1939, this party's candidates
took 80% of the votes. Shortly after this victory for the Trotskyites
and defeat for the ICP, an unnamed informant (probably from the
ICP) provided the French security police with the names and
addresses of all Trotskyites in the country. Their leaders were
quickly arrested and deported. The party's head, Ta Thu Thau, was
later executed by the Viet Minh.

When Stalin realized the implications of Japan's invasion of Indochina, he sent Ho once more back to China. The ICP had already
formed a front organization called the Indochinese Anti-Imperialist
People's United Front. With Ho, the Party created the Viet Minh
(Vietnam Independence League) at the Eighth Party plenum and

announced it at a meeting sponsored by the Chinese nationalist government in 1941. The Viet Minh's members included the ICP, the grassroots organs of the ICP, a few bogus parties to lend it the appearance of a broad-based alliance and individual members of some nationalist groups. At the suggestion of certain Chinese nationalists, Ho changed his name to Ho Chi Minh in order to fool Chinese officials and Vietnamese not friendly to Nguyen Ai Quoc. The Viet Minh was to be a member of an even broader front, the Vietnam Revolutionary League, which formed a provisional government controlled by the ICP. The leadership of the Viet Minh included Ho Chi Minh, Vo Nguyen Giap, Pham Van Dong and Truong Chinh, all high-ranking Communists.

During World War II the Viet Minh provided information to the British and American Intelligence agents in Indochina, but they took little part in the actual fighting. Ho met with OSS agents and managed to convince some that he was just a nationalist hoping to drive the French out of his country and bring independence and freedom to Vietnam. It should come as no surprise that Ho managed to persuade these officers of his alleged sincerity. Throughout his career with the Communists, Ho had assumed countless false identities, taken on various pen names, donned many disguises and claimed diverse allegiances all to suit his own purposes. The fifty-five-year-old revolutionary who had spent nearly half his life with the Communist movement even convinced some people that he was not a Communist at all. (5)

As the end of the war approached, Vietnam was in political turmoil. The French had been greatly weakened, the Japanese had lost their empire, and the Vietnamese had no solid government, although Bao Dai was still the imperial ruler. The ICP met to organize a "revolution" to take advantage of this situation when the time was ripe. They organized "liberation zones" and local "liberation governments", and prepared to claim the reins of national government. On August 19, 1945, the Viet Minh stomped into Hanoi and declared themselves the new government. They convinced Bao Dai to abdicate and on September 2, Ho proclaimed the Democratic Republic of Vietnam.

Nationalist groups, who had not expected this sudden turn of events, were upset and demanded a piece of the action. Ho knew the

Viet Minh Party was too weak to go it alone, so he was forced to
accept them in the National Assembly and then dissolve the ICP.

But Ho had to contend with the Chinese army, which had been
placed in charge of disarming the Japanese in the northern part of
the country after the war, and the British in the southern half.
Accomodations were reached between the Viet Minh and the French
in 1946 which allowed the Viet Minh to concentrate on liquidating its
political opponents. (See Part 2.)

All this is quite different from the story told by PBS and its Chief
Correspondent, who make use of partial truths, omit serious facts,
and record some rather astonishing falsehoods to glorify the Communists' rise to power. Communist union boss Hoang Quoc Viet's
claim that "the entire country rallied" to the Viet Minh in 1941 is just
plain nonsense. Furthermore, the general Vietnamese population
was not introduced to the name of Ho Chi Minh until after the
August revolution began, and even then there was no proof that this
fellow was the "famous patriot" Nguyen Ai Quoc. It was not until
the late 1950s that Ho felt secure enough to confirm that indeed he
was the notorious Communist leader of the early '30s.

The *Television History* does not relate that the Communist
newspaper *Cuu Quoc* (Save The Nation) was already denouncing
the "American imperialists" toward the end of World War II, before
most Vietnamese knew the meaning of either "American" or
"imperialist" and while Ho Chi Minh was supposedly courting the
U.S. The series' selection of Archimedes Patti as a star informant is
not surprising. In the preface of his book *Why Vietnam?* (1980,
University of California Press), Patti notes that among his friends
and teachers are pro-Hanoi "scholars" Gareth Porter, Mai Elliot,
Ngo Vinh Long, and one Truong Dinh Hung, who was convicted of
espionage against the U.S. in 1982. The producers do not tell us this,
but hope to convince us that Mr. Patti is a good judge of character.

The series refers to Ho's "Declaration of Independence" as
evidence of the old revolutionary's good intentions following World
War II. Yet, one might reasonably ask at what time in his career did
Ho Chi Minh ever follow democratic principles or allow for the
pursuit of "life, liberty and happiness"? Even a casual observer can
tell the difference between a tough dictator and a libertarian.

However, the PBS producers are anything but casual in their defense of Ho Chi Minh, the patriot.

Films of Independence Day celebrations were apparently taken long after the fact since they show bands of strong, healthy youths in a country we were just told was stricken by a devastating famine that killed millions. Individuals who participated in demonstrations at the time were celebrating their country's independence, not the Viet Minh, which few of them had ever heard of. Dr. Tran Duy Hung. is moved almost to tears as he recounts his feelings when Ho Chi Minh led the singing of the national anthem for the first time. He neglects to note that the author of the anthem, Van Cao, was later a victim of Ho's purge of intellectuals in the 1950s.

The doctor's tale about the crowds "enthusiastically" cheering an American airplane flying over the square in Hanoi should not be taken too seriously. As noted above, the average Vietnamese citizen did not know what or where America was or what an American flag looked like. One person informed this writer of an incident that happened in a village outside Hanoi at about this time: The young people were being taken outside to march down the road and as they conducted this organized demonstration a plane flew overhead. A Viet Minh cadre told everyone that it was a Vietnamese plane. Not suspecting the fraud, the young people cheered.

Propaganda films of the Independence Day activities are careful to include shots of the ubiquitous red flag with the yellow star. This may be close to reality, since the Communists had seen to it that theirs was the only flag waved during the ceremony while all other groups' flags and banners were confiscated.

Thus concludes Part 1 of Vietnam's "History." It is no wonder the Vietnamese viewers grew so angry watching it.

The Death of Peter Dewey

Part 1 closes with a lengthy description of the death of Col. Peter Dewey, the first American to die in Vietnam. It is simply worth noting here that more time is spent relating the details of this individual's death than is granted the account of the Communist Land Reform program which resulted in the deaths of many thousands of innocent people. This lends credence to Stalin's contention that the death of one is a tragedy, the death of a million a mere statistic.

Footnotes

1. Hoang Van Chi, *From Colonialism to Communism*, p.39
2. Ibid., p. 31
3. Ibid., pp. 39-40, taken from *Echo du Vietnam*, Paris, July 1960
4. Bernard Fall, *The Two Vietnams*, p. 90
5. Regarding the last point, see Robert Shaplen's article "The Enigma of Ho Chi Minh", which includes comments from an anonymous OSS agent. Reprinted in *Vietnam: Anatomy of a Conflict*, p. 294

Supplements

(Ed. – In pp. 145-6 of his *History*, Karnow tells a tale of how the Vietnamese enthusiastically executed a village official and then murdered certain "henchmen" of the Japanese during the August revolution. The reader might compare this to the following story written by a Vietnamese refugee who calls herself Co Thang Gieng. Here the author recalls her experience when the Viet Minh took over in 1945. Excerpted from "The Bloodstained Hand", by Co Thang Gieng, printed in *San Diego Tin Tuc*, 1983. Translation included by permission of the author.)

When Papa passed his licentiate, he went to work as a district chief. Shortly afterwards, the imperial court in Hue appointed him to be provincial judge in Khanh Hoa-Nha Trang Province.

At that time, the Japanese army had returned to Nha Trang. They disarmed the French and forced the Annamite governor with the French civil service workers into confinement. The province chief's villa had not yet been surrounded, but the Japanese were coming and going daily and they forced the old chief and my papa to do wicked and illegal things, such as take rice from the district and prefectures to feed the horses of the Japanese. What the horses did not eat was then taken out and burned or thrown into the sea. The policy of Japanese rule was to make the Vietnamese suffer and starve. Experience had taught them that people who eat their fill can become obstinate and might rise up against them at any time;

let the people starve and they will be more docile – offer them a bowl of rice and they will do whatever you want. What father and mother was not hurt to see their children hungry or would not sacrifice their lives for the children?

My papa was clearly frightened in those days. His face was drawn from thinking too much He rarely spoke to Mama and didn't hold me the way he used to. I carried his straw slippers and tiptoed to put them on, but he never noticed. Once he just sighed, "The shame! The shame! No reason to kill myself. That would be cowardly. I must do something! Do something!"

A month later he died – not by suicide, but from a stroke. Mama took us away from the villa earlier than planned because the family of the newly appointed judge had already arrived . . .

It was 1945. The U.S. dropped an atomic bomb on Hiroshima, wiping out a part of Japan. With the war lost, the Japanese emperor surrendered. The news stunned and saddened the Japanese army in Nha Trang. They became milder, more conciliatory, handing over direction of the city to a group waving a red flag and calling itself the Viet Minh.

The people in the province were glad and poured out into the streets to cheer and welcome them. This group announced that it had driven the French colonialists out of the country and forced the Japanese to surrender, bringing back independence to our country. They took their megaphone through every street and alley with their propaganda. "Comrades! Stand up and break off the chains of slavery! Overthrow class separation! Tear down the status of rich and poor! Property belongs to the nation! It is shared by all! Anyone who resists is a reactionary! Men and women have equal rights! There is freedom of speech, freedom of marriage."

Gold and silver weeks were organized to raise funds for a noble cause: buying weapons to rebuild the nation. Those who loved their country stood in line to present trays full of bracelets and jewelry to a committee called the Comrades of the People. Persons too poor to own jewelry gave coins to be melted down into bullets.

Our joy at having regained independence and liberty did not last long, however. We learned that the invaders had come – the colonialist French invaders had returned and were out at sea.

The order was spread: all people, men and women, young and old, had to have weapons to fight the invaders. Knives, hammers, and sickles were brought out and sharpened. Poles and canes with sharp points were carried on shoulders like guns. The people practiced every day, following the instructions of the Comrades of the People who showed them how to fight hand-to-hand with the invaders. They stayed on ships out at sea, firing their big guns like rain and killing many people in the city. Nha Trang was more chaotic than ever – it was everyone for himself. By the hundreds and thousands, we fled into the countryside to escape.

Mama and the old maid placed me and the baby in a big basket with rice and clothes and carried us away. But mama had been raised as a lady, so how could she have the strength to carry us? After her shoulder ached too much, she threw the pole away and carried me on her back, following the wave of refugees. But everywhere we went, the shells of the invaders still exploded around us, right over our heads. Each day the invaders' ships came closer to shore and fired more and more. The old maid took Mama to her home village of Truong Lac . . .

While the children played, the grown-ups were terrified. They talked in whispers among themselves.

"You know, sister? The dead lay all over the streets and there was not time to save them. If you want to become a nurse, let me introduce you to the army!"

"Oh! The shells falling in the river sank boats filled with people! Such tragic deaths!"

The next morning while going down to the dock to wash, Mama discovered two corpses that had washed up on shore. The bodies reeked. Sometimes they even seemed to shake because of the fish going after them.

Mama ran back and called the old maid. The old woman gathered the children, took stock of the situation and reported it to the village. I heard someone say, "If you tell the Committee now, they'll make us pull them up and bury them. But how can we bury them right in our yards?" After that, the old maid lit a handful of incense, said some prayers for the two deceased and with her son took a long pole and pushed the bodies out to the middle of the river to float away with the current.

* * * * * *

The refugees fled, leaving house and home, running by day and resting at night, without food or water. The weather was terrible and flies swarmed from the unclaimed corpses along the way. Children became sick, with vomiting and fevers, and there was cholera in some places. Village schools, temples, village houses and markets were soon overcrowded. It was hard to find any place for the children to lie down for the night. Due in part to fatigue and in part to hunger, the people ceased believing in those who dreamed of chasing out the French and Japanese. People whispered about going back to the city, their homes, and just to escape the artillery shells from the battleships out at sea. Refugees who had no food started heading back toward Nha Trang. One armed "people's squad" wearing red scarves wanted to punish those going back. They stopped the refugees on the road and confiscated their belongings. After checking each person's background, the squad accused them of betraying their country and decided that two people should be executed as a warning to the others. Those first two victims were a messenger who had swept floors at the governor's office and a girl who sold perfume and powder and had been the girlfriend of a French security policeman.

The announcement was made all over the village for everyone to go see the executions of the two Vietnamese traitors in the field the next morning. The people looked at each other in fear and dared not say a word. Mama was quite terrified and didn't want to go, but the old maid finally persuaded her. The maid thought that if the "comrades" noticed her missing they might check her background. So the maid took the baby and Mama followed with me in hand. Mama was afraid to leave me alone at home, thinking I might run outside and fall into the river behind the house. The baby and I laughed and played, just having a good time as if we were going to a show. Mama gave me a look that told me not to laugh and made a gesture with her hand that said I should not even speak. She made her way through the crowd and sat down like the peasant farmers.

The field was full of people, but I could not see a single smiling face. Instead, everyone looked downcast. In the middle of the field was a long table covered with a red cloth. There sat the Revolutionary People's Court wearing khaki shirts with high collars like those in the pictures of old Ho. Behind them hung a red flag. By the execution place stood a group of vanguard youths wielding sharp bamboo sticks and making their rounds with a commanding presence. When the time came for carrying out the sentence against the two prisoners, there was a long drumroll that made our stomachs churn. The two criminals were dragged out into the execution place and forced to kneel. The woman could hardly walk and fell to the ground. The comrades then chained the two to stakes so they wouldn't fall over. The woman wept pitiably for a time, then kept still. Perhaps she had fainted from terror.

One member of the execution team brought out two baskets filled with sawdust. These were set in front of the faces of the criminals. Another person solemnly read the decision of the People's Court, declaring their death sentences. A female cadre, her face fresh as a flower, ran up. She took hold of the long black hair of the female prisoner and lifted it forward, exposing the woman's white neck.

Then the executioner came up carrying a big knife that glistened in the sun. The entire People's Court and the crowd there stood up cheering and applauding the patriotism of the executioner. I took a close look at the man with the knife and saw that he was still quite young, though his face was pale.

There was a moment of silence. The old maid shut her eyes and recited prayers. Mama closed her eyes, too, and put her hand in front of my face so that I should not see. But I kept my eyes open and peered through the slits between her fingers.

There was a thud and the head with a bun of hair dropped into the basket of sawdust.

Suddenly the male prisoner began to shout.

"Down with the bloodthirsty Communists! I vow my soul will come to avenge my death on you! Long live Vietnam! Immortal Vietnam!"

The executioner, still drunk from the first killing, chopped at the head of the second prisoner. Maybe the knife was too dull or the man's neck too stiff, but the executioner's arm shook and it took three or four slashes with the big knife before the head finally came off. As the head fell, three spurts of blood shot from the victim's neck and onto the face, body and clothes of the executioner, staining them red.

Mama squeezed my hand and pressed me to her bosom to hold

back her own terror. Her hands were as cold as ice and her whole body trembled.

The audience went home in silence. Their faces were ashen, as if lifeless. They were like ghosts making their way down the village road.

PART 2: THE FIRST VIETNAM WAR (1945-1954)

Ho Chi Minh's government holds office uneasily for a short time while the French return to renew their claims to the colony. Ho negotiates the return of the French in the North to replace the Chinese, but tensions escalate and war breaks out in late 1946. Gen. Giap leads Viet Minh guerillas in the countryside and with Chinese assistance, organizes modern forces. Bao Dai is reinstalled as emperor by the French and the U.S. begins to directly support France's war effort in order to halt Communist expansionism. The war drags on until 1954 with the Viet Minh victory at Dien Bien Phu. At the Geneva Conference, an agreement is made to divide Vietnam into two parts with elections on reunification to be held later. The United States does not bind itself to this accord.

The Mysterious Disappearance of Cambodia and Laos

French Indochina comprised three countries, namely Vietnam, Laos and Cambodia. Each of these countries is distinct from the other. Each has its own language and customs. The French returned to Indochina after World War II, hoping to regain their position in Asia. They did not come back merely to Vietnam, but to Laos and Cambodia as well. The war that resulted involved all three countries and is described by historians as "The First Indochina War." To the producers of the *Television History*, however, Laos and Cambodia did not even exist at that time. The two countries do not appear at all in the series until Part 9. At that time, their place in the history of the second war is tied solely to the actions of the Americans, implying that nothing of interest happened to them until the Americans got involved. For now, the First Indochina War becomes the "First Vietnam War." The omission of Laos and Cambodia is critical because what happened in those countries during the 1940s and 1950s had an impact on the future of Southeast Asia that is still being felt today.

Following is a summary of just the essential background of Laos and Cambodia omitted by the series. (1)

Both Cambodia and Laos have a history of animosity towards the Vietnamese. Until the French arrived to colonize Southeast Asia, Vietnam had been making territorial advances into both of its neighboring countries. The southern region of Vietnam along the Mekong Delta was once a part of Cambodia. During the mid-1800s Vietnam and Siam (present-day Thailand) shared a joint sovereignty over the Cambodian kingdom. The ill feelings were further reinforced during the colonial period when France brought educated Vietnamese into the two countries to serve in the administration of the colonies. The Lao and Cambodian people developed a resentment toward the Vietnamese, who often seemed insolent and arrogant towards the local people. By the end of World War II, both countries, as well as Siam to the west, feared the Vietnamese would try to inherit the administration of Indochina from the French, whose colonial power appeared to be on the wane. It is interesting to note that when Lao resistance forces were training young soldiers to fight the invading Japanese, many of the youths participated enthusiastically because they thought they were being trained to fight Vietnamese, not the Japanese. (2) Some Vietnamese residents in the two countries served as spies and informants for the invaders while others supported the resistance.

The Vietnamese populations in some areas of Laos and Cambodia proved to be important to the Viet Minh during the war with France. Vietnamese in Savannakhet and Thakhek helped the Viet Minh in battles in those two Laotian towns. Vietnamese residents of Cambodia formed the basis of a Communist movement that appeared in that country in the middle of the war. Lao-Vietnamese troops were recruited by the Viet Minh in Siam where many refugees had fled the fighting in Laos. The Viet Minh bribed Siamese police to arrest and kill any Vietnamese who refused to join Ho Chi Minh's army. In many cases, the Viet Minh were able to rely on these Vietnamese residents for support in their political and military activities.

Prince Souphannavong of Laos was courted by the Viet Minh and backed by Vietnamese troops when he created the Pathet Lao in the 1940s. The prince met with Ho Chi Minh, Gen.Giap and Pham Van Dong as they planned strategies to disrupt the Royal government. The Pathet Lao's political aim was described as driving out the French colonialists and American imperialists. Lo Faydang, a Hmong tribal leader who had a grudge against the French, was one of the early leaders of the Pathet Lao forces (most of the Pathet Lao were hill tribes, not lowland Lao). In March 1951, the Pathet Lao joined with the Viet Minh and a Vietnamese-sponsored resistance group in Cambodia in making a statement declaring their shared aim of opposing French colonialists, American imperialists, and national traitors while establishing "true independence" in the three countries.

On the non-Communist side, the Lao Issara (Free Lao) movement and its leader Prince Phetsarath forced King Sisavang Vong to establish a constitutional monarchy in Laos in 1946. Prince Souvannaphouma tried to form a compromise between the political factions in order to keep the country at peace. This was opposed primarily by the Pathet Lao and Viet Minh, who wanted to take control of the government. The Pathet Lao created a revolutionary government in the northern provinces of Laos in 1953. Meanwhile, Viet Minh were using opium from the highlands to pay the Chinese for their military aid. Gen. Giap's troops were attacking the Royal Lao forces in early 1954 when the Viet Minh were supposedly concentrating on Dien Bien Phu.

There were important political conflicts in Cambodia at the time as well. King Sihanouk was chosen by the French to succeed Sisowath Monivong on the throne because Sihanouk was young and considered easy to manage. Sihanouk was opposed by reformers almost from the time he became king. Son Ngoc Thanh, a nationalist leader, headed the Khmer Issarak which demanded a more progressive government and opposed the French. King Sihanouk passed a treaty with France over the objections of his consultative assembly.

The Viet Minh conducted military actions in Cambodia and formed a "Joint National Front" directed by the Viet Minh. Vietnamese Communists engaged in political activities in Cambodia. In April

1954 the Viet Minh staged an invasion of Cambodia to gain a foothold in that country before going to Geneva.

After the Geneva Agreements forced the Viet Minh to withdraw from Laos and Cambodia, the Vietnamese Communists took with them thousands of youngsters from both countries for training in preparation for the time when the Vietnamese would return. Some of these boys even went to Hanoi, Peking and Moscow for "study."

To the producers of the *Television History*, who boast they have made "perhaps the most exhaustive historical documentary in television history," all the above information is irrelevant. This omission supports their narrow view that the Viet Minh was simply a nationalist group, that the war with France was simply a Vietnamese nationalist war and that there was no real trouble in Laos and Cambodia until America entered the picture. The last point is brought out in Part 9. For now, the viewer must forget that there is a Laos and a Cambodia.

The Nature of Vietnamese Resistance Against the French

The *Television History* presents the Viet Minh as the model of anti-French resistance in Vietnam. It was inspired by Ho Chi Minh, whom the series alleges was "famous as a patriot for a quarter of a century." Gen. Giap's "ragtag army" battled France's "modern army with modern weapons." The Viet Minh's support from the peasants is evidenced by interviews with two Communist cadres, Duong Van Khanh and his wife Do Thi Bay (the couple who exchanged notes in piaster bills). "To the Front," a song by noted Vietnamese composer Pham Duy, is cited to reflect the nationalist spirit of the people. A propaganda film of girls jogging up to an overturned truck engulfed in flames and plucking rifles off the corpses of unfortunate French soldiers is used to show how the Viet Minh obtained their weapons. Nguyen Thi Dinh, heroine of the National Liberation Front, reminds us that the patriots also used bamboo spears. Only in 1950 did the Chinese come rumbling to the border to offer succor to the struggling Viet Minh.

The producers do not become involved enough in their project to investigate what was behind the anti-colonialist struggle of the 1940s and 1950s. The Vietnamese tasted a brief period of independence with the end of World War II, but the political scene was chaotic. Japan's authority had collapsed and France seemed too weak to resume its ambitions. The Viet Minh was not well known in 1945 and those who knew of it were wary of supporting Ho's government. As war appeared imminent, many Vietnamese joined the resistance movement. Young people were among the most enthusiastic recruits. In the early days, people joined because they believed they were fighting for independence. The Viet Minh government was obscure to most Vietnamese, but it was their government, not France's. Except for the hard-core cadres and some of the intellectuals and older nationalists, no one knew what Communism was. When the majority fought, they did not fight for Communism, but for independence.

This point is extremely important because it explains why many of those who joined the resistance movement left the ranks of the Viet Minh by the end of 1954 once they became enlightened as to the reality of the fanatic Ho Chi Minh and his Communist government. It explains why peasants who supported the Viet Minh in the early years of the resistance fled their ancestral homes when the Communists took power in the North. It explains why Pham Duy's "To the Front" was later sung by South Vietnamese soldiers training to fight the Communist army of the North during the Second Indochina War. It allows us to understand why many nationalist leaders found themselves forced to collaborate with Bao Dai's royal government rather than side with the Viet Minh, concluding that working with a weak king was better than risking the destruction of the country under Communism.

Many different types of people followed the Viet Minh in those days. There were some intellectuals who believed that Communism offered a workable model for reform and modernization. Others disagreed, but felt that as nationalists they should support a Vietnamese government against foreign rule. Some peasants who had suffered for generations in poverty were convinced that a new system would give them prosperity, wealth and power. There were adventurous youths who saw the struggle for independence as a noble cause. And there was the mass of people in the middle whose notions of nationalism were vague and who could be persuaded, cajoled and coerced into supporting the resistance. As the war dragged on, coercion became more and more necessary.

The Vietnamese Communists used the Viet Minh as a front to exploit the various sentiments of the people while pursuing the ultimate goal of transforming Indochina into a socialist state. Hoang Van Chi gives credit to the Communist Party for "skillful leadership, provided by the Comintern, the sound organization at the core of the Party, and the courage and determination of its members." The Communists, says Chi, were able to attract both intellectual idealists and underprivileged peasants with promises of a better future. However, he concludes: "Its final success was due in large measure to the suppleness of its tactics which enabled it to appear Communist or Nationalist as changing circumstances demanded, while keeping well concealed the unchanging strategic objective." (3)

The Communists mobilized the people with nationalist slogans, shed the blood of non-Communist nationalists to achieve victory over their enemies, and later betrayed those loyal to the nationalist cause by denying them freedom, and often their lives. Through the front of the Viet Minh, they took advantage of foreign repression, oppressive mandarinal rule and the hopes of ignorant peasants to attract followers to the cause of independence only to use those followers for the socialist revolution.

The producers of the *Television History* have missed this point entirely. In their series, they have provided an oversimplified picture of Vietnam, based primarily on mythology. Their "First Vietnam War" is inaccurate and unrealistic, but produced in such a way as to mislead those who know nothing about this part of Vietnam's history. Viewers will easily come to the conclusion that Ho Chi Minh was popular, his movement sincerely nationalist and his efforts to mobilize the people entirely successful. This presentation helps set the stage for the series' contention that America's later involvement in Southeast Asia was unjust and unpopular.

(The Chief Correspondent interchanges the terms "nationalist" and "Communist" almost as skillfully as Ho Chi Minh. In the end the reader cannot tell them apart. At the same time, Karnow appears to recognize a difference between Communist "ideology" and "nationalism." Contradictions are inevitable. Ho is credited with seeking support from the United States prior to the war with France – this would be considered "nationalistic" rather than "ideological." Yet Ho bemoaned the refusal of French Communists to assist his struggle, complaining they were "more nationalistic than ideological." (p. 154) Later, Karnow would explain Vietnam's invasion of Cambodia in similar terms.)

The Viet Minh and Nationalists

In order for the producers to maintain that the Viet Minh was essentially nationalist in nature, they must ignore the activities of Ho Chi Minh's group in the years immediately following World War II. In fact, that is exactly what they do. And the viewer, unaware of Vietnam's history at this time, will not know how important an omission this really is.

Vu Van Thai is a former administrator for Ngo Dinh Diem's government, adviser to the U.N. Secretariat and ambassador from South Vietnam. In a 1966 article on Vietnam entitled "Development of the Revolution," Mr. Thai answers the suggestion that Ho Chi Minh was primarily a nationalist by stating, "If it were really true, this interval (after World War II) would have been used by Ho Chi Minh to strengthen the national union and not to liquidate its non-communist fellow travelers." (4)

Ho Chi Minh's August Revolution government was only moderate and conciliatory on the surface. In fact, it was firmly controlled by the Communist Party. The Chinese and French found Ho's proposed government unacceptable. Ho formed a new "Government of National Union and Resistance" the next year. Opposition leaders soon discovered they had no power in this administration and virtually all resigned. (5)

Ho realized the Viet Minh was not strong enough to prevent the French from returning to Vietnam. He sought an accommodation with the colonial power. The result was two agreements with the French – the Sainteny Accord (March 1946) and the *modus vivendi* at Fontainbleu (September 1946). Ho was able to present the Viet Minh as the legitimate government of Vietnam and himself as a moderate leader and thus buy time in which to eliminate his political opponents and secure his position, even if it meant selling out the country.

Taking advantage of this accommodation with the French, the Communist Party proceeded to liquidate its opposition. The main targets were the Nationalists, the Dai Viet (which had been somewhat discredited by its collaboration with the Japanese), the Trotskyites, and other serious political groups. Political leaders were killed, including Truong Tu Anh (of the Dai Viet), the writer Pham Quynh, Bui Quang Chieu (of the Constitutionalists), Huynh Phu So (founder of the Hoa Hao), Ta Thu Thau (Trotskyite leader), Ngo Dinh Khoi (brother of Ngo Dinh Diem), and countless others of high and low rank whom the Viet Minh wanted to get rid of. Nationalist Party leader Vu Hong Khanh, who signed the Sainteny Accord with Ho Chi Minh, was forced to flee for his life. The methods of eliminating these figures varied. Many were bound hand and foot and thrown into a river. Some were buried alive. At least once the Viet Minh ambushed a group of Nationalists and buried them, then later dug up the bones and displayed them to show the people what they alleged was an atrocity of the Nationalists! (6)

Besides outright murder, there were other ways to weaken the opposition. Persons who had supported the Japanese or French at some stage might become discredited by means of rumor and innuendo. The Viet Minh were promoted as the only true nationalist group, creating polarization among the Vietnamese— one was either for the Viet Minh and the true cause or for the French and hated colonialism. Those who had any connections with the French were branded "traitors."

The Communist leaders also eliminated non-Communist fighters by placing them at the front line. Vu Van Thai gives the example of the Hanoi Self-Defence Force, composed of youths aged 15 to 20, left to defend Hanoi while Communist troops retreated. (7)

During the period between 1945 and 1950, there were those who believed in and were loyal to the Viet Minh. The struggle for independence took priority over other political issues. But as time went on, the situation was to change and even formerly loyal followers of Ho Chi Minh would begin to question why they were fighting and for whom.

(Karnow's *History* gets particularly lively for a while. The months of August and September 1945 are described as chaotic. There is some violence mentioned, especially in the South, but in all cases the author is careful not to implicate his hero, Ho Chi Minh. There is no discussion of systematic assassinations or any explanation as to why the immensely popular Viet Minh suddenly became disorganized and, at times, murderous after taking power. Karnow's assertion of Ho's "widespread popularity" is certainly an exaggeration (p. 151). Strangely, Karnow, does not tell us where "Viet Minh bands" got the idea to stage "phony people's trials" or murder mandarins (p. 151), although such activities require careful training and preparation. The Vietnamese Nationalist Party is accused of trying to kidnap and kill Viet Minh members, but apparently the Viet Minh did nothing to deserve this horrible treatment (p. 152). In any event, the political rivalry suddenly seems to have quieted down by the end of 1945!)

The War With France

In describing the fighting between the French and the Vietnamese, the producers fail to point out that most of the Vietnamese fighters, whether within or outside the Viet Minh, were non-Communists. Few of the resistance fighters had any knowledge of or love for Communism. They struggled for the goal of independence and an end to colonialism. As a consequence, when the first few years of war went by with no sign of success against the well trained and equipped Europeans and Legionaires, many Vietnamese grew dispirited and quit the ranks to return home and rejoin their families. Others began to realize the true nature of the Viet Minh leadership – authoritarian, brutal, deceptive, power-hungry – and felt betrayed. No longer were they fighting for their country, but for the ambitions of a few stubborn and demanding fellows at the top. Some of these nationalists then made the painful decision to go to the other side, the Bao Dai government, which they had previously denounced, but now felt was the only alternative to the greater problem, namely Communism. By 1950, the people were becoming discouraged and the Viet Minh resorted more and more to forced conscription and propagandizing among the idealistic youth.

The war further disheartened the general population, which suffered from both Viet Minh terrorism and attacks by the French. As often happened in South Vietnam more than a decade later, guerillas fired at the French from populated villages, drawing in French troops who, of course, could not distinguish the guerillas from the villagers. Thousands of civilians became victims of atrocities on both sides, due as much to Viet Minh provocation as anything else.

The *Television History* turns away from common sense and factual history to tell us that despite the length of the war and its human toll, the people of Vietnam discounted the sacrifices, the privation and the suffering all for the sake of Ho Chi Minh's dream. The series suggests that the Vietnamese have inherited a wild form of single-minded nationalism that causes them to forget everything else in life as they pursue it. This idea reveals a lack of understanding about war and about human nature as well.

Like some historians of both Indochinese wars, the television series romanticizes the revolutionary fighters. The Viet Minh take on ghost-like qualities. "The guerillas seemed to be everywhere... and nowhere." "The French controlled the day, the Viet Minh the night." One gets the impression of spirits moving in to take over villages as the sun goes down. Descriptions of the Viet Minh lack substance and this adds to their mystique.

But the resistance fighters were not ghosts. They faced a number of significant problems, among them: food shortages, malaria, lack of proper medicine, few doctors, high casualty rates, separation from loved ones for extended periods of time. The war became tedious and many of the units lived in the mountains. Some hard-core cadres remained devoted to the cause, but this was often due to the traumatic indoctrination they received (see Supplements). There were other devices for keeping order in the ranks, among them the system of organized cells. In his companion book, Stanley Karnow adopts the idealized description of the 3-man cells as they applied to the First Indochina war. He calls the cell "a system designed so that each would fight, not for ideological abstractions, but to gain the respect of his comrades." The three eat together, sleep together and fight together, cadres as well as privates, to promote equality and a sense of mutual responsibility. (p. 182)

Actually, the three-person cell is an internal control and security measure. The Communist system relies on mutual distrust and surveillance in order to maintain strict control of thoughts and actions. Members of a cell are comrades in name only – Communism discourages the "buddy system" or close relationships. Personal emotions and sentiments are threats to the Party, which demands the complete loyalty of the people. Each cell member must keep an eye on the other two and report to their cadre daily. Any sign of unhappiness, discontent or insubordination is included in the report. The cells come in conjunction with regular self-criticism and group-criticism meetings in which each person's behavior is brought to light before larger groups and discussed along ideological lines. Those who fail to meet the system's standards are singled out and subjected to physical and/or psychological abuse until they conform. There are no secrets allowed since everything one does is laid bare and dissected by group members. The cell is a reinforcement tool for the control process. It monitors each person's daily activities and also makes desertion very difficult. Members are held responsible if one of the cell disappears, so they keep close watch on each other.

During the first few years of the war, the Viet Minh had to settle in the frontier areas. The survival of Ho's troops depended greatly on the mountain tribes, perhaps more so than on the Vietnamese peasants. Ho's movement had some support, but it was limited and, as Stalin knew, there was little hope for success. (8) Military aid from China and adverse public opinion to the war in France were two important keys to the ultimate success of the Viet Minh.

The Viet Minh victory at Cao Bang-Lang Son (in late 1950, although the television series says 1951) was not simply due to Giap's new offensive tactics. There were other important factors, such as the French government cutting the number of troops patrolling the frontier and a French officer's mistake in disobeying orders. The entire battle lasted for months while both sides suffered heavy losses. (9)

The series does not adequately describe the Viet Minh's military defeats in 1951. "Gen. Giap, who had overextended his fledgling troops, was stopped cold and forced to return to hit-and-run tactics." Actually, Giap's attempts to win big in the Red River Delta coincided with the re-emergence of the Communist Party (officially dissolved in 1945 as a move to placate non-Communist nationalists) and Ho's promise to return to Hanoi by February 1951. The Viet Minh were looking for the big victory and were badly defeated, then forced to retreat back to the mountains where they had more success. France's victories over the Viet Minh in this premature offensive almost caused the replacement of Gen. Giap as head of Ho's forces. The Viet Minh concentrated on the highlands, not the lowland villages, and in 1953 Giap invaded Laos.

Readers may look to Bernard Fall or other historians for details of the war with France. The producers of the *Television History* have apparently relied on Communist accounts for their summary of the war. The Viet Minh seem to have magical powers and the morale of the troops never diminishes. With popular support, they rally and defeat the French. Very neat and simple. But the television version is not quite the way it was.

(The written history of the war is somewhat more sober. Karnow uses anecdotes and brisk battle scenes to skim through the war. He discounts the "ragtag" image of the Viet Minh as "pure romanticism" (p. 184), but his own description of the Viet Minh is, if not pure, still heavily romantic. His understanding of the cell unit, mentioned above, is one example. Karnow also states the Viet Minh troops "plunged into battle ready to sustain frightful casualties," as they fought "virtually a holy war" against the French. (p. 182) The *History* is made for readability and entertainment. As a consequence it runs from scene to scene without achieving depth. There are important questions suggested, but not answered by Karnow's writing: Why did Ho's forces go to the mountains instead of establishing bases in the lowlands? What type of mentality permits the deaths of thousands of people, including civilians, just to achieve "victory"? How did the fighting affect the masses? If Ho Chi Minh was so skillful in playing sides, couldn't it be he was more opportunistic than nationalistic? Karnow credits Ho Chi Minh with a number of social accomplishments, including "land reform, education, health care and other programs . . . that would broaden participation in the struggle." (p. 188) If Ho Chi Minh's "reforms" did anything, they alienated the masses rather than attracted them. (See next chapter.) Karnow incorrectly states that Ho changed the name of the Communist Party to the Workers Party to emphasize "the nationalist character of the war" as opposed to the Marxist struggle. Actually, the Party had been underground for several years and was re-emerging in 1951 to guide the course of the war.)

Dien Bien Phu

The battle at Dien Bien Phu is presented in all its propaganda glory for the Communists. Capt. Cao Xuan Nghia tells how he marched forty-five days to reach the valley. Capt. Tran Van Ngo stoutly declares his troops enjoyed high morale and courage which enabled them to defeat the French. The narrator blandly tells us that 51,000 Viet Minh soldiers hauled guns and supplies on their backs and on bicycles while peasants volunteered to build roads for Chinese and Soviet trucks. Major Nguyen Van Vinh relates the tale of Comrade Hero Phan Dinh Gop who threw himself over a foxhole so the soldiers could charge. A Russian propaganda film made afterwards shows how soldiers dug trenches at high speed in the midst of exploding bombs. Uniformed soldiers heave big guns up the mountainside. Steely eyes peer from trenches as the morale of the French troops in the compound collapses in the rain. Finally, the liberation flag is raised as the Viet Minh army achieves its greatest victory.

The viewers are, naturally, not given the same version of the battle Gen. Giap offered a delegation of Hungarian diplomats visiting Hanoi in 1959. At that time, Giap told his Communist visitors that Dien Bien Phu was a last gasp for the Viet Minh. The troops were exhausted. Rice supplies were low. The people were tired of fighting and didn't want to go to the front. Morale had plunged. Transportation of artillery was provided by elephants and buffaloes. Officers had to reassure the terrified troops. (10) The viewers do not get a complete and realistic idea of how Chinese aid saved the day for Giap's forces; instead the Chinese are blamed for the failure of the mad human-wave attack that started the battle. We do not hear about the assistance of T'ai tribes who served as porters and guides in the mountains. We are not told that the "legendary heroism" of the Viet Minh shock troops was made possible through intensive indoctrination that fed into fanatic faith. No Viet Minh

officer is available to tell how the soldiers felt watching thousands of
their comrades die, or what it was like sitting in trenches or hiding in
the trees during the long weeks of rain. The French, we are told,
were demoralized. But not the Viet Minh supermen.

In the end, the French could hold out no longer. Jean Pouget,
a French paratroop captain, was wounded. But a Viet Minh behind
a surgeon's mask told him, "We will take care of you." Take care
they did. The Viet Minh had a record of mistreating their prisoners
of war, 65% of whom perished in the prisons and camps. This was
due in part to shortages, but also to "the contempt for human life
displayed by the Viet Minh command in their conduct of the war."
(11)

Visual images make a strong impression on the viewer's mind.
By showing propaganda films, the *Television History* presents the
Communists at their best, even in a brutal and horrible battle. The
Viet Minh suffered more deaths than the French, but you cannot tell
this by watching it on television. Viewers will remember the glory of
alleged volunteers throwing their bodies over foxholes, but not learn
how hard the battle was fought by both sides.

The total number of deaths in the war is never mentioned. This is
perhaps a minor, irrelevant detail for a 4.6 million dollar history
project. Bernard Fall, whose books can be borrowed for free from
the library, writes that the war "had cost the French Union forces
a total of 172,000 casualties... The Viet Minh's casualties probably
ran three times as high and perhaps another 250,000 Vietnamese
civilians were killed during the fighting." (12) Such huge losses, of
course, meant nothing to the patriotic Viet Minh of television.

Geneva

The controversial agreement that eventually emerged from the
Geneva Conference in 1954 was an agreement for cessation of hostilities. Its contents covered troop withdrawals, movement between
the two zones marked off in Vietnam, administrative measures,
a ban on the introduction of fresh troops and ammunition, a ban on
the creation of new military bases, return of prisoners and supervision by the International Control Commission. The *Television
History* does not bore us with the details of the agreement, but
concentrates on the partition of Vietnam, America's "observer"

status, and the refusal of America and the State of Vietnam to sign the Agreements. Since the articles on troop movements, introduction of new soldiers and weapons, and the establishment of bases are not mentioned, the producers do not need to bother us with the fact that North Vietnam violated these provisions over the next few years. Their focus is on the United States and South Vietnam, whom they see as the real villains.

The series also hopes to portray Ho's government as an innocent victim of the major powers at Geneva, pushed around by the United States, France, Russia and China. Whatever the Viet Minh was, it was hardly innocent, having played partisan politics in the past and being prepared to play again in the future. The portrayal, however, suits the producers, who would like the viewers to feel sympathetic toward the Communists in anticipation of the big war with the United States.

There were separate agreements for Laos and Cambodia at Geneva. Viewers are not told that from May to July Viet Minh delegate Pham Van Dong held up proceedings by stubbornly insisting on recognition of the Khmer Communists and the Pathet Lao, claiming these groups had liberated vast territories and were establishing democratic governments while raising the standards of living for their people. The Cambodian and Lao delegates denied there were any "liberated territories" and French Foreign Minister Bidault suggested the Viet Minh withdraw its forces from those countries. Pham Van Dong continued with his demands until the Chinese pressured him to keep quiet. British Foreign Minister Eden proposed that Laos and Cambodia be made neutral buffers between Vietnam and Thailand. French troops were to leave, as the Viet Minh and Pathet Lao forces withdrew to the northern provinces of Laos; eventually the Pathet Lao was to be integrated into the royal army. The Viet Minh were forced to leave Cambodia, as were the French. Participants in the conference pledged to "respect the sovereignty, independence, unity and territorial integrity" of Vietnam, Cambodia and Laos. (13)

Since Laos and Cambodia do not exist in the television war, they are also not involved in television's Geneva Convention. Communist activity in both countries and North Vietnamese violations of Lao and Cambodian borders completely disappear. The stage is then set for a limited war between Vietnam and America.

(The Chief Correspondent seems to enjoy describing the big power politics at Geneva, from the American delegation "limping in . . . its legs shackled by Eisenhower and Dulles" and France's Bidault, "puffy and dissolute", to the "grim old Bolshevik" Molotov and "brilliant diplomat" Zhou Enlai. Karnow notes "the Viet Minh's attempts to control Laos and Cambodia", although he attaches no significance to this, even retrospectively, after Hanoi has indeed taken control of the two countries. In the end, the Viet Minh get "double-crossed" by Zhou, in the words of Pham Van Dong, who is not one to admit that the history of the Vietnamese Communists is riddled with incidents of double-crossing their allies. Karnow describes the Geneva Conference as "an interlude between two wars – or, rather, a lull in the same war." pp. 199-204). Describing the First and Second Indochina wars as one and the same is risky business. America's goals were hardly the same as those of colonial France. The Saigon regime was not in the same position as the Bao Dai government. Ho's forces were fighting their own people, not Legionaires. And so on. But Karnow sees no need to explain these presumably trivial details.)

Footnotes

1. See *Area Handbook for Laos* and *Area Handbook for the Khmer Republic,* Foreign Area Studies, American University; Hugh Toyles' *Laos: Buffer State or Battleground;* and Bernard Fall, *Laos: Anatomy of a Crisis*

2. For one description of this period, see *Lao Issara: The Memoirs of Oun Sananikone,* tr. John B. Murdoch, Data Paper No. 100, Southeast Asia Program, Cornell University, 1965

3. Hoang Van Chi, *From Colonialism to Communism,* p. 29

4. Vu Van Thai, "Development of the Revolution", reprinted in *Vietnam: Anatomy of a Conflict,* p. 262

5. Douglas Pike, *History of Vietnamese Communism,* p. 73

6. See Vu Van Thai, "Development of the Revolution", and I. Milton Sacks, "The Indigenous Roots of Vietnamese Nationalism", in *Vietnam: Anatomy of a Conflict;* also Bernard Fall's account of this period in *The Two Vietnams*

7. Vu Van Thai, Note 4 above, p. 262

8. See Janos Radvanyi, *Delusion and Reality,* Chapter 1, "Stalin's Vietnam Policy"

9. Fall, work cited, pp. 109-111

10. Radvanyi, Note 8 above, pp. 8-9

11. Donald Lancaster, "The Emancipation of French Indochina", reprinted in *Vietnam: Anatomy of a Conflict,* p. 55

12. Fall, work cited, p. 129

13. Lancaster, Note 11 above

Supplements

(Ed. – Life among the Viet Minh was arduous and at times frightening. In a three-volume work entitled *Jungle of Reeds,* author Doan Quoc Si relates his experiences with the Viet Minh during the wartime. In the following excerpt, he describes how hard-core cadres were indoctrinated on the Chinese frontier. The reader may note striking similarities to methods used by fanatic religious cults. Translation.)

After the seventh session had gone through half the process, the Chinese adviser to the division commander suddenly encouraged Brig. Gen. Tran B. to apply the Chinese experience to the Vietnamese soldiers. This was the criticism movement. According to this adviser, by means of criticism the Chinese Communist Party had uncovered a multitude of reactionary elements who directly or indirectly were spying in order to destroy the Party. The progression of the study session went:

– First, the participant revealed what he was thinking and what he did in each event.

– Relying on the self-denunciation of the participant, the comrades in the "intimate cell" in the battalion and regiment would bring up questions and cross-examine him to light up the path and seek out his disease. There were different kinds of diseases: avoiding action, pleasure-seeking, wavering attitude, promiscuity,...

– Relying on the results of the above, the leaders would apply the "light of Marxist reasoning" to determine what category the participant fell in.

The criticism of the participant's philosophy of life in these waves as they applied to the case of Vietnam used 1945 as a time marker to divide history into two stages: everything before 1945 belonged to the old society; everything from 1945 on was the new society. The hard-core cadres were assigned to Committees for Research and Investigation. The first task of each committee was to make a blacklist [sic] with the names of those people comprising the element with the most serious crimes (in the opinion of the committee) to prepare them for the "surgery table" (i.e., for criticism). The committee prearranged the questions to be repeated over and over and rehearsed them to learn how they should react with each participant. The committee wisely appointed a number of volunteer Party members to go on the "surgery table" first as models, to prepare the spirit of those who were to go later.

The criticism movement began.

Slogans were hung everywhere, reminding everyone of the importance of the criticism movement. Any and all means go to serve the criticism movement! Each study battalion went to a separate house and absolutely no one was to speak to another person outside his battalion.

The "model" went and sat in a small room covered all around with black cloth to review his past life prior to the revolution. This would prepare him to write his personal confession beneath the dim light of an oil lamp. The "model" went barefoot, wore a shirt without buttons and trousers without a drawstring, ate plain rice and assumed the appearance of a sad and miserable individual, remorseful of his crimes.

One model person denounced himself for three times thinking of surrendering to the French. Being in the resistance was so hard, he said, it would be better to be a prisoner in the enemy's jail for a while and then go home to the French-occupied zone.

Another model denounced himself as an informant for the French. He said he hung mirrors in the treetops to mark places for the French planes to bomb.

There was a model who denounced himself (oh, the horror!) for thinking of sleeping with his sister. During this criticism, the speaker talked for a while, then fainted... went on and fainted again... but this time for real! Finally he stood up and blamed the old society for bringing on such depravity. He then praised the new society with the "light of Marxism" for leading humanity from the deep abyss of crimes up to the pinnacle of virtue.

The author would like to note that only six months later, during a review of the errors of the criticism movement, these same models confessed that the above crimes came entirely from their imaginations. They thought that the bigger their crimes, the more they would prove they had overcome pride and liberated themselves from individualism so they might know only loyalty to the Party. The crimes may have been imaginary, but these men were truly remorseful because they believed the old society must have been full of such crimes. If they could not see the crimes stimulated in them by the old society, they could not become enlightened and absorb the ideas of the Party. Could any cadre be trusted by the Party so much that he would be assigned as a model if he had not absorbed the thoughts of the Party?

That is why the models competed with each other in enthusiastically denouncing themselves for the most grievous of crimes.

Following these plants, there came the persons named on the blacklist. These were the principal victims, the real goal of the movement.

There were cadres who had been guerrillas in enemy territory. Others had been arrested by enemy intelligence and nearly tortured to death. Some cadres had risked their lives in countless campaigns and received the highest award (of these, the biggest number were the regional cadres of the Party). But, confronted with stupid questions such as "Why this and why that?" they, too, became confused— the state of mind of a "counterrevolutionary exposed in his schemes". Even though it was winter and there was snow in the mountains, some men were stripped of their clothing and dunked in cold water for half an hour, then left naked like that with a sign around their necks reading "counterrevolutionary". They were ridiculed in front of the "school personnel", male and female alike (among the staff there were some Chinese women). The strangest thing was that the leadership board carefully maintained two contradictory faces in the same study session. The participant made a personal confession. The members of his unit showed sympathy for the confession, then began to question and cross-

question, insult and abuse, in order to make him feel miserable . . .
After the criticism, the participant was consoled with the reminder
that only by self-revelation and abuse by his fellow unit members
could the old vestiges of slavery be washed away and he could serve
the Party and the people. . . .

Usually when the criticism ended, the victims were near collapse,
crushed both in body and mind, their faces hanging with sadness as
if they had just learned that all their families had died.

But it was not yet over! After criticism session, the spirit was not
yet released. Following a session, if the participant could still eat
and sleep as before, that meant he had no shame for his crimes. If he
ate less or stopped eating altogether, he was lacking in honesty and
harbored resentful thoughts (for the Party) inside. Instead, he had
to do whatever he could to show deep suffering, misery and remorse,
while still talking with his comrades, even going to the field with
them to join in a game. Immediately after that, he would go to the
room draped in black, sit beneath the dull glow of the lamp, hold his
head and think, trying to recall other criminal actions to prove his
criminal thoughts in order to respond to legitimate questions from
his unit members . . . Then with full devotion he would write new
pages to supplement his previous personal confession.

All the above activities, and even stopping briefly to relieve himself, were performed under the harsh scrutiny of the cell of
"intimates".

Arriving at another stage, many of the participants were led to
the brink. Once, when their nerves were on edge, they suddenly
exploded, like a mine blowing up under the weight of a tank. They
screamed.

"Yes, I am a counterrevolutionary!"

"Yes, I am the secretary of Vu Hong Khanh!"

"Yes, I am a counter-agent for French intelligence!"

"Yes, I struggled only for individualism, for heroism!"

Le K., the son of Mme. Cat Hanh Long, was then assistant political commissar of the study group... The suicide movement started
and Le K.'s regiment was well-known for having the most suicides.
Some used ropes and hanged themselves. Others broke razor
blades and swallowed them with water, then ran out to play sports,
collapsing and dying half-way through . . .

(Ed.- One method the Viet Minh used to raise revenue for their activities was smuggling opium through Laos. Below is a brief account of a cadre's report regarding his activities in this regard. Taken from *Jungle of Reeds.* Translation.)

...Hang had been an offical Party member for a little less than a year up until the day of the criticism movement. His achievements in the struggle were too brilliant and his loyalty was not questioned by any comrade. Hang was one of those upright fellows who spoke what he believed, lived as he spoke, and if he trusted in someone, it was without condition or suspicion... But despite his brilliant accomplishments and his undisputed loyalty, Hang was placed at the head of the blacklist! Why? . . .

Perhaps because the Party ranked him among the old intellectual elements (he had one part of his law degree) and he was the son of a landlord. The Party still paid special attention to his spontaneous character. He was sure that having left his family, joined the Western Movement and fought in difficult conditions, been captured and imprisoned by the French and tortured – surely the Party could not force him to denounce himself for any action or thought that went contrary to the revolution . . .

In his personal criticism describing his tasks in the Western Movement regiment, Hang wrote briefly, succinctly. If the contents did not contain hard facts, people would suspect he was adopting an insolent attitude toward the group.

"The 150th Battalion of the Western Movement regiment camped at Bat Co plantation, about 8 km from Nho Quan. Our task was a daring economic one: smuggling opium. We did it for the group. If unfortunately we were caught in places where the group could not intervene because it was too much in the open, then each individual had to accept responsibility in court. Our itinerary was as follows: from Nho Quan past Kim Tan to Cam Thuy by road; from Cam Thuy by La Han to Hoi Xuan upstream on the Ma River; then across to Samneua [in Laos]. In the first months, we had to purchase silver coins at Phat Diem, Phu Ly, because the Lao would only trade opium for coin. When we ran out of coins, we tried to persuade them to take the paper Indochinese piaster bills. Going past La Han, Hoi Xuan, to the contact bases near the Lao-Vietnamese border, we were often

ambushed and surrounded at night. Flares lit the sky, machine
guns screamed and swept through the brush. If a comrade died, we
left his body, but we took any of his coins or money. Arriving at
Samneua, we often had to wait two weeks before the goods were
delivered. We ate dried manioc. Dysentery and malaria were two
common diseases. That was around 1948 and the beginning of
1949. When the goods came, only the company commanders on up
could use the card. The Security Police district chief alone was
allowed to inspect the goods in private and sign the papers. We
established contact with the Chinese at Bac Hai. They brought
stuff smuggled from Macao and Hong Kong."

PART 3: AMERICA'S MANDARIN
(1954-1963)

*Ngo Dinh Diem returns to Vietnam to head the South
Vietnamese government. Supported by the United States,
Diem resettles 900,000 refugees from the North and secures
the authority of his government by defeating political and
military opponents. The United States strives to further its
image as defender of freedom for the world with Vietnam as
a testing-ground. Diem hopes to establish a base of support
among the people while brutally repressing his opposition.
But, relying heavily on his family, he becomes increasingly
isolated from the people. The National Liberation Front
arises and gains support against Diem. The strategic hamlet
program fails to stop the Viet Cong. The Catholic leader
encounters problems with the Buddhists. His unpopularity
grows and America becomes concerned about his future.
In 1963 Diem is assassinated by his generals.*

Ho Chi Minh Takes Charge of the North

The *Television History's* producers apparently wish to give the
impression that Ngo Dinh Diem's government in the South
functioned in a vacuum, totally unrelated to all that was happening
at the same time in the North. No serious description of the events
that unfolded in North Vietnam after 1954 is ever given in the series;
the cursory view given in Part 6, "America's Enemy", is hardly
sufficient to tell the whole story. This omission is one of the major
faults of the series.

In order for the reader to get a better understanding of the time
and circumstances in the North as Pres. Diem was coming to power
in Saigon, we include the following outline, taken primarily from
Hoang Van Chi's *From Colonialism to Communism.*

The Viet Minh had been both militarily and politically active during the resistance war against the French, preparing themselves for the assumption of power once the war ended. From 1946-1949, Ho Chi Minh tried to rally the people behind the banner of "the Fatherland above all!" For the Communist Party this meant a temporary alliance with different political parties whenever possible and respect for private landlords and businesspeople.

In 1951, the Communist Party came out in the open and announced the "anti-imperialist, anti-feudalist" struggle. This ushered in a new stage in the socialist process aimed at the liquidation of "reactionaries", ie., landlords and anyone even remotely connected to them. It began with a tax system designed by Mao Zedong in China which involved both a progressive income tax and a "village tax" that went to support the Communist Party. The exaggerated tax rates, bullying and oppression that ensued led to the impoverishing of the people under Viet Minh control. (These are the marvelous "reforms" referred to by Stanley Karnow, already noted in the previous chapter.)

A "political struggle" was put into effect in February 1953. Those who had not paid their taxes as determined by the cadres were tortured, beaten and sometimes killed. Not only were the tax debtors terrorized, but also anyone who was implicated by them while under torture. Actually, the cadres conducting this campaign started out with a list of those the Party wished to see punished. The interrogations were simply an excuse for the torture and arrest of the necessary victims. Hoang Van Chi describes some of the tortures: "The victim was compelled to kneel down, supporting on his head a basket filled with heavy stones.

"He was forced to hang by his thumbs or feet from a rope thrown over a rafter. In this position he could be beaten or, by pulling on the rope, jerked violently up and down.

"His thumbs were wrapped in a cloth soaked in oil which was then ignited." (1)

During this nightmare, the Party kept itself hidden to avoid any blame in the terror. It lasted for two weeks during the New Year period and led to the miserable deaths of many innocent people. The campaign was obviously not intended to collect taxes, but to clear out of the way those persons who might interfere with the coming

Land Reform Program. Among the victims were the parents of Col. Dang Van Viet, who had defeated the French at Cao Bang-Lang Son three years earlier. Ho Chi Minh apologized for the Party's errors and asked local cadres for a full report. Party members who had refused to participate in the campaign were congratulated for their prudence, then sent to prison until the Land Reform was over. The following months, Ho sent the same cadre teams down to Viet Minh territory in the South to repeat the gruesome ritual.

This wave of terror had the effect of "encouraging" erstwhile reluctant citizens to enthusiastically volunteer to assist the Viet Minh. The Party's claim to authority was thus founded on fear. Many people began to have second thoughts about the "patriot" Ho Chi Minh and his Party. The French, they reasoned, had exploited the people, but they were not madmen.

To justify the terror, the Communist Party staged trials of certain "traitors", which included mandarins, landlords, clergy, merchants and so-called "bourgeois compradores" (persons who traded with foreigners). Some of these poor souls were sentenced to death and executed before cheering mobs. Others were only thrown into prison.

The Party also had to deal with intellectuals and others of reason who waxed wary of what was happening. Only fear prevented these intellectuals from expressing their disillusionment. The Communists relied on them for support in the resistance and could not afford to lose them and their influence with the people. Consequently, they resorted to an ideological revolution.

The Communists use different methods of ideological training. Criticism and self-criticism sessions form the basic type. Participants are urged to confess to specific "crimes" under group pressure. In some cases the victim is subjected to shouting, cursing and other forms of violent psychological abuse until he or she confesses. Denunciations come as a result of mutual surveillance of group members.

Careful ideological training is applied to prepare cadres for imminent policy changes. In this type of re-education, cadres are brought into a controlled environment, a schedule of manual labor, poor nutrition and division into small discussion groups. There are many meetings and conferences. "Students" are guided into making strong objections to selected lessons, then broken down through

"Marxist logic." At the end of the term, the students are ordered to write down their confessions and life histories. The "life history" is an important part of the Communist security process for the author must describe in detail all activities, relationships, contacts and crimes (real or imagined) which may possibly be used against the author or the author's family at a later date.

In 1953, the Party pursued a special training program of five parts. First, the student was to adopt the proper attitude toward the training. Second, Vietnamese history was defined for the student in terms of the "evil" (the colonialists) and the "just" (Marxism-Leninism and the Communist Party). Third, the student was to realize the significance of the new task ahead, namely, establishing a "people's democracy", eliminating reactionaries and collaborating with socialist brother countries. Fourth came the purging of "diseases" from the Party members and cadres; these diseases included deviationism, opportunism, desire for personal freedom, romanticism, adultery, etc. Finally, there came the indoctrination for the Land Reform. Here the students were taught the wickedness of the enemy (landlords and imperialists), the necessity of the Communist struggle, as opposed to simply the anti-imperialist one (thus connecting the resistance war to the liquidation of landlords), the method of giving free hand to the masses in carrying out the program with reassurances of safety to those who followed the Party line.

The Land Reform Campaign had two stages: the rent reduction and the actual "land reform". Their purpose was to destroy in two strokes the landowning class and establish a dictatorship of the proletariat. Both stages were carried out in basically the same manner, although the second was more violent. The proper peasants needed to carry out the campaign were selected by specially trained cadres who were quartered with the peasants (by means of the "three together" system: the cadres ate, slept and worked with the peasants). Then the villages were classified by Land Reform Battalions according to their presumed wealth while the Communist Party once again disappeared from sight. Landlords and those of relative wealth who had supported the resistance hoped to be given favorable treatment, but eventually they were all victimized. The head of each landlord household was arrested and his family forced to pay a "people's debt". This debt was impossible to pay, so the family's property was confiscated instead. Peasants were taken to group meetings and persuaded to denounce the landlords. Persons related to the landlords by blood or socially might also become victims and many of these were punished by ostracism (in time many starved to death), exile to the frontier regions or other means. Those peasants selected to denounce landlords were rehearsed under the guidance of cadres and the formal denunciations took place before crowds gathered for that purpose. At each denunciation, a stage was set up with special seats for 14 "clerks" (all but one of whom could neither read nor write) and seven presidents (including a token woman "police chief"). At the top of the stage were portraits of Ho Chi Minh, Mao Zedong and Soviet leader Malenkov, with the appropriate national flags. A dramatic ceremony took place as the accused was brought forward on his hands and knees as the crowd shouted at him. Once he arrived on stage a parade of denouncers would step in front of him shaking their fists and reciting lines practiced for days in advance. Alleged crimes included beatings, rape, murder, various types of abuse of the peasants and betrayal of the country. Most of the crimes were fabricated and the accusations groundless. This could go on for several days until the accused "confessed" amid the condemnatory roar of the mob. When this was completed, mobile tribunals came to the villages in the district to conduct "people trials". The accused was permitted no defence before the all-peasant jury; his signed confession was taken as his testimony. Some landlords were executed and their deaths marked by compulsory parades. Others were thrown into jail while their property was confiscated. Many persons committed suicide. Others perished in exile or starved to death during the ostracism.

During the time spent in this activity, farms were neglected, homes left unattended and the people uncared for. The peasants became frightened to work too hard because now it was a crime to have a little more than others.

Persons who had escaped denunciation during the rent reduction stage were often the victims in the second stage, the Land Reform. Party members were purged and conflicts between old and new cadres arose. There were more suicides during this period and more victims to fill fixed quotas. The peasants' land and property were taken away. The people were made to realize that only the Party could save them by its arbitrary justice. This stage was temporarily halted in 1954-1955 when nearly a million refugees fled the North, taking advantage of the Geneva Agreements' provision for free movement between the two zones.

How many people died in this campaign? Bernard Falls tells us that "probably close to 50,000 were executed in connection with the land reform and at least two times as many were arrested and sent to forced labor camps." (2) Wesley Fishel, of Michigan State University, echoed this account. (3) In his *History of Vietnamese Communism*, Douglas Pike says, "Estimates range from 50,000 to 100,000 dead." (4) Huong Van Chi quotes from Gerard Tongas, a French professor in Hanoi up to 1959, who said "This indescribable butchery resulted in one hundred thousand deaths." (5) In Part 6 of the *Television History* we are told: "Possibly between three and fifteen thousand were executed."

(Stanley Karnow's modest version of the land reform can be found on p. 225 of his *History*.)

The Land Reform Program was intended to shatter the spirit of ownership in order to pave the way for full collectivisation of property. It was also a purge of the population aimed at uncovering the "enemies of the people" while terrorizing others to underscore the Party's authority. The slogan of the land reform was "better to kill ten innocent people than to let one enemy live."

In 1956, on behalf of the Party, Gen. Giap announced that some "errors" had unfortunately been committed during the program and these would have to be "rectified". This new campaign, actually conceived prior to the start of the Land Reform itself, was intended to provide a period of calm after the storm, to allow the country to settle down again after months of violence. No explanation was given as to why the Party had done nothing to stop what it called "excesses" during the long period of torture, trial, denunciation, and execution. The strategy was to let the people share in the blood guilt and keep the party's hands clean, maintaining its reputation for moderation. The peasants were told they were "masters of their own fate", that what had happened was their own doing rather than the manipulation of their fears by the Party.

During the "rectification", Party Secretary Truong Trinh "resigned" and some prisoners were released after being admonished not to retaliate against those who had unjustly denounced them. However, feelings ran bitter and Party members were disillusioned. Confiscated property could not always be returned and the wives of some Party members had already been forced to marry new cadres (an indication of how women are treated as property under Communism, despite claims to the contrary).

Conflicts arose between old and new Party members. Fighting and arguments were common and there were lynchings, stabbings and shooting in some areas. Some cadres who had unjustly denounced others had their tongues cut out. There were passive revolts against the regime, such as peasants refusing to follow orders or not attending meetings. Active revolts took place in Nghe An, Bac Ninh and Nam Dinh. In Nghe An, for example, 20,000 peasants fought against a division of Viet Minh troops. To avoid more trouble, the Viet Minh stationed troops in the homes of peasants in sensitive areas and metalsmiths were isolated to prevent them from secretly making weapons that could be used against the regime.

The intellectuals in the North were baited by a "Hundred Flowers Campaign". Intellectuals and educated persons who had supported the resistance had been mistreated during the war and consequently were becoming increasingly unhappy with the turn of events. Critics of the regime aired their complaints until the government closed offending newspapers and periodicals. Dissidents were jailed, executed or placed in "reform through labor" (a euphemism for slow death by hard labor), condemned as traitors or saboteurs. Some were sent to the mountains and mines where many eventually perished.

Stanley Karnow and the producers of the *Television History*, while passionate in denouncing the "tyranny" of Ngo Dinh Diem, have surprisingly little to say about this period of Communist history.

The Rise of Ngo Dinh Diem

Once the producers have assured themselves that all the essential information about North Vietnam has been neglected, they set about creating the image of Ngo Dinh Diem as an unpopular and oppressive leader who represented America's effort to halt Communist expansion.

All of this is done with select scenes, careful editing, and a number of doubtful generalizations about the U.S. and South Vietnam. America is treated as the prime mover of history – the derogatory reference to Diem as "America's Mandarin" makes that clear from the beginning. Between insinuations of America's "exceptionalism" and key interviews with "objective witnesses" regarding the policies of the Diem government, the viewers are not given much opportunity to decide for themselves what this period of history actually meant for the people involved.

First, we see Eisenhower and Dulles, whose speeches about stopping the spread of Communism are intended to reflect what the producers see as America's paranoid attitude towards Communism. Then, Diem is introduced: "a little-known nationalist . . . appointed by Bao Dai, the playboy emperor picked by the French. He had few allies in South Vietnam." Diem's Catholic background is noted, along with the fact that he was in the U.S. during the early 1950s "secluding himself in a New Jersey seminary."

Thus in a few seconds of airtime, Pres. Diem is discredited as a viable political figure before he is even shown lifting a finger to carry out the duties of his office. In fact, all of the statements above concerning Diem are oversimplified and misleading. To say that Diem was "little known" is only partly true. Most leaders in underdeveloped nations are not well known to the general population before they assume power. (Despite Communist tales to the contrary, Ho Chi Minh was hardly famous when he tramped into Hanoi in 1945 and made himself head of state.) Diem was known to many nationalists and political figures of his time, including the Emperor Bao Dai and Diem's primary adversary, Ho Chi Minh. Diem had proven himself as an administrator by the early 1930s as governor of Phan Thiet province. In 1933 he was appointed Bao Dai's Interior Minister, but soon resigned, decrying the emperor as an instrument of the French, whose colonial rule he could not accept. The series fails to mention that Diem's brother, Khoi, was killed by the Viet Minh (another brother, Nhu, fled to Hue to avoid a similar fate). Diem was well informed about Ho's methods and goals. He helped reinstate the emperor in 1949, but refused to take an active part in the government. During the 1950s, while in the U.S., Diem did not remain behind closed chapel doors, as the television series implies, but spoke at several sites around the county and made contact with political figures to solicit their support for his cause. Thus, when Diem returned to Vietnam in 1954, he was not without a political background. Whether or not Bao Dai was a "playboy" is irrelevant to the selection of Diem as head of the government; there is no serious reason for mentioning it here. Diem had a reputation for incorruptibility and nationalism; this point is not brought up in the series. (6)

(Karnow tells his readers that Diem, despite his honesty, courage and "fervent fidelity to Vietnam's national cause", could not compare favorably to Ho Chi Minh. Indeed, no human being who ever lived can match the Chief Correspondent's saintly Ho, whom Karnow believes was a hero to everyone. (p 213)

Passage to Freedom

One of the more insulting segments of Part 3 is the portrayal of the refugee exodus from North Vietnam in 1954-5. Nearly one million people took advantage of the Geneva Agreements' provision regarding free movement between zones to move to the South. The *Television History* sorts them into two classes: those who had worked for the French and feared Communist reprisals, and those who expected favorable treatment in the South from Catholic Diem. They left their homes, we are told, because of pressure and CIA propaganda. The incident is further abused by an American newsreel taken 30 years out of context which makes the dangerous and tragic flight of the refugees look like nothing but a cheap political game, a "touching symbol of the Cold War."

The program emphasizes the propaganda effort of the CIA in encouraging Northerners to flee. A former CIA agent, Edward Lansdale, is quoted to the point. Yet, the series never describes the persecution of the Catholics by the Viet Minh during the 1950s or explains what was in store for the Catholics had they elected to remain in their homes. The series brushes off the exodus as opportunism, forgetting that the refugees were largely peasants, many of whom had supported the resistance movement against the French.

They had sided with the Viet Minh until Ho Chi Minh's new order oppressed them worse than the French had.

Never before in Vietnamese history had there been such a massive flight of refugees. The number 900,000 only counts those who were successful in reaching the South. Thousands more tried to flee, but were prevented from doing so by the Viet Minh, who were thereby violating the Geneva Agreements. The Viet Minh established road blocks, forced refugees to take indirect routes to refugee camps, issued provincial "passports" with early expiration dates, beat and shot those who tried to flee. (7)

The Communists brutally repressed the Catholics, in part because of Marxist hatred for religion, but also because the Catholics were socially powerful. Priests were considered a threat to the system for they often commanded the loyalty of whole villages, making Communist control weak in some areas. To terrify the people, the Viet Minh tortured and executed priests, nuns and lay leaders, while making it impossible for religious services to be held. In time, the government created bogus religious organizations; only clergy approved by the Communists were allowed to preach. Such repression extended to the Buddhists and others.

The refugees fled quite simply because it was impossible for them to live under Communism. As for propaganda, the series fails to describe the grotesque propaganda compaign conducted by the Communists to discourage the people from fleeing to the South. Furthermore, the influence of America's propaganda was diminished by the refugees' fear of the Americans, whom they still identified as supporters of the colonial French. The refugees had no way of knowing that the Americans were not the monsters depicted in Viet Minh propaganda leaflets. This makes their flight all the more amazing. They left their native homes because they believed it was better to die seeking freedom than to live under Ho Chi Minh's government. The truth is so simple it's pathetic.

(Former CIA agent Edward Lansdale is quoted on the series as he describes how the CIA "urged" people to flee. That Lansdale is only half quoted can be found by reading Karnow's *History*. After playing up Lansdale's CIA activities to the hilt, Karnow comes to a terribly brief story of the refugee flight, at the very end of which he allows Lansdale to put everything "in perspective": "People don't just pull up their roots and transplant themselves because of slogans," Lansdale explains. "They honestly feared what might happen to them, and the emotion was strong enough to overcome their attachment to the land, their homes and their ancestral graves. So the initiative was very much theirs – and we mainly made the transportation possible." (p. 222) This transitory quote – the only justification given to the refugees – is then dropped without further comment. Tradition and strong family feelings are not exciting subjects for journalists. Later, an indignant Karnow will invoke images of peasants being "uprooted from their native villages and ancestral graves" by Diem's agroville program, an effort hardly comparable to the refugee flight of 900,000 people.

(At one point, Karnow remarks that the Catholics are "fanatical anti-Communists." (p. 224) He seems to assume they had no reason to be. Nor does he deign to note that the Communists are fanatical anti-Catholics, anti-Buddhists, anti-Taoists, and anti-any religion.)

The First Republic

Pres. Diem faced many challenges during his term in office. These included consolidating power in a chaotic country just coming out of war, organizing a new government, promoting a new patriotic sentiment, resettling a million refugees, and so on. True journalists, the producers of the *Television History* concentrate on the most visible and spectacular aspects of Diem's republic and ignore the rest. Mme. Nhu makes for a better show than, say, minority problems in the Central Highlands.

At the same time, the producers wish to emphasize Diem's alleged unpopularity and failures in symbolic ways. We see, for instance, crowds gathered on his behalf and demonstrations organized by aides, which, we are told, were necessary because the president was not a man of the people. (Of course, the series never acknowledges that Ho Chi Minh's demonstrations were planned and staged.) In order to highlight the dictatorial nature of Diem's regime, there is even a short clip of young people giving Diem a raised-arm salute reminiscent of Hitler. Diem defeats the gang-lord Bay Vien, but this is qualified; he does it only with American aid and because he is stubborn and "would *never* compromise". (sic)

The truth is, Diem treated his political opponents harshly. There are many persons, victims and witnesses, who can testify to this. Some of them were former supporters who turned against Diem when it became clear he did not intend to soften his ways and lead South Vietnam towards a more open democratic republic. The producers of this series would have had little problem finding persons to give frank and objective criticisms of Diem's political career or express sincere grievances and complaints about his government.

Instead, they interview a pair of Communist cadres they picked up on their guided tour through Vietnam. One of them, Le Minh Dao, accuses Diem of seeking "revenge" against those who "had directly fought against the French" or "had helped organize the resistance." This is nonsense. Diem was strongly anti-French and had no reason to seek "revenge" on "resistance fighters." His main targets in the political clean-up were the Communists and their allies. The other "witness", Dr. Pham Thi Xuan Que, remarks with a wry smile how Diem sent his "hounddogs – this was our term for the secret police" to throw her ancestral altar out on the street and force her to become Catholic. This, too, is absurd. Diem may have had strong prejudices about his religion, but to say he compelled baptism is ludicrous. Not only that, Vietnamese society is founded in Confucian tradition, where ancestor veneration is of extreme importance. All Vietnamese Catholics had ancestral altars in their homes. There is just no basis for claiming that Diem went against his people's tradition by ordering the desecration of family altars, as the "witness" charges.

It can be seen that instead of talking to sincere critics of the Diem regime, the producers chose to use the testimony of two people who clearly hate the man and will even lie to discredit him. The resentment of the Viet Cong toward Diem is not surprising – for all his failings, Diem was, in fact, more successful in stopping the Communists than any other leader in South Vietnam and the Communists will never forgive him for that. For their part, the producers can be criticized for being so intent on making Diem look bad that they accepted any testimony that supported their opinions. These same producers who assert that refugees are not reliable witnesses to Communism because of their antagonism to that system do not hesitate to take evidence from Communists critical of the arch-enemy of Communism, Ngo Dinh Diem.

The series might also have mentioned that many of the harshest tactics employed by the Diem government were those they copied from the Communists. The president believed (as do many of his ilk) that the only way to deal with the brutality of the Communists is to offer them more of the same.

(Stanley Karnow likes to describe Diem through graphic details of the president's repression. Strangely, he does not show the same morbid curiosity with regards to the Communists.)

Geneva Realities

According to the television series, Ho Chi Minh's followers inno-cently expected country-wide elections in 1956 to reunify Vietnam and bring them to power. Actually, that was their rhetoric in those days. Since the Geneva Conference, the Communist leaders never seriously believed elections would actually come about. But, the issue did make for good propaganda material in attacking Diem.

The *Televison History* focuses soley on this issue of the Geneva Agreements because the producers wish to imply that only America and South Vietnam are responsible for the failure of the accords. (Again, it is a Communist cadre who makes this point.) Since neither the State of Vietnam (Bao Dai's government) nor the U.S. signed the agreements, it can be debated forever to what degree they were bound to implement them.

What is not debatable is that Ho Chi Minh's government did sign the accords and clearly violated the major provisions without con-cern for public reaction. This is not mentioned in the program, suggesting that the producers consider North Vietnamese violations to be irrelevant. For the record, a 1962 report from the International Supervisory Control Commission charged with overseeing com-pliance of the Agreements, concluded that North Vietnam violated the principles concerning complete cessation of hostilities, the pro-hibition of the use of regroupment zones for the renewal of hostilities, the guarantee of neutrality for the demilitarized zone, respect for territory controlled by the other party, and the pledge that all its military personnel would comply with all points of the Agreements. North Vietnam increased its military capacity, allowed military cadres to remain behind in the South while their family members regrouped in the North, sent arms and personnel into the South aimed at the overthrow of the Saigon government, and violated the territorial integrity of Cambodia and Laos to pursue military hostilities. The Commission reported that South Vietnam had violated the articles regarding taking increased military aid not deducted from its credit of worn out equipment. Both sides were criticized for interfering with the investigation. (8)

A separate agreement was made regarding Laos which called for the withdrawal of Pathet Lao forces into two northern provinces and the Pathet Lao's integration into the Royal Lao Armed Forces. Peace in Laos was never realized. The Pathet Lao eventually secured its own administration in the nothern provinces and infiltrated the southern part of the country. The Pathet Lao forces, supplied by the Communists, grew in number of arms and soldiers while Pathet Lao radio broadcast from Hanoi. The Lao government responded to the problem by accepting American aid. The U.S. began training Hmong tribesmen as guerrilla soldiers to fight Communist infiltration in the highlands.

A second Geneva Conference on Laos was held from 1961-2 to deal with growing problems. This second cease-fire was only temporary as the Pathet Lao and Vietnamese resumed their military build-up and the Vietnamese increased traffic down the Ho Chi Minh Trail.

In the meantime, the Vietnamese began using Cambodia as a safe haven along the southwestern end of the supply route. Further Communist proselytizing was carried out and Vietnamese infiltrators lived among the resident population in Cambodia.

Somehow, on the television series, the Communists come out looking like Mr. Clean.

With regards to the 1956 election promise, there are several statements from Pres. Diem to the North Vietnamese government noting Diem's willingness to participate in free elections any time the North agreed to actually comply with the Geneva Agreements, put an end to terrorism and intimidation and grant political liberties to the people of the North. Naturally, the Communists were not ready to accept these suggestions.

And yet, despite the political repression in the North, the concentration camps and prisons, "people's courts" and executions, Ho Chi Minh comes off in the television series as the patron saint of democracy simply because Ngo Dinh Diem refused to play his game.

(Although Karnow considers the Geneva Agreements to have been "hastily contrived" to prevent war from expanding while providing a "temporary truce between France and the Viet Minh", he seems to lay all the burden of compliance on Diem and the U.S. At one point, Karnow offhandedly remarks that Diem "reneged" on the reunification elections. (p. 226) As the author should know, this is not quite right; Diem could not "renege" on something he never agreed to in the first place.)

The National Liberation Front

The viewers are introduced to the National Liberation Front (NLF) by an NLF film with marching people shouting and shaking their fists. Background commentary by the Vietnamese speaker is not translated. One might assume that they are denouncing Diem, their primary opponent. In fact, the speaker is railing against "the American imperialists, the most dangerous imperialists of all!"

According to the series, the NLF was nothing other than a "communist-organized coalition of anti-Diem forces", created in response to the failure of reunification elections to take place and because of repression by Diem's police. The series never explains that the NLF was designed and organized in the North and not the South, and that its activities were directed from Hanoi. Furthermore, according to Bernard Fall, the NLF's leaders were not even identified until April 1962, fully a year and a half after the Front's formal "creation." "Even so," Fall continues, "the leaders . . . are hardly the caliber to constitute a 'shadow government' ready to take over from the Saigon regime at the first sign of disintegration." (9) As a political organization, the NLF was not the formidable opponent of the Diem regime that the series (and Cohen's *Anthology*) would suggest. It was, from the beginning, dependent on Hanoi. Nor was it a true "coalition." Its main constituent was the People's Revolutionary Party, which was the new name given to the southern branch of the Vietnamese Communist party. Says one scholar, "The People's Revolutionary Party called itself the Marxist-

Leninist party of South Vietnam, the principal member of the NLF, the vanguard of the struggle against Diem, the soul of the NLF, the engine of the revolution." (10) The Front was never able to attract serious opposition groups in South Vietnam and was less a political threat than a military one.

(Karnow admits that the NLF was controlled by Hanoi, but still insists that the U.S. might have exploited regional differences among the Communists to some sort of advantage. (p. 239) While asserting one more "lost opportunity" by the U.S., Karnow forgets that he himself was unaware of regional conflicts among the Communists until he visited Vietnam in 1981.)

Strategic Hamlets

One of the series' symbols for the failure of Diem's regime is the strategic hamlet program. The "strategic hamlet" is a counter-insurgency device used before in Malaya by the British. As described by its mentor, Sir Robert Thompson, the principal aim of the strategic hamlet is to isloate the insurgents both physically and politically from the population. Applying Mao's analogy of guer-rillas living among the peasants being like fish in water, this isola-tion is intended to keep "all the 'little fishes' out of the 'water' ", ie., prevent insurgents from getting support from the population. (11)

The *Television History* relates that the strategic hamlet program in South Vietnam was a disaster. First, the peasants were "already resentful" because of Diem's "half-hearted land reform." (An ironic statement. The producers downplay the Communist land reform and yet chide Diem for being "half-hearted" about his! Perhaps they think the Southern president should have attended to the task with the same zeal Comrade Ho applied in the North.) Now, the villages are being "forced to relocate" into hamlets that would become "targets of Viet Cong attacks." "Life inside the spiky peri-meter didn't measure up to the ideal." In part 4, the viewers will see films of peasants vigorously tearing these hamlets down after Diem's death. ("The structure he had created with American support was being smashed.")

Looking beyond this rather derisive depiction of the program, one might ask: What exactly happened to the strategic hamlets? If the program failed, why? What went wrong?

Some South Vietnamese who were connected with the program claim the hamlets were in fact effective in stopping the Viet Cong infiltration, altough there were problems in the beginning. Literature on the program generally indicates that the hamlets encountered serious problems in method, organization and goals. (12) One of the more revealing criticisms comes from Sir Robert Thompson himself, who complained of the manner in which the program was being implemented. According to Sir Robert, the Vietnamese effort lacked overall strategic direction and was carried out too hastily. As well, the hamlets were being spread too thinly; as such, they could not provide a secure defense line in the countryside. Moreover, the hamlets were created in areas already heavily infiltrated by the Viet Cong, while they should have been in more secure locations. (13)

Perhaps the most interesting news about the program comes almost twenty years later in the writing of none other than Stanley Karnow. According to Karnow, Ngo Dinh Nhu's "chief lieutenant in carrying our the strategic hamlet program was Col. Pham Ngoc Thao, the secret Communist operative." (p. 257) Col. Thao "deliberately propelled the program ahead at breakneck speed in order to estrange the peasants and drive them into the arms of the Viet Cong."

From this information, one might conclude that the strategic hamlet program failed, not necessarily because of inherent weaknesses, but because of internal sabotage. Col. Thao and his comrades in Hanoi most certainly had been aware of the program's effectiveness in Malaya and were afraid of its potential success in Vietnam. Therefore, they decided to defeat and discredit the program before it would do much damage. This logic, however, is lost on the producers of the television series (and Stanley Karnow), who continue to maintain that the program was a misguided, repressive action doomed to failure from the start. It provides a good symbol: the barbed wire fences lock in the poor peasants who later liberate themselves from the shackles of Diem's tyranny by beating those fences down!

(Karnow's description of the strategic hamlets and the earlier agroville "scheme" is filled with judgmental language that one might easily mistake for contempt. Peasants were "uprooted" from their homes and ancestral graves, and "corralled into stockades."

The government feared the peasants would "bolt." Meanwhile, "the Viet Cong stood back, watching the regime fumble." The Chief Correspondent also becomes Chief Mindreader as he persists in his irritating habit of explaining the psychology of the Vietnamese peasants and their resentment against Diem. Regarding the direction of the program, Karnow claims that Sir Robert Thompson "disavowed" the Vietnamese strategic hamlets. (p 256) In fact, the British advisor was aware of the problems and detailed these in reports to Pres. Diem. As late as September 1963, Sir Robert expressed confidence that the program would work once it was implemented properly. (14) Years later, he would still swear by the program as a tool in combating insurgency.)

The Fall of the First Republic

While Pres. Diem had some success in pulling South Vietnam together, his regime disillusioned many people and he made no few enemies. The Diem government's political problems and errors resulted in the November 1963 coup that left Diem dead and the army in power.

Some observers feel that the media played a part in bringing about Diem's fall. Pierre Salinger, Kennedy's press secretary, complained about this in 1966. Gen Westmoreland felt the press was looking for all the negative aspects of the Diem regime in order to discredit it. "Finding fault was one way to achieve sensationalism," the general writes, "and finding fault with an Oriental regime with little background in or respect for Western-style democracy was easy." (15)

If charges of dictatorship were not enough, there was the Buddhist problem. Self-immolations and demonstrations provided the right type of showbusiness. No Communist propaganda statement could hurt Diem more than Mme. Nhu's "barbecue" remarks. American reporters (who even now show little interest in religious persecution by the Communists) were outraged and shared their fury with the world. Newsmen became instant scholars of Buddhism; the political side of the problem never emerged.

The *Television History* is no more enlightening on the matter. In fact, it may obscure the viewers' understanding more with its tales of forced baptism. If there were Buddhist leaders, including monks, with political ambitions, the viewers would never guess it. If dissident Buddhists had learned to use the American media with English-language banners and announcements of up-coming demonstrations, that suggests something of the role the media played in the politics of Vietnam. The series does not deal with these issues or the simple matter of South Vietnam's need for a stable government, which could not avoid some criticism and difficulty. A thoughful series might have tried to explain why the only stable governments in Saigon were led by Catholics (Diem and Thieu).

Meanwhile, there are plenty of other clever images included in the series to give an "objective" historical appraisal of this time. Pres. Kennedy is shown unable to give lucid responses to reporters' questions about Vietnam until he suggests that the U.S. might pull out. Eisenhower is quoted out of context to tell viewers what a popular guy old Ho Chi Minh was. A film taken from Michigan State University is used as an example of America's flimsy attempt to cover up its support for Diem's "police state." And is it not irony one hears when the series quotes Capt. Edmond Fricke to say, "As you know, it's the man who gets the support of this farmer who is going to eventually win this war," since the producers believe it was the Viet Cong who got the support and not the American invaders?

By this time, the series has already concluded for the viewers that the Communist struggle was a just and honest one. America's support for the Saigon government was thus mistaken and a losing proposition from the the start. Once this idea has settled in the viewers' minds, it becomes easy to follow the rest of the series, which simply takes off from these themes.

(Karnow devotes an entire chapter to the fall of Diem. It is not possible to review it in detail in this small space. Although Diem's repression was by no means as fierce as that of Ho Chi Minh in the North, Karnow's Vietnamese loathed Diem but revered Ho. Unless the Vietnamese are inordinate masochists, there is no sense to this conclusion.

(Karnow's disgust for Diem the Tyrannical is apparent in the way he describes Diem's republic. His summary of Vietnam's reaction to Diem's overthrow is typical: "At the time, Saigon welcomed his downfall. Crowds tore up his portrait and slogans. Political prisoners, many scarred by torture, emerged from his jails. The city's nightclubs reopened with a vengeance. In the countryside, peasants demolished the strategic hamlets." (p. 311) The sun shone once again over South Vietnam!)

Footnotes

1. Hoang Van Chi, *From Colonialism to Communism*, p.92
2. Bernard Fall, *The Two Vietnams*, p. 156
3. Wesley Fishel, Ed., *Vietnam: Anatomy of a Conflict*, p. 83
4. Douglas Pike, *History of Vietnamese Communism*, p. 109
5. Hoang Van Chi, Note 1 above, p. 166, from *L'enfer communiste du Nord Vietnam*, Les Nouvelles Editions Debress, Paris, 1960, p. 22
6. For biographies of Ngo Dinh Diem, see Denis Warner, *The Last Confucian*, and Bernard Fall, *The Two Vietnams*
7. See Dr. Tom Dooley, *Deliver Us From Evil*, for a description of the refugee flight and America's effort to help the refugees.
8. See Kenneth T. Young, "Geneva Machinery in Retrospect", reprinted in *Vietnam: Anatomy of a Conflict*, pp. 102-117
9. Fall, Note 2 above, p. 356
10. Pike, Note 4 above, p. 122
11. Sir Robert Thompson, *Defeating Communist Insurgency*, pp. 123-4
12. For example, see *Strategic Hamlets in South Vietnam: A Survey and Comparison*, by Milton E. Osborn, Data Paper No. 55, Southeast Asia Program, Cornell University, 1965
13. Sir Robert Thompson, Note 11 above, Chapter 11
14. Ibid., p. 138
15. Gen. William Westmoreland, *A Soldier Reports*, p. 79

Supplements

(Ed. – In *Jungle of Reeds*, Doan Quoc Si describes scenes from the Land Reform Campaign.)

In the early months of 1953, the Northern Provinces officially instituted the denunciation campaign, beginning with Mme. Cat Hanh Long... Mme. Cat Hanh Long, a landlord from Thai Nguyen, had been with the revolution since its underground days. Until the denunciation, she had been praised as a model mother of a warrior, a model benefactress of the resistance. Now the Party deliberately brought her out for public trial to be the first sacrifice to demonstrate to the peasant classes that no matter how much merit the landlords had with the resistance, they could still be punished by the Party, in the name of the power of the people. Twice the denunciation began, and twice it failed because the cadre could not whip up enough enthusiasm. The peasants felt no resentment toward her; they went home disappointed, silently complaining that the government was being overzealous.

The Workers Party resigned itself to the idea that twice the people had been a little apolitical, but they were wise to avoid a great apolitical error of executing Mme. Cat Hanh Long on the spot.

Once more, at all the agencies a criticism movement was organized to enlighten and strengthen the stand:

"You must know how to cultivate and practice the valor of the working class. The working class always knows to place its sympathies in the right place. Knowing how to love the people means knowing how to hate the enemies of the people, including the landlord class, the principal enemy."

The third denunciation session was successful. For three straight hours the wives and children of tenant farmers took turns charging up to Mme. Cat Hanh Long, jabbing her in the face while shouting curses. Once in a while, the whole field rose up in the cry:

"Down with the great wicked landlords!

"Down with the obstinate landlords, trained dogs of the pirates!"

Mme. Cat Hanh Long was denounced in turn as a spy for the fascist Japanese, then a spy for the French colonialists, then for

killing three tenant farmers, and for having relations with a French
envoy in Thai Nguyen.

"The people" demanded the death sentence. And "the
people" were satisfied.

The "three-with" cadres established roots according to the
following principle. They would never fix roots with a person who
had become poor simply because of falling on hard times. The
wretched peasant had to be the current generation of ignorance and
stupidity going back for three generations with no connections to
the French administration. After fixing roots, there was a period of
investigation, usually lasting about a month. Then the cadre
selected a village to conduct an experiment. At this village, the
cadre mobilized the masses by calling a general meeting to classify
each person. The landlord class was immediately isolated, meaning
that it had to report all property and request permission to move
about; relatives coming or going to visit would be searched to ensure
that they were not taking anything away. Often when a landlord
was isolated, his friends and neighbors avoided him like a leper. If
he greeted them, they did not answer. If he tried to sell something
he did not need, no one bought it. Or, if he wanted to purchase some
item, no one sold it to him. In other words, he was treated as a
criminal. But, while a criminal in the free world is confined to a jail
made of brick or stone to cut him off from outside contacts, here the
criminal was imprisoned in a novel type of jail – a jail constructed of
his own people; his fellow villagers became the wood and stone or
tried to be like wood or stone. There is no loneliness more horrible or
tragic than this!

The home of the wretched peasant was used as a headquarters for
all groups in the village to come daily to learn and practice their
complaints. Here the special "three-with" cadre incited the class of
wretched peasants to fury against the landlords to prepare them for
the day they would appear at the trials. The "rich peasant" element
could not attend these lessons because they were not friends of the
wretched peasants. The Party's strategy was: "Rely on the
wretched peasants, ally with the middle peasants, neutralize the
rich peasants, and repress the landlords!"

Mien [a character in the story] and a number of her friends in the agency were appointed to attend criticism sessions of landlords at some nearby villages, it was said, "to get experience." Through these experiences, Mien observed there were pure peasants who still preserved their unpretentiousness and loyal souls. Perhaps they had truly been oppressed, but when it came time to denounce others they said they knew nothing, despite attempts by the cadres to put words in their mouths or lead them on. On the other hand, the most resolute were the hoodlums. They eagerly spoke badly of those who previously had refused to lend them money or had been too clever to fall into their deceitful traps. There were cases of resentment among in-laws . . . They stood up and made their complaints, hoping to take advantage of this fortunate oportunity to steal the victim's property. Finally, there were the young people who had not completed their education . . . Through their behavior and speech they flattered the right people, believing that by doing so they would be promoted to cadre in the intervillage group or the district.

The third time Mien went to the denunciations, the victim was Mme. Luan, a widow with two sons who had gone to school in Hanoi. Mme. Luan had also raised two orphans from a neighboring village. She had found a wife for the first boy; later he joined the resistance and died in battle at Vinh Yen. The younger boy was just 13 years old at the time of the denunciation. The cadre assigned him to guard his foster mother. During the criticism, he forced her to call him "sir."

Pointing to her face, he asked her in succession: "Why didn't you let me go to school, but forced me to tend the buffalo? Do you remember when you made me stand in a hill of red fire ants? Do you remember the time you thought I'd stolen money and you poured fish sauce down my nose?"

The fury rising in her old and miserable face, Mme. Luan denied the charges, her voice resentful, but also clear and resolute.

Mien decided that the simplest question this cruel child should ask before any other was, "Why, Mme. Luan, did you bring me and my brother to your home and raise us instead of leaving us to starve or become beggars?"

The cadre bent over and explained to Mme. Luan at length. Mien was sitting too far away to hear what was being said, but only knew that the second time the child thrust his finger in the old woman's face and repeated the charges, Mme. Luan answered in a choking voice.

"Respectfully, sir, yes!"

Just those three words – "Respectfully, sir, yes!" brought so much shame and anguish for the person who suddenly realized she had raised a snake in her home.

(Ed. – CIA agents were not the only Americans involved in the evacuation of refugees from the North in 1954-5. Dr. Tom Dooley, a Navy lieutenant, was assigned to Vietnam to assist in the transportation and care of the refugees in an operation called "Passage to Freedom." Dr. Dooley's eyewitness account of this event made him well known in the U.S. as well as Vietnam. Below are a few of the scenes and experiences of Dr. Dooley with the refugees as described in his book *Deliver Us From Evil.*)

As the first boat filled with refugees came alongside the U.S.S. Montague, Dr. Dooley was shocked to see the crowd of sick and frightened people. The refugees did not leap on board in joy, but held back, hesitantly waiting to see what was going to happen. One elderly man came on board first, his only possessions being the clothes on his back, a bamboo pipe and a picture of the Virgin Mary. After the elder, the others came up, eyeing the Americans warily. More than 2,000 persons were crowded onto the Montague on its first shuttle to the South.

Dr. Dooley found out the reason for their reluctance to get on board. "They had been told in great detail by followers of Ho Chi Minh . . . that Americans were scarcely human. The whole evacuation, they were told, was a trap. American soldiers would throw the old people overboard, cut off the right hands of the newborn, and sell the comely girls as concubines to capitalists." Before they left their villages, they had been shown propaganda leaflets of American sailors roasting a child alive, a doctor injecting deadly germs into a victim's arm, and a boat spewing people out into the open sea. One leaflet depicted Hanoi as the target of an American atomic bomb.

It was not long before the refugees lost their fear of the Americans. But it was not easy for the doctors to treat the physical conditions they were seeing. Besides starvation and disease, the refugees had injuries inflicted by the Communists. Asks Dooley, "What do you do for the children who have had chopsticks driven into their inner ear? Or for old women whose brittle collarbones have been shattered by rifle butts? How do you treat an old priest who has had nails driven into his skull to make a travesty of the Crown of Thorns?" There were the children of Bao Loc province near the Chinese border who needed ear amputations; the Viet Minh had torn their ears partially off with pincers and left them dangling. This was the punishment for listening to prayers.

Dr. Dooley took part in the construction of refugee camps in the Hai Phong area as the number of people fleeing soared. While treating their medical problems, Dr. Dooley was to find out about life under the Viet Minh. Many of the refugees had supported the Viet Minh, trusting them to be nationalists. They believed there were to be "agrarian reforms", but the new taxes were so heavy that the people became poorer than they had been before. Farmers were forced to pay high rent for the use of water wheels to irrigate their farms. Conditions grew worse. Meanwhile, the Viet Minh taught the people about the barbarism of the French and Americans. The propaganda had produced doubt and fear. Dr. Dooley recalls one radio broadcast from Voice of Vietnam on the topic "This is an American." He quotes the text: "His head is a blockhouse. His beard is barbed wire. His eyes are bombs. His teeth are dum-dum bullets. His two arms are guns and from his nose flames shoot out. A vampire, he sucks the blood of little children. His forehead is a nest of artillery and his body is an airfield. His fingers are bayonets, his feet tanks. He puts his fangs out in order to threaten, but in his hideous mouth he can only chew scrap iron because he has against him the powerful forces of our people of Vietnam, who are valiantly fighting. All things considered, the American is a paper giant."

The French and Americans were accused of raiding villages to kidnap the peasants and take them to the South. The Communists also declared that Americans poisoned the water and used poison chemicals in other ways on the refugees. The propaganda had some effect as one mother, thinking a penicillin shot had hurt her baby, came with a stick and a few friends to beat up the doctor, fracturing his ribs. After her child began to recover from his sickness, the woman realized her mistake and apologized profusely.

More than a thousand refugees sailed on fishing junks from Cua Lo. Under the Communists they had suffered from famine, family denunciations, self-criticism, distrust and cruel government. The refugees fled entirely on their own, without outside aid or encouragement. They left behind a boy whose brother had been beaten and burned alive because he had been the head of a Christian youth movement. The refugees sailed for five days with little food before being rescued.

In the town of Phat Diem, residents remained in their church for ten days until the ICC team arrived to receive their petitions to leave. The Viet Minh had tried to force the refugees home by starving them out of the church. The ICC protested and demanded that the Viet Minh let them go. The Communists continued to harass and brutalize the people before some of them were able to reach the camps.

PART 4: LBJ GOES TO WAR (1964-1965)

As Lyndon Johnson becomes the president, he takes on Kennedy's commitment to defend South Vietnam from Communist aggression. At the same time, the new president is concerned with domestic policy and his war on poverty. The Vietnam war escalates with the unstable political situation in South Vietnam. Viet Cong infiltration along the Ho Chi Minh Trail increases as regular North Vietnamese troops join in the fighting. LBJ receives bipartisan Congressional approval for his Gulf of Tonkin Resolution and he gains full military authority in Southeast Asia. Retaliatory bombing raids are started in North Vietnam. Johnson wins the 1964 presidential election. Viet Cong attacks continue and Johnson orders heavy bombing of the North. The South Vietnamese leadership changes hands and the White House is skeptical of its strength. More American troops are committed to the fighting and the draft is instituted. In 1965, Gen. Ky takes control of the Saigon government. The war grows.

Tiger Squadron Splatters a VC

Parts 1, 2 and 3 took the viewers on a restricted tour of Vietnamese history. Part 4 continues the process as it reviews America's deepening involvement in the war. Its goal is still to direct the viewers' attention along a fixed course and its principal instrument in this effort is the television camera. For example, the *Television History* makes little secret of its desire to portray the United States as an arrogant Goliath trying to sweep away poor, defenseless David (the Vietnamese Communists) by the might of high technology, all in the name of some sort of moralist imperialism. The irony is that this very series uses its own arrogance in television technology to attack – either blatantly or subtly – those with whom the producers find fault, without permitting the victims an opportunity to defend themselves or tell the other side of the story. And this is done in the name of free speech and "history."

The opening scene in Part 4 reflects this quite pointedly. A Tiger Squadron helicopter gunship bears down on a field chasing VC sampans. A suspect is spotted running along a dike. There is gunfire and then voices:

Voice #1 (excited): I saw you splatter one right in the back with a rocket!

Voice #2 (modestly): Roger. Got lucky I guess.

This shocking scene ends right there with no explanation as to why it is being presented. Since this program alleges to be historical and educational, we might seek some manner of educational value in this incident. An editorial value is obvious, but as objective history it leaves much to be desired.

Let us assume that the producers want to show the remoteness or insensitivity of technological warfare and how it can make soldiers into killers. Perhaps there is some merit to this. But the producers might then have balanced this with scenes of guerrilla violence in which VC agents coldbloodedly murdered civilians. A suggested true-life scenario might go like this: A Viet Cong unit moves in on a South Vietnamese outpost. These heroic troops decide not to charge the fort headlong as their brave comrades did at Dien Bien Phu. Instead, they grab villagers – including old people, women and children, usually the relatives of the Southern soldiers in the fort – and use them as a defensive shield as they move in. Some of the civilians get killed in the fighting.

A balance of this nature might remind the audience that the brutality of war extends to both sides, not just one. The producers chose not to take this course, but rather, to extract a gruesome scene out of context in order to successfully condemn the Americans. They apparently feel no responsibility to explain their purpose, which must be obvious to them.

Double-Standard Journalism and the One-Way Camera

Part 4 looks at how Lyndon Johnson took on the war in Southeast Asia while at the same time striving to create his "Great Society" in America. Johnson becomes a dual figure – on the one hand he is sensitive about domestic needs and hopes to find a solution to a troublesome war; on the other hand, he is the clever politician working to get reelected and fighting hard not to be the president who loses the war. The difficulties Johnson faced, the controversies, the deceptions, the ironies . . . are all shown. Several of his advisers are interviewed, some agreeing, some disagreeing with his policies, some just explaining the background of some of his decisions. The series tries to present a complex man, although it hardly gets beyond the superficial stage and one never really knows what to think of him when it's all over.

But then there is Ho Chi Minh, the leader in North Vietnam and Johnson's counterbalance. Ho Chi Minh is never analyzed. His advisers and detractors are not interviewed. His mistakes are not brought out into the open. His deceptions are not exposed. There is no debate over his decisions and policies, no quarrel about his stubbornness. Instead, we see Ho handing out cigarettes to the troops, chatting with the peasants and observing his people marching about in perfect unison. It would be logical for viewers to conclude that the American leadership was divided and uncertain while the Vietnamese people were all united against us, and consequently we should never have been there.

For example, there is the issue of government deception. A considerable amount of time in Part 4 is spent dealing with the Gulf of Tonkin Incident. We learn the background of Johnson's war powers resolution and how the resolution was shelved until the incident in the North Vietnamese gulf. We hear of Johnson's political motives in seeking bipartisan congressional approval of his war policies. There is a detailed analysis of the U.S. Navy newsreel which describes the alleged "unprovoked attack" of the U.S.S. Maddox and the question of a "second attack." The reactions of Congress and the "man on the street" (sic) are given. In the end, Johnson gets his resolution, removes the war as an election issue and becomes the winner of the 1964 presidential contest.

As the series tells it, LBJ and his staff lied to Congress and the people about what happened at Tonkin Gulf in order to pursue political goals. The CIA was conducting covert operations in the waters off the North Vietnamese coast. The attack by the North Vietnamese was not "unprovoked", though assertions of this allowed the President to get what he wanted. The viewers might justifiably feel their government betrayed them when the Congress granted him full military powers in Southeast Asia.

In the other direction, we see Hanoi. Throughout the course of the war Hanoi denied there were any North Vietnamese troops fighting in the South or that Hanoi was directing the affairs of the National Liberation Front. Like the account of a second attack in the Tonkin Gulf, Hanoi charged that U.S. claims of North Vietnamese infiltrations were "fabrications" invented by the White House and Pentagon. In 1967, Harrison Salisbury made a celebrated trip to Hanoi where he interviewed high-ranking North Vietnamese and NLF leaders. Speaking for the NLF, Nguyen Van Tien told Salisbury that the Front was independent of the North, that "the North cannot speak for the South" and that the "direction of the struggle is run by the South, not the North." He even claimed that supplies were not passing through the North before reaching South Vietnam! (1) Although there is not the slightest bit of truth to these statements, they were published at the time to reinforce views critical of the president's policies. Deceptive statements by the Communists and their propagation through persons such as Salisbury had an impact on the public relations of the war. Yet not a word about this is ever mentioned in the television series, which keeps its cameras fixed on America alone while allowing the Vietnamese Communists to get off scot free. Based on the series, one might surmise that Washington told lies while Hanoi only gave an honest appraisal of the war.

This double standard is brought to a head by the use of a USN newsreel version of the Gulf of Tonkin incident. The film gives the government's version of the alleged attack on the USS Maddox. The narrator of the *Television History* notes: "The film charged an unprovoked attack. But it left out crucial facts." These facts are then presented with maps and arrows and an explanation of what really happened. We are even reminded that Hanoi "always

denied" the second attack on the Maddox, once again suggesting
that Hanoi always told the truth. It is odd that the narrator has
nothing to say about crucial facts left out of Communist films provided to the television series. Scenes of proud North Vietnamese
troops marching off to join the fray, young ladies leading artillery
attacks without even wearing protective helmets, Viet Cong boats
slipping through the water reeds carrying supplies through a rain of
"bombs" – all these scenes are shown without comment. The East
German film of supply boats stealing down the waters is even
affirmed by the narrator, who whines, "Its message is true. The
bombing campaign was not working." No mention of the crucial
fact that many of the supplies from the North were coming along the
sea route to Cambodia or that Hanoi denied there even was a Ho Chi
Minh Trail. When Pham Van Dong accuses the United States of
interfering in Vietnamese affairs, opposing the Geneva Agreements
and replacing the French in Vietnam, no comment is made about
such crucial facts as North Vietnamese infiltration into the South
and military buildup – violations of the Geneva Agreements – as well
as the true position of the U.S. which was hardly similar to that of
the French during colonial times. Apparently some crucial facts are
more crucial than others.

The series strikes at Pres. Johnson with its scene of his April 3,
1965 White House speech. On this occasion, Johnson is speaking of
"trying to do the reasonable thing, to say that power and brute force
and aggression are not going to prevail..." As he speaks, we watch
U.S. Marines move into a hamlet, pull peasants out of their homes,
blow out a VC tunnel and burn hootches before our eyes. Again,
there is an editorial flavor to this presentation which is not matched
by similar scenes of "gentle" Ho Chi Minh talking of liberty while
oppressing his people, ordering political opponents to be murdered,
locking people up in concentration camps and approving terrorism
in the South. Johnson is attacked without being given a chance to
defend himself. Ho Chi Minh literally gets away with murder.

Compare the way difficult decisions were made on each side.
After much deliberation, Johnson elected to bomb the North. He
considered different options, talked to many people. Some agreed
with him, others dissented. Or the problem of extricating the
country from Vietnam – there were views on different sides. But

when Bui Tin talks about North Vietnam's commitment to liberate the South, the vote is unanimous – the "decision of our party, our leaders and our Supreme High Command" – with only the Chinese advisers dissenting. One might argue that of course there must have been discussion of the issue and debate among the Communist leaders. Yet the producers did not seek out, and consequently did not find, such differences of opinion, thereby portraying the North Vietnamese as single-minded and strong, while America was divided and weak.

Naturally, the military front is not exempt from this one-sided research. Battles are shown in relation to how much damage is done to U.S. or South Vietnamese forces while no mention is made of the casualties suffered by the Viet Cong. The fact that thousands of North Vietnamese were dying every year is of no consequence to this series, since the producers believe that only civilians were affected by American action, and, too, the daring Vietnamese were unaffected by such trivial matters as the massive loss of human life. The climax of this presentation is the final scene of Part 4: the battle at Iadrang Valley in the Central Highlands. This confrontation, described as "the first time... Americans fought the North Vietnamese face-to-face", proved to be tragic for both sides. The camera shows us the Americans preparing for the fight, then the North Vietnamese moving in. The Americans cover their turf as the North Vietnamese fix their positions. A battle is engaged. B-52s are called in. In the end, American soldiers lie dead. Bleeding American soldiers are evacuated by helicopter. Wounded Americans lie in the grass... The narrator does not tell us the outcome of the battle. The visual impression is that America met its match and lost heavily. Not a single North Vietnamese casualty is shown despite the fact that nearly 1,200 North Vietnamese soldiers died at Iadrang. Furthermore, in the week of November 14-20, 1965, fully 2,262 Viet Cong and North Vietnamese lost their lives in the fighting. (2) By watching television, one would never know the Viet Cong suffered a scratch.

Thus the *Television History* gives a misleading and distorted impression of the war by focusing its cameras in only one direction and applying subtle language and commentary along one line. The viewers should already be convinced that the Communist struggle

in Vietnam was just, that America made a mistake in getting involved in the war, that many Americans were dying for no reason while
their enemy never suffered and the American government lied to the
world. This image has now been recorded for history.

The Bombing of North Vietnam

Pres. Johnson ordered the bombing of North Vietnam with three
objectives. The first was retaliation for attacks against the
Americans. The second was to obstruct the supply route and
make it more difficult for the North to assist the armed movement
in the South with men and equipment. Lastly, the U.S. hoped it
could force Hanoi to give up its goal of liberating the South and
begin negotiations to end the war.

During the war and afterwards there has been considerable
debate as to the actual effects of the bombing on the people of
North Vietnam and on Hanoi's ability to continue the war. Mythologists claim that the morale of the Northerners never flagged;
with nerves of steel they became more determined to carry out the
fight. These observers seem to say that it was almost a pleasure
for the people to spend their time and energy shifting all their
factories to the countryside or rebuilding the bridges attacked
time and again by American pilots.

These myths are supported by Hanoi's propaganda since the
Communists would never admit that they were really in trouble
while the bombing was going on. Hanoi and the mythologists
never mention what really happened or how North Vietnam
became totally dependent upon Communist bloc aid as a result of
the bombing's devastation. At the same time, more informed
persons, such as George Ball (quoted in the series) had reserva-
tions about the value of the president's strategy.

During the 1960s, Janos Radvanyi, a former Hungarian diplomat
who was close to the peace negotiating process between the U.S. and
Hanoi, met with Gusztav Gogolyak, then the Hungarian ambassador
to North Vietnam. In their talk, Gogolyak kept repeating to
Radvanyi that "the situation in North Vietnam was not good. The
American bombing was hurting, and there was a shortage of food
and medicine. The bombed out industrial compounds had to be
abandoned" as only the smaller plants could be moved to the

villages. Resources were thus scattered and difficult to concentrate. "The morale of the population was low in Hanoi, Haiphong and some parts of the countryside. Criticism of Ho Chi Minh's decision to resume fighting in the South was growing and the police had found it necessary to make wide-ranging arrests to stem opposition and prevent disturbances." Gogolyak explained how it was difficult for the North Vietnamese to move supplies to the South. They could only move at night and through "crude jungle roads and complex waterways." Thousands of people had to be mobilized for this effort. "Gogolyak concluded that the Vietnamese survived only because the socialist countries had substantially increased their aid to the DRV." Soviet Foreign minister Gromyko confirmed this later at a Soviet bloc meeting held prior to a session of the U.N. General Assembly. "The Soviets informed their Eastern Eurpoean colleagues that the intense American air bombardment in Vietnam had inflicted heavy damage and had badly shaken the morale of the populace." Gromyko urged his comrades to seek a way to stop the bombing in order to give North Vietnam time to strengthen its air defenses. (3)

Radvanyi also reports that during the first six months of 1966 Hanoi resorted to force to contain opposition to its war policy. The Hungarian embassy in Hanoi informed Budapest that a "rectification campaign" had been launched. The People's Security Force "arrested and deported 'suspicious elements' to remote mines, while the disciplinary organ of the Communist party, the Control Commission, carried out, under guidelines of the Politburo, a large-scale purge at different levels of the party organization." The purge began in February 1966 with an article by Le Duc Tho, entitled "Let Us Change the Trend and Step up the Party Building Task in Order to Insure Successful Carrying Out of the Anti-U.S. Struggle for National Salvation." Tho attacked those who had adopted "pessimistic" views of the war situation, who were reluctant to engage in the protracted war and who, in Tho's words, had "made an incorrect assessment of the balance of power between the enemy and us." (4)

While statistics of the movement of supplies down the Ho Chi Minh Trail into the South indicate that the bombing did not meet the objective of halting infiltration, Radvanyi's account suggests that the situation in the North was hardly as idyllic as some people would like to believe. The bombing was disruptive and the people did suffer. Opposition arose to Hanoi's war policy, which was causing such grief to the people of the North. Presumably George Ball would agree with this since he wrote the introduction to Radvanyi's book. The *Television Hi.. :ory* – whether deliberately or out of laziness – does not thoroughly investigate the reaction of the North to the bombing, but reinforces the myths with half-truths and selective information. The program backs up the tale of undaunted courage with films supplied by the Communists: anti-aircraft guns with no comment on where they came from, boats sneaking down the waterways, and aerial views of the Thanh Hoa Bridge being hit several times during the war. The impression given is that the Vietnamese were ever cheerful in their fight, untouched by feelings of frustration and despair.

It is not the place of this book to take sides on the bombing issue; that is the role of strategists, politicians and moralists. What this book would like to do is suggest that historians record the facts and not the fantasy.

The South Vietnamese Soldier

Thus far the *Television History* has ignored the Army of the Republic of South Vietnam (ARVN) and its role in the war – except for the times the ARVN was defeated by superior Viet Cong or North Vietnamese forces. The omission is typical of the news media's handling of the South Vietnamese, and especially so for television. Since television is a visual medium, it requires visible images of its subjects, without which it ceases to have a function. As a rule, American journalists did not follow ARVN units during the war, but remained with the Americans. The result is that there are many pictures of American GIs available for review, but far fewer shots of the South Vietnamese soldiers.

Gen. William Westmoreland complains about the media's neglect of the South Vietnamese in his book *A Soldier Reports.* "The American news media contributed to a false image of the ARVN's performance. Serving an American public, the U.S. press and television understandably focused on American units, seldom covering ARVN operations unless something sensational happened, such as heavy losses." As an example, the general cites the battle at Dak To in November 1967 where "several ARVN battalions were in the thick of the fight", yet they were barely covered by newspaper reportage. (5)

The fact is that the ARVN were in the war; they were fighting and dying. Millions of Vietnamese actively participated in the conflict. Every year, many thousands perished. They should not be ignored simply because there were no American cameramen around to take their pictures (the proverbial tree falling in an abandoned forest). The *Television History* tells of American advisers, but who were they advising? The Americans were sent in to support the fighting, but who were they supporting? As far as the South Vietnamese are concerned, the viewers see only the scattered dead at Dong Xoai.

The series might have at least considered the numbers. In 1964, there were 514,000 South Vietnamese troops in action, as compared to 23,310 Americans in the country. When the Americans began to move in more troops, the Vietnamese still outnumbered them, reaching 643,000 by the end of 1965 and eventually surpassing one million men. (6)

Although trained and supplied by the U.S., prior to 1968 the South Vietnamese were not receiving weapons on a par with their wealthy allies. The ARVN used older weapons of the World War II era, especially the Garant M-1 and the Carbine. While the Viet Cong were already using the Soviet AK-47 automatic machine gun (a highly respected weapon), the ARVN did not begin to receive the comparable M-16 until after the Tet Offensive, when the Americans began preparing for withdrawal. Likewise, the Viet Cong were also being supplied with rocket launchers, mortars, land mines and other munitions, making reliance on home-made weapons minimal by 1964. The ARVN, however, lacked the appropriate arms and equipment to adequately face these weapons and often were at a disadvantage in fighting the VC.

Still, the ARVN continually improved. One veteran journalist who had covered both the Korean and Vietnam wars concluded that the ARVN was "strikingly more effective" than the Koreans had been. Unfortunately, they did not appear this way in the American media representations because the media was friendly to the Koreans in the 1950s but "antagonistic" toward the ARVN. (7)

The media helped give the ARVN a reputation for cowardliness and incompetence by emphasizing the problems rather than the strengths of the South Vietnamese military forces. The PBS series echoes the derogatory sentiments later in the series with its exaggerated stress on desertions and an alleged lack of loyalty to the government. This opinion of an inept South Vietnamese army was not shared by all observers and the ARVN provided countless instances of heroism and determination in battle that gained little publicity, if only because the editors in the United States were not interested in them.

Australian journalist Denis Warner recounts cases of the courage and strength shown by the ARVN as it improved during the war. For example, the ARVN First Division consoldiated into a strong fighting unit that was considered the best army division in the country by 1968. One American adviser, Major Michael Ferguson, told Warner that during the Tet Offensive "when we met the NVA (North Vietnamese), they were better equipped than any American division, and we beat the hell out of them." The ARVN First fought back against two North Vietnamese divisions at Hue. "240 men in the division's elite Black Panther Company fought without rest or relief for 72 hours. At the end of that time there were only 19 men left, and they were still fighting." If one should question their loyalty to the government, consider the story of the company commander in Hue who, "with tears streaming down his face", ordered his gunners to fire on his home and family surrounded by the Communists. (8)

Like the First Division, the ARVN Rangers and Paratroopers were also well regarded for their courage and staying power. It is true, of course, that not all the ARVN troops were outstanding warriors and the South Vietnamese did have problems, similar to those experienced by the armies of any emerging nation. The local forces were not given the training and support enjoyed by the regular troops. There were "deserters", including men who returned to their homes to tend to their families and farms; many of these persons joined the local forces so they would not have to be separated again (a point not brought out in the PBS series' "educational" expose of ARVN incompetence in Part 8). It was rare, however, for South Vietnamese soldiers to defect to the other side (a point contradicted by the PBS series, which makes defections appear to be a common and natural occurrence). A number of officers took advantage of their positions to acquire personal wealth or benefits (as do some people in the journalistic profession in the U.S., although that is not something they like to talk about). The Vietnamese had an image problem with the American soldiers, who fought in separate units and only infrequently saw the ARVN in action.

There were personal matters that affected the South Vietnamese soldiers as well. The troops were poorly paid and their families often lived in worse conditions than those of poor peasants. The dependents of some ARVN soldiers lived near the military bases, a situation which divided the soldiers' loyalties between duty and family when the fighting threatened their loved ones. On the other hand, many of the professional soldiers were away from their families for long periods of time and this added to the hardships they faced while serving their country.

Taken as a whole, the ARVN cannot be fairly criticized by generalizations of their shortcomings. Despite being underpaid, underequipped and thrust into a complex war in difficult circumstances, the South Vietnamese army continued to function for twenty years as it fought against an aggressive and determined enemy. By 1965, the South Vietnamese had sacrificed over 35,000 men in battle (cf. U.S. battle dead 1,636 at the time). By the end of the war, well over 200,000 South Vietnamese soldiers had given up their lives in the terrible conflict which the American news media hardly gave them credit for fighting in.

For now, the *Television History* depicts the South Vietnamese soldiers as nothing more than corpses on the battlefield.

The Allies

Viewers of the *Television History* might be surprised to learn that other nations besides the United States supported the war on behalf of South Vietnam. South Korea, Australia, New Zealand and Thailand sent combat troops to help in the fighting. South Korea was the most generous in this respect, offering to send soldiers as early as 1954. During the period from 1967 to 1971, the number of South Koreans in Vietnam came to around 50,000 each year. (9)

The Philippines sent a civic action group along with its own security force.

Aside from military support, 34 nations sent food, medicine, advisers, educational material, economic aid, training aid and other forms of support to South Vietnam. (10)

The exhaustive *Television History* and Stanley Karnow's "complete" account of the war do not even mention these facts, which do not coincide with their view of a totally "American war."

Viet Cong Repression

If the increased presence of American troops and the bombing of the North were supposed to have united the Vietnamese against "American imperialism", one wonders why it was necessary for the Viet Cong to engage in terror tactics in the South in order to get the support it needed.

An important part of Viet Cong strategy – and one only hinted at in the *Television History* – is the use of "repression" by the Viet Cong. (11) "Repression" is the term used by the Communists to describe the systematic application of violence aimed at terrorizing or intimidating the Vietnamese people. The tactics included assassination, execution, abduction, imprisonment in "thought reform" camps, forced indoctrination, village confinement, short-term confinement, hostage-taking, warnings and threats. Victims of repression were primarily persons connected to the Government of Vietnam (GVN) or to the Americans, especially civilian and military officials, security and intelligence personnel, political leaders, school teachers, and Rural Development cadres. Relatives and personal contacts of any of these individuals could also become targets for repression. Villagers fleeing to the government side during a raid might too become victims. Targets were typically referred to as "tyrants", "reactionaries", "traitors" or "enemies of the people."

The purpose of Viet Cong repression was to facilitate the break-down of the South Vietnamese government. First, the Viet Cong hoped to eliminate or demoralize government personnel and thereby weaken the GVN's base in the countryside. Secondly, terrorism helped give the VC an image of all-pervasiveness, a ghost the government could never get rid of.

Because the activities were terrorist in nature and not full-scale attacks, the number of agents needed to carry out each assignment was relatively small. Nonetheless, these few persons could effect damage on the minds of the population. In charge were the Armed Reconnaissance Units – mobile units responsible for collecting intelligence, indoctrination, sabotage, mutual surveillance and the direction of terrorist activities. In 1965 these teams were small: 3 cadres per district and six for a province. The Armed Reconnaissance Units belonged to the Viet Cong Security Section, which in turn was controlled by Hanoi. The Security Section has been described in this way: "Estimated at between 15,000 and 20,000 members in 1966 ... this highly professional, ruthless organization operates in all areas of South Vietnam (Viet Cong-controlled, contested, and GVN-controlled) under close supervision from Hanoi." (12) Key posts were held by Northern-trained officials down to regional, province, district and village levels.

In North Vietnam the government of Ho Chi Minh held undisputed authority and had at its command a large and well-trained army. Consequently Hanoi had a free hand in carrying out programs such as the Land Reform based on calculated mob violence. The situation was different in the South. There, the Communists were not in control of the government or army and did not have enough troops at their disposal to conduct large-scale campaigns of this sort. Furthermore, the Communists needed to protect their image as moderates, which any sort of blatant bloodbath would quickly dispel. Their "heroic cause" would be sullied by any rash and uncontrolled actions such as occurred in the North. The strategy in the South required greater caution.

At the same time, the murders, kidnappings, detentions, etc. in the South were not simply incidental abuses of the system or "excesses" committed by overzealous cadres. Terrorism and intimidation were an actual part of the strategy of the Viet Cong, which did not have sufficient military strength to defeat the government forces in combat. "Far from being a mindless and random bloodletting, (repression) is, according to Viet Cong doctrine, a carefully calculated and controlled process designed to support the immediate objectives in each phase of the revolutionary struggle

and closely integrated with other political-military operations."
(13) This caution was to be lifted during the Tet Offensive of 1968.

Viet Cong repression was used to break down the government set-up and establish control over a particular area. The terrorism had a political goal as well, namely, to purge the countryside of so-called "reactionaries" and "tyrants", that is, government officials, landlords and anyone who opposed the revolution. Security cadres rounded up the populace for indoctrination sessions where the peasants were taught the virtues of joining the revolution and the wickedness of the Saigon government. In the indoctrination sessions, "Viet Cong propagandists dwell on the many 'inhuman' and 'barbaric' atrocities allegedly committed by the Americans and their 'GVN henchmen', the wanton destruction of homes and property, and the 'rape', 'murder' and 'torture' of innocent men and women." (14) The cadres tried to induce hatred of the Americans and the South Vietnamese government while inciting the peasants to get "revenge" for alleged crimes – a more controlled form of the purge of "tyrants" conducted in the North in the 1950s. Government officials were characterized as "'Vietnamese traitors' who 'fatten their lives on the blood of the peasants'." In the meantime, the peasants were made responsible for one another, forced to keep an eye on each other and report regularly the goings-on in the village.

The indoctrination and intimidation served to polarize the peasants into two classes: those who served the government and those who served the revolution. This had a dual purpose of making the war easy to understand for the uneducated peasants and fulfilling the dialectical requirements of Marxism.

To facilitate control of the people, security cadres wrote up blacklists of individuals in each village, classifying villagers into various categories (such as "wicked personnel", "bad elements", and "reactionaries"). This helped clarify the targets for repression so as to avoid confusion or indecision on the part of the person charged with carrying out the sentence. "Crime", in the Viet Cong lexicon, meant anything that got in the way of the "liberation struggle." Consequently, persons who may have had outstanding reputations personally would still receive the same treatment as the corrupt or oppressive members of the government, simply because of their association with the government. Nor were family and friends safe. The Viet Cong often obtained the cooperation they needed for a specific task by taking a person's family members hostage; villagers would cooperate in order to save their wives and children. When a target could not be eliminated by other means, the Viet Cong might kidnap or keep close watch on the target's family, with the warning that any unfriendly action would lead to a sad end for the hostages. (This tactic continues to frustrate refugees today. Virtually all refugees have close relatives in Vietnam; they are afraid of what might happen to them if they speak out publicly against the Communists.)

Communist blacklists also provided a master list of "enemies of the people" who were to be taken care of once the Viet Cong took control of an area. These lists were used during the Tet Offensive.

The scale of Viet Cong repression increased over the years. From 1958 to 1959, the total number of assassinations and abductions in South Vietnam came to about 1,000. (15) From 1958 to 1965, there were at least 46,500 such incidents, including 9,700 murders and 36,800 abductions. (16) Nearly the same number were victimized between 1966 and 1969.

Despite these figures, indications are the Security Service "manifested continual dissatisfaction with the success of repression." (17) There are several reasons for this failure. The Viet Cong did not have firm control over many areas so that their targets were often well protected. GVN counter-operations led to the arrest or death of many VC cadres. Local cadres were sometimes too weak to carry out their orders. The system suffered from poor training and mismanagement.

The fact that the war lasted so long is an indication that the Viet Cong did not win over the hearts and minds of the peasants through their repressive tactics. The fact that repression had to be utilized at all casts doubt on the claims of some "scholars" that the war was won by the "will of the people."

Observation

There are many issues about the war in the mid-1960s that need to be reviewed in order for people to get a better understanding of those difficult years. A few of these issues include: the justification for continuing America's commitment to Southeast Asia; the roots of escalation; the effects of the Great Society on Americans' attitudes concerning foreign wars; political, economic and social problems in North Vietnam; the Soviet Union's commitment to support Hanoi; views of South Vietnamese regarding the political turmoil in their country; how the American public understood the war. The list could go on. None of these issues is adequately dealt with in the *Television History* – some are not even brought up at all.

It is hoped that future historians of the war will concentrate on serious matters and skip the theatrics.

(Karnow's account of this period is more anecdotal than analytical, reflecting once again his journalistic, rather than scholarly, background. President Johnson's vulgar language and "primitive blusters" feature more prominently than any detailed study of world and domestic affairs. The Chief Correspondent cannot detach himself from his personal opinions long enough to keep from calling South Vietnamese President Nguyen Khanh a "sleazy surrogate" (p. 335) and a "mischief maker". (p 336) North Vietnamese Col. Bui Tin's description of a trek down the Ho Chi Minh Trail reads like a child's safari and gives the reader little idea what life was really like for the North Vietnamese soldier. (p. 331-332) Particularly revealing of Karnow's shallow understanding of the Communists is an ironic quote from Pham Van Dong in a 1981 interview. Premier Dong vented his anger against the Chinese for waging a proxy war in Vietnam by saying of Mao Zedong, "He was always ready to fight to the last Vietnamese." (p. 329) Karnow does not point out to him how the Vietnamese Communists were always ready to sacrifice the lives of non-Communists for the goals of the revolution – using nationalists to fight the French and then purging them; inducing the Lao to fight against Lao and then taking over their country; creating a barbarous Khmer Rouge that pitted Cambodians against Cambodians until that country became so weakened the Vietnamese could invade with little fear of resistance; and now Vietnam is padding its northern border with Cambodian teenagers to stand in the way of an attack by China . . . Such details are totally meaningless to the Chief Gadfly.

(The *History* includes another ironic quote from Pham Van Dong, made in 1965. At that time, Premier Dong was explaining Hanoi's reluctance to participate in negotiations. The Vietnamese, he said, had learned "a lesson on relations with the imperialists", who sign agreements in order to "gain time to prepare their military forces for further aggression." (p. 419) The premier naturally forgot how the Viet Minh used negotiations with the French to buy time needed to liquidate Ho's political opponents or how the Geneva Agreements gave the Communists a chance to catch their breath and regroup in preparation for the liberation of the South. And, of course, he was not looking forward to 1973 when the Paris Agreements would serve to get rid of the Americans while the North prepared to continue the war.

(Karnow admits that the Communists stretched the truth a bit when they claimed there were no North Vietnamese troops in South Vietnam during the war. (p. 330) He does not see any value in playing up this or other Communist deceptions the way he does the deception of an American president, or a South Vietnamese official. The matter merits only one paragraph in his book while his account of the Tonkin Gulf resolution covers about twenty pages.

(The Chief Correspondent rather remarkably claims his 1981 interview with Viet Cong commander Tran Do "dispelled the myth, in which many Westerners then believed, that the Viet Cong was essentially an indigenous and autonomous insurgent movement." (p. 401) This statement is surprising because intelligent analysts had been saying that for two decades prior to Karnow's interview. Readers would benefit more by learning why "many Westerners" clung to their misguided belief despite evidence to the contrary.

(Karnow, too, buys into the stereotypical image of the intrepid North Vietnamese whose sole reaction to intense bombing was to become more determined than ever to oust the American imperialists. There was no problem mobilizing his North Vietnamese to repair damage again and again or move supplies down the Ho Chi Minh Trail. The human element of the war – the terror, grief, sense of loss, dislike of one's own government as well as hatred for the enemy, and general war weariness – are replaced by a fairy tale.)

Footnotes

1. Facts on File, *South Vietnam: U.S.–Communist Confrontation in Southeast Asia, 1966-1967,* p. 254
2. Facts on File, *South Vietnam: U.S.–Communist Confrontation in Southeast Asia, 1961-1965,* p. 188
3. Janos Radvanyi, *Delusion and Reality,* pp. 51-2
4. Ibid., p. 188
5. William Westmoreland, *A Soldier Reports,* p. 305
6. Shelby Stanton, *Vietnam: Order of Battle,* pp. 275-6, p. 333
7. Robert Elegant, "How to Lose a War", *Encounter,* August 1981
8. Denis Warner, *Certain Victory,* p. 56
9. Shelby Stanton, Note 6 above, p. 333
10. William Westmoreland, Note 5 above, p. 311
11. The following is based on Stephen T. Hosmer, *Viet Cong Repression and Its Implications for the Future*
12. Ibid., p. 6
13. Ibid., p. 21
14. Ibid., p. 17
15. Ibid., p. 6
16. Ibid., p. 42
17. Ibid., p. 74

Supplements

(Ed.- The *Television History* shows only the faceless corpses of the
South Vietnamese at Dong Xoai, but reveals nothing of the human
agony of the battle there. Below is an excerpt from *Dau Binh Lua*, a
book by South Vietnamese writer Phan Nhat Nam, published in
Saigon during the war. Here the author recounts the battle at Dong
Xoai in its worst moments. The reader should note that the
Communist atrocity described below – the murdering of wounded
soldiers left lying on the battlefield – was repeated at Ia Drang
Valley, although at that time the victims would be American soldiers.
Naturally, the incident is not mentioned in the PBS series.
Translation.)

"Reporting. We cannot advance any further. The enemy is too
thick. Give us some artillery."

I almost shouted these words to the company.

"We cannot give artillery. There are civilians and a church by the
plantation."

"Civilians, my ---!" I shouted back, my lungs nearly bursting.

"They're not civilians. They're all Viet Cong!"

"The command decided no fire. Go complain to them."

The company leader was as perturbed as I was.

Some men from the 5th Infantry Division, captured by the VC on
the 8th, ran from some homes nearby.

"You can't get in!" they shouted at us. "They've got a regiment
in there!"

We could not pull back. We had come this far and there was only
the road ahead. In the center of the plantation was a chateau d'eau
beside the runway. We were on a hillside. The terrain ahead was
wide open. Dung's and Do's platoons received orders to turn left to
avoid the enemy's fire and cross the runway to take the center of the
plantation. Up to then, there had been no gunfire coming from the
left or behind us.

The rain had started falling and the wind had picked up. The
plantation was dim, as at sunset. The rain poured harder and the
jungle grew darker. The companies used their firepower to cover

the two platoons crossing the runway. Dung's and Do's men crossed the airstrip swiftly, using all the strength they had. Halfway across, gunfire erupted. From the chateau came the incessant fire of machine guns. The soldiers of the two platoons toppled over each other like falling trees. Do died on the spot. Dung, with a wound in his arm, tried to move toward the left. He had made about three steps when a hail of bullets riddled his chest. He fell motionless. The two who survived crawled back.

Now, there was gunfire coming from all directions. In waves the shout "Assault!" echoed from the darkness. The noise of the rain and thunder were drowned out by the sound of guns and shouting. Dark figures appeared from the jungle shadows.

"Surrender! Surrender!" the Viet Cong shouted as they advanced.

We fired back, but it was too late. The bullets poured from the guns in the flash of an eye and before a clip was loaded another gun was staring us in the face. We retreated to the rubber trees and fired again. The men of the 72nd and 74th Companies raced to the right. On that side was a low open slope with a bamboo grove. No other way. In front of us, to the left, in the rear, the enemy's AKs drowned out our Carbine M-2s. A few soldiers of Company 71 ran up. But the Viet Cong had tanks. M-F-... there was no way to fight them.

Mr. Ky from Company 71 was dead. Our communications equipment was out. Each man had to fight on his own.

Out of the last banana grove on the hill we met a barbed wire fence that blocked the way. As the troops were about to pass through it, machine guns opened up from the north. I could make out the sound of 12.7mm machine guns. Our squad dropped in the first moments. That was it – we had reached the end of the line.

I ran back to the south where the scene was painful and terrifying. It looked as if nearly everyone from Company 73 had been wasted. Maybe two squads were left, firing as they advanced toward us. It was a sad meeting. A section of Company 73 came in from the right. The company commander, Lt. Hop, pointed to the left.

"That road is okay. Take the men there."

I nodded and led the remaining soldiers in the direction he had indicated, trying to avoid the fire coming from the enemy's machine guns by the barbed wire. Only one way. If we were lucky, we would survive. Otherwise, . . .

As I mulled this over before going into the wire, a volley of bullets flew and I dropped like a dry leaf.

It was dark and rainy in the jungle. The gunfire had stopped, but all around I could hear the wounded moaning. I realized then that I had been hit in the face and arm. The wounds appeared to be light, so I was alert. This was not good, because the Viet Cong checking the area would find me and either kill me or take me prisoner – in either case, it was a bad scene.

I listened to the screaming in the night, miserable howling like echoes from hell. Suddenly tears flowed from my eyes as I recalled those who had died that day and now I would witness further the last moments of my friends. During these final moments, a dying man does not think of himself, but all his thoughts go to his parents, wife and children... The soldiers cried for their wives and children, the sound cutting deep like a knife. I wanted to shut my ears to keep from hearing it, but in the still night, the terrible moans never ceased.

There was whispering and I heard someone coming. It was time for the Viet Cong to "collect". Their cursing and insults mixed with the dry crisp sound of gunfire. They were abusing and killing the wounded. I never hated them more than I did at that point. War is the law of life and death, but once the opponent has fallen, who can continue to abuse him like that? It was like they had no souls. We had taken prisoners many times. We gave them cigarettes and food. The paratroopers had a reputation for toughness, but they never abused a prisoner, let alone a wounded one. But here, the VC were like soulless beings with no more human feelings. The Viet Cong were of the same blood and race, though war had made them enemies in battle. But what had happened to generate such hatred? Still, I could easily hear their obscenities in the night and the final gasps of those who died with a cruel thrust of a bayonet or a bullet aimed at their heads.

I crawled quickly to the right along the slope. Everywhere were cold, stiff corpses and the warm bodies of those who had not yet died. I bumped into someone. Who is it? Me, Cam. Save me!

Footsteps. Someone was coming. VC. Let me save you, he

laughed barbarously. A bitter bullet exploded in Cam's head.

I lay still, with my face hidden in the rubber leaves. I pretended to be dead when the Viet Cong soldier kicked my leg. Flares were falling. The corpses of the sad victims appeared in the light that filtered through the trees, terrifying and wretched like a scene from hell.

A plane appeared. Bombs fell. The plantation trembled like there was an earthquake. Fire glowed. The wounded tried to get up and run, but staggered and fell. I made my way to the top of the hill and slipped through the barbed wire, climbing over a heap of corpses. About four o'clock in the morning I fell exhausted when I knew I was on the road by Dong Xoai.

(Ed.- Later in the same book, Phan Nhat Nam compares the ARVN Paratroopers to their military partners, the American First Air Cavalry.)

. . . The First Air Cavalry was the best thing to come from Secretary of Defense MacNamara and the finest product of modern technological warfare. (No other American unit could stand up to it, not even the Marines, the heroic symbols of America's forces.) The First Cavalry had nearly 500 helicopters and three brigade commands with independent combat capability, each of which could take charge of a field of responsibility usually given to a division. Each paratroop brigade coordinated with an air cavalry brigade....

The areas of responsibility covered by each battalion of paratroopers and air cavalry combined to spread over three provinces – Phuoc Long, Binh Long and Tay Ninh. By principle we were to coordinate operations, consequently our areas of responsibility were of equal breadth, measure and strength.

But that was in principle only. The reality was a far cry from that. The capability of the air cavalry was unlimited, that of the paratroopers was limited . . . . The American fire base was a compact city with a hospital station, a helicopter pad for Chinooks, VIP choppers, with paved roads, a cook to give hot meals to the whole battalion and a private helicopter for the battalion commander, the armed choppers receiving complete supplies. The helicopters covered the air space of each battalion to give support the moment there was contact with the enemy.

Although the Vietnamese paratroopers were supposed to be coordinated with them, they did not enjoy the absolute priority of the Americans. Their fire base was built by their own hands and their resolve on the field lay in the muzzle of each man's rifle.

(Materially, too, the two forces were far apart.) For the Americans, their dirty uniforms were carried off by helicopter to Tay Ninh to be laundered. The soldiers spent two weeks in the jungle, one week at the home base, one week to rest in Tay Ninh. At night they had good, warm food.

For the paratroopers, their clothes were patched with wire and tape. They drank water from bomb craters and once a month they returned to the base (each battalion had one base) so they could see the sky without trees in the way and drink water from a cistern brought from Tay Ninh, each man getting one helmetful.

Of the same degree on the battlefield, with the same speed of operation, carrying out the same responsibilities, though with much fewer resources and lacking even necessities, the paratroopers had to give it everything they had – the honor of their army and nation was at stake.

PART 5: AMERICA TAKES CHARGE (1965-1967)

America's military presence in South Vietnam increases as the number of U.S. servicemen reaches nearly half a million in two years. America takes charge of an expanded war. The selected stories of a few individual soldiers are given.

In Country

The American soldiers fighting in Vietnam were young, sensitive and impressionable. In general, those who entered the war in its early years held a fundamental trust in their government and a sense of duty to their country. But the politics of the war were complicated and the experiences of the soldiers did not always mesh with the things they had been told by their commanders. Strategies were not always successful, the war dragged on, and more and more young men died or were wounded. When America began pulling out, it appeared to many that the war was lost. Some of the soldiers who had risked their lives at the call of their government felt they had been betrayed and lost faith in their government. Perhaps worse, their trust in themselves was shattered as well.

When the war is discussed among Vietnam veterans, invariably many diverse feelings erupt. Pride, pain, loss, anger, frustration, grief. The feelings lie deep inside; even today it is hard for many to draw them out and expose them to others. The negative emotions (generically described as "shit") may have been inside them for ten or fifteen years. They may be too powerful for some veterans to face. There are different ways to protect oneself from them: changing jobs frequently, avoiding contact or discussion with other veterans, submerging oneself in family or employment, drifting, abusing alcohol or drugs. The proud soldiers who have made their adjustment experience many of the negative emotions too. There is the sense of loss and pain as well as the pervasive feeling that somehow they are responsible for the war's outcome. They feel that society has placed a burden on their shoulders and then left them by the wayside.

They came into the war in a very critical period of their lives. The average age of the Vietnam soldier was 19, seven years younger than that of the average World War II fighter. While the 1940s hero had achieved some individual stability and maturity, his Vietnam counterpart was still in his formative years. Indeed, some veterans refer to their war experience as their "rites of passage" into adulthood. Many were away from home for the first time in their lives. In just one day they were transported from the most modern nation in the world to a farming country of rice fields and jungles. They were not prepared for what they found. The people of Vietnam looked different, behaved differently, the language was incomprehensible and the culture seemed strange and primitive. It is no wonder that some soldiers felt they were on – or from – Mars. The soldiers were told little about the war and even less about the history and culture of the people they were fighting for. These young men were being asked to fight a war that even their fathers did not fully understand or agree about. Still, they did their duty.

The environment and conditions of their abrupt arrival fixed the soldiers in a state of limited shock, part of the coping mechanism of significant life changes. It was not a textbook war. There were few fixed battles and no frontline. Days or weeks could go by without their contacting the enemy. One veteran describes his experience as "hours and days of boredom" punctuated by "minutes of terror." In time, the soldiers became conditioned to their environment and learned how to deal with the daily tensions. But they were always wound up and thus vulnerable to the war's psychological effects. As in any war, the soldiers in Vietnam had to pad themselves to keep from facing directly the reality of what was going on.

They were confronted with the basic questions of life and death. They laid their lives on the line, watched their buddies disappear and took the breath away from others. Killing was not a game for them. If the soldiers adopted a new jargon to describe

of earlier wars chastised them for "not going out and winning it." Anti-war demonstrations troubled and confused them – their doubts and fears multiplied as they asked themselves, "Were we really the bad guys? Was it all a big mistake?" Television news coverage displayed their worst side – drugs, VC ears for souvenirs, massacres... In later years movies would depict them as deranged killers and psychotics. Criminals in television programs would turn out to be Vietnam vets. Their own generation did not understand them.

Shaken and uncertain, many turned in on themselves. Emotional disorders are common among the veterans. Some have blocked out their feelings and have difficulty maintaining relationships. The divorce rate is high among Vietnam veterans, as is the suicide rate. Employment turnabout prevents many from attaining stability in their lives. Although a decade may have gone by, many veterans still cannot discuss their war experiences with others. They still cannot reach inside and pull out their "shit" to examine it and overcome or learn to live with it. They may have trouble accepting the refugees from Vietnam, whom they identify with that traumatic period of their lives. Many still don't feel as if they fit into society.

They were not playing war. They lived it and it still lives in them.

In the first four parts, the *Television History* has already made it clear that the United States was the aggressor in Vietnam. The American government misjudged the nationalist struggle in Vietnam and became involved to halt what it thought was Communist expansion. The government lied to its people and sent helpless boys to fight for a mistaken and losing cause.

Now is the time to show sympathy for the Vietnam soldiers, to condescend and allow them a few minutes to talk and give their side of the story. But let the viewer never forget that they are guilty of burning homes, dragging women around and beating up innocent villagers. Brute force and aggression will not prevail!

Vietnam: A Television History offers only a very limited view of the American Vietnam veteran. It allows room for guilt and shame, but not for pride or a sense of purpose. It shows how Americans caused death and destruction, but does not indicate what the Americans were responding to. The viewers find scenes of Marines trampling through a village, mistreating civilians and leaving burning heaps of thatch behind them; it omits the weeks or months of trouble eminating from that village – sniper fire, night raids, the murder of government workers. Americans become beasts for having deprived farmers of their homes. But one does not see school teacher's raped or disembowled by the Viet Cong or gain even a hint of the VC drawing fire into a village that refuses to cooperate with the "revolution." The Americans lose ground, lives and popularity . . . at least according to the series. There is never a scene of an American success in helping a village set up a medical unit or build a schoolhouse. The Americans just stumble through, leaving death and destruction in their wake.

The series' symbol is a fleet of helicopters and the sound that introduces each of the 13 parts is the clatter of the choppers' propellers. Helicopters seem to represent robots of death in America's technological war. Gunners shoot down at apparently helpless people below. Music plays from a radio and targets are "splattered". The shadowy machines terrorize the Vietnamese.

But in a talk with this writer, one helicopter crewman defended his unit. The Air Mobile, he said, was the "heart and link of everything that happened in Vietnam." Helicopters transported troops and supplies, made ammunition drops, served as a communications base and evacuated casualties. Without the helicopter units, Vietnam combat deaths would certainly have been much greater than they were. Meanwhile, gunners were not out on shooting sprees, zapping villagers for the pure joy of it. If they fired, it was because "it was a hot LZ." They were being fired upon and people were dying. The series only shows Americans shooting, but not getting shot at. It is obvious who the villain is supposed to be.

The handful of soldiers interviewed in Part 5 hardly seem to have been selected at random. There are three main speakers – Pvts. Mark Smith, Bill Ehrhart and Charlie Sabatier. Rather than reflect differing views about the war and their experiences, the three support each other through their words and impressions. The viewer might get the image of an organic whole rather than a sampling of diverse opinions (in fact, the voices of the three men are so similar that the viewer almost cannot tell who is speaking unless the face is shown). The soldiers come off stereotyped: innocent boys taken from a little farm town and trained to become killers in a senseless war. Charlie Sabatier represents the "Draftee": trained to kill, afraid to die and uncertain what he's fighting for.

One must admire the three interviewees for their courage in facing the cameras and telling their stories to the public. Their sincerity and candor cannot be questioned. Perhaps the most sensitive and moving point is when Bill Ehrhart admits to having nightmares about shooting down an unarmed old woman. The viewer can only guess what inner strength it took for the veterans to open themselves as they did and expose themselves to us.

It is unfortunate that the producers have not made better use of their interviewees and developed a deep, penetrating analysis of the Vietnam veteran experience. Such a study is sorely needed for the benefit of both the veterans and the general public. But the producers have opted for shallowness and stereotype, assuming that representing an image of something is the same as bringing understanding of it. Even the inclusion of one black, Pvt. Jack Hill, suggests tokenism. Pvt. Hill is given little opportunity to talk about the war, but is thrown into the uncomfortable position of having to defend his unit against charges of massacring civilians. No other minorities will appear on the show until Part 8, "Vietnamizing the War", when the topics of racism and black market are similarly displayed as scandalous specimens. Whether the issue is race, drugs, massacres, the conduct of operations or general impressions of the war, it should be dealt with in a careful, objective and discerning manner. In preferring tokenism, the series has opted for the easy way out.

Attitude Toward the ARVN

U.S. troops were sent in large numbers to Vietnam beginning in the mid-1960s. To Gen. Westmoreland and other senior officers, America's role in the war was an advisory one to support the effort of the South Vietnamese government and military. In the eyes of many American GIs, however, the Americans seemed to be carrying the brunt of the fighting while the ARVN sat on the sidelines and watched.

The different impressions are based on their varied experiences. Gen. Westmoreland dealt with both the U.S. and South Vietnamese military commands. He met with Vietnamese officers and watched the ARVN in action in various capacities. Westmoreland offered counsel on issues related to the Vietnamese military, including the training of soldiers and officers, the draft, logistics, care for disabled ARVN soldiers, etc. During his term in Vietnam, Westmoreland emphasized that he was acting as an adviser, not taking over the job of the ARVN.

Meanwhile, the average American soldier had very limited contact with the Vietnamese, military or civilian. Large units operated independently of the ARVN. The vast majority of American soldiers were rarely in a position to see the ARVN in action. Few GIs ever met with civilian families. Only rarely did American units settle in with a village for any extended period of time. During their year-long tours, many GIs never even visited Saigon or other major cities or learned anything about the people. American bases were self-contained little worlds barely related to the rest of the country or the local populace. Americans saw Americans fighting and dying, but they did not see the Vietnamese. It is not supprising, then, that many Americans should have felt that the Vietnamese were supporting them rather than the other way around.

While in Vietnam, a number of Americans developed negative feelings toward the ARVN and the Vietnamese people in general. In particular, there was the feeling shared by many that the ARVN "wouldn't fight", that the South Vietnamese were "chicken" and did not fight the way the VC did. These are the comments of Bill Ehrhart included in the *Television History* and since no one else is questioned on the matter, the viewer may safely assume that the producers consider Ehrhart the final and authoritative voice on the ARVN. The producers make no effort to explain Ehrhart's impressions or place them in perspective. To them, the answer is obvious: The VC were fighting for a noble cause, while the ARVN fought for a corrupt and oppressive regime. The VC fought voluntarily, while the ARVN were puppets and mercenaries. The VC had popular support while the ARVN were generally hated.

Self-assured in their theories, the producers do not send their staff of researchers out to investigate the issue any further. They allow Ehrhart's remarks to stand uncontested, and end all discussion right there. Furthermore, they reinforce the worst images of the ARVN by cutting into films of South Vietnamese soldiers torturing a prisoner by dunking his head under water and later shooting him on the run. More derogatory scenes of the ARVN appear elsewhere in the series in case the viewers have not yet gotten the point. As far as the producers are concerned, the case is closed even before it is opened.

As a matter of fact, there is much more to be said about impressions of the ARVN's fighting ability. Remarks by both American and South Vietnamese veterans are included in the supplementary readings that follow this chapter. The readers will perhaps find it interesting just how narrowly the producers of the *Television History* limited their study and ask themselves how that narrow mode of research has affected other topics covered in this series.

Attitude Toward the Enemy

Part of the weakness of the American war strategy stemmed from the failure of people in the government and military to know their enemy. Few Americans were interested enough in the war to try and find out what the Viet Cong were all about, what motivated them and how they operated. For the U.S. soldiers who had to fight them, there were many complicating factors: the Americans were on foreign soil while the VC fought on their own "turf"; the language and culture of Vietnamese were quite different from those of the Americans; the VC were better equipped to deal with the local people's values and beliefs; and so on. Despite an overall technological superiority, the American soldiers suffered from a psychological disadvantage which actually robbed the technology of much of its weight. The Americans were strangers in a strange land, hence the "Martian" syndrome.

One result of the psychological disadvantage is that some Americans tended to see the Viet Cong in generalized or mythological terms. The Viet Cong became ghostly rather than human – they fire and then retreat, fire and retreat, fire and finally disappear into the black-haired populace.

The VC were often not viewed as a group of individuals, but as one person, the ever-elusive "Charlie." Charlie shoots from the left ... now Charlie is on the right ... Charlie is everywhere at once and yet ... nowhere. And no matter how many times Charlie is killed, Charlie always manages to come back again to harrass the GIs.

The frustrations compounded when the Americans entered a village and encountered icy silence from the peasants. Perhaps a helicopter had been fired at from the village or there had recently been a number of hit-and-run attacks in the area. The GIs knew that the villagers knew who was involved. But the peasants said nothing; no one would point out Charlie. The GIs could not communicate and they failed to recognize what sort of reprisals were in store for the villager who fingered the local VC cadre. To many American soldiers, this apparent lack of cooperation meant only one thing: that the villagers supported Charlie and hated the Americans. And these were the people America was supposed to be protecting!

As a result of all the frustration and lack of understanding, a folklore developed which popularized the VC fighter as a superman – invulnerable, immortal, indefatigable, able to leap tall bamboo groves in a single bound . . . Charlie became the product of speculation and vivid imagination, an absurd creature of another world, totally removed from reality.

PBS reinforces the image of the phantom Communist soldier through an interview with Major Vernon Gillespie. The major describes how the U.S. 9th Cavalry caught the 22nd NVA (North Vietnamese Army) Regiment on the coast and "proceeded to eliminate them . . . primarily through the use of awesome firepower." Three times the U.S. troops encountered this NVA regiment, and three times they "tore 'em up." But six months later the enemy was back, "completely refurbished – a new regiment", and the process would be repeated again.

According to PBS, this is an example of how the United States "brought to bear the power of its industry and technology" to "break the will of the enemy", and failed. Whether this story says just that is debatable. What it does say is that the U.S. firepower wreaked havoc on the North Vietnamese Army and forced Gen. Giap time and again to recruit more young men and boys to fight his brutal war. Readers should bear in mind that the North Vietnamese soldiers were not all enthusiastic volunteers whose will power was not to be broken by the force of modern technology. They were draftees, told that if they refused to fight, then back at home their families' food rations would be cut. They went, often believing they were fighting for their country. And while the Americans knew what had happened to the old 22nd NVA regiment, you can bet your bottom dollar Gen. Giap never described its fate to his new recruits.

Another example of the type of speculation that colored the Viet Cong is given through the comments of Everett Bumgardner, former U.S. Civilian Adviser in Vietnam. Bumgardner facilitates the conversion of the passive Vietnamese peasant-farmer to vicious Viet Cong killer quite neatly. For generations, he explains, control of the government and economy rested in the hands of "maybe three to five per cent of the population." Peasants found it almost impossible to break from the traditions handed down from their fathers and grandfathers – the assumption being that they wanted to break from them in the first place. Then, as if descending from a cloud, the VC came and invited the peasants to "revolt" and "change the system!" "Many young men and women voluntarily, willingly, joined the Viet Cong" and so became instantly "a savior of his village and family – a super nationalist." Though the peasant might be "an extremely sensitive young man, maybe even a Buddhist," he underwent a "complete metamorphosis" from farmer straddling a buffalo to "savage fighter," engaging in terrorism and assassination.

While this image of the "super nationalist" is accepted by some observers (including the producers of this series), it is difficult to justify. Certainly not all the peasants thought of the Viet Cong as heroes and saviors – not even Stanley Karnow believes that. It is true that, within the limitations imposed by the Communists, many people did "willingly" join the Viet Cong. But they did so for numerous reasons, more often personal than political. (See discussion of Part 6 below.) Proponents of the indigenous "revolution" theory have yet to prove that peasants in a traditionally serene agricultural society harbor deep-seated yearnings to "change the system." Bumgardner does not explain why his

village "saviors" had to resort to chopping off the heads of
government officials or Rural Development Workers in order to
become popular. Nor does he explain why more impressionable
young people did not decide to become village and family heroes,
and why it was necessary at times to use terrorism to recruit more
"saviors." He says nothing of the incredible obstacles involved in
a "complete   metamorphosis" from   sensitive   Buddhist   to
"savage" terrorist. He assumes that every task performed by the
villagers in support of the VC was done "voluntarily, willingly" by
grateful peasants happy to serve their saviors, not recognizing that
many tasks, especially the most dangerous ones, were performed
under force by civilians, quite often the relatives of ARVN soldiers
or government workers; forced labor saved the VC from doing all
the dirty work and implicated all the villagers in the anti-government effort, sharing the responsibility in case of retaliation. For
Bumgardner and others like him, the myth of the Viet Cong's
pervasive popularity prevails.

Pvt. Bill Ehrhardt follows Bumgardner, describing his frustration with "Joe, the rice farmer" who never looks up when the
Americans sweep through the area and does not twitch an eyelash
when a mine explodes. Obviously, "Joe" must be a VC or "VC
sympathizer." Like most GIs, Ehrhardt was not in any village long
enough to learn about the people and realize that if Joe did not jump
up and shake Ehrhardt's hand each time the Americans stomped
through the rice fields, Joe didn't do it for the VC either. The
peasants learned early that the best policy is not to associate with
either side, for to do so is to court trouble. A peasant who showed
sympathy for or interest in the Americans left himself open to
reprisals by the local VC. For merely lifting his head, Joe might be
executed that night. Likewise, if Joe was actively involved in
supporting the VC, he could be arrested by the government forces.
So, Joe did his best to avoid conflict, just hoping to survive. Joe
knew, too, that while Americans came for a few minutes or hours
and then left, the VC would still be there keeping an eye on him.
What were Joe's options in such a war?

Finally, there is draftee Charlie Sabatier who asks in bewilderment, "What the hell is Communism?" There he lay with a bullet in
his back wondering if he were "going to die for killing a bunch of

people 'cause they happened to be Communist!" He began to respect the enemy for living in a "stupid jungle" and in tunnels "for ten years" just to fight the Americans. To this soldier, "Communist" was nothing more than a meaningless label, a tag placed on the enemy to identify a target. Sabatier sees no danger in Communism overthrowing a government, since obviously – to him at least – the revolution is a popular one.

What would Sabatier and other American soldiers like him think if they were to return to Vietnam today and see what Communism has done to that country? What would they say about the re-education camps, prisons and labor camps? How would they respond to the hundreds of thousands of refugees who have fled their homeland because the government "happens to be Communist"? The *Television History* never poses these questions. Perhaps the producers would be embarrassed by the answers.

Sabatier reflects a segment of the population that knows little about Communism and its dangers. He cannot understand why some people oppose it or why he was in Vietnam fighting it. He would probably be suprised to hear a story told by the refugees: If the American soldiers were to return to Vietnam now, they would all be killed – the people would be so glad to see them that they would hug them to death!

For the *Television History*, the history of "America's war" is simply the tragic tale of bumbling Americans crashing through little Vietnam with bombs and bulldozers, turning pretty villages into "parking lots", destroying property and killing people with no rhyme or reason. In Part 5, America's "enemy" is really America itself.

The "Massacre" at Thuy Bo

The producers of this series appear to have worked under the assumption that the war was full of American atrocities and massacres. My Lai was only one instance. Rather than do a careful study of My Lai (which most observers agree was the exception in the war and not the rule) and risk getting involved in controversy, the producers have taken a safe way out by finding another atrocity, happily supplied by their Communist tour guides. This is the incident that occurred in January 1967 at Thuy Bo in Central Vietnam. (The exhaustive historical documentary fails to inform its viewers of the name of the site, noting only that it is "ten miles from where U.S. troops first landed in 1965," a comment which suggests that pacification had not extended very far during the preceding two years. Stanley Karnow identifies the place for us: "Thuybo, a complex of hamlets straddling an intersection of rivers about a dozen miles south of Danang." (p. 468) "Complex of hamlets" is journalistic jargon for "village.")

The *Television History* provides two versions of what happened at Thuy Bo – one from two Marines involved in the operation and the other from three witnesses, residents of the village itself. The two accounts differ markedly. The Marines claim they were pinned down for one night by heavy enemy gunfire from the village. The next morning, after 36 hours without food, water or sleep, they moved in and encountered more gunfire. They entered the village for a short time, clearing the people out of their huts while looking for the Viet Cong. Sometimes villagers were rooted out with grenades or rifle fire. When the enemy could not be found, the Marines withdrew.

According to the witnesses, it was just another day at Thuy Bo. People were going about their normal routine when suddenly the Americans came. Bombs fell and shells exploded. Soldiers came into the village and murdered entire households. They shot off ears and splattered guts, smashed heads with rifle butts, laughing as they did. The Americans, we are told, burned "everything, even dead children." They killed the pigs and chickens and thoroughly terrified the population. Only some lucky people survived.

Discrepancy between the two stories is to be expected. The witnesses came from both sides of a traumatic conflict. Needless to say, no one was taking notes at the time. Furthermore, the incident happened about 14 years prior to the interviews. The memory of Pvt. Jack Hill, who bears most of the responsibility for defending the Marines, is notably hazy. Several times he uses the term "chaos" loosely to describe general confusion or the atmosphere of the event. His unit "dropped a couple of grenades" and "cranked a couple of rounds" into the huts to draw people out. Another time he says they dropped "plenty of grenades" into tunnels. Pvt. Hill was being interviewed cold and had not been given any opportunity to clear his mind before his statements were recorded. By his demeanor, the viewer can tell he becomes troubled by questions regarding the killing of women and children. In the end, Pvt. Hill is forced to concede that he "can't account for every Marine that was there and what they done," leaving the impression that while Hill himself might not have slaughtered unarmed civilians, his buddies might have.

On the other hand, the Vietnamese villagers seem to be blessed with total recall, even of the least significant details. Nguyen Bay was on his way to school when he heard the Americans were coming. He ran back and "hid (his) things" as airplanes flew over and bombs were falling. Le Thi Ton recounts how she got up to greet the Marines, only to be laughed at scornfully. The soldiers responded by throwing a hand grenade into the hut and shooting up the bodies.

A number of Vietnamese who listened to the program have remarked to this writer that the testimony of the three villagers lacks the spontaneity of a cold interview and gives the appearance of having been rehearsed before the American cameramen came to the village. The charge is not far-fetched. Countless times during the war so-called victims of alleged atrocities made public statements prepared in advance for them by Communist officials to guarantee that the proper charges were made in the authorized manner. During the Land Reform, for example, peasants were taught to accuse their landlords of every sort of crime ranging from robbery and extortion to murder, mutilation and rape. Tens of thousands of persons were executed on the basis of charges that were totally fabricated. It is not unlikely that these three peasants (whom we are led to believe are innocents, although the young man, Nguyen Bay, gives every appearance of being an official cadre) had been given instruction by their leaders on what to say when the Americans came and how to say it. Even as Thuong Thi Mai raises her cupped hand to show how she could only find a "handful of bones" – the remains of her three children whose corpses were allegedly burned – we are reminded of the rehearsals of the Land Reform where every gesture, clenched fist and grimace was practiced by the "witness" for days before the denunciation session. The bizarre nature of their tale also lends itself to suspicion. Wounded villagers going to their beds to rest in the midst of a terrible slaughter? Soldiers beating and shooting the wounded in gruesome, sadistic ways? Burning dead children? It certainly sounds a bit contrived.

The producers forget that it is common practice for interviewees in Communist countries to make fraudulent charges to discredit their enemies. Stanley karnow, who derides Ngo Dinh Diem's strategic hamlets as "Potemkin villages," seems all too willing to believe that Communist villages prepared for foreign guests are exactly what they purport to be, i.e., typical residences of typically innocent civilians who express typical complaints about the monster Americans. Yet the fact is that in any Communist country – whether it is Vietnam, China, or the Soviet Union – the stage has been set beforehand and witnesses are rehearsed so that what the visitors get is a manufactured tale approved by the government. The producers of the *Television History* refuse to accept this reality in their zeal to expose American atrocities. Thuy Bo seems to provide a good example of what the PBS crew wants to believe. The story is certainly as good as any other.

But in viewing this account of an alleged atrocity, suspicions are further heightened by modifications of the villagers' testimony made by the translator. At times, their comments are condensed or adjusted. Their statements are smoothed out, omitting repetition or hesitancy. Sometimes, words are explained to us: Le Thi Ton tells how the Marines grinned at her "showing their white teeth"; this is translated "they laughed when I (greeted them), they seemed to hate us." As Nguyen Bay recounts the litany of abuses performed by the Americans, he remarks, "The wounded went to lie down on their beds . . . their hands cuffed, they lay down on their beds"; in translation, this becomes: "Some of the wounded people went to their beds to lie down. The soldiers shot their ears."

If this is not enough to cast doubt on the authenticity of the villagers' testimony, there is, as well, an item mentioned in Stanley Karnow's *History* which is not presented in the television series. According to Karnow, "a local Communist cadre" (Ed. – Nguyen Bay?) asserted the Marines had slaughtered as many as 145

unarmed civilians! (p 469) The inclusion of this outrageous figure
(flatly denied by Capt. Banks in Karnow's book) would have lent
much to the argument that the "massacre" story was false. Its
omission makes one wonder about the editorial sense· of the
producers.

Lest there be any misunderstanding, this writer is not claiming
that there were no atrocities committed during the war or any
brutality from the American side. The very nature of war dictates
that such things will happen. This is no less true for a war lasting
two decades and involving numerous complex factors, including
human psychology, cultural differences, disparate military
strategies, the use of "tactical weapons", and an enemy that
thinks nothing of sacrificing old women and young children for
the "great cause." But, as one writer put it, "War is not fought by
abnormal men. Rather, it is fought by normal men in abnormal
circumstances." In reviewing those circumstances for history, the
least we might ask is that we be given a sensitive and honest account
of the events so that we might balance the facts and learn for
ourselves the relevance of these events to our lives. This requires
extra caution on the part of those presenting the story for us, to
ensure that the information we receive is unbiased, truthful and
reasonably complete. This writer feels the *Television History* has
failed to fulfill these basic requirements.

POWs

Neither the *Television History* nor Stanley Karnow's companion
book does justice to the American POWs held by the Communists
from 1964 to 1973. (In fact, Karnow hardly brings them up at all and
is careful to balance his admission of Communist torture with the
recognition that mistreatment of prisoners happened on both sides,
with emphasis on the South Vietnamese.) Yet the POWs might have
a lot to tell us about North Vietnam and the mentality of their
captors as well as their air operations during the war.

In the TV series, POWs do not enter the picture until Part 6 when
select interviews with Everett Alvarez and Robinson Risner are
used. Alvarez was the first pilot shot down, a triumph for Premier
Pham Van Dong to recall with amusement. Both POWs tell stories
that reflect the "righteous wrath" of the North Vietnamese

toward the aggressor pilots (Alvarez' hate rally and Risner's half-blind old man pointing a loaded pistol in his face). Except for Risner's description of rope torture, there is no other evidence in the series of the brutal treatment the POWs received at the hands of the Communists. Throughout the war, as the Communists boasted of their "humane and lenient treatment" of prisoners, the American POWs were being starved, shackled, locked in tight leg stocks for prolonged periods of time, beaten with clubs, hung from the ceiling by their arms wrenched behind their backs, kept in solitary confinement for years, left in vermin-infested cells and refused medical treatment for wounds, infections, dysentery, malnutrition, and so on. They were subjected to psychological abuse, harangued and cursed, forced to write confessions and biographies, and to inform on other POWs or reveal military information. The POWs were treated well only when it was politically expedient for the North Vietnamese, for example, just before the prisoners were to be released.

In the TV series, the South Vietnamese, along with their American advisers, are shown in graphic films or interviews abusing and torturing Viet Cong or allegedly harmless peasants. No scenes even suggesting systematic abuse of prisoners by the Communists are presented. It is not true that such films do not exist. There is, for example, the 1966 press conference of Jeremiah Denton in which he blinked the word "torture" in Morse Code into the cameras. Or the famous scene of Richard Stratton repeatedly kowtowing before his press interviewers. The series' producers have chosen not to include such footage, preferring instead films of South Vietnamese torture supplied by the National Liberation Front, films which are, so we are told, objective and unbiased.

Honors

Part 5 concludes with an awards ceremony for meritorious service and for soldiers wounded in battle. This appears to be the producers' way of honoring the American soldiers for their efforts and sacrifice during the war. Considering that at the same time the series depicts the GIs as "stumblebums" and killers, this scene comes off as somewhat hypocritical and, consequently, rather insulting. This is especially true in light of the poor way in which the media treated the GIs during the war. Any honors come many years too late and from the wrong source.

In any event, this scene reminds one of a third-grade ceremony where the teacher passes out gold stars to all the children in the class to make them feel good. Such is the attitude of the producers toward the American soldiers, an arrogance which presumes the right to honor or dishonor anyone at will.

Supplements

(Ed.– On Februray 6, 1984, the editor met with a small group of American Vietnam war veterans at a local counseling center in San Diego. The veterans were asked for their opinions of the *Vietnam: Television History.* About ten veterans participated in the discussion, which lasted one hour and extended into topics beyond the series itself. The responses, summarized below, are not intended to be a statement on behalf of the Vietnam veteran community, but the personal opinions of the discussion participants. Their purpose in being presented here is to give the reader some initial insight into the attitudes of veterans and the information they hold in their heads.)

Image of the American Soldier – There appeared to be a consensus that the television series showed only one side of the brutality of the war. Comments by the veterans included these: It seemed as if the Americans "pulled all the atrocities." The American soldiers came off as "brutal individuals" who went to Vietnam "with one intent in mind." The series showed "the same scene time and again" of Americans going through and burning a village. The program did not say that "for the past month that village had cost the lives of 50 to 60 people," that everybody knew it was a "VC ville." The series never showed what motivated the Americans to act as they did – if, for example, you see a schoolbus full of kids get blown up by the other side, "you get a feeling inside." Meanwhile, the program did not depict "what the VC did for shits and giggles" – the maiming, beheading and castration. Particularly abhorrent to the veterans was the booby-trapping of children. Knowing that every American is a "sucker for a kid," the

VC planted handgrenades on the children and sent them out – this was not shown on the series. In short, the program presented only the brutality inflicted by the Americans, not by both sides. One person remarked that while both sides were subversive, at least the Americans "weren't maniacs like the Communists." Another veteran expressed respect for the Americans in the series who "owned up" to their actions, no matter how terrible, unlike the Communists, who could not admit to killing nearly 3,000 people in Hue.

Beyond the brutality, some veterans indicated that the series presented the Americans as "looking like assholes," while the VC were professionals. The veterans did not deny the mistakes, difficulties and foibles that occurred among the American troops, but objected to the overemphasis of these in the series as well as the omission of similar incidents among the VC. Some veterans pointed out the films of the other side came from propaganda sources (which one referred to as "Ho Chi Minh's Archives"), were reenacted and staged out. One person noted that no one smiles when he's "humping 150 pounds on his back," yet the program showed Communist soldiers hauling heavy artillery up the side of a hill with big smiles – for the cameras. Another veteran said that a lot of North Vietnamese officers were interviewed. There was a comment that the veterans have been waiting for years to find out what happened in the war and now all they're getting is "Hanoi's side" of the story. All in all, the North Vietnamese "got the better show."

The Americans and the South Vietnamese– Some veterans expressed dissatisfaction with the performance of the ARVN during the war. One had particularly strong opinions about this. He said the ARVN "were not doing a goddamn thing" when he was in Vietnam in the Vietnamization stage. The South Vietnamese "were supposedly doing their thing after we left," but he claims he never saw this. This individual was extremely distrustful of the Vietnamese, including those on his own side. He said the ARVN "wouldn't learn" and eventually got dropped from patrols. In his opinion, the United States should not be blamed for losing the war; the U.S. had done its job, but the ARVN could not hold the country only two years after the Americans left.

Another veteran was more sympathetic. The ARVN did fight, he said, but the Americans pushed them aside, walked in and made it our war, then "backed out." Instead of supporting South Vietnam during the war, Americans took responsibility for it, leaving the Vietnamese in the lurch.

A third person felt the Vietnamese were not cooperating. They knew if there were VC in their village and would have told the Americans if they had wanted to. The South Vietnamese "didn't get behind patriotism"; they wouldn't fight and just were not "in it together."

The veterans agreed that one problem they faced was their lack of knowledge about the people. The soldiers went to Vietnam "without knowing anything about the culture and language" – just how to use a rifle. Americans had no interaction with the Vietnamese civilian population and many never even met a Vietnamese family. Instead, the soldiers were "thrown off" the boat, left on their own, and did their duty hoping to survive for 395 days so they could go home in one piece.

One person remarked that there are all kinds of Vietnamese; they are not all the same. Before he forms an opinion about any Vietnamese he meets, he tries to get some background information about them first. He asked the group: How would we react if we were at war and a bunch of individuals from another country came here? How would we feel?

After meeting with some Vietnamese in his hometown, one veteran came to the conclusion that most Vietnamese would rather be in their own country, but are only here because of circumstances. He said that both sides were duped by their leaders.

A veteran who had attended a Vietnamese New Year celebration in San Diego recounted how a Vietnamese refugee came to him and thanked him for what he had done in Vietnam, then asked him to join the refugee's family for a picture. The veteran was deeply moved and described the experience as being "welcomed home." He pointed out that the person who expressed gratitude was "not one of us" (i.e., not American).

War Policy – The individuals in this discussion had several views about America's involvement in the war, the government and policy.

Some complained of the political, or "diplomatic," war going on at the same time. The governemnt should have let the military "clean up" the situation first, then let the politicians come in. One person spoke of his frustration at learning that the U.S. government planned to get out as early as 1965, but kept sending men in while trying to re-establish a political status quo.

Some veterans said they felt sold out. The government put them in Vietnam, left them there, then pulled out of the conflict. This was "good for any propaganda film for any Communist country in the world."

Some said the U.S. "fucked up" politically. It lied to the soldiers about Communist aggression. One mentioned that he had been given the "normal propaganda" about the domino theory, but what he saw happening was not what he had been told. Another person called the U.S. a "third party" trying to impose its way of thinking on people who probably did not want it in the first place. Another declared that the U.S. gave the Vietnamese an opportunity to choose what they wanted – if they wanted Communism, they got it.

One person said that if there was anyone to blame, it was Kissinger.

According to one veteran, the war was lost by the leaders who did not "control the war right militarily."

Another said it would have been great if the leaders had "had the balls to say, 'We made a mistake and we're pulling out'." He likened the war to the big guy on the street egging on a smaller boy to fight for him. (The big guy would say, "See him over there? Go beat him up. If there's any trouble, I'll back you up.") Another noted that the television series interviewed "top people" on both sides, people who were doing well later and not suffering from the burden of responsibility. The veterans felt that they were being held responsible for the war and that this was not right.

(Ed. – Among the Vietnamese refugees living in the U.S. are a large number of former soldiers. Some were asked to respond to the PBS series and to criticism about their ability and will to fight. Below are some of their responses. Not suprisingly, the Vietnamese defend their military and resent what they consider unfair criticism of the

ARVN. Readers who consider the testimony of the Vietnamese to be too biased for honest assessment may disregard the following.)

Re the Television History: Before anything else, those Vietnamese refugees questioned expressed outrage at the series' portrayal not of the ARVN, but of the American military. They felt the series depicted the Americans as "senseless killers" and showed them in the worst of situations without doing them justice. The Vietnamese felt that the honor of the war and the "noble sacrifice of the American soldiers" was being insulted. The refugees said the GIs had fought to protect their freedom and deserved better treatment.

Although they strongly disagreed with the portrayal of the ARVN in the series, the refugee veterans did not emphasize this. They are used to such treatment by the American media and do not feel inclined to protect themselves. Their greater disgust was in the insult done to the Americans, whom they call their "allies", and to the image of their "just cause" in struggling against the Communists. They are astonished that American television can show American soldiers in such a bad light.

Response to Criticism of the ARVN: The *Television History* brought out some sensitive points about the ARVN through comments expressed by American veterans. The refugees were upset by suggestions of cowardice or lack of patriotism. One officer remarked that he had been in the military for 21 years, virtually all of his adult life. "The last battle of the war," he lamented, "was lost before it was even fought." Although he escaped as a refugee, his shame was "not worthy of those left behind". He described as "nonsense" contentions that the ARVN were not patriotic, could not coordinate into military operations and could not fight. Such criticisms, he said, emanate from the American media and some U.S. soldiers. These opinions are subjective, one-sided and express personal resentment. Nonetheless, they are understandable because the Americans subconsciously rejected the war and were not in a proper position in which to see the South Vietnamese fight. For a period during the 1960s, American combat units were given responsibility for assault operations while the ARVN were placed in charge of pacification. American units were separate from the ARVN;

consequently, American soldiers only saw their own people doing
the fighting.

Another refugee remarked that the Americans only saw Vietnamese when the Americans were chasing Viet Cong or when the
ARVN was being overrun by heavy VC forces. By the time the
Americans reached ARVN bases to help, the main VC units were
gone, and the Americans would find the ARVN in a bad condition.
This refugee noted that the ARVN were not as well equipped as the
Americans. It was necessary for ARVN units to have an American
advisor because only an American could call for air or artillery
support and hope to get quick response. If a Vietnamese called for
support, it would be late in coming.

The images Vietnamese soldiers have of American soldiers are
not always complimentary. The GIs fought for 365 days with two
periods of R & R in Manila or Hong Kong in which to "screw
around." Helicopters brought in drinks to the field and the GIs got
warm meals. A laundry truck was there to serve them. At night the
Americans would walk around as if in a daze and when they slept
there was ice underneath the cots to keep them cool. Some refugees
remarked that the Americans looked foolish wandering around in a
village or in an open field – easy targets for snipers – or tramping
around in 100-degree heat in the middle of the day when it made
more sense to sit in the shade. Frankly, sometimes the Americans
just looked ridiculous. It might be disrespectful to talk this way of
their allies who sacrified 50,000 lives, but it is true nonetheless.

Meanwhile, the ARVN soldier might not see his wife for years.
The South Vietnamese were not simply fighting for one year, but for
decades, never knowing when the fighting would end. Their soldiers
were not discharged, but served until they were severely wounded
or killed. If anyone wants to know how the ARVN really fought,
that person should ask the American advisors. They saw the
airborne troops, the marines, rangers, infantry and armored units.
The advisors are "living and dead witnesses of the great heroic
struggle" that was carried on by the South Vietnamese with a sense
of responsibility, resoluteness and durability.

As for patriotism, one officer asked how patriotism can be
measured. He recalled how in the spring of 1966 as an inspecting
officer he visited a platoon of the Popular Forces at Go Dau Ha.

There, he talked with the platoon leader about the status of the troops. The previous night the post had been attacked and one third of the men lost. But, they had not given up the bridge. The platoon leader was paid 1,400 piasters per month, plus rice and cooking oil. That was equivalent to about $15. During the day, the men caught fish to supplement their meals. At night, they guarded the bridge. They had pushed back a company of main force VC even after it had broken through the second perimeter. The officer had shown off the shell marks on his jeep and joked about how, as a member of the general staff, he received $20 a month. He asked, "Where in the world could you purchase mercenaries at that price?" The officer and the platoon leader knew why they were fighting. Their patriotism could not be measured by their salaries but by the duration of their lives.

Now, thousands of their comrades are in Communist prison camps. They must be there for some reason.

(Ed. – The producers of the PBS series were clearly amazed by the heroism of Gen. Giap's soldiers. In Part 2, they include the story of one Viet Minh soldier at Dien Bien Phu who threw himself on a foxhole so that his comrades could charge. Perhaps these producers would be surprised to learn that stumbling American soldiers could be heroic, too. In *A Soldier Reports*, Gen. Westmoreland names a number of those who earned the Medal of Honor. A few are listed below.)

Capt. Paul Bucha, 101st Airborne Division. Knocked out a bunker single-handedly as his company advanced to an enemy base area. As a human wave attack forced the Americans to retreat, Capt. Bucha covered the withdrawal, although wounded by a shell fragment.

Lance Corporal Joe C. Paul, 3rd Marine Division. Diverted the enemy's attention so that five wounded Marines could be evacuated. He was killed in the fight.

Corporal Jerry Wickham, 11th Armored Cavalry Division. Charged and knocked out three enemy bunkers before being killed.

Capt. Robert Foley, 25th Infantry Division. Though wounded, he charged the enemy, destroyed three machine guns and saved several wounded comrades.

The following persons threw themselves on grenades to protect the lives of their buddies:

Specialist 4 Daniel Fernandez, 25th Infantry Division.

Pvt. First Class Leslie Bellrichard, 4th Infantry.

Staff Sergeant Frank Molnar, 4th Infantry.

PFC John Barnes III, 173rd Airborne Brigade.

Specialist 4 Dale Wagrynen, 101st Airborne Division.

PFC Milton Olive III, 173rd Airborne.

To name just a few of the people the *Television History* was obviously not interested in.

PART 6: AMERICA'S ENEMY
(1954-1967)

The history of the Vietnamese Communists is given from the partitioning of the country to the Tet Offensive.

History or Propaganda?

Gloria Emerson has described Part 6 of the *Television History* as the "most exceptional" of all the episodes in the series explaining that "in it we see and understand at last those Vietnamese who defied us." (1)

Indeed, Part 6 is most exceptional, but not necessarily for the reason given by Ms. Emerson. The viewer may look back on this segment and wonder about the strange Vietnamese and especially the followers of Ho Chi Minh. It is most astonishing that in this description of the Communists not a single non-Communist Vietnamese is interviewed to give a critical opinion about the North Vietnamese or Viet Cong in the South. Viewers must make an extra effort to find any word or phrase that might be construed as less than complimentary toward the Communists and their activities. The result is a biased – and at times outrageous – picture of the Communist Vietnamese and their handling of the "revolution." Persons looking for a balanced and open description of "America's enemy" will be greatly disappointed, for in the PBS series, common sense and decency have been thrown to the wind. When the hour is done and the "information" has been presented, the viewers are left with only tall tales and mythology.

What is most exceptional about Part 6 is that it got on the air at all.

Victory at any Cost

In an interview with a group of Vietnamese students, Hoang Van Chi compared the intellectual foundation of Western thought with that of Marxism. The West, said Chi, has a long-held tradition of rationalism out of which evolved scepticism and then scientific analysis. Marxism, on the other hand, is irrational and, therefore, unscientific. (2)

Americans attempting to look at the Communists by comparing them rationally to Western democratic countries will find it difficult to understand how the Communists act and why they do things as they do. The Communists have their system of beliefs and values which do not always coincide with those taught in American schools and homes. Candor and sincerity, for example, are highly valued traits in American society, but they are disavowed by fervent Communists seeking to incite "revolution" or fighting against "imperialist aggressors." Because Americans value morality and the rights of individuals, they may question their government's involvement in war and demand an accounting of their military's actions. On the other hand, the Communists have little concern for the lives and rights of individuals, which must be sacrificed for a greater cause. For this reason, the Communists will pledge to fight "ten years, twenty years or longer until complete victory." This is why Gen. Giap could tell a French officer that great destruction and the deaths of a million Vietnamese are "not important", but victory is. To the producers of the PBS series, this senseless obstinacy is something to be admired, although it has in fact led to the deaths of millions of people.

When one accepts the fundamental irrationality of the Communists, it is only a short step further to grasping the unethical quality of Communist strategy and tactics. In fact, one of the greatest strengths of the Communists is their total lack of ethics. They will prevaricate, assassinate, terrorize, torture and cover up their atrocities all without batting an eyelash as long as it serves their purpose. The Vietnamese Communists have simply and single-mindedly pursued their goals with no concern as to how many corpses they trample on in the process. The current conquest of Laos and Cambodia are perfect examples: While decrying American "imperialism", Hanoi plotted and orchestrated the occupation of both of its neighboring countries and has begun exterminating their people and cultures. To those who try to interpret the Communists rationally, these actions have come as a surprise. (It was frequently predicted after 1975 that Hanoi would concentrate on rebuilding the Vietnamese economy and not engage in an aggressive foreign policy.) On the other hand, Hanoi's attempt to dominate Southeast Asia is not surprising to those who have emphasized the brutality, arrogance and senselessness of the Communists. The latter group, however, is usually denounced as narrow-minded and bigoted, obsessed with a limited vision of Communism born in the 1950s. No one dares explain why these anti-Communists have a better record of predicting Communist atrocities than more progressive observers.

The brutal fanaticism of the Vietnamese Communists is identified by the television series as "fervent nationalism." This so-called "nationalism" has taken on peculiar forms over the years. Strapping hand grenades to little children is an odd way of promoting the superiority of one's country. (Perhaps the children may be said to be emulating the "heroic shock troops" attacking Dien .Bien Phu!) And Ho Chi Minh's famous saying, "There is nothing as precious as independence 'and liberty" (quoted in Part 6 as an example of his patriotic idealism) presumably cannot be translated into Cambodian or Lao. To critics of the Communists, Ho Chi Minh's statements are nothing more than hypocritical rhetoric. To the producers of the *Television History*, they are pearls of wisdom.

The reader should understand that this book does not pretend to justify America's wartime policies or actions. The U.S. performed its share of brutal and senseless actions – from the widespread spraying of defoliants to the overwhelming destructiveness of its bombing raids. The *Television History* spares no effort in pointing this out. At the same time, the series' portrayal of the Communists is unacceptable if it dares to characterize Communist terrorism as an effective psychological tool and makes deception and betrayal no more than an amusing footnote to history. The Communist "will to win" needs to be placed in perspective, and this the *Television History* does not do.

"Cruel and Reactionary Tyrant"

After reciting "victory" statements by Ho Chi Minh, Pham Van Dong and Vo Nguyen Giap, Part 6 launches into its description of the political situation in Vietnam after the Geneva Agreements. This book has already looked at some of the salient features of the agreements and Communist violations of the basic principles noted in the accord (all of which are carefully omitted from earlier episodes of the *Television History*). Part 6, too, says nothing of these violations, while leaving an impression of sincere compliance by the Communists. Ho's forces, we are told, regrouped in the North, as their families and unarmed cadres remained behind in the South waiting for reunification elections. There is no description of the weapons hidden in the South, the military build-up in the North and Communist extension of influence into Laos. Instead, we learn that "Ho Chi Minh wanted a political solution" – just as in Part 12 we will hear that the Communists wanted only a political solution following the 1973 Paris cease-fire. But those American war-mongers would have nothing of it.

Referring to the 1956 election, Mme. Nguyen Thi Dinh says, "The people in the South truly believed that there would be a national reunification in two years." Did they still believe it after 900,000 Northern refugees left their homes to resettle in the South, a foolish move if the country was about to be joined in harmony under Chairman Ho?

Ngo Dinh Diem returns to the scene as the narrator explains how the South Vietnamese president "rigged a referendum" to set up a separate state. There is no mention, of course, of any political maneuvers "rigged" by Ho Chi Minh and that no honest election was ever held in the North. Instead, Pham Van Dong appears to remind us that Diem was "a cruel and reactionary tyrant" who was "extremely barbarous" in suppressing the "revolutionary movement." In case one Communist leader is not proof enough of Diem's barbarity, two more are brought in to lend a helping hand. The first is the NLF's Nguyen Thi Dinh, who accuses Diem of repressing "former participants of the resistance against the French." Then comes Major Duong Sang, who explains that he was so moved by stories of "people in the South . . . being killed in droves" that he volunteered to go fight. The narrator tells how Diem "shunted" peasants into strategic hamlets. And an NLF film "shows government officials torturing (Viet Cong) suspects by electric shock and hanging."

Thus in Parts 3 and 6, the *Television History* presents five Communist officials who condemn Ngo Dinh Diem, their testimony supplemented by propaganda films, selected statements by Americans and loaded language from the narrator. Meanwhile, not a single individual – Vietnamese or American – is asked for an opinion of Ho Chi Minh. Instead, we get the unsupported statement from the narrator that Ho "personified the nationalist struggle, even for Vietnamese who feared Communism." That is the last word we get on the character of good old Uncle Ho, who slapped a repressive government on North Vietnam and directed a campaign of terrorism in the South. According to PBS, it is perfectly all right for biased Communist officials to condemn Ngo Dinh Diem and glorify Chairman Ho, but it is unfair for non-Communists to put in a few words about the barbarity of Ho's regime in the North! The producers claim that their program is balanced. If this is so, this peculiar style of balance has not yet been explained by the laws of physics.

But no matter. Eventually Diem is killed in a coup "encouraged" by the U.S.

Land Reform

The *Television History* finally gets around to the Land Reform Movement in Part 6, although this version is considerably briefer and softer than the event merits. According to the series, the movement was intended to raise food production and to break the political influence of "the old landowning class." Peasants were invited to describe how they had been exploited. Landlords were put before "people's courts" and "those found guilty of actual crimes were sent to jail." The narrator adds that there were fixed quotas of "criminal landlords" and admits that "perhaps three to fifteen thousand" people were executed. Hanoi was "alarmed" at the "excesses", which it said were "serious mistakes."

As pointed out in our discussion of Part 3, the Land Reform did not aim at distributing land to poor peasants to end exploitation and raise food production. The distribution of land was a temporary measure leading to collectivization. The ultimate economic aim was to impoverish the people to make them realize that all people must depend on the State to survive. Land distribution actually had little practical value in the North where even the "rich landlords" were not very rich. (3)

As for the political goal of destroying the influence of the landlords, the series says nothing of the brutal sweep made through the villages by the government teams or the torture, terrorism, and mock nature of the trials. There is no mention of concentration camps, forced starvation, or exile in the jungles. The Polish film of an irate peasant shaking his fist at a landlord wearing traditional robes and turban resembles reality only in that both the film and actual denunciation sessions were rehearsed prior to the show. As for the executions, the series makes the most extraordinary claim that only 3-15,000 people were killed! This number is extremely low and perhaps deliberately vague, as if the producers do not want to commit themselves. But while the producers boast of the competence of their research staff, it seems strange that the same people who went out of their way to calculate how many dollars the South Vietnamese spent on cosmetics cannot tell us how many people were murdered by the Communists!

This rather tolerant version of the Land Reform Campaign is apparently based on the "scholarship" of consultant Gareth Porter, a long-time apologist for the Hanoi regime. One of Dr. Porter's research efforts is an essay entitled "The Myth of the Bloodbath: North Vietnam's Land Reform Reconsidered" *(Bulletin of Concerned Asian Scholars, No. 5, 1973)*. The author's main premise is that traditional descriptions of the Land Reform came from unreliable sources (Diem's government, for example), while more trustworthy statistics are available from official Communist sources. In 1976, Porter used the same reasoning to discount reports of Khmer Rouge brutality after the Communists took over Cambodia. Said Dr. Porter: All those tales of butchery, torture, executions and starvation caused by the Khmer Rouge are simply propaganda bunk supplied by Western anti-Communists who want to discredit the Communist revolution in Cambodia. Although Porter fell flat on his face, the producers of this "historical" series still seem to trust his analysis.

For Porter's sophisticated analysis of the Khmer Rouge, see *Cambodia: Starvation and Revolution*, Monthly Review Press, 1976, written with George Hildebrand. The book is not mentioned in Porter's credits as "consultant" for the series.

All reference to the Land Reform ends with Hanoi's "alarm." The purging of intellectuals and the repression that characterized North Vietnam since those early years presumably never happened. We learn instead, that "North Vietnam's economy, ravaged by war and neglect, was being rebuilt" – until the bombing started ten years later. The narrator might have added that the "neglect" was due to the Party's forcing peasants to spend all their time denouncing "criminal landlords" and attending meetings so they could not take care of their fields and homes. Meanwhile, the Communist leadership, unable to deal with the practical realities of running a government, turned its attention to "liberating" the South.

In Praise of Terrorism

Mme. Nguyen Thi Dinh tells us that the war for liberation began when a band of peasants captured a "notorious police garrison" with their bare hands. The NLF comes into the picture without any mention that the creation of such a front was recommended by Le Duan in Hanoi after his 1958 fact-finding trip to the South, or that the first official announcement about the Front's existence came out of Hanoi several weeks after its creation. (4) There is never a word that the "coalition of Southern forces opposed to the Diem regime" was directed from Hanoi and never included any serious opposition groups from South Vietnam besides the Communists.

The alleged Southern roots of the movement are reinforced by the words of Cadre Tran Nhat Bang, who claims that on Aug. 1, 1964 his village "liberated itself" without the aid of guerrillas or regular forces. The people set up a "revolutionary administration" that just happened to resemble a Communist administration. They spontaneously began to carry out activities that by chance looked just like Communist activities. And they started using language that by pure coincidence sounds exactly like Communist jargon. The producers do not try to explain this peculiar phenomenon or show why people should be "delighted" to dig trenches and tunnels as protection against enemy artillery. Bang later declares that comrades from the North came to help out their brothers in the South in a coordinated effort against the enemy. He makes a special point of noting that "there were never any problems between Southerners and Northerners," a sure sign that problems did indeed exist.

Popular support for the struggle is shown through propaganda films of peasants making punji sticks and road mines. Although the series has been stressing the importance of the Ho Chi Minh Trail as a supply route, it does not explain why peasants were still fighting with homemade weapons. Rather than admit that the VC eagerly threw away their homemade weapons once imported machine guns from China and Russia became available, the program likes to promote the image of a technological Goliath being defeated by peasants using sticks and stones.

Le Thi Ma gives us a big grin as she describes how to make anti-tank mines, much as one would expect Julia Child to prepare a souffle. However, typical home-made weapons were of much smaller caliber. These included anti-personnel explosives placed in cans and bottles, the spring action "Bouncing Betty" (or "frog mine") that leaps up and severs the victim in two, punji sticks and other booby traps.

In a display of brazen deception, Comrade Duong Sang informs us that old people and children *volunteered to retrieve and defuse high explosives!* "Have you heard of Mrs. Nguyen Thi Ranh, who was over 80 years old when she became a military heroine?" Comrade Sang does not mention that peasants become "heroes" after they have died, thus the unfortunate Mrs. Ranh likely achieved her honor after being blown to bits while digging up an artillery round. "The children were more active and creative," the Major continues with pride. This appalling statement conceals the fact that the children did not *make* the bombs and mines – they *were* the bombs.

As if these horrendous scenes are not enough, the program accepts terrorism as a legitimate military strategy for the Viet Cong. Throughout the series, terrorist acts are given the same prominence and tactical value as major battles, even though terrorism is usually a sign of the perpetrator's weakness. The producers expect us to listen with awe as Lam Son Nao tells how he "transformed anger into action" by planting a bomb in the U.S.S. Card in a speech obviously repeated many times for foreign tourists coming to visit Vietnam. Like the attack on the Brinks Hotel given earlier in the show, this act is glorified by the telling, the only apparent purpose being to make the viewers realize the cleverness of the Viet Cong.

Even Earl Young's description of Viet Cong terrorism in the villages is given the air of a proper political action. As Young talks of beheadings to mobilize the population, we are shown scenes not of gruesome terrorist acts, but of peasants sabotaging a bridge in support of the glorious cause. In a moment we will see actual torture – committed by the South Vietnamese, of course! All this is to show how the Communists are great psychologists.

It would appear that even when the Viet Cong are at their worst, they are still better than anything the South Vietnamese or Americans have to offer.

Return of the One-Way Camera and the Spirit of the Revolution

It is curious that in all the battles shown in Part 6, Viet Cong never die. Binh Gia, 1964: "The Vietcong destroyed two South Vietnamese battalions, killing 158 soldiers and five American advisers." The program could easily have added that Viet Cong casualties numbered in the hundreds, but somehow this minor detail is omitted.

But if the VC soldiers never died, not so the innocent villagers. When GIs went tramping into a village you could be sure that "Wherever the Americans went, they burned, destroyed and killed. I didn't see any guerrillas being killed, only villagers." This is the word from Le Thi Hien of Cam Ne, and Comrade Bang adds with a satisfied smile that he and his guerrilla fighters ran away when the fighting got rough and left the women and children to take the raps. So much for the courageous Viet Cong.

To supplement our images of the ugly Americans, we are shown GIs taking photographs of corpses or standing by ARVN soldiers applying water torture to enemy suspects. And no account of the Americans' brutality would be complete without sufficient footage of bombing and the cheers for napalm, "Look at it burn! Look at it burn!"

The viewer hears nothing about Viet Cong soldiers chopping the finger off a prisoner to steal a wedding ring, gang-raping a village chief's wife and daughters, throwing a hand grenade into a movie theatre full of children, starving prisoners to death or committing any of a number of other horrible deeds, which if performed by the Americans or South Vietnamese would immediately be labled "war crimes."

The series would have done well to explain how the Communists gained and maintained support in the villages. Typically, cadres from outside would agitate the population by playing on personal as well as local grievances. For instance, the Communists were strong in the central lowlands because the villagers there were quite poor and had nothing to lose by radical political change. At the same time, individuals dissatisfied with the local government or victims of abuse by the military often joined the Viet Cong. At times entire villages supported the VC because their neighbors, rivals in fishing or marketing, belonged to the government side. Many people trusted the strength of the VC over that of the Saigon regime in the long run. Some villagers thought the Americans were trying to replace the French as colonialists while others who had more contact with the Americans considered this idea nonsense.

Once in a position to control a village, the Communists employed a number of techniques to ensure that their control would be deep and long-lasting. First, there was terror. Villagers would be gathered around in the village square or other public place to witness an execution. Contrary to myth, not all persons executed were tyrannical officials hated by all the villagers. Many honest and dedicated people, including youths, were murdered, if only because they threatened the control of the Communists. It was not necessary for executions to touch every family. One public execution was enough to let the people know that at any time the same thing could happen to them. The execution of an innocent person was most effective; it reminded the people that no one was safe. There were people who supported the VC, but ultimately, they had no choice. They cooperated or they died.

The Communists could also ensure compliance by holding hostages. Families who had sons or brothers in the Viet Cong were afraid to disobey the orders of the VC cadres, since at any time their loved ones could be killed or punished. Likewise, VC soldiers were kept in the ranks by the knowledge that if they fled, the safety of their families would be jeopardized.

While the villagers were thus subdued, they were given extremist propaganda. Americans murder old people, rape girls and sell babies – these were typical tales. The fact that some atrocities did occur helped reinforce the fanatical urgings of the cadres. Isolated from the rest of the world, villagers had no access to more responsible or alternative information.

The people were worked to the limits of their physical ability. Everyone belonged to a "team" or "brigade," a woman's group or other organization. Youths dug tunnels, old women sewed clothes and cooked food for the soldiers, others made booby traps or carried rice. In this way, the people were kept constantly busy and worked to the point of exhaustion. At the same time, they were implicated in the village's actions and no one could claim innocence if the government soldiers came by. The VC also used *kiem soat bao tu*, or "stomach control." Dietary standards were kept low, and this, coupled with continual labor, weakened the peasants and made them more susceptible to indoctrination.

Privacy was severely restricted. Meetings were held at night after work and the villagers were given extra chores to keep minds and hands from idleness. Conversations were to be conducted in the open and with a voice loud enough to be overheard. The killing of a chicken or pig had to be reported to the local cadre, who kept records of the villagers' possessions. Through criticism sessions and mutual surveillance, the villagers learned they could trust no one. This played into the hands of the cadres, who preached total reliance on the Party and the Party only.

These factors (terrorism, isolation, starvation, exhaustion, forced labor and indoctrination) ensured the participation of the people in the great struggle for liberation.

Time after time, the *Television History* remarks on the alleged growing popularity of the liberation movement. The reader may be suprised to learn that in actuality the exact opposite was taking place. One scholar, Wesley Fishel, of Michigan State University, regards as "myth" the idea that the Viet Cong was "an embattled popular army of patriotic peasants" or "simply honest peasants

who rose in righteous wrath against an oppressive government and
. . . gained the support of the vast majority of the population." (5)
Fishel does not deny the South Vietnamese peasants had grievances
against their government or claim that the Viet Cong had no
support. As in many emerging nations, he says, the South Vietnamese government did not always manage itself properly, and it is
natural to see some resentment arise. Beyond this, the Saigon
government did little to promote a nationalist spirit among its
people. Finally, the presence of Americans "bolstered the xeno-
phobic propaganda of the Viet Cong and . . . the NLF." (6) Still,
Fishel's "wonder" is that despite the political advantages, the Viet
Cong never gained much popularity at all.

In an article entitled "The Faceless Viet Cong," George A.
Carver, Jr. indicates that by the mid-1960s the Viet Cong were losing
support in the rural areas due to rising taxation, forced conscription, "and the Viet Cong's manifest inability to deliver on political
promises of earlier years." (7) Furthermore, in one year 800,000
refugees were fleeing contested areas to areas controlled by the
government and this was not simply because of American bombing.
Carver notes, too, that more than half the rural population
participated in the 1965 provincial elections, despite a boycott called
by the Viet Cong.

Carver points out that the Viet Cong were weak in the cities,
although they had terrorist capability. The author adds that the
NLF was not joined by any urban political groups and proved
unable to bring groups such as the Buddhists and students into its
fold. "Just how weak the Viet Cong are in the cities," he says,
"was demonstrated twice . . . (on October 15 and December 19,
1965) when two public calls by the Viet Cong for a 'general
strike' went totally unheeded and produced no visible change
whatsoever in the pattern of urban life."

Carver further discounts Communist propaganda regarding the
rallying value of concepts such as American imperialism and
reunification. On the latter point, he notes, "The concept of
reunification has relatively little appeal for peasants who regard
someone from the next province as an alien." Nor did Southerners
buy into Viet Cong claims of "independence and freedom" from
control by the North as long as Northern troops ran the war.

The television series tells us that the greatest motivating spiritual force within the Viet Cong was patriotism – the people would give up everything for their country. But as Douglas Pike points out in his classic on the NLF, *Viet Cong*, the essence of NLF indoctrination and the single emotion the NLF could count on to mobilize the people was hatred. (8) Viet Cong propaganda and activities were geared around the exploitation of the hatred that supposedly was boiling in the masses. The peasants were instructed to hate anyone connected with the Saigon government. They were taught to hate the "pirate imperialists" and their "lackeys" and "puppets." They were taught to hate white people, who represented colonialism and exploitation. Destructive hatred was easier to foment in peasants than something as vague and remote as nationalism. It was easier to teach: simple black-and-white, friend-and-foe terms are more understandable to uneducated peasants than the complexities of international politics. If the Viet Cong ever fought well and hard, it was due in part to the intense hatred cultivated inside them by their cadres and leaders by means of exaggeration and deceptive propaganda.

A good example of how hatred is used in Communist society can be seen in the hate rallies perpetrated against the American POWs in the North. One such rally is brought out in the television series, the "Hanoi Parade" of July 6, 1966. Everett Alvarez describes how he and other prisoners were taken out in new uniforms to march in the streets before crowds shouting and shaking their fists. The crowd turned into a mob with sticks, bricks and bottles being thrown at the prisoners while some groups were pulled out of the audience to beat the "war criminals." The citizens became hysterical. (The series does not mention that the man who hit Alvarez in the back of the head was a Cuban, not a Vietnamese.) (9) In the case of the *Television History*, the Hanoi Parade is used to display the righteous wrath of the Vietnamese against the Americans who killed their people; it might have been more constructive to help the viewers understand the methods and psychology of the Communists.

Another way the Communists displayed their hatred was through torture. The closest the series comes to portraying Communist torture is Robinson Risner's account of the "rope trick" ordeal. Risner tells how his arms were tied and pressed together behind his back until the pain broke his strength. Unfortunately, Risner's soft voice and edited description do not reveal the severity of the punishment or the sadism of the men who performed it. The account is used to show how an American prisoner breaks under torture brought on by the righteous indignation of the North Vietnamese who wished to avenge the deaths of their wives and children occurring in the "terrorist" raids of "pirate" American pilots. Shortly afterwards, the producers give us a parallel interview: Nguyen Thi Anh, a Viet Cong spy, was tortured by the South Vietnamese, with American advisers at either side. Despite the electrodes on her nipples and needles under her fingernails, she never gave in, as visions of her people's suffering passed before her eyes. The lesson is not one of the brutality of war, but of the alleged spiritual strength of the Viet Cong.

From watching Part 6, it would appear that the producers are not interested in educating the viewers, but in conducting a spiritual crusade. However, no matter how intrepid were the VC in the South, they still needed aid from their brothers in the North.

Resistance in the North

The *Television History* relates how the liberation movement in the South grew so popular that it could "pressure" Hanoi into supporting it. Northern troops poured down the Ho Chi Minh Trail in marching armies cheered on by local crowds. As the U.S. began bombing above the 17th parallel, "North Vietnam was under attack, its developing economy threatened." But the Rolling Thunder campaign was thwarted by bearded old men clanging gongs when they saw the bombers coming and cute young girls firing away at the pirates. The civilian economy suffered, but not the military spirit of the people (termed "strange" by Ho Chi Minh's physician). Blind to the terrible force of the bombs, the North Vietnamese were mobilized by Ho's sayings and their morale was never broken. Friendly "sister countries" helped out too, giving aid to brother Vietnam under attack by the imperialists. Operation Rolling Thunder garnered a big goose egg.

Once again we get a grade school account of the war in the North, filled with simplistic claims and a total disregard for common sense. The Vietnamese, living in an underdeveloped country and enjoying relatively little modern education, had never imagined the destructive power of the American military and were naturally awed and terrified by their experiences. To suggest that they viewed the bombing with stoic courage buttressed by official pronouncements from their repressive leaders is begging our imagination.

As depicted in the PBS series, the bombing campaigns did more damage to civilian areas than military targets. This disregards the precautions taken by the U.S. military to ensure that civilian areas would be avoided. Photographs and intelligence reports were consulted prior to each mission so that targets were properly identified. A number of American pilots were shot down precisely because they lingered over a site too long while trying to stay clear of non-military areas. Realizing that the Americans were avoiding civilians, the Communists deliberately planted bases near residential areas for protection. Still, Hanoi was able to convince visitors such as Harrison Salisbury and Mary McCarthy that the U.S. was conducting a terrorist campaign against civilians.

To underscore the horror of America's bombing, the series informs us that "North Vietnamese doctors became adept at treating burns, . . . removing bomb pellets and splinters." These clever physicians are apparently not the same medical personnel who treated (or rather mistreated) the American POWs from 1964 to 1973. Those "doctors" sawed up injured limbs, left broken backs untreated, could not clean wounds properly, kept the prisoners in unsanitary conditions and confidently declared that the rats in the cells could not be rabid because rabies is a "European" disease. After the war the South Vietnamese population was to experience these same physicians, whom they would learn to regard with disgust as ignorant and inept.

Yet the bombing did not stop the Northern "volunteers" from running to the aid of their comrades in the South. The viewers might wish to compare the Communist troops to the American and South Vietnamese soldiers they fought against. The series satisfies this curiosity by giving a balanced and objective appraisal of the two sides – told entirely from the point of view of the Communists! While the narrator tells us how the North Vietnamese were such disciplined and good fighters, three North Vietnamese captains come on the screen to explain how comradely the three-man cells were, how the South Vietnamese were "only mercenaries afraid to die," how the Americans were "rather naive and clumsy," and how one small man in an ambush could kill three big Americans with his bayonet! The narrator adds the supposedly well-informed opinion that the South Vietnamese troops were "despised by the North Vietnamese and Viet Cong as puppet troops" and the ARVN casualty rate is insinuated to be due to the cowardly and mercenary nature of the South Vietnamese army.

All of these obviously one-sided views are reinforced throughout the series. The Communists are seen fighting for a noble cause rooted in their people's tradition of nationalist fervor. Meanwhile the South Vietnamese are paid by foreign dollars on behalf of a police state supported by American invaders. The Americans trip all over themselves while killing and bombing only innocent civilians.

The North Vietnamese and Viet Cong described in this series are such supermen that in all of the battles and confrontations they engage in they never die! Viewers see bleeding Americans and the corpses of fallen GIs. Civilians describe the alleged barbarity of America's war actions which never caught the elusive VC. Propaganda films show Northern soldiers with grins on their faces marching off to liberate the South from foreign aggression.

But the simple statistics of Viet Cong and North Vietnamese battle dead are never given. And scenes of Communist casualties are not shown to suggest that there was indeed a military nature to the Allied war effort, that it was not all just a cruel campaign to eliminate women and children from the face of the earth.

The Viet Cong were being beaten as thousands of troops were being sent from the North to fight in the South. These soldiers were not being sent because of any technical skills but to serve as cannon fodder in an escalating war. As time went on, North Vietnam was forced to rely on younger and younger boys to do the fighting. For one thing, the number of older men was dwindling as the death toll among Northern troops rose excessively during the mid-1960s. As well, the younger boys were easier to prepare for war, more docile and impressionable, more gung-ho about fighting for their country, while the older folk were becoming weary of war. The youngsters often fought well and with spirit. They also lacked maturity and broke just like American youths sent to fight a terrible war. By 1975, there were soldiers as young as 13 or 14 in the field.

Despite the incredible losses they sustained, the people of North Vietnam never wavered in their determination to struggle. Or so we are told. The series does not mention that Hanoi opened a special office to forge letters signed with the names of dead soldiers sent to their homes so that the families would believe their sons were still alive. Nor does it discuss the effects of radio broadcasts from the South announcing the names of Northern soldiers who died in combat.

What we are told is that the people of North Vietnam valued patriotism so highly that they would accept sustained poverty, the abuses of a totalitarian regime and the deprivation of all human rights in order to drive out the American imperialists. They were willing and eager to cast aside centuries of tradition, all family ties, social relations, religious ideals and beliefs and embrace Marxism in order to liberate the South and share their socialist paradise. And, most incredible of all, they were happy to sacrifice the lives of their sons, husbands and brothers all for the glory of Ho Chi Minh! By the beginning of 1968, they were even ready to start "a fresh ambitious offensive – the Tet Offensive!"

Rallying to the Cause

In describing the alleged popularity of the liberation movement, the series makes yet another unsupported statement through the narrator, namely that: "Artists, writers and musicians rallied to the National Liberation Front. . . . Many actors, dancers, singers, filmmakers and poets joined in the fight against the Saigon administration and the Americans."

This is, purely and simply, nonsense. The Communist Vietnamese have a long history of repressing the artistic and intellectual community. It is safe to say that artists are probably the last people who would rally to a group obviously controlled by the Communists. The *Television History* shows only a tiny sampling of the "artistry" of the North, where the performers never had the freedom to "rally" to whatever group they chose. The producers cannot explain why most talented artists of South Vietnam are currently refugees, living in concentration camps or dead.

We challenge the producers of the *Television History* to back up their claims that writers joined the cause by naming real names and giving real evidence. Rather than wait for a response, however, we might take a look at the history of Communist Vietnamese "love of the arts."

Poetry is traditionally the most popular form of literature in Vietnam. The Vietnamese language is often thought of as poetic, almost made for rhyme and rhythm. This literary form is often used by the Communists for the purpose of spreading propaganda and Ho Chi Minh used to write poems on special occasions. (He is also alleged to have written a book of prison poems in the 1930s, but there is serious question as to the authenticity of his authorship.)

The poet laureate of North Vietnam is the old minister To Huu, a writer who is best known for the eulogy he composed for Josef Stalin upon the Soviet dictator's death in 1953. Below are excerpts from that famous masterpiece:

Forever Remember You

The other day, a mother showed
Her small child a picture
Of Mr. Stalin beside a little child.
Wearing a white shirt, surrounded by red clouds,
With gentle eyes and a smile on his face.

On the broad green field
He stood with the child
Who wore a red scarf on his neck.
Toward the future
The two of them gazed together.

Stalin! Stalin!
How much I love it when I hear my child
    learn to say your name!
The first word he can speak is "Stalin!"

In days past we were chained and mistreated.
With You alone was there freedom every day!
Tomorrow, people will have fields to plow.
Tomorrow independence. Who will we remember for this?

This favor falls on two shoulders –
One Uncle Ho's, and the other Yours . . .

This incredible work is punctuated with a refrain that will likely never be forgotten:

I love my papa and mama, I love my husband
And myself just once. But You I love ten times!
I love my child, I love my country and race.
However much I love, I love You so much!

Dear Reader, this is not a joke; these are the actual words of To Huu's poem. The writer could not have made a greater fool of himself if he had walked up and down the streets of Hanoi with his drawers hanging down at his knees. And this great poet is currently a high government official in Hanoi! (Stanley Karnow would likely call this a "nationalist poem.")

How about the pro-Communist writers in the South? In 1975, Hanoi published a review entitled *Literature of the Southern Liberation* (Van Hoc Giai Phong Mien Nam.) The author – with the unlikely name of Pham Van Si (Pham the Literature Scholar) – names the "best" writers of South Vietnam before 1975, his list including Huynh Minh Sieng, Tran Hieu Minh, Nguyen Trung Thanh, Anh Duc, Huong Trieu, Thanh Hai, et. al. Most of these are unknowns. All of them received training in the North and some are even ranking Communist officials. Huong Trieu (or Hieu Truong) is the pen name of Tran Bach Dang, head of the Communist artists association. If these writers never achieved popularity, it is not because of censorship. The fact is their work is terrible and the readers of the South, as in the rest of the civilized world, had no taste for socialist literature.

Most artists of talent in the North were quietly disposed of in the 1940s and '50s. In coming to power, Ho's government "dispatched large numbers of intellectuals to army camps, factories, production units, and so on" where they were forced to write propaganda under the supervision of uneducated cadres. (10)

After the Land Reform, Ho Chi Minh's government instigated a phony free speech movement to lure intellectuals into the open and then crack down on them. Ho's old enemy, Phan Khoi, provided innocent bait when he attacked the government and Party as well as the Communist Arts and Letters Association, which had been producing nothing of artistic value since its creation. Hanoi pretended to advocate freedom of the press just long enough to learn who its "enemies" were. The intellectual publications, especially *Nhan Van* (Humanities), *Giai Pham Mua Thu* (Autumn Literary Works) and *Tram Hoa* (One Hundred Flowers), continued to criticize the government until all were suspended, their editors and contributors accused of "sabotage," "revisionism," debauchery and anything else the government writers could think of. Writers and artists were imprisoned or forced to "go to the countryside, factories, mines and army units, to perform manual work and study the practical life of the people." They were mistreated and many of them died. Three hundred actors and actresses were sent to perform hard labor in the countryside (perhaps we should say they "rallied" to the countryside) and the Ministry of Culture rewarded up to half its personnel with the same fate. (11)

Some of the figures in this intellectual movement included Tran Dan, Phung Quan, Van Cao (who wrote the national anthem used by Ho's government), Quang Dung, Tran Duy, Nguyen Huu Dang, Thuy An, Bui Quang Doai, Hoang Cam, and others.

Meanwhile, literature in the non-Communist part of the country enjoyed an opportunity to develop. While the Saigon government was not without its critics, the difference between North and South was like night and day. For example, Saigon had more than 40 different newspapers during the time of the 1971 presidential elections, a number Hanoi could never even begin to compare with.

A prime example of the gross unpopularity of Communism among artists is the story of Nhat Linh. One of the most famous writers of the modern Vietnamese era, Nhat Linh was co-founder of the group called the "Self-Strengtheners" which brought literature, national

pride and modern ideas to Vietnamese society. Nhat Linh was
involved in politics and even served briefly with the Viet Minh
government in the 1940s. Unable to accept the Viet Minh's
Communist leaders, he quit his post and fled, chased by an
assassination squad. Eventually the writer settled in the South
where he continued to create novels and short stories; his works
were part of the required curriculum for literature study in the
schools. Nhat Linh, however, was opposed to the Diem government
and implicated in an unsuccessful plot against Diem in 1962. To
avoid being arrested he committed suicide. While he could have
joined the NLF in opposition to Diem, he preferred to die rather than
cooperate with the Communists.

Among the talented writers of the South from 1954 to 1975 were
these: Vu Hoang Chuong (poet; died in a Communist re-education
camp); Doan Quoc Si (author; served term in a prison camp); Vo
Phien (author and scholar; a refugee); Duyen Anh (prolific
author of novels and short stories; spent several years in a re-
education camp, now a refugee); Nha Ca (woman author especially known for her portrayals of how the war affected the common
people; recently arrested and sent to a re-education camp for the
second time); Nguyen Manh Con (died in prison); the list goes on
and on. These writers, of course, are not mentioned in the television
series. Perhaps this is because their names are not to be found in
the Communist literature books, which seem to be the only
resources used by the producers of Part 6.

Nor do the producers note that after "liberating" the South the
Communists began a campaign to confiscate and burn books
opposed to the Party line. Even today the authorities continue to
arrest and punish individuals who publish and sell "reactionary"
material.

Now, let us ask again: Artists and writers rallied to the cause?

(Karnow's views of the Communists up to Tet appear here and
there throughout the book before Chapter 12. The Chief Correspondent admires the courage and determination of the North
Vietnamese and tells their story with sympathy. For a moment,
reading the accounts of teenage nurse Tran Thi Truyen, or napalm-
victim Ho Thanh Dam, one might even believe the North Viet-

namese are human after all. (pp. 455-8) But Stanley Karnow does not let us down; as the narrative continues, he smothers his subjects in speculation and mythology until they regain their phantom-like characters. For instance, Karnow claims that the North Vietnamese and Viet Cong regulars needed no persuasion or indoctrination before going off to fight, for nationalism is second nature to them. "They had been raised on the legends of Vietnam's resistance to Chinese rule, and their fathers or uncles or older brothers had fought against the French. They were thus convinced from the start of the righteousness of their mission." (p. 460-1) Such overstatement ignores reality. How many uncles, fathers and brothers died in war? How many more should be sacrificed and how long should the war go on? And what about the many fathers and brothers who learned to hate the Communists during those years of oppression? Did nothing move these people? Were they made of stone?

(Historically, the Vietnamese Communist leadership has never had much regard for human life. Neither Gen. Giap nor Ho Chi Minh cared how many people had to die as they pursued their goals. The Communists risked the lives of their own civilians by locating military bases right in their back yards or forcing them to retrieve artillery rounds or working them to death in the jungles. Thousands of soldiers perished in the big offensives waged throughout the war. Thus it is with great scepticism that we consider Pham Van Dong's tears for "the suffering and losses" of his people. (p. 458) Even now Premier Dong shows no trace of compassion for the Hmong he is slaughtering in Laos or the Cambodians his soldiers are trampling on, not to mention the thousands of Vietnamese in concentration camps in his own country.

(Karnow's description of criticism and self-criticism "forums" makes them resemble Sunday school classes rather than political training. It is hard to believe that Karnow lived in Hong Kong for many years, right on the threshold of Mao's Communist nation.)

Footnotes

1. Gloria Emerson, review for *National Catholic Reporter*, September 30, 1983
2. Vu Tue, "Two Hours With Scholar Hoang Van Chi", *Xac Dinh*, No. 1, April-June 1983
3. For reviews of the Land Reform, see Bernard Fall, *The Two Vietnams*, Chapter 8; Hoang Van Chi, *From Colonialism to Communism*, Chapter 15; Douglas Pike, *History of Vietnamese Communism*, Chapter 6
4. George Carver, "The Faceless Viet Cong", reprinted in *Vietnam: Anatomy of a Conflict*, pp. 322-3
5. Wesley Fishel, *Vietnam: Anatomy of a Conflict*, p. 289
6. Ibid., p. 290
7. George Carver, Note 4 above, p. 332
8. Douglas Pike, Note 3 above, pp. 283-4
9. Hubbell, *P.O.W.*, p. 188
10. P. J. Honey, "Ho Chi Minh and the Intellectuals", reprinted in *Vietnam: Anatomy of a Conflict*, p. 159
11. Ibid., pp. 165-6

Supplements

(Ed.- The following poem was written in North Vietnam by the writer Le Dat. The poem was intended to describe Chairman Ho, consequently its author was arrested, a prelude to the anti-intellectual movement. A lime pot is a little bowl in which lime is kept to be mixed with the ingredients of a betel quid. It is a common implement often found outside the village gates in North Vietnam.)

> *Those who live a long life*
> *Are just like the lime pot.*
> *The longer they live, the worse*
> *   the shape they're in.*
> *And the shallower they get inside.*

(Ed. – Writer Hoang Cam was born in 1921 in Hai Duong province, North Vietnam. He joined the anti-French resistance and became a member of the Communist Party in 1951. So strongly was he influenced by Marxist ideology that he denounced his own earlier writings and adopted the Communist style. His enthusiasm for Communism waned after two short years, especially after the brutal Land Reform. Hoang Cam returned to his former ways and began criticizing the Party. The editors of *The Hundred Flowers in North Vietnam*, published in Saigon in 1959, wrote: "The story of Hoang Cam is proof that a person with the soul of an artist who truly loves freedom can never fit into the Communist mold." Three decades later, the situation had not changed. On August 20, 1982, Hoang Cam was arrested in Hanoi for having given a collection of his poems to a foreign visitor. Amnesty International has named him a "Prisoner of Conscience.")

Little Child of Six

I.   The little child of six
     Searches for something to eat.
     His papa executed as a bullying landlord
     To pay a blood debt before the peasants.
     His mama left him on his own
     And escaped to the South.

     When first he was born,
     He ate well and had a bed to sleep in,
     A flowered blouse and clothes enough.
     He was so happy then!

     Then the great wave rolled in
     And no one gave a thought to such
                         a little one.
     But people with other people
     Still know how to have compassion.

A hungry man
Hobbles off, looking for crabs.
He sees the child, his papa and mama
            gone now
And he so scrawny.
He feels pity for this orphan
And gives him a bit of rice.

His arms and legs are like twigs.
His belly is swollen and his neck is narrow.
His eyes are round and red
As he gauges life in bewilderment.
"Please, Grandma, a bowl of rice soup.
A little rice for me, sir."

II.   *There is a female cadre*
      Active in the village movement.
      All at once the young woman turns
                  to an alley
      Hearing the sound of lost crying.

She shudders now to recall
A long time ago when she, too, was hungry.
She was only five then,
Licking the food wrappings fallen
            on the ground in the market.

The young woman runs to the alley
And takes the little child to her home.
A handful of rice she has saved —
She breaks off half for the child.

A female peasant and key cadre,
Turns away with tears in her eyes.
"He is a landlord's child.
So small, what does he know?
The other day I gave him a bowl of soup.
They investigated me for three days."

This cadre of the Land Reform drew back
Looking on the little orphan child,
Searching him for a sign of the enemy
But seeing only a human being.

When the little child had eaten his fill
And lay on the floor asleep,
The young woman thought, "When I marry,
I hope I have a baby as pretty as this."

III. The cadre is discharged from duty
      Because of this incident.
      In a cold dark room late at night,
      The lamp glows as she composes her
          self-denunciation.

      By a tongue that has no bones
      So that it can be twisted any way,
      By eyes so puny
      They cannot see very far,
      By brains so lazy
      Whose color is that of rust
      Sleeping soundly for many years
      On the silent pages of a book,
      By robot people
      Full of thews and sinews but lacking a heart ...

IV. "Associated with reactionaries!" they say,
     "Lost vigilance in her ideology!"
     For nights she weeps unceasingly
     As the lamp shines dimly
     And she asks herself the question,
     "Why did I love the enemy's child?
     If I had hated him,
     My heart would be at peace now!"

(Ed. – As this book was being written, it became known that author Doan Quoc Si was arrested by the Communists for the second time since the fall of Saigon. His first prison term lasted from 1976 to 1980 and he had been released only after protests from international humanitarian organizations. News of his recent arrest came from his daughter living in Australia. Translation excerpts from one of Doan Quoc Si's works can be found following Parts 2 and 3 in this book.)

PART 7: TET 1968

The Communists launch a major offensive in South Vietnam during the Lunar New Year. The biggest battles are at Hue and Khe Sanh, as fighting erupts even in the capital. Although the offensive is both a military and political defeat for the Communists, it proves to be a turning point in America's war effort. President Johnson begins de-escalation of U.S. involvement and decides not to run for re-election.

Fresh Ambitious Offensive

The Communists lost big with their Tet Offensive of 1968. The Viet Cong were crushed. Every attack was thrown back and none of the political objectives was met. The effort failed to rally popular support for the Communists or topple the Saigon government, contrary to Hanoi's predictions. Tet 1968 proved the ultimate weakness of the revolutionary movement.

This should seem surprising to those who viewed the first six parts of the *Television History*. Up to now the series has shown the Communists as popular heroes with a just cause, namely that of expelling foreign aggressors. They are able to mobilize the masses simply by uttering the sacred name of Ho Chi Minh. A stalwart tribe, the North Vietnamese and Viet Cong remain undaunted amidst the heaviest bombing in world history. The people's patriotism is maintained by an iron-clad will to win. Meanwhile, the other side is inept, clumsy, unpopular, dependent on American aid and bound to lose anyway. Had viewers been asked to predict the outcome of Tet based on this information, they might have concluded, as did Stanley Karnow in Hong Kong during the early days of the Offensive, "Only time will tell. But so far the Communists have shown that if they lack the strength for a clear-cut victory, they are dynamic enough to stave off defeat." (1)

M. Karnow's assessment proved incorrect, yet after 14 years and despite subsequent revelations he apparently has not changed his opinion.

The *Television History* makes no attempt to reconcile its rosy portrayal of the Communists with their utter defeat at Tet. Rather, the series tries to make the defeat look as glorious as possible – the Viet Cong may have lost, but they sure looked good doing it! We see snipers in the Embassy Compound holding off defenders. VC raiders seize the Saigon radio station. Valiant North Vietnamese battle it out for a month in Hue and divert valuable American troops at Khe Sanh. The narrator remarks, "The consternation was indeed maximum," thereby playing mind-reader for the entire country of South Vietnam. A map with blinking lights illustrates how the Viet Cong "hit nearly every province and district capital across South Vietnam." Comrade Dang Xuan Teo relates how his men occupied the radio station and eventually sacrificed themselves by blowing up the place when reinforcements did not arrive. North Vietnamese Capt. Tran Dinh Thong describes the objectives at Khe Sanh: "to inflict casualties on the enemy . . . thus compelling him to shift more of his forces there from the southern part of the country" so the South could be liberated.

The series does not mention that the Embassy was cleared out in only a few hours, power at the radio station had been shut off while Saigon broadcasting took place from an alternate site, nearly every attacking force was pushed back in one to three days and the majority of the fighting across the country was done by South Vietnamese troops. The battles were so brief in some places that many people (including some Viet Cong attack units) had no idea a major offensive was supposed to be taking place. (Where's the "consternation"?) The attack touched 36 of 44 province capitals and only 64 of 242 district capitals, not "nearly every" one. (2) No one asked Dang Xuan Teo how he escaped from the radio station or what happened to the expected reinforcements in his magnificent raid. As for Khe Sanh, there is no comment on the huge number of casualties suffered by the North Vietnamese; instead we are told how clever they were for allegedly diverting a small number of U.S. troops from other areas!

Thus, by distorting some essential facts and substituting flashy scenes of fighting along with an overestimate of the striking force, the series gives a less than accurate impression of the Tet Offensive. The important questions about Tet are ignored. The producers might have asked: Where was the general uprising the Communists expected? Why did the Communists murder thousands of people in Hue? What good was the sacrifice of 10,000 or more men at Khe Sanh if the only purpose for fighting was to direct attention away from other areas where the Communists were losing badly as well? What happened to the "genius" of military strategy, Vo Nguyen Giap?

Not a single one of these issues is investigated. Nor does the series try to find out why a devastating defeat for the Communists should be perceived by many Americans as a defeat for the U.S. This issue is hinted at right at the beginning of Part 7, through comments by Walt Rostow and Harry McPherson, but then removed from our attention by the scene of Gen. Loan blowing the brains out of a Viet Cong in the streets. Gen. Loan becomes the symbol of all that was wrong with the war while Dang Xuan Teo, who ran away while his comrades died, represents the heroic Communists!

This is the oddity of the *Television History*: its perspectives and priorities baffle and amaze, much like a circus act. But "Tet 1968" is nòt a turning point for this series; it is just one of 13 similar events.

(Karnow's companion book is a study in hyperbole. The reader learns that the "audacious" Viet Cong launched a "carefully coordinated series of attacks" that "exploded around the countryside like a string of firecrackers." The Communists "hurled" a division at the U.S. base at Bien Hoa. Rockets "ripped" into a place called "Locbinh," where they supposedly blew an ammunition dump "sky high." Masterfully ignoring the Allies' superior air mobility, the Viet Cong "blocked roads to prevent American and South Vietnamese reinforcements from reaching Saigon." As American officers were "dazzled" by the "dimensions of (the) offensive," Communist forces "crashed" into Hue. And so on. The only thing that could put a halt to the Communists' genius attack was "overwhelming American and South Vietnamese military power, its destructive capacity brought to bear with uncommon fury." (pp. 523-529) If this type of sensationalized reporting is typical of war histories, then writers may have to destroy journalism in order to save it.

(Furthermore, one might question Karnow's sources of information. His reference to a place called "Locbinh" could not be confirmed by this writer; perhaps he meant Long Binh, near Bien Hoa, the U.S. Army base which was attacked by a Viet Cong regiment and defeated by the efforts of Col. Frederic Davidson, of the 199th Infantry Brigade. Likewise, Karnow must be joking with his contention that the Viet Cong were able to block American and South Vietnamese reinforcements heading for Saigon. The Chief Researcher apparently neglected to read Gen. Westmoreland's account of the Tet Offensive, in which he notes that "American battalions took positions on roads leading into (Saigon) lest enemy reinforcements seek to enter." (3) Mr. Karnow does not seem to know who blocked whom.)

Saigon: Once in a Lifetime

The narrator tells us that just prior to Tet 1968 Pres. Johnson had "orchestrated a campaign of optimism" about the war situation. At the same time, Ho Chi Minh "approved a bold offensive" that was expected to shake up the war and "open the way to power" (this phrase is not explained). Ho's own campaign of optimism to encourage the troops to engage in this major battle is sidestepped by the series. Likewise, there is no mention of Ho's predictions of a general uprising, which, of course, never materialized. But Viet Cong attacked the U.S. Embassy in Saigon, and "the center of American power in Vietnam had come under fire." The heroic VC also took the radio station in an effort the interviewee calls a "once in a lifetime assignment." It proved to be so literally, since all of his comrades perished in a suicide explosion. The scene closes with a lingering shot of an ARVN soldier picking the pocket of a corpse (this scene symbolizing "looting").

The radio station and Embassy were just two of many "key targets throughout Saigon" that the Viet Cong were to attack. There were others not mentioned in the program whose results deserve attention. A dozen Viet Cong attacked the Vietnamese

Naval headquarters; all but two died within a few minutes . . . of course, before television cameras could arrive to record the scene. A Viet Cong battalion sent to "liberate" prisoners in the Saigon jail got lost and ended up fighting for their lives in a cemetery a mile away from their objective. Two Viet Cong battalions overran ARVN guards at the Armored and Artillery Command only to discover that the tanks they were looking for were gone and the artillery had been rendered useless by having the breechblocks removed. For a while, attackers did occupy the Phu Tho racetrack; to this day military analysts are trying to unravel Gen. Giap's unique genius in selecting this strategic site. The attack on Tan Son Nhut airbase was quickly stemmed while the Viet Cong took on heavy casualties. (4) But these instances of VC bungling do not find their way into the PBS series' version of Tet.

While the series glorifies the attack on the Embassy, it neglects to mention that the VC were unable to carry out orders to assassinate top government officials in Saigon. These key targets included Pres. Thieu, Gen. Nguyen Ngoc Loan, Gen. Linh Quang Vien (head of Central Intelligence), Lt. Col. Nguyen Van Luan (a high police official) among others. Americans such as Ambassador Bunker were also fingered. (5) The execution of a VC agent in the streets suddenly seems less appalling when one considers that the VC had orders to actively seek out and assassinate "reactionaries," "tyrants," and "traitors," among whose numbers Gen. Loan was counted. Had the tables been turned and Gen. Loan made the victim, would international attention have been paid to the incident? Would Stanley Karnow have batted an eyelash?

Eddie Adams was the photographer who won an award for his still shot of Gen. Loan executing the VC prisoner. He later recalled the awards ceremony in Holland when "tears came to my eyes – but they weren't tears of happiness. They were for Gen. Loan." Adams believed that by recording the scene of a soldier killing his enemy during wartime, the photographer had destroyed the general's life. Now, to the Communist Vietnamese, Adams is a hero; a copy of his photo is displayed in Hanoi's war museum. (6)

Now too the incident has been recorded for history by PBS. Neither Hanoi nor the television series finds it important enough to talk about what the VC agent had been doing before his summary execution.

The worst fighting in Saigon took place in the residential sections of the city. The Viet Cong were cleared out by the ARVN and Saigon police, with assistance from the Americans. The Viet Cong had moved into the populated areas to use civilians as a shield. In the fighting, isolated parts of the city were destroyed, only a small part of the total area of Saigon. The fighting threatened civilians more than it did the South Vietnamese or American forces, which says something about Viet Cong military tactics. However, this point never enters into the discussion of the Viet Cong offensive. Instead, the documentary gives the impression that the Viet Cong effected a master military stroke in the capital city.

(Karnow calls the attack on the capital the Communists' "boldest stroke" in the offensive. The Chief Correspondent goes so far as to describe it as an "upheaval." (p. 529) Dang Xuan Teo and his suicide squad get full coverage, of course, but not those who won the battle. Gen. Loan is professionally painted as a "crude cop" whose "fierce" mood at Tet was due to the fact that "Communist invaders had killed several of his men – including one gunned down with his wife and children." (p. 529) That is all Karnow says about Gen. Loan's motives for shooting a VC agent, but he uses this incident as an example of how his book "can get into complexities" while the *Television History* is more limited. (7) One wonders why the television series could not have mentioned even that brief sentence. In the Fox Butterfield review of the series, Karnow is quoted as saying the series provides no commentary on the execution because that would not be "the adult way." (8))

Hue: The Hidden Massacre

During the occupation of Hue, Viet Cong and North Vietnamese soldiers conducted a massacre of the city's residents. Thousands of bodies were later found in mass graves. Some of the victims had been buried alive; others were beaten or shot. There remained thousands more who were not accounted for even when more graves were discovered long after Tet. The story of the massacre was hardly covered by the news media at the time and as a consequence a good number of Americans never knew that it happened at all.

In pursuit of "balance," the *Television History* provides two accounts of this awful massacre. One comes from a refugee, who refuses to let her name be used to avoid jeopardizing the lives of her relatives in Vietnam. The other is from two Communists, neither of whom is identified as such by the program. (One, Pham Thi Xuan Que, is noted as a "Viet Cong" in the transcript for Part 7. The other, Hoang Phu Ngoc Tuong, is well known by those who were in Hue at the time.) The refugee relates how her father was taken away to a "study session" and never heard from again. The two cadres stress their attempts to maintain discipline during the Communist occupation, to prevent reprisals, but according to one, "The people (of Hue) so hated those who had tortured them in the past that . . . they rooted out those despots" like "poisonous snakes" to keep them from committing further "crimes."

Thus, the Communist version of the massacre is that "the people of the city took justice into their own hands" and so systematically murdered thousands of people. But it leaves out crucial facts. The series says nothing of blacklists and their widespread use in South Vietnam by the Communists. Such lists were prepared for Hue and other cities for Tet. Nowhere is there mention that if the Communists had managed to take control of other cities and towns similar atrocities would have occurred there as well. There is no hint that in the takeover of Hue the Communists gunned down civilians who refused to cooperate with the "revolution" by turning over their Honda motorcycles or helping carry ammunition. The program does not identify Hoang Phu Ngoc Tuong, a Communist agitator among the college students and member of the local revolutionary government when the "revolution came to Hue." Comrade Tuong personally led Communist troops to the homes of assassination targets. The series says the victims were officials, officers, priests and students, but omits the others: women, children, old people and foreigners. None of the above information is secret, yet the producers apparently consider these things irrelevant. Communist reports of the incident mentioned the killings and even described them as a "victory." (9)

And the series does not explain why the American news media all but ignored reports of the massacre while concentrating instead on damage to the city caused by the U.S. forces trying to pound the occupiers out of their entrenched positions. Communist killings do not seem to make headlines.

(Karnow tries to be "balanced" about the massacre, astutely concluding that "the Communist brutality did take place – perhaps on an even larger scale than reported during the war." (p. 530) However, he claims that "clandestine South Vietnamese teams slipped into Hue after the Communist occupation to assassinate suspected enemy collaborators" and throw their bodies into the graves alongside the victims of the Communists! (p. 531) Karnow does not cite his source for this, but it would be interesting to hear how the "clandestine teams" got into Hue, dragged their victims several kilometers outside of the city, located hidden graves in "riverbeds, coastal salt flats, and jungle clearings," dug up the graves, dumped the victims in, recovered the graves and then slipped away without telling anyone that thousands of people were being murdered by the Communists! Karnow notes that Communist Gen. Tran Do called pictures of the massacre "fabrications" and said the whole thing never happened. (p. 530) The Chief Correspondent describes as "paradoxical" the little attention given the Hue atrocities by the American public which was preoccupied with the My Lai incident. (p. 530) It might make more sense to wonder about the news media, whose reports were all the American public had to learn about the war from.)

The inclusion of the Hue massacre in the series serves two purposes, other than the obvious historical one. First, it makes up for the gross omission of the event by the news media at the time, thereby covering up one of the major failings of Tet news reporting. Secondly, the story of an alleged Communist atrocity "balances" off an earlier story of an alleged American atrocity (Thuy Bo, Part 5). By citing atrocities of both sides, the producers apparently feel they have fulfilled their responsibility for treating the war in an even-handed manner. However, they fail to take note of significant differences in the two presentations, differences which may influence viewer perception of the events.

In the account of the Thuy Bo incident of 1967, we hear from three witnesses who are alleged to be victims of the American atrocity. Two of them are elderly women – who is going to argue with a couple of grandmothers? The third witness is an apparent Communist cadre, identified only as a person who had been in the fourth grade at the time of the slaughter. The American side is defended by Pvt. Jack Hill, who admits that he cannot speak for everyone in his unit, and to a lesser extent by Capt. Edward Banks, who led the American unit into Thuy Bo. Through Parts 4 and 5, the viewers have already seen the Americans as killers, sometimes taking delight in their tasks, which include burning homes and the harsh treatment of villagers or zapping running prey from helicopters. Villagers have always appeared as innocent civilians. Part 5 had just shown one American veteran describe having nightmares because he killed an unarmed 60-year-old woman. The killing of civilians is echoed later in the program as well, further supporting the image of the American soldier-killer. In short, the whole atmosphere of the program works against the Americans.

As for the Hue incident, the viewers see only one single victim, a refugee too afraid of the Communists to give her name in public. Her insistence on remaining anonymous is never clarified for the viewers, most of whom likely did not pay attention to the fact that her name does not appear on the screen. The woman is countered by two Communists, neither of whom is identified as such. Throughout the program, unidentified Vietnamese informants are used without any comment as to their credibility – why should these two be any different? The series has not given any indication that the Communists had a policy of liquidation throughout the war, consequently there is no reason for doubting one cadre's claim that the local people rose up in indignation and took justice into their own hands. The program omits reference to relevant information, including blacklists and official Communist directives. As a result, a case can be made in support of the claims made by the cadres to at least diminish their responsibility for the slayings.

But the issue is more sensitive than that. Available evidence places responsibility for the massacre squarely on the Communists. This suggests that the two cadres interviewed were lying. If the producers accepted the guilt of the Communists at Hue, are they then suggesting that Jack Hill and Edward Banks were lying when talking about what happened at Thuy Bo? And are they concluding for us that the Marines were guilty of an atrocity there? Let the readers decide.

The story of the Hue massacre ends with a reference to

predictions of a bloodbath, which many feared might occur once the Communists took over South Vietnam. The producers will return to this theme in Part 13, pointing out that indeed there was no publicized bloodbath on the same order as the Hue massacre. The impression given is that the Communists were restrained and disciplined, enough so that Hue was just an aberration. Meanwhile, for the Americans, burning hootches, killing chickens and pigs and dropping handgrenades into holes to root out peasants was just part of the procedure.

Hue: Saved but Destroyed

Hue was rescued from the Communists, but large sections of the city were left in ruins. Marine Capt. Myron Harrington explains that the Americans did not use their firepower indiscriminately, but "when we had to destroy a house, we destroyed it." As one would expect, the captain is followed by a Hue resident, Nguyen Thi Hoa, who describes how her neighborhood was destroyed in what the viewers might surmise was an unnecessary fashion. Homes using "kerosene and gasoline" (sic) burst into flames when hit by rockets. And what report from the Communists would be complete without the horrible deaths of "old folks – children and pregnant women who could not flee"? One is reminded of the words of old Mrs. Ngo Thi Hien in Part 6 who said, "Wherever the Americans went, they burned and destroyed and killed. I didn't see any guerrillas being killed, only villagers."

No one questions that American firepower caused damage in Hue – it was the military's method of rooting out an entrenched enemy. It is not suprising that residents should be upset about the destruction of their homes and property. But the series says nothing of the damage caused by the Viet Cong – the holes punched in the walls to facilitate house-to-house fighting; the B-40 rockets; dynamite at the Citadel. The producers could have spoken to a responsible witness who would tell us what truly happened from a sincere sense of grief and loss. Viewers get only the common refrain about the killing of innocent civilians. Nguyen Thi Hoa was not afraid to let her name be used with her testimony because she was doing exactly what the Communist government wanted. Had the producers interviewed refugees about the destruction, there would be less cause for complaint. What is hard to understand is why they insist on talking to people approved by the Communists to describe what ogres the Americans are.

The series gives complete credit to the Americans for freeing Hue, saying nothing of the 11 ARVN battalions involved with the three U.S. battalions there. From the show it would appear that the ARVN did nothing but raise the flag when the battle was done. The series once again fails to note the extent of losses suffered by the Communist forces: 5,000 dead inside the city, 3,000 lost nearby. This compares with 384 South Vietnamese and 142 Americans. (10)

Khe Sanh: A Costly Diversion

The Khe Sanh outpost was located just below the Demilitarized Zone in the mountains by the Ho Chi Minh Trail. North Vietnamese troops laid seige to the base from late January until March. While the Communists never seriously threatened Khe Sanh, the seige received considerable news coverage. Every battle of the Tet Offensive except Hue was over and done with within days, but Khe Sanh was sustained and enjoyed "inherent dramatic values" that "filled a journalistic need" for the news media. (11) For weeks the media speculated as to whether or not Khe Sanh would be America's Dien Bien Phu.

The *Television History* declines to deal with the Dien Bien Phu analogy, largely promoted by the media at the time. It also refuses to mention how many North Vietnamese soldiers perished in the fighting around Khe Sanh with intensive U.S. bombing to protect the outpost, losses estimated at 10,000 to 15,000 by Westmoreland. (12) Instead, it attempts to turn this gruesome disaster into a strategic victory for the Communists! From Capt. Tran Dinh Thong of the North Vietnamese Army we learn that the Communists' "real purpose in fighting there" was not to seize the place but to divert American forces away from the southern part of the country so the liberation forces could accomplish their task. Westmoreland guessed wrongly – and that is the last we hear of the battle! Aren't those Communists clever?

Actually, the North Vietnamese Army's purpose in concentrating on Khe Sanh was never really clear. This may have been due to the loss of a North Vietnamese headquarters "in a limestone cave in Laos" that was bombed in January. (13) The headquarters was out of commission for two weeks and that strategic loss may have accounted for the confusion that resulted in the North Vietnamese strategy. Westmoreland was prepared for a major engagement and later listened with "wry amusement" to claims that the North Vietnamese had intended to simply tie up American troops on the hill. The general points out that more than 15,000 Communist troops were tied down at Khe Sanh in the early stage of the battle and more came to reinforce their comrades; the North Vietnamese eventually suffered tremendous casualties.

Compare this to the allies defending the base: one reinforced American regiment of about 6,000 men, comprising just one-sixtieth of the total U.S. and Allied battalion strength in South Vietnam. The general concludes, "How can anybody legitimately question who was tying down whom?" (14) The television series seems to consider the word of a Communist captain more valuable than that of an American general. Yet even the comments of Capt. Thong suggest that the North Vietnamese had hoped to score a major victory at Khe Sanh. The captain concedes, "But because we drew larger enemy forces into Khe Sanh, and allowed them to supply and reinforce themselves, *we could not turn the encounter into a final big battle.*" (Emphasis added) This may be the closest the Communists come to admitting their Dien Bien Phu failed.

(Karnow implies that Westmoreland feared Khe Sanh would be similar to the Dien Bien Phu siege, an idea he calls "preposterous". (p. 540) In fact, Westmoreland personally studied comparisons of the two situations and emerged confident that the U.S. could not suffer a defeat similar to that of the French. The general also received letters of encouragement from French officers who had served at Dien Bien Phu. (15) But Karnow clings to the "diversion" theory and states that "Westmoreland fell for the enemy's ruse" (p. 542). The Chief Correspondent's total of North Vietnamese troops at Khe Sanh is 40,000, twice as many as Westmoreland suggests, thus making the question "who was tying down whom?" even more relevant.)

The ARVN at Tet

In his assessment of the Tet Offensive, General Westmoreland concludes: "In the main, the Tet Offensive was a Vietnamese fight. To the ARVN, other members of the South Vietnamese armed forces, the militia, the National Police – to those belonged the major share of credit for turning back the offensive. Some officials failed; an occasional commander proved incompetent; but over all, when put to a crucial test, no ARVN unit had broken or defected." (16)

Peter Braestrup, commenting on the ARVN's performance during Tet remarks: "The South Vietnamese units' performance varied widely under the shock, but, overall, their stout resistance was an essential factor in Hanoi's military failure." (17) Furthermore, contrary to predictions by observers such as John Kenneth Galbraith, the ARVN did not "collapse." (18)

In the *Television History*, Elsworth Bunker states that the "Vietnamese armed forces . . . have demonstrated their capability (and) turned in an excellent performance."

Bunker's comment, presumably his personal opinion and not that of the producers, would appear to be a joke, at least when compared to the scenes of the ARVN shown in Part 7: a soldier steals a wallet from a corpse, ARVN troops raise their flag at Hue while the Americans are doing all the fighting. The ARVN are rarely seen fighting in Tet, even though they played a major part in the battle. Why is this the case? That is part of the big story.

The Pen is Mightier than the Sword

The Tet Offensive proved to be a considerable defeat for the Viet Cong. Yet most people in the U.S. received the impression that the battle was a defeat for the U.S. and South Vietnam. This discrepancy between reality and impression has been generally attributed to the distortion of news coverage of Tet.

In his study of media coverage of Tet, Peter Braestrup concludes that news stories of the event were "a distortion of reality," relaying to America a message of "DISASTER IN VIETNAM." (19) This the author calls a "failure in crisis journalism" where the "special circumstances of Tet" overwhelmed journalism's "special susceptibilities and limitations." Some of the unique factors at play include: the initial shock and the personal impact of the offensive on correspondents' lives, the inability of reporters to cover all points and thus give a complete picture, gaps in information and uncertainty about the scope of the attack, the professional expectations of journalists for dramatic and compact stories, lack of coordination among news sources, the narrow focus of the journalist (as opposed to say, professional researchers), shortcomings in knowledge about Vietnam, limited personal contacts with the Vietnamese (especially the ARVN), the failure to follow up on events and so possibly alter the "disaster" image to a more accurate one, the use of second- and third-hand reports, and a tendency to interpret or explain the offensive to their audience. Braestrup sees no malicious intent on the part of reporters; it was not an "antiwar" sentiment that led to a media conspiracy against Pres. Johnson. But the author does note correspondents' overall lack of optimism about the war's progress and their resentment against Johnson, who they felt had manipulated them in the past. The author also blames Johnson for not "seizing the initiative" in dealing with reporters. This variety of factors brought about the "disaster" of Tet.

Examples of media distortion of Tet as uncovered by Braestrup include the following: exaggerating the force of VC attacks, especially in first reports; emphasis on destruction wrought over the actual successes of the U.S. and South Vietnamese troops; minimizing the enemy's defeat; concentration on the big battles (Hue and Khe Sanh); dramatization of the offensive; depictions of doomsday at Khe Sanh; ignoring or discrediting of ARVN troops; and failure to modify early impressions about the offensive and its meaning. Reports were also tainted by speculation and interpretation (suggesting, for instance, that official spokespersons were being overly optimistic in their reports or commenting on the "unpopularity" of Pres. Thieu). Not all media sources were responsible for the same distortions, nor did they commit errors to the same degree. However, the general impression being given was that of defeat for South Vietnam. So apparent was this idea that one NBC official was later to remark that "Tet was already established 'in the public's mind as a defeat, and therefore it was an American defeat'." (20)

The news was part of the news at Tet.

Peter Braestrup is listed as one of the consultants for the

Television History. The influence of his book is evident in some aspects of Part 7. (The offensive is described by the narrator as a military and political failure; scenes are shown of reporters' involvement at the time.) Yet the series also commits some of the distortions Braestrup points out (minimizing the enemy's failure, discrediting the ARVN, focusing on destruction) and covers up other media errors (depiction of Khe Sanh as America's Dien Bien Phu, inaccuracies in media reports). It pokes fun at television correspondents giving breathless reports as shots are being fired around them, but does not discuss the doubtful merits of interviewing a Marine in the middle of battle. (The soldier talks to a bodiless microphone: "Just hope you can stay alive, day to day. Everybody just wants to go back home and go to school. . . . The whole thing stinks, really." What does one expect the man to say as he loads his rifle for the next round of fire?) Or what of the effects of idle speculation regarding the enemy's motives or methods? (Eg., Stanley Karnow in Hong Kong: "The experts contend there is probably considerable plausibility to the communist thesis that the Vietcong raids could not have been possible without widespread support, particularly in cities and suburban areas." (21) Explain the phrase "probably considerable plausibility" and name your "experts," please.)

Perhaps the most important omission is the issue of how Tet coverage influenced public opinion and the government. Harry McPherson was stunned by the discrepancies between official cables and the television news. Dean Rusk heard from his cousins in Cherokee County who wanted to know "when this war was going to end." Something was up, but the *Television History* declined to find out what.

The media may not be able to tell people what to think, but it can provide a framework in which people can shape their thoughts. Through the sights and sounds of Tet, the news media provided the images and opportunity for those who had doubts about the war, but lacked a vehicle by which to express them. The question of that vehicle's accuracy or inaccuracy is not a trivial one, especially if one intends to educate the public about the past in order to avoid similar problems in the future. Such is apparently not the intention of the PBS series.

(While citing Braestrup's work, Stanley Karnow concludes that "whatever the quality of reporting from Vietnam, the momentous Tet episode scarcely altered American attitudes toward the war." (p. 545) Gazing mystically beyond public opinion surveys, Karnow divines not only the thoughts, but also the feelings of the American people. Prior to Tet, "a plurality of Americans had concluded that the United States had 'made a mistake' in committing combat troops in Vietnam." Most of this number were "dispirited" because Johnson had not prosecuted the war strongly enough. Tet was followed by "a predictable display of patriotic fervor" only to be followed by "despair" as the fighting continued.

(In Karnow's view, not only is it not true that the news media influenced public opinion, but he says, the exact opposite was taking place. Using Walter Cronkite as his prototype, the Chief Correspondent says, "But Cronkite, *like all other journalists*, was lagging behind the American public – reflecting rather than shaping attitudes." (p. 548) (Emphasis added.)

Footnotes

1. Stanley Karnow, "What Are the Viet Cong Trying to Prove?", Washington *Post,* Feb. 2, 1968; quoted in Peter Braestrup's *Big Story,* p. 168

2. Westmoreland, *A Soldier Reports,* p. 399. The total reflects Karnow's estimate: The Viet Cong "surged into more than a hundred cities and towns." (p. 523)

3. Ibid., p. 399

4. Ibid., pp. 396-7

5. Stephen Hosmer, *Viet Cong Repression and Its Implications for the Future,* p. 46

6. Eddie Adams, "The Pictures That Burn in My Memory", *Parade,* May 15, 1983

7. Robert Wells, "New Book Puts Vietnam in Perspective", book review for the Milwaukee *Journal,* October 1983

8. Fox Butterfield, "TV Returns to Vietnam to Dissect the War", New York *Times,* Oct. 2, 1983

9. Stephen Hosmer, Note 5 above, p. 48

10. Westmoreland, Note 2 above, p. 402

11. Peter Braestrup, *Big Story,* p. 257

12. Westmoreland, Note 2 above, p. 422

13. Ibid., p. 385

14. Ibid., p. 412

15. Ibid., pp. 409-10

16. Ibid., p. 403

17. Braestrup, Note 11 above, p. 338

18. Ibid., p. 335

19. Ibid., p. xi

20. Ibid., p. 509

21. "Vietcong Mount Political Offensive", Washington *Post,* February 4, 1968, quoted in Braestrup, *Big Story,* p. 372

Supplements

(Ed. – Author Nha Ca, a part-time resident of Hue, was in that city
during the Tet Offensive. She subsequently wrote an account of the
Hue experience entitled *Giai Khan So Cho Hue* – Wear a Mourning
Band for Hue. The novel became so well known that after the fall of
South Vietnam in 1975, North Vietnamese soldiers looked for the
book because they, too, wanted to know exactly what happened
during Tet. Following are excerpts from the book. Translation.)
(From the author's preface)
. . . The waiting period has come to nearly two years now. Two
years. The remains of ten thousand people of Hue slaughtered,
buried in shallow graves in the brush, thrown in the rivers and
streams, have slowly been collected. The mass graves have grown
over with grass. The ruined houses have stood still for a time. The
lamentation of Hue, the jumbled words about Hue, thus, have lost
some of their clamor.

Here, this is the time when together we can put on our mourning
bands once again, relight the small incense sticks in the vast dark
night of war and mourn, reminiscing about Hue.

Many shots and many types of mourning exploded and destroyed
Hue. That undertaking – I don't know where it originated, but no
matter – the atrocity of the destruction of the historic city of Hue is
something that our generation, our era, must take responsibility
for.

In our generation there was Doan, a girl I once went to school
with, sitting in her university seat in Saigon. Suddenly she was
returning to Hue with a red armband, carrying a gun at her side,
eagerly pursuing this person and shooting that one, becoming an
evil spirit in Hue's last gasp.

In our generation there was Dac, a young, enthusiastic student.
Previously, Dac had written poetry and struggled, and finally he
went off to fight. Then, back in Hue, he set up people's courts,
handed out death sentences to whole groups, and with his own
hands dug a pit, took an old classmate with whom he had had
disagreements and forced him to stand beside the pit to carry out the
death sentence. The young classmate, whose name was Mau Ty,

held up his red armband, the insignia of the liberation forces, and begged.

"Please, Brother! I'm on your side now! I'm wearing the red armband! Long live the revolution! Long live Ho Chi Minh!"

But regardless of how Mau Ty pleaded or cheered the revolution, Dac deliberately fired at his little friend.

In our own generation, crowds of people, hundreds of them, priests and monks, old and young, staggered into the city full of fire, each person grasping a white flag to surrender to either side. They ran, this way and that, until nearly all of them fell.

And, too, in our time, after more than twenty days of this last gasp in Hue, a small dog caught in the crossfire ran barking toward the riverbank. He became the target, the sport of guns perched on the other side of the river. They fired at the terrified creature until he fell into the river. Then they fired at the banks that the dog paddled desperately to reach. The shots were not fired in order to kill him, but only to tease him as he floundered in the stream, just a joke in the war. Hue city – and perhaps our whole miserable country – how is it different from that small dog floundering in the river? Our generation, the generation that prefers the most beautiful words with which to boast, not only must put on a mourning band for Hue, and for our country that has been destroyed, but must bear the crime of Hue, and of our country, too. . . . (pp. 9-12)

* * * * *

Every family, everyone sat together in a group. They looked up warily at the soldiers from the North, whom they were permitted to call the Liberation Army. The soldiers went back and forth, their expressions sometimes earnest, sometimes grave and secretive.

They dared not answer any questions put to them by the strangers.

The people of the neighborhood were also suprised to see not infrequently some of their neighbors, whom just the day before had been wishing them a happy new year, now carrying guns and wearing red neck scarves, watching them with threatening, arrogant eyes. They went openly to visit the neighborhood. One man, a blacksmith, had gotten drunk the night before and exchanged curses with some girls getting water at the well. Now he, too, carried a rifle as he went from home to home. His face broke out into a smile whenever he met someone.

"Don't worry, comrades!" he blustered. "Don't worry, friends! In a few days Uncle Ho will be here and you can celebrate!"

"You don't know?" he said to another. "I've been with the liberation army for a long time! I've been underground!"

The people looked at him and turned pale. They were all frightened. Before they had seen him as a harmless blacksmith. Each night he got drunk and talked bad, picking a quarrel with the children or the girls at the well. But who could say he was not harboring a grudge against someone in the area?

The young sons of a lady who sold pork in the market were also carrying guns for the liberation. An old beggar who used to sit in front of the teahouses had a bright face that day. He went to each house, loudly proclaiming, "The liberation army is here! And I'm so happy! I tell you – no one has done anything here that I don't know all about!"

It was like a threat. The people looked at each other, unable to conceal the worry and sorrow.

At noon, the liberation army came and made everyone go out to the yard. They called on all the young men to go and carry ammunition and the girls to carry the wounded. From age 15 on up – everyone had to go. Only the mothers, whom they called "liberation mothers," women who had just given birth, pregnant women, whom they called "liberation sisters," were to stay at home and help by cooking for the soldiers.

The weeping rose pitifully. In many houses, civilians were dying because of a lack of medicine and bandages. A young soldier standing guard at the crossroads listened, then lit a cigarette ... The weeping grew louder. He had another smoke and frowned. Hesitantly, he decided to enter the nearest house ... The door was ajar and it swung open when he knocked. He walked straight in. Two women looked at him in fear. The children ceased crying. The guard came close and stared at the bodies – not one, but two dead. They were the corpses of a man and a child of about three, his face bruised and covered with blood. A woman stood up as if to shield the corpses from his sight, her eyes imploring.

"Oh, sir! They're all dead. There's no one else for you to take!"...
And she began to cry...

The Northern soldier unwrapped his neckerchief and patted the
man's head. Then he removed his handkerchief and wiped the face
of the little child. He pulled the mat carefully over the child's face....

There was a gunshot – just one – then silence. The liberation
soldier raced outside to the crossing and looked around. Another
soldier standing guard in front of a house about ten meters away
pointed to some bushes by the road. The soldier looked and saw a
young man struggling to crawl onto the road. He had been hit. The
blood trailed behind him on the ground. The soldier ran up to
him...

"Is he dead?" his friend called.

The soldier nodded... Two female cadres came up behind him.
They laughed at their friend.

"Comrade Thu! What are you doing here? You're supposed to
be on guard over there. Go back to your post. Maybe tonight we'll
retreat to the mountains."

One of the girls looked at the corpse.

"What happened? Who shot him? You?"

"No."

"He tried to run away," the friend explained. "I saw him
creeping behind the bushes and shot him."

The other girl looked at the corpse and laughed scornfully.

"He's so fat. Probably drinks American milk!"

The young soldier held his hands in front of his face and stared at
them. He returned to his guardpost... (pp. 122-132)

(Ed. – One important figure in the Tet Offensive was Lt. Col. Tam
Ha, a Communist officer in charge of the assault on Saigon. His
story is not included in the *Television History* or Stanley Karnow's
companion book.)

Tran Van Dac, also known as Tam Ha, was born in Phu Yen
province, Central Vietnam around 1924. In 1945, Tam Ha joined the
Viet Minh to participate in the resistance against the French. After
the Geneva Agreements, Tam Ha regrouped in the North and

received further training. In the late 1950s, he was selected to command a special military battalion of the regular Northern army. This special battalion was composed entirely of officers ranking second lieutenant or higher. Each officer was assigned to organize and command a local military unit in the South. As for Lt. Col. Tam Ha, he acted as secretary and political commissar, making him both a military commander and Party leader. Tam Ha was the first regular unit commander to be sent to the South. While in the Central Highlands, his contacts with the local population began to make him doubt the things his superiors had taught him and the rightness of the cause.

The Communist high command placed Tam Ha in charge of the attack on Saigon during the Tet Offensive of 1968. His headquarters were located in an underground hideout dug beneath a Catholic church in Xom Moi, one of the so-called "Catholic enclaves" created by Pres. Diem more than a decade earlier. The location was very secure, since no one would suspect a Communist operation was being commanded from right underneath an anti-Communist area.

Prior to the Tet attack, Tam Ha moved about the city trying to feel out the mood of the people of Saigon in order to determine how they would respond to the general offensive. He came to the conclusion that the people were not behind the revolution and dutifully reported this to his superiors. The high command reprimanded him for "lacking spirit" and ordered him to continue with plans for the attack. The Tet Offensive was a disaster for the Communists.

A few weeks after Pres. Johnson's television speech in which he announced he would not seek a second term as president, the Communists launched a minor offensive. Not trusting Tam Ha, the high command took precautions to keep him in his headquarters during the attack. However, Lt. Col Tam Ha persuaded the other members of his three-man cell of the futility of the fight. "As one man" the three defected.

PART 8: VIETNAMIZING THE WAR (1968-1973)

The number of American troops in Vietnam decreases as the burden of the ground war falls on the South Vietnamese. American bombing creates three million refugees. Black marketeering, prostitution, and drugs become a part of life in South Vietnam. American soldiers are confronted with new problems in the ranks, including racism, drug abuse and lack of discipline. Presidential elections are held in the South in 1971. The CIA launches the Phoenix Program to identify Viet Cong suspects. The North Vietnamese wage a major offensive in 1972.

The Sick Man of Southeast Asia

Throughout its 13 parts, the PBS series gives evidence of how misleading recorded histories can be if the direction and viewpoints of the historian are narrowly guided. Nowhere is this more apparent than in Part 8, where the one-way camera is applied in its most abusive form. For here the camera focuses primarily on those matters which place South Vietnam and the United States in the most unfavorable light, while denying these matters perspective and proportion. It is like looking at a small ulcer and declaring that the entire body is corrupt. With the sophisticated technology of television, stereotypes may be reinforced and half-truths made whole. All this works to the advantage of the carefully edited *Television History* and its antiwar themes.

The Ugly American

After the Tet Offensive, the war went on and the tragedy of war continued. Through the strategy of Vietnamization, America's role in the ground war decreased, but the presence of large numbers of U.S. troops, the flood of American dollars and merchandise, and new social values and attitudes brought from the States affected the U.S. military and the people of South Vietnam in many ways.

Through interviews with veterans, the *Television History* discovers for its viewers what life in the U.S. military was like during the later war years: It was a comfortable war, with nine-to-five hours, air conditioned bases, air mattresses and beer. Patrol units turned away from known VC positions – the so-called "search and avoid" missions. Unit officers endured frustration along the chain of command. The ARVN would not shoot, or they ran away, leaving the Americans to fight alone. Marijuana cigarettes, soaked in opium could be traded for a box of Tide. Prostitutes were introduced by cab drivers. In some places blacks and whites seemed to be at war with each other. Low ranking soldiers slugged officers; in some cases, attempts were made on officer's lives . . .

It goes without saying that the majority of American soldiers did their duty, obeyed orders and made no attempt to murder their comrades. The majority of soldiers, however, are not exciting enough for television, and so they are not discussed at all in this episode. At the same time, it is true that there were problems in the military during these war years and they merit some attention. But these issues must be reviewed through careful study, not merely by representing bald examples of presumably typical situations based on popular notions. Looking at the issues faced by the military in the late 1960s and early 1970s, what one finds is not exactly what the *Television History* portrays as truth.

In the post-Tet period, the U.S. military was undergoing a "crisis," many of whose symptoms are suggested by the PBS series. The program declines to deal with the problems in any depth, preferring instead to concentrate on the "Vietnam experience" as related by veterans, without adding any explanation or overall context. On the other hand, the series does imply that the problems within the military were unique and inherent offshoots of America's involvement in Vietnam, stemming from the unjust nature of the conflict and growing antiwar sentiment. Since the series does not look at other possible reasons for the military crisis, one might question whether the series' inferences are justified or simply one more unsupportable indictment of "America's war." At this point, it might be helpful to look at some of the issues and review their context to the war.

Drug abuse became a serious problem within the military during the war. A Department of Defense survey showed that in 1971 "50.9 percent of Army personnel in Vietnam had smoked marijuana, 28.5 percent had used narcotics such as heroin and opium, and 30.8 percent had used other psychedelic drugs." (1) Drugs were cheap and easy to obtain, yet according to one observer, "the percentages of drug users (in Vietnam) were not much higher than in other theaters of command" and the majority of these soldiers had used drugs prior to their Vietnam tours. (2) Abuse of drugs and alcohol continued in the military for years even after the war and problems were still being reported in the early 1980s.

Racial consciousness spread in the United States during the 1960s and 1970s, often with militant expressions. Many blacks brought their racial consciousness with them to Vietnam as symbolized in their speech, gestures and close contact with "brothers." The most extreme type of racial identification was the creation of segregated "cities" within some bases. Tension was fed by charges made by a number of black activists in the U.S. that the proportion of blacks dying in the war greatly exceeded the proportion of whites. Not all observers agreed with this. Comparing the Vietnam conflict to previous American wars, Gen. Westmoreland says that the Vietnam war was "the first war in which no vestige of the nation's long-standing social inequality was condoned." (3) Guenter Lewy concedes that there were fewer black officers and a larger proportion of blacks were placed in ground combat units; this, he feels, was a result of "social class and educational differentials" rather than race. Among servicemen in Vietnam, the actual percentage of black soldiers never exceeded 12.5 percent, while in 1973 the percentage of blacks of military age was 13.5 percent of the total population. By the end of the war, blacks had accounted for 12.3 percent of all combat deaths. (4)

Racial concerns were also expressed in relation to the Vietnamese, whom some blacks regarded as "brothers," or victims of racial oppression. Communist propaganda leaflets fed this attitude by urging blacks to stop fighting the "white man's war" and go back home where blacks had their own battle to fight. Black soldiers have reported that at times North Vietnamese units passed them by on patrols or did not snipe at them as they did the whites. All this reinforced the idea of racial solidarity. For the most part, however, blacks and whites fought a common enemy.

General problems in military discipline arose during the later years of the war. Challenges to command ranged from disputes over hair length to demands that soldiers be allowed to unionize. AWOL and desertion rates increased. There were cases of soldiers refusing to obey orders and avoiding contact with the enemy. The number of fragging incidents increased even as the number of American soldiers in the country decreased. In 1969, 126 incidents of fragging were reported; in 1971 the number was 333. However, the total actual deaths from such attacks fell dramatically from 37 in 1969 (or about 33 percent) to 12 in 1971 (less than 4 percent) and intended victims were not always readily identifiable. (5)

At no time did these and other problems reflect the actions of the majority of the U.S. armed forces in Southeast Asia. However, they were serious enough to affect the way the war appeared to Americans.

Still, these problems cannot be fairly seen as the result of America's allegedly mistaken involvement in the war or a reflection of antiwar sentiment. There was little active resistance to the war among GIs and antiwar organizations failed to generate mass support from the troops. Most soldiers seemed to feel they were in the service to do their job on behalf of their country. However, demonstrations and antiwar statements made by officials and other Americans may have hurt the morale of the soldiers, causing them to question their purpose and role in the war and wonder if their sacrifices were being appreciated. The problem was aggravated by the recognition of America's withdrawal from Vietnam and the inability of many government officials to clearly define the goals of America's involvement. Some soldiers were reluctant to risk their lives when everybody else seemed to be going home anyway. As one veteran told this writer, many GIs were becoming survivors, not fighters.

As suggested above, drug and race problems were related to

social conditions in the United States. The same could be said of general discipline problems. Soldiers opposed military dress codes and behavior regulations, which differed markedly from the free life they had been accustomed to at home. Arguments and insubordination mirrored an attitude of disrespect for authority that was growing in the U.S. among young people; it was manifested in the military outside of Vietnam as well.

Deserters or soldiers going AWOL were usually not acting for political reasons. Guenter Lewy writes: "The vast majority of those going AWOL and most deserters during the Vietnam era, as in previous wars, absented themselves not for political reasons but because of personal or financial problems or inability to adjust to military life." (6) That the problem extended beyond the war is evident from the fact that AWOL and desertion rates among the Marines reached a peak in 1975, while figures for the Navy were highest in 1976, a few years after America's role in the war had already ended. (7)

As the military attempted to provide better opportunities for disadvantaged youths, it lowered recruitment standards to attract more people from lower income and educational classes. While this effort was intended to assist youths, it also increased problems: rates for disciplinary problems and court martial convictions among these recruits ran at almost double those for other soldiers. (8) Lower standards and the policy of granting deferments to college students accounted for deficiencies within the leadership ranks. Many unit officers were young and inexperienced, thus inequipped to recognize problems or act to correct them in a timely manner. Being as young as the men they commanded, some unit commanders sought peer approval by becoming lax on regulations. Some officers had chalked up fewer combat hours than the men they commanded; consequently, they were not always greeted with respect and at times their orders appeared foolish or fatal to the battle-wise men. Some soldiers did not see their questioning of orders to be insubordination; they were simply using their heads. Fragging incidents often occurred when personal grudges got out of hand or when soldiers were stoned or drunk.

Another factor contributing to the breakdown of morale was idleness. In 1971, a reporter for *U.S. News and World Report* remarked, "The most persistent enemy the U.S. soldier faces in South Vietnam these days is not the Communists – it seems to be boredom." (9) As the level of military activity declined, soldiers were idle for longer periods of time. The empty hours made many restless and discontented. As if to underscore this, discipline problems tended to occur more in rear line or support units rather than combat areas.

Taking the above ideas into consideration, it can be seen that there were a number of factors leading to troubled conditions in the military after 1968. Describing the matter solely in terms of America's involvement in the war may be a convenient generalization for criticizing the war, but it fails to deal with the more complex realities that presented themselves at the time. The *Television History* is happy to provide a forum for this and other flimsy generalizations, as will be seen below.

In the meantime, it should be kept in mind that despite the difficulties, frustrations and complaints, the Americans and South Vietnamese were still able to hold off the allegedly superhuman forces directed by the "genius" Gen. Giap and his crew from the North. The PBS series makes no attempt to explain this phenomenon.

Deliberate Bombing

Death and destruction in civilian areas is a tragedy of war – all war. During the war in Indochina, critics of American policy charged that the U.S. was conducting a policy of deliberate destruction as a terror tactic with little regard for the lives or wishes of the people of Southeast Asia.

Like other war critics, the *Television History* charges the U.S. with "deliberate" destruction of civilian areas in the effort to drive out the Viet Cong and North Vietnamese. Even as the series makes no attempt to support the claim, which it views as an obvious fact, it never raises questions regarding the war methods of the Communists: using civilians as shields and for forced labor, storing weapons and supplies in the homes of peasants, locating military bases and artillery sites in residential areas, dropping mortars and rockets indiscriminately, killing unarmed refugees, liquidating political opponents, etc.

In *America in Vietnam,* Guenter Lewy compares civilian suffering during the war in Vietnam to that which occurred in World War II and the Korean conflict. (10) Civilian deaths and the destruction of residential areas was considerable during World War II, the result of aerial bombing and ground attacks by both sides. The situation in Korea was proportionately worse, as major cities in that country were devastated and perhaps 70 percent of all lives lost in the war were civilian. By Lewy's reckoning, the proportion of civilian deaths during the Vietnam war was "substantially lower" than in either of the two previous conflicts, although many unfounded claims were being publicized to criticize America's involvement in the war.

Furthermore, Lewy argues that it would be unfair (and unsound) to charge the U.S. with total responsibility for civilian casualties and the disruption of civilian lives. The volume of U.S. bombing has frequently been cited as a measure of America's wanton destructiveness. However, much of the bombing during the war was conducted in sparsely populated areas, particularly in the latter years of the war. Consequently, the proportion of civilian casualties from U.S. air attacks could logically be seen as decreasing during that time.

For their part, the Viet Cong were continually engaging in deliberate terrorist attacks on the civilian population – including assassinations, firing rockets and mortars into villages and refugee camps, mining village roads, etc. The number of civilain deaths caused by these actions would at times be "appallingly high." Meanwhile, the U.S. and South Vietnam conducted no comparable activities and the Viet Cong alone carried out a policy of terror.

With all this in mind, one might well ask why the U.S. was singled out for blame and so earnestly condemned as a criminal during the Vietnam war. Part of the answer seems to be that charges made against the U.S. were based on the emotional attitudes of the accusers instead of on objective facts. Once again, Guenter Lewy compares the situation in Vietnam with that in World War II. During the earlier conflict, says Lewy, the Allies used "terror-bombing" and paid little attention to civilian losses. Still, few people objected to these tactics, which were considered part of the "moral crusade in which the Allies could do no wrong." The eventual victory also vindicated the use of such actions. On the other hand, the war in Southeast Asia was a protracted fight with no clear victory or even the popular image of being a conflict between "good" and "evil." Too, the activities of the Americans were exposed to the world while the Communists pursued their side of the war in secret, with only controlled revelations of their performance. Thus, when the war was reviewed, the U.S. got the worse rap. (11)

Lewy does not feel that Allied military tactics in Indochina were beyond reproach. For instance, he notes the failure of the U.S. to ensure a consistent application of the "rules of engagement," directives regarding the limits on firepower to minimize destruction and death among civilians. Nonetheless, Lewy concludes that charges of systematic and willful criminal behavior on the part of the Allies in Southeast Asia are unsupportable and based on, among other things, ignorance of battlefield conditions and a "tendency to construe every mistake of judgment as a wanton breach of the laws of war." (12)

The PBS series seems to ignore Lewy's findings – a curious move, since Lewy is supposedly a consultant for the program. Perhaps the producers of the series disagree with the style and methods of the U.S. military in the war. They may scoff at evidence of enemy presence in villages and hamlets which precipitated military actions. And they may not be satisfied with Guenter Lewy's arguments regarding America's policy or tactics. Yet it seems difficult for them to justify the use of unsupported statements condemning the U.S. while at the same time neglecting to deal with the dubious activities of the other side. War in all its destructive forms is undesirable. To look at the tragedy of war in an educational manner, the least one might ask for is balance and perspective, not careless and flippant generalizations.

The Ugly Vietnamese

Up until now the viewers have gotten only rare glimpses of the people of South Vietnam, the ones America was supposedly fighting for. These few instances have included anti-government demonstrations "proving" the unpopularity of the Saigon regime, and interviews with presumably innocent civilians who suffered from

America's war policy. We have been told that the U.S. interfered with the wishes of the Vietnamese people and killed civilians, never Viet Cong.

Finally, in Part 8, we get a broader view of the Vietnamese people as the series hopes to record them for history: pimps, whores, dope pushers and black marketeers!

"The American-financed war overheated the economy," says the narrator, and this blank statement is backed up by responses to "key questions" aimed at exposing the rot and corruption of Vietnamese society caused by America. Greedy peddlars make "enormous dope deals" with GIs. Girls shamelessly toss off centuries of tradition and morals to sell themselves for American dollars. One interviewee casually remarks that he "did not see anything bad at all" about selling goods on the black market – obviously a typical response from a typical Vietnamese. In the end of the program, America has abandoned the country, leaving a heap of electrical appliances for a bewildered nation more concerned about cosmetic surgery than warfare. Truly an objective and clear-minded portrayal of a country, is it not?

When the producers selected their "key questions" about Vietnamese society, did they think about the millions of Vietnamese who did not work for the Americans or pilfer from the PXs? Or the vast majority of girls who never entertained thoughts of dishonor-ing their families by becoming prostitutes? Or the people who did not barter drugs or contraband in the streets? And what about the general population who just wanted to survive in peace and raise their families without losing sons or husbands or brothers in war? These questions never came up, for the likely responses would belie the image of total decadence and upheaval in South Vietnam that the producers and Frances Fitzgerald feel very comfortable with.

One might responsibly argue that America's influence on the economy affected the Vietnamese in many ways and disrupted *segments* of the population. One can argue, as well, the relative merits of displaying abundant wealth to an underdeveloped nation without taking into account social values or the necessity of such goods. One can complain, as many have, that America's investors did little to help the South Vietnamese economy develop so that it need not become a one-way funnel for American dollars. But to do as the *Television History* does and describe all of South Vietnam as a land of corruption and greed is senseless, and the Vietnamese who have viewed this episode might rightly feel insulted.

Responsible scholarship might have taken note of the enormous difficulties involved in trying to build and stabilize a small emerging nation in the twentieth century – difficulties made worse by the fact that a hostile, terrorist regime was intent on subverting the development of that nation. South Vietnam's centuries-old traditional society and agricultural economic system were suddenly thrust into a modern world of international markets, expanded social opportunities, new ideas and freedoms, and increased awareness of the human potential. The demands for modernization grew as the people of South Vietnam – like people everywhere – sought to enjoy the benefits of prosperity. It is hardly peculiar that the Vietnamese began to compare their own situation with that of their American visitors. People saw more and wanted more, and there is no great mystery in this.

In such circumstances, it was impossible that there should not have been some negative side effects, some abuses in the process of monumental change. However, it is grossly unfair to view these side effects as the sole and inevitable result of the alleged decadence of American capitalist society. While capitalism has its weaknesses, only the most bigoted observers can conclude that this system has brought nothing positive or worthwhile to America, South Vietnam, or any other land it has touched. Thus, instead of giving credit to the South Vietnamese for the advances they made in education, health care, economic development and political freedom, the PBS series collaborates with the crowd of short-sighted critics who never crept out of their holes to see that there was a good deal of sunshine in South Vietnam. To these critics, South Vietnam was nothing but a cesspool of wickedness and corruption.

Beyond the matter of common decency and good sense, there is, too, the question of balance. "Key questions" concerning corruption and prostitution were asked of Nguyen Cao Ky and Ambassador Bui Diem of South Vietnam. But no such questions were posed for Pham Van Dong or Gen. Giap in the North. The Communists, we might assume, lived sanctified lives in their socialist paradise inspired by the saintly Ho Chi Minh. But is this image true?

The truth is that Communist officials, too, could be corrupt and ambitious, seeking to enhance their own personal positions rather than sacrifice themselves for the people. The sons of North Vietnamese officials were exempt from the military service. Cadres and government workers who stayed behind in the North often visited the wives of soldiers out in the field. The Communists were not shy to become involved in the black market or sell gold. After the new administration took power in 1975, the fact of Communist corruption was exposed for the world to see. Property was confiscated and taken for personal use. People were often required to bribe officials in order to get business done. A constant complaint heard from refugees who left their country after "liberation" is that the Communist government is "more corrupt than Thieu." Perhaps the worst atrocity in this regard is that the people must pay in gold for the privilege of risking their lives to flee the country! Communist corruption and abuse were real even before 1975, but they were not a "theme" of the war, and so there is no mention of such things in the *Television History*.

Vietnam's political situation is treated with no more sensitivity or balance. "Years of fighting failed to topple the American-supported Saigon government," says the narrator, along with several other reminders about who is paying for the war. The program shows demonstrations against Thieu, charges of corruption and protests of Thieu's refusal to hold free elections. As Thieu celebrates his uncontested victory, the narrator comments, "The only effective opposition to Thieu was the Viet Cong, which now called itself the Provisional Revolutionary Government."

At no time does the narrator speak of what had been happening in the North all this time. While Ho Chi Minh boasted of a paradise north of the 17th parallel, there was no free press, no freedom of assembly, no right to dissent or demonstrate. The series never says that no free elections had ever been held in the North since the Communists took over and any "effective opposition" to Ho Chi Minh was quickly imprisoned, sent to labor camps or liquidated. The people of the North were impoverished and abused, as Chinese and Soviet aid went to building up Hanoi's war machine.

How does this compare with the South? Thieu was no angel and his government had its share of corrupt officials and selfish generals. Some political opponents were jailed or killed. Yet, overall, the people of South Vietnam enjoyed far greater freedom than their cousins in the North. The South had dozens of independent newspapers. There was freedom of movement and the right to conduct business without being intimidated. Millions of people did not betray their officials or throw handgrenades at buses. Many realized a higher standard of living and improved opportunities for the future. And countless Vietnamese would agree with Le Tan Nhan, whom the series quotes: "If I have to think about supporting Thieu or the Communists, I will vote for Mr. Thieu any time." Unfortunately, these people have already been discredited as war profiteers and cheap whores whose accomplishments are easily erased by constant references to some reliance on American aid.

There is always room for criticism of the Saigon government. Vietnamese refugees can speak for themselves of the problems with the government, many of which helped facilitate the fall of the South in 1975. But narrow-minded and exaggerated dramatizations, one-way censure and interviews with black marketeers and prostitutes do not teach us anything other than the terrible power of the limited media and the bias and irresponsibility of the series' producers.

Security and Vietnamization

Post-Tet South Vietnam was characterized by increased security in most of the country. By 1971 the level of fighting in most provinces had dropped significantly as the war seemed limited to a few areas. Government strength was apparent in some places that had formerly been contested. Large numbers of refugees were being resettled or returned home. Pacification efforts helped curb VC activity in the countryside. The Communists were on the defensive.

It is true that government claims of "control" or "popularity" in many areas were often difficult to justify. By the same token, one cannot conclude that all villagers who failed to wave the Saigon flag or sing the South Vietnamese national anthem every five minutes were VC sympathizers. Over the years, the Viet Cong had been increasingly effective in alienating the population of the South by their cruel tactics, taxation, forced labor and conscription, and their inability to bring security and prosperity as promised. If the Saigon government could be accused of mismanagement and abuses in its pacification programs, the Provisional Revolutionary Government was hardly proving itself to be an exciting and popular alternative. At many times and in many places, it would be seen that whenever the ARVN and U.S. forces stayed put in an area for a considerable period of time, the population would offer its support to the Allies in preference to the Communists. (13)

The overall military situation had been changing as well. From 1965, the Communists had been moving more toward a regular forces war, putting "insurgency" in the background. North Vietnamese soldiers replaced Viet Cong guerrillas, whose ranks were being depleted through death, arrest, and defection. Concedes Stanley Karnow: "By early 1970, almost two-thirds of the estimated 125,000 Communist regulars in the South were North Vietnamese." (p. 601) The proportion would continue to increase in years to come.

Asserting the contrary, the PBS series maintains that the war was still a Southern insurgency. More Northern battalions were coming to the South, says the narrator, "but most of the enemy troops were native Southerners fighting in Viet Cong units." Perhaps the producers forgot to read Karnow's companion book.

The series claims that on the political front, too, the Communists were strong. The Provisional Revolutionary Government was the "only effective opposition" to the dastardly Thieu. To support this remark, the series interviews Jane Barton, a Quaker volunteer who lived in an unnamed province in South Vietnam at an unnamed time. (A number of Quakers actively supported Hanoi during the war through demonstrations, donations and volunteer action; it would not be too unfair to suspect that Ms. Barton was one of these.) The "civilian volunteer" declares in all innocence that "of course, the PRG in the area were not, as people thought, the North Vietnamese . . . but were really the people themselves." (sic) Barton recounts how the local South Vietnamese government "closed up" every afternoon as the PRG came to help the people by sifting rice, "talking" to the villagers and bringing movies. However, she does not explain why she was admonished to "go home" when the local Communists came to work these marvelous deeds.

The series indicates that the peasants were opposed to Saigon's pacification programs. (There is a scene – obviously selected at random – of a peasant approaching an ARVN soldier with a defiant look on his face.) Jane Barton returns with movies of her own of jails holding women and children, including a 67-year-old grandmother who had been tortured. William Colby's defense of the Phoenix program is "balanced" by such gruesome scenes, as well as the tale told by an Intelligence officer who was quite disturbed by the body-count contests and other abuses of the program.

There are, naturally, no films of VC torture, or stories of how the Viet Cong attacked villages with flame throwers or how the North Vietnamese killed civilians by throwing hand grenades and satchel charges into bunkers (a tactic they would repeat in Cambodia in 1983). The viewers learn nothing of VC taxation, coercion and indoctrination, only that the PRG "talked" to people and showed "movies."

Meanwhile, the war was being Vietnamized. Here again the series shows the ARVN at its worst: mercenaries ("paid with American aid, armed with American weapons"), deserters, timid, cowardly and inept fighters. Oh yes, a couple of units did stand and fight – a tank driver curls his lip at Quang Tri. However, as the narrator says, "loyalty to the Saigon government was difficult to measure," which comment is followed by the testimony of Lt. Peter Mahoney, who relates how one night 29 self-defense trainees "walked off and joined the NLF" with three cadres who had come to visit.

Once again the series deals in unfair generalizations. The ARVN had problems, and desertion was one of them. But the South Vietnamese army had continued to improve over the years and Australian Denis Warner found that by 1972 "the ARVN was a much better fighting force overall than it had been in 1968." (14)

What then of the ARVN desertions, which figure so prominently in the minds of PBS producers? Upon inspection, one finds that there is no basis for claiming that the ARVN desertion rate was a reliable measure of the government's alleged lack of popularity. As Gen. Westmoreland describes the situation, "many were not deserters in a true sense, but were taking French leave to look after their families or the rice crop or were re-enlisting in Regional or Popular Forces, so they could serve closer to their families." (15) The general points out that "hardly any of these men were defecting to the enemy," and this is supported by Guenter Lewy, who notes that "defection to the enemy was rare." (16) Even the series' own *Anthology and Guide* slips in a brief sentence on the subject: "Very few (ARVN) defected to the enemy, however." (*Anthology*, p. 226)

Yet, on the TV series the viewers get the impression that defection was typical of the ARVN forces and desertion a sure sign that soldiers disliked their government. Had the producers been on the ball, they might have pursued Lt. Mahoney's story further, inquiring, for instance, if the South Vietnamese trainees who picked up their weapons and walked off might have done so because the VC cadres had threatened to kill their families if they refused.

The producers of the *Television History* have shown that they are not interested in scholarship, but rather in simplistic themes, easy to identify and present to the public. Unfortunately, the themes of ARVN's alleged mercenary nature, incompetence and lack of patriotism simply do not reflect the real situation. But by ignoring reality in pursuing these themes, the PBS series has taken one more step backward in the understanding of the war in Vietnam.

Cambodia and Laos

From 1965 on, the war was becoming a battle of main forces. North Vietnamese forces were being sent south and supported in the sanctuaries in "neutral" Cambodia and Laos. Those two countries entered more largely in the war after Tet as the U.S. and South Vietnam conducted spoiling raids across their borders. (Cambodia and Laos are dealt with in Part 9 of the series.)

In implementing his Vietnamization strategy, Nixon had two goals: to ensure that the South Vietnamese would be able to hold up against the Communists once the Americans were gone and to protect American troops as they departed. In Hanoi, the plan was to hasten America's departure while interfering with the improvement of the Saigon forces. Hanoi decided the best way to do this was to launch offensives, for which they would rely heavily on their sanctuaries in Cambodia and Laos.

In 1969, Nixon ordered the secret bombing of military targets in Cambodia. The following year, after the coup in Phnom Penh, approval was given for a massive raid into Cambodia. Nixon was optimistic, believing the military could "clean up" the sanctuaries, destroy the COSVN (Central Office of South Vietnam) headquarters from which the North directed their end of the war, and disrupt the flow of supplies coming to Communist troops through the port of Sihanoukville.

The effort succeeded in killing thousands of Communist troops, putting thousands more to flight, destroying large quantities of supplies and uncovering "enough foodstuffs . . . to feed 25,000 men for a year." (17) Viet Cong military activity dropped markedly in the areas near Saigon and the Mekong Delta. Lon Nol, the new Cambodian leader, shut off Sihanoukville to enemy supply vessels. Continued bombing helped deter the Viet Cong from rebuilding their sanctuaries. ARVN morale was bolstered by the success as they "demonstrated increasing ability to conduct operations with a diminishing reliance on U.S. logistical support." (18)

Westmoreland describes the situation following the raid: "With the closing of Sihanoukville to supply ships, with the bombing of supply depots, and the American and South Vietnamese naval patrols still sealing the coast, the North Vietnamese had to depend for supplies almost exclusively on the Ho Chi Minh Trail." (19) The North Vietnamese attempted to fortify the trail and heavy stock-piling was reported west of Khe Sanh in the area around Tchepone, Laos. It was apparent that the Communists were planning a major assault on South Vietnam's two northern provinces.

To forestall such an offensive, a raid into Laos was planned for early 1971. Due to Congressional restrictions on the use of U.S. ground troops outside South Vietnam, the operation, called Lam Son 719, was to be carried out by the ARVN with U.S. air, artillery and logistical support. The base at Khe Sanh was reactivated as the operation began in late January.

Lam Son 719 achieved initial success. The ARVN advanced into Laos and located North Vietnamese supply bases. However, North Vietnamese forces were thickly concentrated in the area and heavily supplied with sophisticated Soviet weapons. Tchepone was reached on March 6, after a month of hard fighting as the ARVN and

U.S. air support encountered greater resistance than expected. Intense ground attacks halted the ARVN advance and pinned the South Vietnamese down in several positions. Meanwhile, bad weather and heavy antiaircraft fire often prevented American helicopters from moving in supplies for the ARVN. Some units were left facing the enemy without food or water, let alone ammunition. Communist troops "clung to the belts" of the ARVN to evade the bombing. The decision was made to end the operation and evacuate the ARVN.

This withdrawal was severely hampered by inadequate planning and lack of coordination between the troops and support system. The senior American and ARVN commanders were located at different points. Some ranking ARVN officers performed poorly and field commanders had difficulty arranging for fire support and resupply. Despite the problems of command and logistics, many ARVN units fought well, even though outnumbered and outflanked by the enemy. Some units were never heard from again as their posts were overrun by waves of Communist troops and Soviet tanks.

The evacuation of the ARVN was carried out amid intense enemy fire. American helicopter pilots maneuvered their craft in for the pick-up.. Out of ammunition and stunned by the force of the North Vietnamese counterattack, some of the ARVN panicked. Desperate troops clung to helicopter skids during the pullout. Journalists were on hand to record the scene of the "cowardly" and "incompetent" ARVN returning home from the "rout."

As depicted in Part 9 of the *Television History*, the Cambodian "invasion" resulted in nothing more than the deaths of civilians, a few VC and 350 Americans. American and ARVN troops looted the villages. One U.S. spokesman is quoted to the point that the tons of captured equipment had reduced pressure on American troops in South Vietnam; this statement is tempered by the suggestion that the operation was responsible for everything that happened later in Cambodia. The narrator declares bluntly, "A plan to save American lives had plunged Cambodia into full-scale war." In Part 10, the narrator will summarize the results of the raid in a single sentence: "The (COSVN) control center was never found." Period.

Regarding the Lam Son operation, the series shows the familiar scene of ARVN troops hanging from a helicopter while the narrator remarks only that "without American combat troops beside them, the South Vietnamese forces fled in disarray. They took 3,000 casualties in the first week alone." As indicated above, the truth was not so simple. Although the ARVN suffered heavy losses, this writer could not find confirmation of the series' 3,000 in one week. According to the 1971 Facts on File publication, during the first week of the operation (from January 31 through February 6) the ARVN suffered 345 killed and 805 wounded (total 1150). The following week saw 478 killed and 1159 wounded (total for two weeks 2787). (20) Reliable figures are hard to come by, but it is generally agreed that the North Vietnamese took on very heavy losses as well during those weeks of terrible fighting. On the television series, they never suffer a scratch. (A few months later, the North was hit by unusually hard flooding of the Red River. However, if we are to believe the PBS series, no disaster, natural or man-made, ever fazed the iron people of North Vietnam.) Although the Lam Son raid failed to achieve its goals, it did delay North Vietnamese operations for several months and forced Hanoi's men to move their supply trail further into the Lao interior. But once again, we realize that such details as these are inconsequential to history.

The Easter Offensive

By 1972 the Communists had failed to make any firm gains in their drive to take control of the South. The Viet Cong had been severely hurt in the countryside and most of the fighting was being carried out by Northern troops. It was then Hanoi decided to launch a full-scale invasion of the South. The Communist leaders were betting that the ARVN would not hold up without American forces on the ground with them. A victory at that time might also influence the 1972 presidential election in the U.S., where Hanoi believed the peace vote would force Nixon out of office and bring on a more flexible leader. Significant gains would give North Vietnam a stronger hand at the Paris peace talks.

Since the bombing halt, the North had been building up its forces

along the DMZ and in Laos. Their weapons included tanks, anti-
aircraft guns and artillery that far outranged the American
howitzers used by the ARVN. The offensive struck at three points:
the northern provinces of South Vietnam below the DMZ, the south
by the Cambodian border, and at Kontum in the Central
Highlands.

With the initiative as the attacker, the North Vietnamese charged
across the DMZ and from Laos with three divisions and 200 Soviet
tanks. They quickly overran the northermost ARVN posts. After a
month of bloody fighting the ARVN 3rd Division, newly created and
untried in battle, collapsed. The ARVN command was unprepared
to coordinate its ground troops with the Marines and armored units,
and this confusion aided the North Vietnamese advance. On May 1,
1972, Quang Tri city fell and most of the northern province was in
Communist hands. The ARVN lacked an orderly withdrawal plan
and some leaders abandoned their troops. Soldiers joined civilians
in a flight south on Highway 1 toward Hue. On the way they were
pummeled by North Vietnamese artillery and tanks. Thousands of
corpses lined the road on what became known as the "Highway of
Terror".

In the South, the North Vietnamese moved toward the town of An
Loc on the way to Saigon. Their guns pounded the town, destroying
much of An Loc and killing civilians as well as ARVN troops.
Outnumbered and outgunned, the ARVN dug in and waited for
reinforcements. (The series inaccurately locates the fighting in this
area as occurring in the Mekong Delta. Actually, An Loc is north of
the Delta, between Saigon and the Cambodian border.)

Finally, the Communists attacked Kontum, where the ARVN
22nd Division fell, to be replaced by the sturdier 23rd.

One week after the offensive began, Nixon ordered the resum-
ption of full scale bombing of North Vietnam. Air and naval strikes
aided the South Vietnamese. On May 8, Hai Phong and other
Northern ports were ordered mined. By the end of June the ARVN
had regrouped in the provinces to begin their counterattack. The
Communist assaults at An Loc and Kontum were turned back and
Quang Tri was retaken on September 15 after much destruction.

The North Vietnamese offensive failed for several reasons. The
Communists' large, heavily armed units depended on open supply

lines. They required several thousand tons of ammunition and gasoline each day. But accurate and devastating American bombing disrupted the flow of supplies. The large Communist units were also vulnerable to bombing and shelling; their losses were enormous. American airpower is generally considered to be the decisive factor in the invasion's failure.

Hanoi's strategy and field command suffered from weaknesses. After years of deathly fighting, experienced field leaders were in short supply and fighting units were not always properly coordinated. Hesitant to move, the Communists trapped themselves in static battles. Tanks rumbled on without infantry support; many ran out of gas, their drivers chained helplessly inside in their suicide assaults. Persistant human wave attacks resulted in huge losses that diminished the North's numerical advantage over the ARVN. Many of the Northern soldiers were teenagers fighting far from their homes and dispirited by the horror of war.

After a poor start, the ARVN managed to hold off the Communists on the ground. Their reliance on U.S. air support is undeniable, yet that support would have been meaningless if the ARVN had not held its ground in the end.

The North Vietnamese had employed 14 divisions and 26 independent battalions in the offensive, "nearly all of their armed might" (21) but failed to prove that the South could not survive. There were no mass uprisings to greet the Communists, but the fighting generated nearly a million more refugees, who apparently were not convinced of the good intentions of the Northerners. The ARVN was not destroyed and the U.S. continued its withdrawal. To pay for this offensive, an estimated 100,000 North Vietnamese mothers "willingly" sacrificed their sons for the glory of Stalin and Ho Chi Minh.

"All this means, of course," writes Guenter Lewy, "that the 1972 offensive did not really constitute a conclusive test of Vietnamization." (22)

The *Television History* version of the fighting does not bore us with details. It remarks only that Hanoi decided on a "dramatic change in strategy," "an all-out offensive." (Note how the narrator carefully avoids the term "invasion.")

The series concentrates on Quang Tri, where the ARVN had the most trouble. Thieu aide Hoang Duc Nha (never one for under-statement) called the attack a "debacle" for South Vietnam and "one of the darkest hours in our history." Sgt. Tho Hang recounts how soldiers fled the Communist advance as American advisors took off in helicopters. As told by the series, the name "Highway of Terror" comes from the fear generated in the South Vietnamese by the flight of the American advisers! There is not the slightest mention that an estimated 20,000 people were slaughtered by the Communists in this horrible event. The producers are clearly not interested in any atrocities that are not committed by the Americans.

But the Communist offensive was halted. "Masses of American equipment and massive American bombing made the difference." There is no mention that massive Soviet and Chinese aid made the Communist invasion possible in the first place. In the end, Quang Tri is pulverized, as a South Vietnamese flag flies once again over the rubble.

The narrator recounts the toll: 40,000 South Vietnamese died, 5,000 of them in the week of Sept. 15. In that same week, no Americans died. These casualty figures are then taken to represent the goal of America's war policy as the narrator blandly concludes, "The war had been Vietnamized."

Of Bombs and Cosmetics

Part 8 concludes with scenes of Saigon and motorbikes, Bob Hope's last Christmas show and a woman receiving surgery to round her eyes. Along with this comes the note that the South Vietnamese spent more money on foreign cosmetics than the country gained through exports. These scenes are placed in contrast to the dogged Viet Cong who "still exploded their bombs."

Meanwhile, before departing, the Americans have forced Pres. Thieu to accept their cease-fire agreement with Hanoi; the story is related in lively fashion by Hoang Duc Nha.

The narrator concludes: "America had viewed Vietnam as a crusade, as a challenge, and finally as a burden. Now, like the Chinese, Japanese and French before them, the Americans were leaving."

The scholarship is astonishing. The producers show more interest in the financing of cosmetics than the number of civilian casualties caused by the Communist ambush on the Highway of Terror. Plastic surgery is treated as a symbol of decadence whereas the act of terror bombing is almost admirable. And too, how do the producers justify comparing the U.S. to China, Japan and France, each of which came to Vietnam for different reasons and likewise left for different reasons?

If this is not enough, Part 8 repeats a quotation from former Ambassador Bui Diem, who notes the bewilderment of the Vietnamese who put their trust in the Americans, never believing that after so much investment the Americans would one day just "call it quits." Earlier, this quote was recorded and played over the face of the speaker; the second time it is played over scenes of heaps of goods left behind by the untrustworthy departing Americans.

All this is done, we have been assured, without any intent to editorialize.

(More concerned with the politics of the time, Karnow devotes little space to the "personal" aspect of the war. He attributes problems in the military to "the sense of futility that seeped through the ranks of the American armed forces." (p. 631) The obvious solution, he says, was to "end the war and repatriate the GIs, for whom the conflict had become as pointless as it had for the rest of the people." (p. 632) In his "research," he quotes only from helicopter pilot Fred Hickey – the series gives his name as Frank – making the reader assume that Hickey's unit, where everybody was "doing heroin," fragging lieutenants and participating in race wars, was typical for the service as a whole.

(The Chief Correspondent's portrait of Saigon might have come straight out of a cheap detective magazine: "Saigon at the height of the war had stunk of decay. Its bars were drug centers, its hotels brothels, its boulevards and squares a sprawling black market hawking everything from sanitary napkins to rifles – all of it purloined from American warehouses. Soldiers from Ohio and Georgia and Oregon, black and white, their pockets filled with cash, strolled streets covered with whores and pimps, beggars, orphans, cripples, and other victims of devastation. South Vietnamese army generals, enriched by silent Chinese partners, possessed gaudy villas not far from putrid slums packed with refugees, and government officials and businessmen connived constantly, shuffling and reshuffling the seemingly endless flow of dollars. It was a city for sale – obsessed by greed, oblivious to its impending doom." (p. 35) This is the story of the Naked City! A foreign visitor cruising Sunset Strip in Los Angeles might come away with a similar impression of America. The question is: Is it realistic?

(In discussing security, Karnow notes both the successes and abuses of the Phoenix Program, although suprisingly he does not dwell on the abuses the way he did those of Ngo Dinh Diem. Apparently the admission by Communist officials of the Phoenix Program's effectiveness sobered him to take a more "balanced" perspective. (pp. 601-2)

(The Cambodian incursion is characterized by Nixon's "defiance" and "jingoism," as well as by the indefatigable drive of the Communists – who, oddly enough, are never guilty of defiance or jingoism. The incursion's "triumph was temporary and, in long-range terms, illusory." The Communists were hardly fazed by the effort and Nixon thus gets full credit for extending the war and bringing on the utter devastation of Cambodia. (pp. 606-610)

(The Lao raid was another mistake, says Karnow. While conceding that in Saigon the rumors of the "setback in Laos were exaggerated," his own hyperbolic account hardly clears the air. "The blunders were monumental." That about says it all. He notes the ARVN's leadership problems – in less than sympathetic terms, naturally – and ignores the other factors in the operation's failure, including foul weather and the profusion of Soviet antiaircraft guns that troubled even experienced American pilots. Karnow goes on to blame Lam Son for everything from demonstrations by Saigon students to arguments following minor traffic accidents. (pp. 629-31)

(The Easter Offensive is described as a strategic victory for the North. Hanoi was "prepared to accept appalling casualties for the sake of minimal gains." The offensive, which lasted for months and brought about terrible slaughter of the North's young men, was, according to Karnow, nothing more than a political move and a rehearsal for the future. (p. 643)

(Karnow blames the slaughter on the Highway of Terror not only on the North Vietnamese but on American aircraft and warships as well. (p. 641) This claim is unique and South Vietnamese who were in Quang Tri at the time speak only of Communist tanks and artillery, not the Americans. That the casualties were civilians and ARVN soldiers adds further doubt to Karnow's analysis of the situation.

(The ARVN stood against the Communist seige at An Loc, Karnow goes on, although the town was shelled "around the clock ... But in the end, An Loc owed its survival to American help." (pp 641-42) The Chief Correspondent does not pause to consider where the Communist Vietnamese got their tanks and long-range guns used to destroy the town; perhaps he thinks the peasants fabricated them in their back yards.

(Looking at Karnow's overall description of Vietnamization – the fumbling ARVN, poor command, lack of will, etc. – one cannot but wonder what happened to his "breed of warriors" theory.)

Footnotes

1. Guenter Lewy, *America In Vietnam*, p. 154
2. Ibid.
3. Westmoreland, *A Soldier Reports*, p. 363
4. Lewy, Note 1 above, pp. 154-5
5. Ibid., p. 156
6. Ibid.
7. Ibid., p. 159
8. Ibid., p. 160
9. Quoted in Lewy, Note 1 above. p. 160
10. See Lewy, Appendix 1, "Civilian Casualties: A Qualitative Assessment", *America in Vietnam*
11. Lewy, Note 1 above, pp. 223-4
12. Ibid., p. 268
13. For example, see F. J. West, Jr., *The Village*, Harper and Rowe, 1972
14. Denis Warner, *Certain Victory*, p. 58
15. Westmoreland, Note 3 above, pp. 120-1

16. Lewy, Note 1 above, p. 172
17. Westmoreland, Note 3 above, p. 473
18. Lewy, Note 1 above, p. 167
19. Westmoreland, Note 3 above, p. 474
20. Facts on File, *South Vietnam: U.S.–Communist Confrontation in Southeast Asia, 1971*, p. 31
21. Lewy, Note 1 above, p. 198
22. Ibid., p. 201

Supplements

(Ed. – Thousands of North Vietnamese soldiers came to the South to take part in the big offensive of 1972. Many of them lost their lives in the fighting. South Vietnamese writer Phan Nhat Nam wrote about them in his account of the battles in that offensive. Below are some of his perceptions of the North Vietnamese taken from his book *Mua He Do Lua* published in Saigon 1973. Translation.)

The residents left their villages for the liberators to stay. They came from the North, from Thanh Hoa and Nghe An, down to Dong Hoi, crossing the border along Tchepone and Muong Nong, gradually moving toward the South, changing course to Kontum or Front B3, or continuing on down to the Parrot's Beak before crossing the border into Loc Ninh, 18 kilometers from An Loc. The travel corridor opened wide with no obstacles. They came to An Loc in the beginning of April after six months of traveling and enjoyed the "privilege" of being chained inside their tanks, or to trees so they could shoot at planes, or to the necks of those next to them so they might fulfill their vow: "Born in the North to die in the South."

Ah, but that was just the exterior, a false, pitiful exterior concealing a spirit torn and shattered by terror. How could they not be afraid? On the night of May 11-12, after 8,000 shells had cleared the way, three regiments, each with three full battalions, accompanied by a tank company from the 203rd and 303rd Armored Regiments, thought they were going to level An Loc and kill all the enemy American troops and leave no civilians alive. Then came 17 passes of B-52s, each pass flown by three planes with 42 bombs

weighing 500 kilograms, 24 bombs weighing 250 kilograms . . . 17
passes just 600 meters from An Loc. The First Paratroop Brigade's
concrete command bunker "traveled" with the spasms of the bombs.
The normal strategy held that bombs could not be dropped unless
there was a safety zone of two kilometers or more between the target
and friendly troops. Just one pass at Trang Bang had been enough
to shake the city of Saigon, 30 kilometers from the site. What human
beings can endure 17 passes over their heads, surrounding them,
not in waves but in heaps, the intensity of the sound going beyond
imagination?

Afraid? They had to be afraid. Though they were made of steel,
even steel will melt. Though they had taken potions to give them
courage, that too would wear off. Marx, Lenin, Chairman Ho, Great
General Giap, are all worthless in that upsidedown horror.

There was fear, so that even if he concealed it in a letter to his
family in Nghe An, Nguyen Dinh Nghiem, secret serial number and
unit HT 810042 S27, while encouraging his family to "work well to
achieve the standards . . . Little brother, practice and progress
according to the guidelines of the Party," could not control himself
in the end and wrote, "Battle conditions are very terrible here,
extremely difficult. I may not be able to write for two or three years,
so don't wait for a letter from your son . . ."

. . . Back in the rear, in the North, the people are comforted with
the joy that "this New Year I will buy for Mama 1.5 kilos of sugar
from the cooperative, the ration for families that have someone in
the service. Mama says to bring over flour and eggs, but that is so
expensive . . . I'll make fifty cakes and one packet of tea . . ."

Good God! Could anything be more pitiful? Sent three years to
liberate the South for the joy of 1.5 kilos of sugar! Who are you
liberating and for what, brother Nguyen Van Huu, serial and unit
number 271003 TB004? Do you liberate your people in the South to
"advance society with one mind" for 1.5 kilos of sugar?

In An Loc, no argument survives. There is only the sound of
tragic sighing that holds back the pain in one's chest as the eyes
blink bitterly, thinking that invisible tears will fall – but one cannot
even weep.

Going beyond the facts of military strategy where the Northeners had the advantages – proximity to their rear lines, a broad corridor for moving their army, mobility, good camoflage, sufficient logistical support, and especially their terrifying fire support, a firepower greater than that used by any infantry in military history. Compared to Tet 1968, Lower Lao, the battles at Tri Thien and Kontum, An Loc beats them all as far as firepower goes... But even with their great military advantage, the Communists still could not take An Loc . . . The strategic objective (stress the word "strategic") of the enemy was broken, completely broken.

The other face of the battle was not in this defeat, but in the shattering of the myths of the North Vietnamese infantry. At no other battlefield did the warring power of the soldiers sink so low. If their ability to fight was weak, it was perhaps due to lack of training and experience in the field. But the main factor that was the basis for the entire weakness was the morale of the Northern soldiers –the high degree of emptiness and despair... At Tri Thien, the Northern soldiers crossing the Ben Hai River rushing down to Dong Ha and Quang Tri still maintained their psychology. Fighting near their homes, they were encouraged in their resolve to liberate it by their resentment towards the people of the South, especially the people in cities and towns. Their psychology remained at its high level as they moved down to Quang Tri and the Northern troops retained their violent extremism to encourage themselves and increase their ability to fight – the ability to kill civilians and soldiers of the South.

At Kontum, though traveling a long way and fighting in a difficult environment, the spirit of the Northeners was still not broken because their battles were in the mountains (Delta, Charlie Hotel west of Highway 14, Chu Pao Pass) and did not involve civilians ... Fighting in the jungles, the soldiers developed to the maximum their ability to kill without regret or sense of error.

But An Loc was different. The Northern soldiers came from the maquis to assault an objective where the civilians outnumbered the soldiers and the people were terrified, frightened, fleeing and dying – what human being could not feel grief when he had brought down an unarmed victim with his own hand? Added to that, Divisions 5, 7, and 9 were the names of regiments of the "front," with cadres and soldiers from the South mixed with those from the North . . .

Comparisons occurred, their talk would reveal it clearly. The
Northern troops recognized their true picture and saw clearly the
senselessness of their leaving homes for a faraway place to throw
themselves into a hopeless war. Boys aged 15, 16 or 17 are easy to
incite, but they become easily discouraged as well. That is the age of
honesty, sensitivity and innocence . . . The spirits of the Northern
soldiers on this front were shattered by the war that revealed itself.
Every day, civilians fled the artillery as death spilled over. Their
courage broken, the Northern troops found themselves caught in an
inhuman battlefield, but it was too late then, for they were already
chained to the others . . . The hour of death had come for the North
Vietnamese soldiers.

(Ed. – The PBS series includes interviews with a number of persons
who were victims of, or witnesses to, destruction caused by
American soldiers and pilots. It pays no attention, however, to the
South Vietnamese who suffered from Communist attacks. At An
Loc there were countless civilian casualties. The plight of one family
is described below, in an excerpt from Phan Nhat Nam's *Mua He
Do Lua*.)

Rockets filled the air and death was all around, spreading like
grass, as in nature, as life must come to death. Death at An Loc was
a natural phenomenon. A family of seven, husband and wife with
five children, huddled together inside a shelter dug underneath
their house with a few boards and sandbags on top. In all, the cover
was about a meter thick. These poor people had no idea of the power
in a 130mm delayed-action shell, or the fatal force of 107mm and 122
mm rockets. So, one short burst and that sad shelter was pulverized,
flying like drops of water when a rock is thrown into a stream.
Dead! Six people dead. The sole survivor gathered the remains,
placing them carefully so that the mother's corpse would not include
a child's arm, so the older son would not find a younger child's leg
with him . . . Slowly, deliberately, the father picked the pieces of his
loved ones' bodies. What was left in that dried out mind? Nothing.
We should not even call it the mind of a human being. The man had
died – human beings all had died at An Loc.

(Ed. – Like most Americans, Stanley Karnow saw only a very

limited part of Saigon, that part frequented by GIs and other American visitors. Karnow's eagle eye failed to gaze beyond the most corrupt hovels, however, to realize that for the vast majority of Saigonese the city was nothing like what he describes in his book. Here are some of the images recalled by refugees when asked about their capital: Saigon was relatively safe from the war. Every day, thousands of people swarmed to the busy Central Market. Hundreds of stalls and booths lined the streets in the market area where vendors sold meat, fish, fresh vegetables and fruits, along with fabrics, leather goods, and other items. Downtown Saigon was most crowded on weekends as people came to relax, browse through the shops or bargain with the sellers. Customers poured onto Le Loi Street to look through the vast array of books for sale. On Le Loi, Le Thanh Ton, and Nguyen Hue Streets, the Vietnamese could buy everything from shoes and sandals to cloth and sewing needles and aspirin. Students and other visitors went to the Saigon Zoo, sometimes just to sit in the shade or relax with a book. Movie theaters were filled with people coming to watch American, French and Chinese films. The Vietnamese *cai luong* opera was popular among some classes. Many people stopped at the sidewalk cafes to drink coffee, have a smoke, chat with friends, or watch passers-by. On hot afternoons, Saigonese might go down to the river to enjoy the cool breeze. Those who liked sports could watch the soccer matches at the stadium or athletic fields.

(One can only wonder where Stanley Karnow was when all this was going on.)

PART 9: CAMBODIA AND LAOS

*America conducts a secret war in Laos as the CIA trains
Hmong tribesmen in the highlands. During the 1960s Laos
becomes the most heavily bombed nation in the world.
The Pathet Lao takes control of the government in 1975.*

*In Cambodia, Prince Sihanouk steers a neutral course,
but war spills across the border from Vietnam.
The Khmer Rouge emerges in the countryside. Pres. Nixon
launches a secret bombing campaign in 1969. Prince
Sihanouk loses power in a coup and the United States
invades Cambodia. The Nixon Doctrine is applied to
Cambodia where Khmer are trained and supplied
by the U.S. In April 1975 the Khmer Rouge capture
Phnom Penh and the capital city is evacuated as the
Communists take power.*

Laos: The Ten-Minute War

The tragedy of Southeast Asia is not limited to Vietnam, but
includes, as well, that country's neighbors, Laos and Cambodia.
From 1954 to the present, both nations have faced pressures from
political forces inside and outside their boundaries. Both are
victims of Vietnamese Communist aggression. Both suffered as
American military activities crossed into their territories. Both
countries are currently occupied by Vietnamese troops and their
governments are directed by Hanoi. And both countries are
enduring further bloodshed at the hands of the Communists.

Laos suffers in silence. The nation received international
recognition in the early 1960s when a world crisis threatened to
develop. But since that time little attention has been paid to

Laos. This adds an extra dimension to the misery of the Lao people who must not only endure the loss of their land, culture and freedom, but also know that the world has forgotten them. Not suffering a terrible slaughter like that in Cambodia, Laos apparently does not merit the dignity of acknowledgment. The entire process that led from French colonialism to genocide by the Vietnamese is given about ten minutes on the *Television History*.

"In 1961, Laos was the major Southeast Asia crisis." So says the narrator, but he never explains why. The political scene – the juggling of the three principal factions, the confrontation between the U.S. and the Soviet Union, North Vietnamese infiltration into the northern provinces and Hanoi's influence on the Pathet Lao – all of this is ignored. Unless the viewers already have a background in the history of Laos, they will not have the slightest idea what is happening.

The three major factions in Laos were the rightists, the pro-Communist Pathet Lao and the neutralists.

In the 1950s the rightists were strongly opposed to Communist influence in the government. Distrusting the Pathet Lao they took steps to prevent the smooth integration of the Communists into the government and military. The rightists were supported by the U.S. and also Thailand, which wanted a Lao buffer state between itself and Vietnam.

Prince Souphannavong, leader of the Pathet Lao, was being directly aided by the North Vietnamese. The Pathet Lao military was composed primarily of tribal minorities in the mountains along the frontier with Vietnam.

In the middle were the neutralists, led by Prince Souvanna Phouma, who tried several times to form a coalition of all three groups. The prince returned from France in 1960 to head the Lao government, but the rightists took power. Souvanna Phouma fled to the Plain of Jars to join Capt. Kong Le, commander of neutralist troops in that area. Eventually the prince was to cooperate with the Pathet Lao.

By the spring of 1961, the Pathet Lao and North Vietnamese seemed poised to take over the country. The U.S. warned that it would not sit idly by if this were to happen. A new Geneva Conference was held and an agreement was reached providing international guarantees of Laos' independence and neutrality. A government was formed under Souvanna Phouma which included leaders from both the left and right.

This was the Lao crisis of 1961-62. The producers of the "exhaustive" *Television History* were apparently too exhausted to spend a few moments giving a brief account of this. Instead, they begin their story with the U.S. and focus solely on those items which have greatest sensational value – America's "secret war"! In characteristic style, Part 9 opens with a clever portrayal of America the Hypocrite: Pres. Kennedy at a press conference speaking of peace and neutrality, followed by scenes of weapons drops for the Hmong in the highlands. This, we are to assume, is where the whole war began.

Not content with ignoring the events leading up to the 1961 crisis, the series goes on to ignore what happened afterwards.

Following the Second Geneva Conference, the new coalition government broke down as Communist Pathet Lao forces attacked Kong Le and drove him from the Plain of Jars. Souvanna Phouma tried desperately to hold the factions together for the next ten years amid coups and changes of government. The Pathet Lao refused to allow the International Control Commission to supervise its territory. The U.S. began bombing the Plain, which was infiltrated by North Vietnamese troops.

In 1960, Prince Souvanna Phouma had opposed U.S. intervention in Lao affairs and he spent two years with the Pathet Lao in the highlands, challenging the rightists. At the time, the prince had little fear of the Communists, whom he apparently felt were just another political faction vying for power. As an ideology, Communism was not suited to the Lao lifestyle. Consequently, the prince expected that the Communists would eventually realize this and rejoin the "Lao family."

However, after staying with the Communists, the prince had a change of heart. He learned that the Pathet Lao were simply being used by Hanoi in the Vietnamese drive to extend their influence. In a speech made in Ann Arbor, Michigan in 1965, Prince Souvanna Phouma characterized the Communists as "fanatics . . . trying to subjugate Laos." He explained that the Communists recognize "no ethics, no international codes of behavior, no rights, no frontiers," and charged them with inciting revolution "wherever they can" while announcing the "advent of a social paradise where classes and state would be abolished." The speech decried the North Vietnamese for interfering in Lao affairs and spreading "chaos and subversion." According to the prince, the 1962 agreements regarding Lao neutrality were being undermined by the North Vietnamese and Pathet Lao; the latter he called "creatures of the Viet Minh." Still, Souvanna Phouma hoped Laos could maintain a stable coalition government with participation by all factions. (1)

Although the prince was often angered by the activities of the United States in his country, he did not have any illusions about the nature and goals of the Communists, as he clearly expressed in the above statements.

Throughout the war in Vietnam, the North Vietnamese maintained bases and supply routes in Laos, blatantly violating the country's neutrality while taking control of territory through the Pathet Lao. Opponents of America's war effort justified Hanoi's actions, saying in effect: If the U.S. can have bases in Thailand and the Philippines, the Viet Cong can have bases in Cambodia and Laos. The reasoning behind this statement is more emotional than realistic. Thailand and the Philippines, bound by treaty as allies with the U.S., can hardly be compared with Laos or Cambodia, whose neutrality was formally recognized by the parties involved in the war. Moreover, war is not a soccer game where both sides start out with equal odds and may the best side win. The major argument in support of Communist sanctuaries seems to be based more on hostility to the U.S. than anything else. Critics considered the Viet Cong to be the "good guys"; therefore, the U.S. (the "bad guys") had no right to interfere with Ho Chi Minh's revolution, no matter where it extended.

Whatever the defense of Vietnam's imposition on Laos, it lost its force with the events following 1975. Prince Souvanna Phouma proved right: the Vietnamese were out to control his country.

In December 1975, the Pathet Lao became the leaders of the government and the prince was removed from power. Apparently Souvanna Phouma spent the remainder of his life in retirement. According to some Lao sources, the prince had been detained in a Vietnamese prison camp near Dalat for a few months prior to his death in January 1984. It is not certain that there was a funeral.

The government of Laos is now directed by Hanoi. Some 60,000 Vietnamese troops occupy the country. Thousands of former soldiers and government officials have been arrested and sent to "seminar camps," the euphemism for concentration camps in Laos. Homes have been confiscated and given over to new Vietnamese immigrants. Vietnamese and Russian languages are being taught in schools and gifted youths receive special training in "sister" socialist nations. Thousands of Lao have fled the oppression of the Communists, risking their lives by fleeing through the jungles and swimming the Mekong River to Thailand.

The Vietnamese occupation of Laos is far more devious and tragic than any scheme concocted by the CIA. Yet, it is never mentioned in the *Television History*. The series talks of how the CIA trained and armed Hmong tribesmen in the highlands. It tells of clandestine flights, heavy bombing and America's "secret war."

The series might mention how the Communists used mountain tribesmen to fight and die for them, to act as forced laborers, for the Vietnamese war. It might note how often the Lao. government protested the presence of North Vietnamese troops in its territory, to no avail. The program might say something about how the Communists are destroying the culture and traditions of the Lao people after taking power and how many people would rather leave their homes than live under their "liberators." It might mention, too, how the Hmong are currently the victims of an extermination campaign by the Communists, who use yellow rain and military attacks to wipe out America's former allies – Vietnam's secret war which it still refuses to admit to.

The series might mention these things, but it does not.

Cambodia: The Neutral Prince

Like Laos, Cambodia was formally recognized as a neutral bystander of the conflict developing in Vietnam. Whether or not Cambodia under Prince Sihanouk was acting as a neutral party remains a matter of debate. It is also debatable whether Sihanouk was acting in the interests of his people (his "servants," or his "children," as he liked to call them) or himself. As one might expect, neither of these issues is dealt with in the *Television History*.

Instead, Part 9 shows scenes of prosperous Cambodia, with its "ancient grandeur" at Angkor Wat, dancers celebrating an "abundance of rice and fish," and nearly all the peasants owners of their land – a sad contrast to the horror that would befall the country after April 1975.

In assessing his country's position after 1954, Prince Sihanouk realized he was caught in a dilemma. He saw how Vietnam's royal government was replaced with a republic once the Americans came and he feared his own loss of power should Uncle Sam become too involved in Cambodia. At the same time, he knew the Communists had little need of royalty and so he hesitated to give full support to either side. In the beginning, however, the prince was convinced that the Communists would win in Vietnam. Playing the "winner," he gave significant aid to the Viet Cong as well as diplomatic recognition in Phnom Penh.

While explaining none of this, the narrator says: Prince Sihanouk "skillfully maneuvered to preserve his country's neutrality." Whatever the prince's alleged skills, they did not include diplomacy. Sihanouk hardly endeared himself to the Americans, whom he repeatedly denounced as "imperialists," "aggressors," and "neocolonialist invaders." Throughout the 1960s, the prince declared that the U.S. was violating Cambodia's territorial integrity (claims reinforced by a notable number of "navigational errors" and other incidents that brought U.S. and South Vietnamese troops or planes across the border) although he denied there were Viet Cong in Cambodia. Sihanouk continually accused the U.S. of "murdering" innocent peasants/women and children/civilians. He created something of an international scandal when he publicly rejoiced over the deaths of Ngo Dinh Diem, Thai Premier Sarit Thamaret, and "the great boss" of "those two aggressors," ie., Pres. Kennedy. More than once the prince announced that the U.S. was on the verge of invading his country and he threatened to establish closer relations with the Soviet Union and China, "to protect Cambodia's neutrality."

To be sure, there was a good deal of political rhetoric in the words of the excitable prince. Sihanouk periodically sounded off against the Communists, but with less vehemence. More importantly, the prince's actions gave an indication of where he stood on the war issue.

Sihanouk allowed the North Vietnamese and Viet Cong to use Cambodia's eastern frontier as a sanctuary for military and political operations. The U.S. military had evidence of several major Communist bases in areas such as the Parrot's Beak jutting into the Mekong Delta, and the territory by Cambodia's border with Laos and Vietnam. Meanwhile, major supply shipments from the Soviet Union and China were coming to the port of Sihanoukville and also up the Bassac River to Phnom Penh for transportation by land to South Vietnam. Cambodia provided a secure and attack-free zone for the regroupment of Communist units, storage of supplies and weapons, and initiating of military activities.

Cambodia's agricultural abundance also interested the VC. According to Gen. Westmoreland, in 1965 "Cambodia was selling North Vietnam, for transmittal to the Viet Cong, 55,000 tons of rice annually, a major portion of the Viet Cong requirements, and the Viet Cong were buying almost double that amount direct from Cambodian farmers." (2)

Prince Sihanouk denied all accusations of complicity with the Viet Cong. In 1966 he took a group of journalists on a celebrated tour of the frontier to "prove" to the world that there were no Communist Vietnamese being harbored in his kingdom. As a matter of fact, he had just made a deal with the Chinese to help deliver supplies to the VC, including arms and ammunition, rockets, food, clothing and medicines. From 1966-1969, the VC acquired through Cambodia eight times the amount of weapons and ammunition they used in their peak year of 1968. (3)

When the Viet Cong Tet Offensive failed, Prince Sihanouk reassessed the Communists' position in Southeast Asia. He was becoming worried about the increasing numbers of North Vietnamese and Viet Cong in his country, aware as he was of Vietnam's ambition to dominate Cambodia. The prince became more cooperative with the U.S. and by most indications he approved of the secret bombing in 1969, although he publicly criticized it to save face.

Meanwhile, there was opposition to Sihanouk among the

intellectuals, generals, and politicians. Reformers sought a modern republic and an end to the arbitrary leadership of the monarchy. Sihanouk's family was accused of corruption. The prince was often chided for his condescending attitude toward the people. The ouster finally came in 1970 when the prince was away getting medical treatment.

The *Television History* tells a different story. Prince Sihanouk is portrayed as a skillful politician whose "prestige and popularity" in the countryside was opposed only by the apparently universal greed of his officers, who "were becoming restless" because they "no longer received American military aid." Too, Sihanouk is the great nationalist, who produced his own films, "all of them glorifying Cambodia." In international affairs, he continues to play the balancing act, with Mao Zedong, Charles De Gaulle, and (the so-called non-alligned) Sukarno. He invited Jacqueline Kennedy to visit Angkor Wat, but did he ever apologize for what he called her husband a few years before?

The series gives no hint that Sihanouk endorsed VC infiltration through Cambodia or that his forces sometimes protected VC units being pursued by Americans and South Vietnamese. There are no scenes of the prince visiting Hanoi for the funeral of Ho Chi Minh and no comment on his relations with Pol Pot and Khieu Samphan before 1970. The viewers witness no television scenes from clever reporters who scanned the Cambodian frontier with their cameras and concluded that indeed there were no VC in that country, just as the prince had told them, thus casting suspicion on the claims of the U.S. military leaders.

And while Cambodia's generals (including Lon Nol) were by no means Puritans, there certainly was more justification for their opposition to Sihanouk than the prince's uncontested notion that they were interested only in a "bowl of (American) dollars." Yet, the viewers never hear of it.

The series' simplistic "history" is understandable. If Prince Sihanouk should come across as a worthy nationalist while his opponents are all greedy and corrupt, and if the activities of the Vietnamese Communists are played down to their barest minimum, then it becomes that much easier for the viewers to conclude that America was to blame for interfering in Cambodian affairs, "expanding" the war, and causing the horrible disaster which followed.

Neat, isn't it?

The Communists in Cambodia

The *Television History* has little to say about the Communists in Cambodia. Early on there is a passing remark that Sihanouk faced trouble from "small groups of Cambodian Communists, the Khmer Rouge, (who) were recruiting some discontented peasants" in the countryside. The series does not explain who these "discontented peasants" were in a land we have just been told "prospered" with an "abundance of rice and fish" and where "nearly 90 percent of all peasants owned their own land."

Meanwhile, according to the series, Communist Vietnamese activities are restricted to the Ho Chi Minh Trail and sanctuaries by the eastern border of Cambodia. U.S. bombing in 1969 is blamed for driving the sanctuaries "further into the country."

The reader may already have guessed that the situation was a great deal more complicated than that.

The first Communists in Cambodia were Vietnamese, agents of the Indochinese Communist Party, created in 1930. The ICP's aim was to establish an independent and socialist Indochina – under the direction of the Vietnamese, who, in turn, were managed by Moscow. Early efforts to spread the word of Communism in Cambodia rendered little success, for several reasons. There were few discontented peasants interested in overthrowing their much revered monarchy. Furthermore, Cambodia's traditions and Buddhist religious teachings were thoroughly opposed to Marxism. Last, and not least, the Cambodians distrusted (and many hated) the Vietnamese, whom they were afraid would try to kill them and steal their land. During the war years, however, the Viet Minh did convert a small number of villages and individuals, including minorities and backward peasants. Some of their bases were in remote locations in western Cambodia, far removed from what would later become the Ho Chi Minh Trail.

Francois Ponchaud describes the years leading up to Cambodia's revolution in his book *Cambodia: Year Zero.* There the author writes that the first ethnic Cambodian "revolutionaries" came not from Cambodia itself but from the southernmost part of Vietnam, called Cochin-China. By Ponchaud's telling, these Khmers were not opponents of the Vietnamese, who took Cochin-China from Cambodia in the 18th century, but of the Cambodian monarchy, which they felt had sold them out to the Vietnamese.

Among the future leaders of the Khmer Rouge were a number of bourgeois intellectuals who received their university education in Paris. There they cultivated their interest in Marxism, some of their more ardent members admiring Stalin and Ho Chi Minh. By the end of the First Indochina War, some of these Khmer Marxists were contemplating international Communism and the creation of a Socialist Indochina without national boundaries.

During the war with France, a segment of the Cambodian population sided with the Viet Minh in their opposition to the colonialists. These Khmer were not politically strong enough to be recognized at the Geneva Conference in 1954. At the same time, several thousand Cambodians were taken away by the Viet Minh for training. The more promising ones went to Hanoi, Moscow or Peking for "study," while others were trained in frontier camps by Viet Minh officers.

From 1954 to 1970, the major Communist force in Cambodia was not the Khmer Rouge, but the Vietnamese Communists, who had established bases and supply routes in the country. Cambodians sold their rice to the Viet Cong and many, by payment or coercion, gave food and shelter to the infiltrators. As in Laos, some Vietnamese living in Cambodia acted as spies for the Viet Cong, collecting information and taking stock of affairs in the cities and towns where they resided. After seizing power from Sihanouk, the Lon Nol government violently repressed the Vietnamese in his country. While many innocent persons were victimized by the brutal campaign, government raids uncovered documents, maps, arms and communications equipment in some homes. It was discovered that some of the Vietnamese residents were actually officers in the North Vietnamese army.

Meanwhile, Prince Sihanouk "continued to juggle" with the different political factions inside and outside his country. He maintained close relations with Hanoi and Peking and hoped to establish himself as a viable leader in the socialist camp. Yet he kept communications open to anyone who might be of use to him. In the late 1960s, the prince became worried about the build-up of North Vietnamese soldiers in Cambodia and in 1969 he re-established diplomatic relations with the U.S.

At the same time, Sihanouk remained in touch with the Khmer Rouge, who had gone underground. Some observers say that Sihanouk drove them out of the cities, while others claim he deliberately sent them to "the jungle" to mobilize the people. In any event, the Khmer Communists had no significant influence among the people until the prince was deposed. Before that time, Sihanouk's feelings seem to have been mixed. As one more opposition group, the Khmer Rouge challenged his power. Still, Cambodian Communists were preferrable to Vietnamese Communists, the latter representing imperialism and animosity to the Khmer people.

Immediately following Sihanouk's ouster and prior to the U.S.-South Vietnamese incursion, the Viet Cong moved deeper into Cambodian territory, inciting Cambodian peasants to riot in some places. The PBS series mentions the incident in Kompong Cham where two members of the Parliment were killed. However, the series does not say that the riot was instigated by Vietnamese and that some of these persons were among the arrested, their detention being protested by Hanoi. (4) In the turmoil, the Vietnamese Communists "invaded two-thirds of Cambodia. In the countryside they wore badges representing the deposed prince, whom they swore to restore to power. . . . The peasants wept with joy and greeted the Vietnamese as their liberators." (5) The Viet Cong organized liberation zones headed by Vietnamese residents. Khmer youth were trained to fight and the people were encouraged by tape recordings of Prince Sihanouk's call to arms from Peking. Some old Viet Minh cadres re-emerged and others who had been training in Hanoi and Peking returned to take charge of the "revolution." Peasants rallied to leaders bearing pictures of Sihanouk and Ho Chi Minh.

The government struck up a propaganda campaign against the Vietnamese residents. Many Vietnamese were slain and bodies were seen floating down the Mekong River. The action was protested by the Saigon government, which negotiated to repatriate

Vietnamese residents in Cambodia. Soon the situation quieted
down and the massacres ceased. Not long afterwards, the
Cambodian government would be complaining bitterly about the
mistreatment of the Khmer inflicted by South Vietnamese soldiers
in the 1970 incursion.

A meeting was held in China in April 1970 where Prince Sihanouk
joined Pham Van Dong of North Vietnam, Nguyen Huu Tho of the
NLF, and Prince Souphannavong of the Pathet Lao in signing a
declaration to drive the "imperialist aggressors" from Indochina.
The declaration received the official sanction of the Peking
government and Moscow. Prince Sihanouk formed a government-
in-exile as he continued to appeal to the Cambodian people to "go
into the jungle" and "join the revolution" against the American
"imperialists" and the "traitors" who had taken the throne from
their "father."

The ranks of the "revolutionaries" swelled, primarily in response
to Sihanouk's pleas. The peasants were deeply devoted to their
king and many were willing to die to restore him to the throne.
Sihanouk's National United Front included a number of Communist
leaders, and these eventually took over the movement. While the
Communist leadership strengthened its organization, the Khmer
Rouge did not reveal their political ambitions to the people, who
knew nothing of Communism.

For a time, the main Communist military force in Cambodia
remained the Vietnamese, who took over a number of villages and
towns, at one time blocking the roads to the capital. They were
repulsed by the combined South Vietnamese and Cambodian forces,
supported by U.S. air attacks. The Vietnamese then gave way to
trained Khmer soldiers and withdrew to their main conflict in
Vietnam. Meanwhile, Khmer killed Khmer, and that suited the
Vietnamese Communists, who would later benefit from the
slaughter. Cambodia became part of the competition between
Peking and Moscow for influence in Southeast Asia.

The *Television History* declines to explain Vietnamese ambitions
in Cambodia or describe the reliance of the Khmer front on the Vietnamese. Instead, it opts for simple themes: America's secret
bombing and "invasion," examples of America's arrogance and the
expanding of the war. Allegedly spontaneous mobs protest the

1970 coup. Lon Nol's army commits "butchery" on Vietnamese residents. The Cambodian army is shown in degrading scenes as Americans train Khmer soldiers to fight the Viet Cong. The Nixon Doctrine leads to the corruption of Cambodian generals and the death of the country.

The series also neglects to take note of the not so strange fact that the Cambodian peasants did not rally to Communism. The Khmer Communists had little significance politically or militarily for many years. Only by taking advantage of Prince Sihanouk's National Front and Vietnamese assistance did the Khmer Rouge achieve strength. In fact, many Cambodian refugees blame Prince Sihanouk for the tragedy that occurred after 1975, not Henry Kissinger or Richard Nixon.

Still, just as in Vietnam and Laos, Communist ideals failed to attract mass support. The peasants understood nothing about Marxism. Trained cadres promised wealth and power, and fed the peasants with resentment against their "oppressors." In the end, Communism brought only misery and death.

Even as the PBS producers concede the obvious fact that the Khmer Rouge were brutal fanatics, they are forced to explain why the Cambodian Communists should be so, while the Vietnamese Communists are (by their portrayal) moderates with a noble cause. The answer is conveniently given in Part 9.

First, we are told that the Cambodians are cannibals. In the context of the riot at Kongpong Cham, Francois Ponchaud describes how the livers of the two Parliament members were grilled in the marketplace. The Khmer, concludes the missionary, "are a race of warriors. And that should not be forgotten."

The producers do not forget, for they note how Lon Nol's troops "butchered" Vietnamese residents and later add that in one town government troops "resorted to cannibalism to survive."

Along with this, a Khmer Rouge "organizer" reports that "ordinary people" (and not the Communists) were shell-shocked by the bombing of B-52s. "Terrified and half crazy . . . they believed whatever the Khmer Rouge told them." As the Communists would say, the hatred they were taught was "transformed into action" in the form of more killing.

So here is the answer: The Cambodians are a race of warriors, cannibals, butchers, all shell-shocked from B-52s. It is no wonder that they killed several million of their own people during and after the war.

But the series never deals with the suggestion that the systematic slaughter along ideological lines that ensued after the Khmer Rouge takeover was due to fanatic Communism inspired by Stalin, Mao and Ho Chi Minh. It is so much easier and satisfying to blame the Nixon Doctrine and U.S. "expansion" of the war for the Communist brutality that is destroying Cambodia. Why admit that the Communists themselves might be responsible?

The Silent Massacres

Following the barbaric "revolution" of the Khmer Rouge, the Vietnamese invaded Cambodia, telling the people that they were being liberated from their oppressors. One would like to believe that life is better for the Cambodians now that the terrible Pol Pot is gone. But this does not seem to be the case.

Cambodia is suffering the same type of genocide that has enveloped Laos. Intermarriage between Cambodians and Vietnamese is "encouraged." The Vietnamese language is part of the school curriculum. Children are being sent to school in Vietnam. Government posts are held by Cambodians who spent years in Vietnam, married Vietnamese women and fathered children who speak only Vietnamese. Some Cambodian children are disappearing and according to some refugees Cambodian youths are providing the first line of defense against China on Vietnam's northern border. The Heng Samrin government is directed by Hanoi and all government posts have Vietnamese "advisers." Cambodians are being killed by yellow rain and other types of lethal gas. The royal palace has been robbed, as have Buddhist temples. The great Ton Le Sap lake is guarded by Vietnamese soldiers and fish from the lake go to Vietnam. Hundreds of Cambodian villages are required to grow rice for the Vietnamese. Relief agency supplies, earmarked for the starving people of Cambodia during the years of famine, were taken away by the Vietnamese and used to feed occupation troops. Vietnamese soldiers have attacked and murdered unarmed civilians. The fighting has extended into the refugee camps and over the border into Thailand. . . .

The tragedy goes on. The Cambodians are still suffering under the Vietnamese Communists, just as they did under the Khmer Rouge. Their land and culture no longer belong to them. They are losing their identity and their lives. They are being destroyed by ambitious Vietnamese leaders who, as Prince Souvanna Phouma of Laos said, recognize no ethics, no international code of behavior, no rights and no frontiers. The nation of Cambodia is being destroyed.

And none of this is mentioned on the *Television History*.

(Stanley Karnow's "complete" history is particularly incomplete with relation to Laos and Cambodia. The former country is brushed off with but a handful of references scattered throughout the book. Laos rarely merits more than a single sentence; its most expansive portrayal is in honor of the ARVN failure in Lam Son 719.

(Cambodia fares little better, although once again it would hardly be mentioned if it had not been for the U.S. bombing and incursion. Sihanouk, we learn, was "the shrewd, nimble, tireless ruler of Cambodia" (p. 44) whose opposition came from the alienated "middle class of Phnompenh, his capital. Envious of Saigon and Bangkok, flourishing on American dollars, they yearned to share in the wealth lavished by the U.S. on its Southeast Asian clients." (pp. 603-4) The generals, too, had nothing but money on their minds.

(While presenting the divisions within the Nixon administration regarding Cambodia, Karnow avoids probing for Vietnamese intentions there. Once again, he attaches no significance to the admitted fact that Hanoi "had been arming and training guerillas of the Khmer Rouge . . . in North Vietnam" (p. 604), making this activity appear about as harmless as going to the beach on a weekend. As for respecting Cambodia's neutrality, the onus falls on the U.S. – naturally – while the Vietnamese Communists seem to be nothing but merry pranksters and Sihanouk their little elf in Phnom Penh.

(Although Karnow recognizes the Cambodians' fear of having their country invaded by the "dynamic" Vietnamese, he does not connect this with the actual invasion by Hanoi troops. Instead, the 1979 invasion is credited to Vietnamese nationalism as the Communist Vietnamese were trying to prevent Cambodia from invading them to take back Cochin-China. (p. 45) It would appear the Vietnamese Communists are quite generous people, since they are striving so hard to share their Vietnamese nationalism with the people of Cambodia and Laos.)

Footnotes

1. Account of a speech by Prince Souvanna Phouma, Prime Minister of Laos, at Ann Arbor, Michigan, October 20, 1965. Reported by Mark R. Killingsworth, in the Michigan *Daily;* reprinted in *Vietnam: Anatomy of a Conflict,* pp. 640-642
2. William Westmoreland, *A Soldier Reports,* p. 219
3. Ibid., p. 221
4. Facts on File, *Cambodia,* p. 67
5. Francois Ponchaud, *Cambodia: Year Zero,* p. 167

Supplements

(Ed. - The following is an article taken from a Geneva-based newsletter of Southeast Asian affairs. *Southeast Asia Review,* Dec. 1983. Copyright 1983.)

Laos: In The Shadow Of Events
   by Prince Mangkra Souvannaphouma

Prince Souvannaphouma, exiled in France, is President of the Lao Committee For The Defense Of Human Rights. His Uncle is the pro-Vietnamese ruler of Laos, Prince Souphanouvong (the Red Prince).

Since 1975, when the three free countries of the Indochina peninsula swung into the whirl of the communist world, within the space of one month, the mass media has been content to relate only to the Vietnamese boat people drama and the incredible Cambodian genocide.

On the other hand, very little news has been given to the West of Laos, tucked away from public view, which leads one to ask whether this country still exists or not?

However, this silence can be easily understood, since the Laotian is well known to be kind and nonchalant, and as he is known to retain a certain discretion toward his sad fate. He can keep an exceptional dignity while faced with the misfortune of the history of his country.

Poor forefather under the French colonization, and spattered further by the Vietnamese conflict, Laos has always been hidden in the shadow of its neighbors who, in turn, try to spread its supremacy over this beautiful country, so rich with its raw materials.

In April 1974, with the investiture of the National Union's provisory Government, international opinion rendered homage to Lao wisdom. But now, the whole world has forgotten the destiny of tens of thousands of civil servants, military and students who have been deported, since July 1975, to concentration camps which are pompously called "seminars" or "popular universities."

In spite of sensibilization campaigns organized by our "Lao Committee for the Defense of Human Rights," and by numerous French-Laotian associations, the detention of His Majesty the King and the royal family has been maintained since 12 March, 1977. International opinion remains indifferent and the intervention of Western embassies still in Vientiane have been fruitless.

Although one can refuse to admit the very obvious domination of Laos by Vietnam, which is still occupied by 60,000 troops sent by Hanoi, none can overlook the physical and moral suffering of the people. The Laotian people continue to suffer from the perpetual oppression and all sorts of humiliation, which it submits to without public protest, being faithful to Buddhism precepts which recommend non-violence and self denial.

With the coming to power of the "reds," a disturbing silence reigns over the whole country; with the exception of the twenty or so "repentants" who were released from the camps, the Laotian-Vietnamese authorities have never published a list of dead prisoners, nor have they communicated news of the survivors. From the refugee camps in Thailand, testimony has been given on the torture and privation of prisoners. According to some rumors, the King has died; the heir Prince together with some fifty high-ranking officers and police officials have been executed. Unfortunately, due to a lack of concrete proof, this information has not been used by the International League for the Defense of Human

Rights, nor by Amnesty International and the International Red Cross.

Supported and encouraged by Moscow, Vietnamese hegemony has become more flagrant as it installs more Vietnamese families inside Laos. It prescribes the Vietnamese language and has forced young Laotian girls to marry Vietnamese soldiers.

The annexation procedure has been well known for a long time, but even those people who say that they are in love of freedom and justice have not intervened to stop this hegemony.

Parallel with these arbitrary imprisonments and executions, the Lao-Viet despots have forced people to flee their country. They have exterminated those who remain refactory (sic) by using massive bombing and chemical warfare, the latter which is condemned by the Montreux Convention.

Of a population which counts less than three million people, 400,000 Laotians have chosen exile, and more than 40,000 are still stagnating in the camps located in northern Laos. The remainder must still suffer under the barbaric yoke of the neo-colonialists. While in 1974 the economy of Laos was witnessing a continuous rise, it today finds itself among the poorest countries of the world, and must await the crumbs that their Vietnamese/Russian masters will throw to it.

In face of what can only be called genocide, a handful of men and women are attempting to save what little rests of the Lao entity. But the apathy and egoism of others makes this struggle against the oppressor an extremely difficult task.

Forgotten in its agony, abandoned by its friends of yesterday, neglected by many of its sons, and left to its fate by all, Laos could soon join those many other countries which do not cease to haunt the world; the gloomy world of the stateless person, the universe of the shadows.

(Ed. - American veteran Al Santoli visited Hmong refugees in a camp in Thailand in 1983. From the refugees, he learned more about the chemical war campaign the Vietnamese are waging against America's former allies. Following is an excerpt from the story "Little Girl in the Yellow Rain," printed in the *Reader's Digest*,

April 1984. Reprinted by permission; copyright 1984 by Al Santoli.)

The Soviet-made MiG jet roared over the Phu Bia mountain region of Laos, leaving an ominous cloud of yellow smoke in its wake. In a rice field below, Chong Yang, a 26-year-old H'mong farmer, cried out to his wife and four small children to run for shelter in the forest.

The youngest boy froze in fear as the deadly mist began coming down around them. Chong ran back for him, and then led his family to the shelter of the thick forest. They huddled there as the yellow rain continued to descend that morning of August 23, 1983. They began to feel dizzy. Their vision blurred, and they started gasping for breath.

Twelve-year-old Shea Vang had been orphaned in the post-1975 persecution of the H'mong by the Vietnamese and Pathet Lao, and now lived with her uncle Chong Yang's family. When the MiG thundered overhead, she was nearing the end of the two-hour walk to her village's rice field. She looked up at the plane, and shuddered.

Shea Vang first witnessed poison-cloud attacks on her village in 1980,·when she was nine. Since then she had lived in fear of the aircraft that periodically dropped the yellow, black, white or red smoke that made people very sick. Some had died painful deaths in hours or days. Following an attack in 1981, Shea had stayed by her brother's bedside for six days, praying for his recovery. But he succumbed to severe fever-convulsing, with blood pouring from his nose and mouth.

After the jet passed, Shea emerged from the cover of dense forest and saw the yellow spots on the surrounding foliage. Suddenly she felt dizzy. Her head began to ache, and her stomach and chest muscles tightened.

When she found Chong and his family, they were doubled up with abdominal pain, vomiting uncontrollably. The parts of their bodies exposed to the sticky golden substance had broken out in itchy red blotches. Shea herself now burned with fever. Crying, she asked her uncle, "Why am I feeling so hot? Am I going to die?"

Immobilized by the sickness, the family spent the night in the

forest. In the cool mist of morning, Chong Yang led them back to
their village. His wife and children all suffered coughing spells,
blurred vision and nausea. Walking slowly on the steep mountain
trails, they held on to one another for support. Every step was
painful.

When they reached home, they found the straw roofs and small
family gardens of their hillside community covered with yellow
spots. The sloping clay streets, usually alive with playing children,
were empty but for the contorted carcasses of dead chickens, pigs
and dogs. From the wood and bamboo houses came sounds of
retching, painful moans and wailing for sick and dying loved
ones.

Within hours the sticky yellow spots had turned to a powder that
was dissipated by the chilly mountain wind and washed away by
monsoon rain. Over the next ten days Shea Vang's fever subsided,
but her eyes yellowed and her stomach swelled as she began passing
blood. Ten others in the area had died.

Each day Shea watched the sky, fearing the aircraft would
return. "Why are they doing this to us?" she asked her uncle.

Chong decided they must escape. The village chief advised him to
take his entire clan. In the past, Vietnamese soldiers had arrested
and punished relatives of villagers who fled.

On September 16, in the dark night rain, Chong Yang assembled
his group of 52 relatives, many of them still suffering residual effects
from the chemical attack. Ranging in age from infants to 60-year-
old grandparents, they carried only a little food and the clothes on
their backs. To avoid Vietnamese and Pathet Lao soldiers
patrolling main roads and trails, Chong Yang and the other men cut
their own trails through the dense foliage.

As they slowly descended to lower altitudes the humidity became
unbearable. Swarms of gnats and mosquitoes harassed them from
dusk until after the sun burned through the morning mist.

They traveled this way for almost two weeks, walking day and
night. Their only sustenance was the rice they carried, water, wild
herbs and an occasional wild banana or pineapple. When the
children and grandparents succumbed to exhaustion, they were
carried by the young adults.

On the twelfth day, as dawn illuminated the valley below, they saw the vast Mekong River, and beyond it Thailand and freedom. They waited until the sun set before descending into the valley. They reached the Mekong at last light and looked across the half-mile of rapid water. A murmur went through the group: "We don't know how to swim. We will drown." Shea Vang was afraid, but obeyed her uncle and helped to organize the younger children for the crossing. Others tied bamboo saplings into rafts. Mothers strapped their babies onto their backs. Old people were tied with ropes to young men.

Shea was trembling with fear when a Vietnamese patrol opened fire on the refugees from the dark woodline. Two teen-age boys grabbed Shea's arms and dived with her into the cold water. The swift current carried them downstream as Shea struggled to keep her head above water. On the river bank, two H'mong men, the only ones with rifles, exchanged fire with the Vietnamese long enough to allow all the refugees to plunge into the river. Chong Yang held tightly to his wife and youngest child, encouraging them to keep stroking.

Eventually, small clusters of refugees began washing ashore on the Thai side. With their last bits of strength, they crawled into the trees and brush. When Chong Yang had accounted for his entire family, he and some others walked to the nearest town, Bung Kan, and asked Thai police for shelter. The officer on duty accompanied Chong to the river bank, where they found the shivering group of exhausted refugees. The officer led them to an empty garage next to the police compound overlooking the river.

(Ed.- The Vietnamese invasion of Cambodia was not a blessing for the Khmer people, although the PBS series will portray it as such in Part 13. The following information is based on issues 1, 2 and 3 of *The Indochina Newsletter*, edited by Stephen Denny, 1979.)

Famine hit Cambodia in 1979. The country had already witnessed barbaric autogenocide by the Khmer Rouge Communists, where perhaps two to three million people had died in three and a half years of terror. But the 1979 invasion of Cambodia by the Vietnamese had been timed to disrupt the rice season. As a result, rice could not be cultivated in western Cambodia as refugees fled the fighting and the two armies seized rice stocks. The disruption continued for months, hurting the planting and harvesting of rice throughout the year. According to the Sept. 24, 1979 issue of *Newsweek*, the main rice crop, usually planted in May and harvested in December and January, had not even been planted.

Aid was desperately needed by the country to prevent the starvation of perhaps millions. Relief agencies were negotiating with the Heng Samrin government for permission to transport food into the country. The government demanded that it be given full control of the distribution. In an apparent effort to prevent foreign observers from entering the country, the Hanoi-controlled government in Phnom Penh refused visas to UNICEF and Red Cross officials. A reporter for the New York *Times* News Service speculated that the Heng Samrin government wanted to tie relief for the starving people to diplomatic recognition. Furthermore, the fighting between the Vietnamese invaders and Pol Pot's army was intensifying at the time.

In October 1979, a reporter for the *Far Eastern Economic Review* said that Vietnamese authorities were requesting that detailed distribution plans be submitted to them and demanding total control of food distribution be given to the Heng Samrin government. "Pol Pot's supporters" were not to be fed.

The U.S. proposed to bring $69 million in aid to Cambodia by truck. Distribution of the aid was to be administered by the Red Cross and UNICEF. The Phnom Penh government rejected the idea, accusing the U.S. of an "imperialist plot" to assist the Pol Pot forces. According to an American relief official, Heng Samrin lashed out at the Red Cross and UNICEF because the two organizations were feeding 600,000 Cambodians by the Thai border. Refugees seeking relief were being stopped or killed by Vietnamese troops guarding the roads. According to an article by Keyes Beech, printed in the L.A. *Times*, Dec. 1, 1979, Vietnamese forces were stealing food relief coming in from the humanitarian agencies and also planting mines in rice fields to control the harvest. Cambodian peasants were being given subsistence rations.

At a press conference in Paris, seven members of the French Parliament reported on their visit to Cambodia and Thailand. They declared that "there is a deliberate attempt to famish the population on the Vietnamese part. The food supplies from Western countries are used as strategic arms to control the population." One deputy remarked that "Kampuchea is still like a concentration camp." (*Southeast Asia Record*, Nov. 23-30, 1979)

PART 10: PEACE IS AT HAND
(1968-1973)

The Paris Peace Talks drag on inconclusively.
Henry Kissinger and Le Duc Tho engage in secret talks.
Ho Chi Minh dies in 1969. More American troops are
withdrawn as the war is Vietnamized. An incursion into
Cambodia takes place in 1970. Antiwar sentiment grows
among members of Congress. Nixon visits Red China
in 1972. The Communists launch a major offensive against
South Vietnam. Nixon responds by bombing the North and
mining Haiphong. There is a breakthrough in negotiations
and Henry Kissinger reports that "peace is at hand."
The agreement stalls as the U.S. forces Saigon to accept it.
Nixon orders the bombing of Hanoi to pressure the North
Vietnamese. Talks resume and an accord is concluded
in January 1973. Lyndon Johnson dies.

The Political Implications of Seating Arrangements

Part 10 deals with the politics behind the scenes of the war
following the Tet Offensive. Like its partner, Part 8, this episode
contains parallel images and comparisons: the funerals of Ho Chi
Minh and Lyndon Johnson; serene reverent crowds paying their
last respects to Chairman Ho while Americans hoot and holler in a
football stadium for Richard Nixon; America's POWs are released
from prison under the mocking banner "Good-bye, Uninvited
Guests" as North Vietnamese prisoners defiantly throw off the
uniforms issued them by the Saigon government; and so on.

Also, as in Part 8, this segment contains serious omissions and
looks at events and issues from only one side, reinforcing ideas

promoted by the series since the very beginning.

The political war is engaged. America, the arrogant bully of the world, is unable to defeat the Vietnamese nationalists (or, as the narrator puts it, "to force the Communist leaders in Hanoi to give up their long-held goal of a unified Vietnam"). The Tet Offensive stuns Johnson, who backs off and goes to the conference table.

The U.S. collars the South Vietnamese and brings them along. The North Vietnamese bring "the National Liberation Front, the Vietcong, the Communist-led movement in the South." Mme. Nguyen Thi Binh, NLF foreign minister, arrives in Paris to cheering crowds. This scene is very precious because it is the last time the NLF will be mentioned in relation to the negotiations. This is unusual, since the PBS series has thus far tried so hard to convince its viewers that the NLF was independent of Hanoi, an outgrowth of spontaneous generation resulting from the tyranny of the Saigon regime. Now, during the talks in Paris, the organization will disappear as all the action comes from Hanoi. How do the producers explain this peculiar event? Quite simply: they don't.

Meanwhile, the discussions in Paris go nowhere. Each side reads a prepared statement to the other. There is a break for lunch. The two parties return. Johnson leaves office as "the diplomats haggled over the political implications of the seating arrangements." Who haggled? Hanoi's delegates. But the series gives credit to both sides.

Months later, the presumably sneaky Henry Kissinger opens secret talks with Le Duc Tho. This seemingly treacherous move was concealed even from "top U.S. officials" – a reflection, one might surmise, of the well known "devious" nature of the Nixon administration.

The war escalates as Nixon orders an offensive into Cambodia. He has other tricks up his sleeve, too. The first is a "television spectacular – a diplomatic bombshell." The president goes to Peking to visit Mao Zedong, "the Communist leader he once reviled." They share a toast and watch revolutionary ballet. The North Vietnamese continue the war by launching a "new and ambitious offensive" (cf., the "fresh ambitious offensive," Tet 1968, earlier in the program). But Nixon mines the ports and bombs the North, then goes running off to meet Brezhnev.

There is a breakthrough in Paris. Hanoi drops its demand that
the Thieu government be dissolved. An agreement is near.
Kissinger sends the word to Saigon. Thieu rejects the agreement,
complaining that it allows North Vietnamese troops to remain in the
South. Nixon tries to push it through him.

By now the viewers should be feeling sorry for poor Hanoi.
Stymied in their long-held goal of unifying the country, they have
been betrayed by their allies, China and the Soviet Union. Now, as
one U.S. delegate suggests, they are afraid the U.S. has "led them
down the garden path" and made them the "victims of the biggest
con job in history." Hanoi goes public with the agreement.

Henry Kissinger follows with a press conference, where he
notes, "We believe that peace is at hand." Nguyen Co Thach,
Hanoi's current foreign minister, interprets this statement as a
political maneuver to boost Nixon's presidential campaign.

But Saigon demands changes in the text of the agreement and
Hanoi backs off on its promises. According to Thieu Aide Hoang
Duc Nha, the U.S. threatens "brutal reaction" if Saigon fails to fall
in line. In the meantime, the U.S. also warns Hanoi that the
bombing will resume if things don't shape up.

The bombing does resume and Hanoi returns to the negotiations.
In January 1973 an agreement is signed by all parties. Pham Van
Dong declares his intention to continue the war for "peace, . . .
independence, freedom and the peaceful unification" of Vietnam.
The episode closes with contrasting scenes of returning American
POWs staggering off in a Hanoi propaganda film and Viet Cong
prisoners tossing off the shirts given them by their Southern captors
as they prepare to continue the fight for Pham Van Dong.

The lengthy negotiations were a complicated affair. Even today
the policies, goals and expectations of the principals in this matter
are debated, and clear answers are not always forthcoming. (1) The
PBS series simplifies everything for its viewers by relying on themes
rather than details and facts. We hear of secret talks, pitiful Hanoi,
victimized Saigon, and so on, but do not learn what really
happened.

Needless to say, not all observers are satisfied with this type of
oversimplified presentation. Commentator Norman Podhoretz

offers his view of the Nixon administration's peace efforts in his
book *Why We Were In Vietnam*. Below is a summary of Podhoretz'
main ideas, which might be compared to those of the television
series. (2)

The author suggests that just as Eisenhower was elected in 1952
due to his pledge to end the Korean War, Nixon won in 1968 largely
because he promised to end the war in Vietnam. America had
reached its limit in Vietnam and the only question remaining was
how to disengage. Elements of the antiwar movement felt that
Nixon might order an immediate withdrawal, possibly justifying
this by reminding the public that the Democrats had gotten the U.S.
into the war and now he was bringing us out. But while Nixon did
plan to end America's combat role, he refused to do so at once or with
such conditions as would give up South Vietnam to the Communists. Unlike many of his critics, Pres. Nixon did not believe the
people of Vietnam would be better off under Communism than under
Thieu. Furthermore, he was concerned about America's image
abroad and how it might be tarnished if the U.S. abandoned its ally
and set up a Communist victory.

At the same time, Nixon declined the option of escalating the
war. Serious escalation would mean bombing North Vietnam's
dikes or using nuclear weapons. Nixon believed such action would
lead to a huge loss of life among civilians and therefore was
unacceptable. Other possibilities included invading the North or
attacking Communist supply lines. These options would probably
cause dissention among the American people, harm his plans to
improve relations with Russia and China, and finally, not offer
sufficient proof that South Vietnam was capable of defending itself
in the future. For these reasons, Nixon opted for Vietnamization.
The key to Nixon's policy of disengagement was his declaration that
the U.S. would "continue fighting until the Communists agreed to
negotiate a fair and honorable peace or until the South Vietnamese
were able to defend themselves on their own – whichever came
first."

The serious negotiating was done in secret by Henry Kissinger
and the North Vietnamese representatives, Le Duc Tho and Xuan
Thuy. Hanoi demanded that the U.S. not only withdraw from South
Vietnam, but also do away with the Thieu government. Kissinger

felt that the Communists were asking the U.S. to do what they themselves were unable to do, and naturally he refused to go along with this. The negotiations remained stuck on this issue for years. Meanwhile, critics in the U.S. blamed Nixon's administration for the failure of the negotiations, although Hanoi had stubbornly been rejecting various proposals offered by Kissinger.

In 1969 Nixon ordered the bombing of Cambodia and the next year he ordered the incursion. He felt these measures were necessary both to ensure that South Vietnam would be able to hold up after America left and to protect the withdrawal of American troops. Although aimed at speeding up the end of the war, these actions were widely interpreted as "escalation" and violently protested. The operation in Laos in 1971 had the same basic goals. However, the results were not as bright. The Lam Son operation probably caused Nixon to doubt the progress of Vietnamization.

The North Vietnamese invasion of 1972 became a challenge for Nixon. He felt that if the invasion were stopped, Hanoi would finally agree to a peace settlement. He did not view it as a test of Vietnamization. Determined that the North Vietnamese should lose, Nixon ordered the bombing of the North and the mining of Haiphong harbor, while putting political pressure on Moscow and Peking. The North's military failure made Hanoi more receptive in the negotiations. Because of America's role in blunting the offensive, and South Vietnam's "uneven" military performance, the invasion offered no conclusions about the progress of Vietnamization.

Both North Vietnam and the U.S. were eager for a quick settlement. Hanoi feared that Nixon might take a harder position after he was re-elected. Kissinger thought Nixon's position might be weakened after the election if the Republicans lost seats in Congress. When Thieu refused to accept the agreements, Hanoi brought them to public attention, hoping to force the U.S. to abide by the accord even without Thieu. Kissinger responded with a press conference in which he stated that "peace is at hand." He was putting pressure on Thieu to go along with the U.S. Kissinger's "peace is at hand" statement was viewed by many as election-eve politicking, although by that time such gimmicks were hardly necessary. George McGovern was doing badly in the polls and was not expected to win.

Thieu was dissatisfied with the agreement for several reasons, even though Hanoi had made major concessions. The North dropped the demand that Thieu's government be replaced; it accepted continued U.S. aid to Saigon; it agreed to internationally supervised elections; and it dropped its demand for a coalition government. Thieu wanted safeguards against a coalition government, which he knew would simply be a free ticket to the Communists to eventually take power. He especially feared the U.S.' acceptance of Northern troops in the South (troops which Hanoi still publicly denied were there). Kissinger claimed that Thieu had previously agreed to the presence of Northern troops in negotiations in 1970. Washington expected that limitations on infiltration and the closing of sanctuaries in Cambodia and Laos would force the Northern troops to return home or disappear through attrition. Nixon promised military aid to support South Vietnam and assured Thieu that the U.S. would assist his government if the North violated the agreements.

But Thieu held firm and Hanoi went back on some of its earlier concessions. On December 18, Nixon ordered the bombing of Hanoi, which lasted until December 30. The North Vietnamese returned to the negotiating table. Thieu was persuaded to accept the arrangement. An agreement was signed in January 1973. In the view of Nixon and Kissinger, the agreement was a victory over North Vietnam. Whether or not the view was correct, it would be unfair to say that Nixon was deliberately deceiving South Vietnam or the world by forging an easy way out of the war for the U.S. within a "decent interval."

The account of the Nixon administration's peace efforts by Podhoretz offers an interesting balance to that given by the *Television History*. On the one hand, we find thoughtful research and careful analysis based on available documentation. Whether or not one agrees with the author's views, there is at least a respectable framework for intelligent discussion of the issues of the time.

On the other hand, the PBS series concentrates on popular themes, not all of which are well founded, or, for that matter, even researched. Part 10 takes its name from the Kissinger statement, which it interprets (through the uncontested words of one speaker) as a deliberate attempt to influence the presidential election and make Nixon a "hero of peace." The series fails to point out that Nixon was already ahead in opinion polls, that his opponent was being severely criticized for announcing that he would virtually surrender to Hanoi as soon as he got in office, and that the whole matter would have remained secret at the time if Hanoi itself had not exposed the agreement in the first place. Depth in analysis is not a characteristic of the PBS series. Although the producers claim their program is intended for adult education, it seems more appropriate for disinterested eighth-graders.

As we will see, shallow political analysis is not the only way Part 10 attacks the U.S. in the last years of the war.

You Are Criminals!

No episode of the *Television History* would be complete without some scurrilous attack on America's conduct during the war. Part 10 is certainly no exception.

Narrator: "Used on Vietnam: explosives, defoliants, fragmentation bombs, napalm."

A chorus of schoolchildren describe how they emerged from their bomb shelter to find trees burnt, houses razed and cattle killed by Nixon's bombing.

Then there is the "Christmas bombing" of Hanoi, December 1972, which Hanoi (and many critics of the war) described as an act of terrorism.

War is sick and horrible. One does not need to be Richard Ellison to figure that one out. But any suggestion that war's horror is one-sided is, to say the least, grossly unfair.

Of course, Part 10 does include a scene of VC terrorism: Viet Cong rockets fall on Danang civilians as the war continues. However, this scene lasts but a few seconds and then fades from sight and memory. The producers decline to give it the meticulous coverage they reserve for America's war actions. There are no statistics regarding casualties or destruction in Danang. No victims or witnesses are interviewed to describe the tragedy of being under attack by the Communists. There is no one to stand up and denounce the VC for killing women and children. Still, the producers believe that a few seconds of vague filmage of a single incident serves to "balance" the gross atrocities of the Americans that they are about to show.

Nowhere does the narrator remind us that the Communists, too, used explosives and fragmentation bombs, and that they would have gladly employed napalm and chemicals if they had had the capacity (as they generously proved later on). Americans did not string landmines around people's necks and watch them explode. The Communists did this in Quang Tri, but the series doesn't talk about that. Only America's weapons are evil.

Adm. Thomas Moorer, of the Joint Chiefs of Staff, is permitted to defend the Christmas bombing. "The targets," he tells us, "selected in the 1972 Christmas bombing consisted entirely of military targets." As one might guess, he is followed by a North Vietnamese doctor dressed in surgical whites recounting how he cut apart corpses with his knife; this comes amid scenes of devastation of Bach Mai Hospital in Hanoi. Add more shots of civilian areas reduced to rubble, interviews with two more witnesses who relate the deaths of their neighbors in the attack, a notion of the bombing tonnage and a tally of deaths, and the viewer should get a pretty clear idea why Le Duc Tho called the Americans "criminals."

Nowhere in the series is there even the slightest hint that the number of civilians slaughtered by the Communists at Quang Tri and An Loc earlier that same year far exceeded the number of those who died in the December bombing of Hanoi. Where are the death tolls, the interviews, the scenes of destruction? The question is pointless.

Still, the December bombing is portrayed as a terrorist act perpetrated against a brave and determined people. We are told that refugees from other bombed towns caused Hanoi's population to swell. Half a million people were evacuated in anticipation of the attack. "The Soviet-made surface-to-air missles, SAMs, were ready for the American bombers." The American pilots were scared, says Capt. Michael Conners, but eager to go. The mighty SAMs shot around the B-52s and defended the courageous little Vietnamese. B-52 losses were high. Bach Mai Hospital was hit twice; "their target may have been a small airfield nearby." A residential district was struck by "some of the bombs." The attack was compared to the atomic blast on Hiroshima; the tonnage was greater, but the deaths (1,318) fewer because the targets were more dispersed.

The impression given by the television series is the same one promoted by critics of the bombing in 1972: that it was a deliberate and devastating terrorist attack that totally disregarded civilian casualties. Richard Nixon's attitude is depicted by a striking picture: as a grieving woman digs among the ruins of what must have been her home, the narrator remarks offhandedly that the president's "main concern, he said, was not domestic and international criticism, but high B-52 losses."

As presented in the series, Nixon's posture is appalling and callous contempt for the victims of the bombing. Taken in its true context, however, Nixon's position is more understandable. The president was not concerned about the criticism because he knew the censure was unfounded. The bombing was, as one observer later wrote, "militarily... the most successful U.S. operation of the war." (3) Civilian casualties were far fewer than had been charged by the critics and in no way comparable to those in the Dresden raids or the Tokyo bombing in World War II. (4) Visitors to Hanoi in 1973 reported that damage to the city was much less than they had expected, given the exaggerated reports that had been thrown about by the media during the attack.

In other words, Nixon was right and his critics wrong. But that is not the way the *Television History* tells it.

Defense Department photographs of Hanoi taken after the bombing would also show that Bach Mai Hospital had not been wiped out, as North Vietnam's propaganda had reported. Only one wing had been partially destroyed and the "small airfield nearby" was described by one source as "an airfield where MiG-21 interceptor aircraft were based, and... also the central control center for North Vietnam's air defense system." (5) Stanley Karnow did not ask the "mastermind" Gen. Giap why he had risked the lives of the hospital's patients (who, strangely enough, had not been among the 500,000 evacuated before the bombing) by locating a military facility so close to the hospital.

In its efforts to describe the December 1972 bombing as primarily a terrorist attack aimed at civilians, the series blatantly ignores the overwhelming military effectiveness of the operation. Prior to the attack, Hanoi had been the most heavily armed missile complex in the world. Such was not the case after the bombing. Writes Allan Goodman: "B-52 evasive tactics had decisively defeated the SAM ... defense system, and when the bombing was ended, not a single SAM was left. The bombing also destroyed the vital military supplies that it had taken Hanoi months to get because of the naval blockade. So effective were these raids, in fact, that consensus was again growing within the highest circles in the Pentagon that a military victory, not peace, might be at hand." (6) Stanley Karnow himself notes that "as I observed in 1981, ... most of the buildings (in Hanoi and Haiphong) were neither demolished nor reconstructed. In fact, the B-52s were programmed to spare civilians, and they pinpointed their targets with extraordinary precision." (p. 653)

Somehow, this message got lost in the production of the *Television History*.

Perhaps the worst "war criminals" in the eyes of the series' producers are the American pilots who "deliberately" destroyed civilian areas in their presumably wanton and senseless missions over all of Vietnam. Fervent war critics liked to say that the pilots who were shot down and captured were the ones who suffered for their hideous crimes.

Col. Robinson Risner, seven years a POW, whose testimony was abused in Part 6, returns to take another slap in the face in Part 10. He talks about the war protestors and how they "only encouraged the Vietnamese, prolonged the war, worsened our condition and cost the lives of more Americans on the battlefield." Referring to his captor's practice of exaggerating information in order to demoralize the prisoners, Risner says, "If 200 people marched on Washington, they made it 200,000." Unfortunately, this remark is placed immediately following the narrator's note that at one time a quarter of a million people did indeed go to Washington to demonstrate against the war. The result of this editing is that Risner is made to look like a fool and anything he says later is discredited.

Later, Risner is shown re-enacting the jubilation of the POWs during the December bombing – "guys jumping up and down and clapping each other on the back. People hollering and shouting. ..."

Risner gleefully told one guard, "They're not trying to kill me, they're trying to kill you!"

Thus is Robinson Risner depicted in the series as a foolish and insensitive killer. He represents all the POWs who flew over Vietnam dropping bombs on innocent civilians (so the series says) with indifference, and even joy.

Adm. Moorer expresses his astonishment when he would tell people of the tortures suffered by the POWs and they would respond, "Well, it only serves them right – they had no business volunteering."

The producers of the *Television History* give every indication of concurring with that opinion.

The idea is punctuated by the words of Le Duc Tho (presumably an unbiased observer of the events): "All you are responsible. And you are criminals!"

Ho Goes to Meet His Predecessors

The Second Indochina War was not yet over when Ho Chi Minh finally passed away in 1969, at the age of 79. Ho had been trained in Moscow and China as a professional agitator and revolutionary and served as an agent of the Comintern. He embraced Marxism and his models included Stalin and Mao Zedong. From his earliest years as a Communist, Ho had advocated Marxist socialism and the international creed of Lenin. When in power, he imposed an alien Communist system upon his people, replacing traditional beliefs with socialist ideology and persecuting those who opposed his views. For more than thirty years he plotted how he might take control of Laos and Cambodia and his agents agitated in those countries as well as Thailand. He fought to transform Southeast Asia into a Communist state within the Soviet Federation.

In May of 1969, with his health failing, old Ho wrote his testament, his message to the people left "in anticipation of the day when I shall go and join Karl Marx, V.I. Lenin and other elder revolutionaries." (7)

In Part 10 of the *Television History*, Ho Chi Minh – Marxist revolutionary, chairman of the Vietnamese Communist Party, oppressor, dictator, terrorist leader, imperialist agitator, radical social reformer, betrayer of popular causes, manipulator of his

people, professional fraud and expert propagandist – is buried as a
nationalist and a hero.

Ho is quoted urging his people on, promising victory and
independence. "We will rebuild our land ten times more beautiful,"
he said.

When Ho wrote those words, he was only raising false hopes, if
anyone really believed him any more. In 1975, North Vietnam
achieved victory – with the aid of socialist sister countries and at the
price of countless lives. Independence is a meaningless word –
Vietnam is a member of the Soviet machine and is dependent on
Russian military and economic aid. Rather than becoming more
beautiful, Vietnam has degenerated to a condition worse than what
it experienced during the harshest days of colonialism.

Ho's secretary, Tuu Ky, quotes from the Chairman's testament –
but not quite correctly. "He said he was only going to visit Lenin
and his other predecessors. And by the word 'predecessors' he
could have meant that he was going to visit past Vietnamese
leaders." (Tuu Ky also named Karl Marx, but the translator
dropped that as an inessential detail.) The producers are satisfied
with the misquotation and twisted interpretation offered by the
Communist spokesperson. The modification reinforces their own
twisted view of Ho as a nationalist rather than Communist going to
meet his "predecessors" rather than "elder revolutionaries." The
producers are also content to display films of old Ho exercising and
visiting the people, and the huge crowd of mourners gathered for his
funeral. Pham Van Dong's "pain" at the loss of Ho Chi Minh
becomes the pain of the nation.

The real pain is that such tales can actually be believed.

A final note: The series fails to mention that immediately after
Ho's death, prison conditions for the American POWs improved
markedly. There were fewer beatings, tortures, interrogations,
threats and warnings. The guards almost began to look human.
Changes seemed to be taking place.

A Tragic Mistake

More and more members of Congress turned against the war in its
later years. For some it became a political affair, a chance to
criticize the incumbent president. Richard Nixon was an easy

target for deprecation, even though he was bringing American soldiers home from the war. It was popular to rave against him, his controversial policies, and his questionable style of politics (the latter would eventually convey him out of the White House earlier than he had expected).

For other Congressmen, however, the war was a more serious matter, for it touched on questions of morality, reason and America's place in a very troubled world. Many felt the long and indeterminate war was not worth the cost and sacrifice already paid. Thoughtful ones, like Senator Mansfield, decided that the war was a "mistake, a tragic mistake" and the best thing for America to do was to get out to avoid adding "outrage to the sacrifices of those who have suffered and died" in the conflict.

To the producers of the PBS series, Sen. Mansfield's passionate speech represents the enlightened view of the war, a view they obviously share since they quote the senator at notable length. Yet for all his sincerity and eloquence, Sen. Mansfield had not grasped the full implications of the Vietnamese "revolution" and the future that Communism held in store for the people of Southeast Asia. Now, the Vietnamese, Cambodians and Lao know first-hand why the war was being fought and what the sacrifice was for. And there is no one quoted to suggest that the tragic mistake was not in fighting the war, but in misunderstanding it and losing.

(Karnow gives a rather hearty political history of the time, relying on the three s's of his style, namely singlemindedness, speculation and sensationalism.

(One side of the battle is waged by unstable personalities: a U.S. president capable of going off the deep end at any moment and "blasting North Vietnam to bits" (p. 651); a secretary of state "inclined to rages" (p. 650); a leader in Saigon who is compared to Vietnamese *collaborateurs* of the 19th century, and who in his career "plotted and juggled incessantly, finally becoming president in 1967, after which he plotted and juggled incessantly," a man characterized as "stubborn and indecisive, suspicious, cunning, yet often naive." (p. 649) The reader will find no such revelatory exclamations concerning the North Vietnamese leaders, who oddly .seem to be forever mentally alert, reasonable, objective, and cool as cucumbers – except when terrorized by mad American presidents, at which time a little emoting is to be expected.

(The Chief Correspondent reports that Henry Kissinger's "attitude toward the Communists was apoplectic: 'They're just a bunch of shits. Tawdry, filthy shits'." (p. 652) One never learns what Le Duc Tho and Pham Van Dong truly thought of the Americans, although they certainly treated their American prisoners worse than animals and actually fed them shit at times.

(For Karnow, the war was an amusement park of "if only's" and "might have been's." If only the American leaders had been more open to this or that. . . . If only the Americans had noted signs of that thing or this. . . . Most of the responsibility for setting things right thus falls on the U.S. Karnow's speculations on Ho Chi Minh are noteworthy. The Chief Fortuneteller writes: If only the "primitive French capitalists" had not been so intransigent, then Ho Chi Minh might have been another Gandhi. (p. 118) If only the U.S. had been more enlightened about Vietnam, then Ho might have become another Tito. (p. 136) Taking his logic one step further, one might conclude: If only Ho Chi Minh had not been a heavy smoker of Philip Morris cigarettes he might have become another Buddha.

(One of Karnow's most pathetic victims is Richard Nixon, who comes out in the *History* as a borderline lunatic ready and willing to use the power at his disposal to wreak utter havoc according to his whims. Let it be perfectly clear that this writer is no fan of Nixon. However, the question being posed here is not should one like or agree with the man, but is it fair to judge him with sensational labels, extravagant phrases and one-sided observations?

(Nixon believed that power was necessary in dealing with the Communists. For this he is respected by many South Vietnamese who say that power is the only thing the Communists understand. Nixon put little faith in the sincerity of the Communist leaders. Over the years, they have proven unworthy of faith, even that of their own people. And if Nixon was ready to bomb the North or cross into Cambodia, was that necessarily madness? For five decades the Vietnamese Communists have been slaughtering their countrymen, as well as the people of Laos and Cambodia. They have great atrocities to their credit, including the massacres at Quang Tri and An Loc in 1972, and yellow rain warfare in the mountains of Laos.

They have approved terrorism, executed their followers, launched rockets into populated areas, bombed refugee camps, and thrown hand grenades at civilians. Yet where in the *History* does Stanley Karnow question the sanity of the Communist leaders? It is foolish to ask.)

Footnotes

1. For example, see the conference report *Some Lessons and Non-Lessons of Vietnam: Ten Years After the Paris Peace Accords*, Woodrow Wilson International Center for Scholars, 1983
2. See Norman Podhoretz, *Why We Were In Vietnam*, Chapter 4 "Why We Withdrew"
3. Allan Goodman, *The Lost Peace*, p. 161
4. Guenter Lewy, *America in Vietnam*, p 413
5. John Hubbell, *P.O.W.*, pp. 592-3n
6. Allan Goodman, Note 3 above
7. From *Ho Chi Minh: Selected Articles and Speeches*, Ed. and with an Introduction by Jack Woodis, International Publishers

Supplements

(Ed. - After being relieved at An Loc, soldier-writer Phan Nhat Nam went to Quang Tri where intense fighting had taken place. He visited Highway 1, known as the "Highway of Terror," where Communist tanks and artillery had ambushed and massacred perhaps twenty thousand persons fleeing the invasion. Below are some of Phan Nhat Nam's personal reflections on the scene. From *Mua He Do Lua*. Translation.)

I was on Kilometer 9 from Quang Tri, in the area of Mai Dang hamlet, Hai Lam village. There is no word, no adjective . . . I could not speak, weep, or cry out at the scene before me then. I could only remain silent, grind my teeth and bite my lip, though I should bite so hard my lip began to bleed. My arms fell useless, my eyes dimmed, my nostrils twitched. My body was new to me, emerging at that atrocious scene before me . . . How could I control the pounding of my heart? None could stop my eyes from blinking, my flesh from creeping, or my temples from pounding . . . I knew nothing, absolutely nothing of my own body . . .

I was no longer a living person, because to live means being among the living, sharing their joys and sorrows, their pains and cares. All around me, before me, there was but one thing, one atmosphere – Death. Yes, only death surrounded and enveloped me. There was only death encompassing all space.

I had lived through the death at Dong Xoai in 1965, at Binh Gia in 1964, had lay and slept with corpses for a long time. But next to the pained silence of those deaths there was still the sound of talking and movement of the living, though it was the agonized wailing or the emotional words of families wearing funeral clothes as they gathered around the swollen bodies before they were returned after seven days lying in battle . . . Scenes of death where there were still living beings – that I could endure, that miserable endurance that only war teaches. And just before, at An Loc, with its anonymous graves and mass graves . . . there were still living creatures beside the dead . . . They lived, though with senseless bodies, moving about as if engrossed in tragedy – people crazed with sadness, crazed to silence, holding their craziness inside, upside-down, deep craziness, heavy in their brain cells. Still, they were alive . . .

But here at Giap Hau, Mai Dang, Hai Lam, it was different from An Loc, a higher level, towering above, a stretch longer, interminably longer. The death on these nine kilometers of road was nine kilometers of heaven and earth dying, death in each grain of sand, death in every leaf, death scattered in each strip of flesh, in each bundle of vertebrae, or bone, death in scattered heads and in bent, blackened hands . . .

So many. Nine kilometers or 9000 meters, on each meter an average of two shattered skeletons – how many in all . . . ? One can only estimate the number. A Red Cross truck lay overturned and smashed, exposing black feet from the back door . . . A Honda motorcycle broken in two – only two pairs of Japanese sandals left, but where are the riders? One could not distinguish this arm, that leg, that skull . . . The army engineers steamrolled the long road. The bodies – no, I must say the bundles of bones crushed together with clothes and everything else, pushed together rattling noisily, the human "trash" moving fast, as a black, slimy grease shone on the tar – the "tar" of human flesh!!!

The bright sun, white field, the silent road, the motors of the earthrollers – it is more correct to call them people-rollers – with their steady sound, the hot air rising on the smooth road, the air with its heavy odor . . . The universe dead in the heart of the sunlight. There was the odor of people in the sunlight. What could I do? Shut my nose, cover my mouth – but it was useless. The air of death stagnated on the skin, slipped into the nose, stuck onto the clothes. It sucked itself into the lungs and flowed in my blood. I stood in the heart of death. How to escape it . . . ? The scenes of mass deaths of the Jews in concentration camps were emotionally powerful because the witnesses could see the corpses – corpses stacked up, neat, intact . . . But on the nine kilometers of highway at Quang Tri, one could no longer use the term "corpses," because they were smashed, broken, and thrown about . . . Death above every death. There were no "dead people" on that horrible piece of road on that tragic ground. Giap Hau, Hai Lam – the names are in my blood so deeply they will never fade from my memory . . .

Abandoned road, the sky threatening, the ground beneath my feet soft with each step, the wind cool and the air vast. I sat down beside the road and reached into a pond to wash each finger. Did I want to wash off part of the death around me?

Strange feeling: I was guilty. I lived. Yes, I had the feeling that I myself had killed and taken the right to live, that my own hand had participated in the cruel game. My mind went from one thing to another – shame, indignation, resentment, pain and . . . lack of sensation. I wanted to have a few words with Gen. Giai – though bound to military strategy, he could not abandon Quang Tri so unexpectedly that nine kilometers of highway would be covered with human flesh. Too, I wanted to curse the Northern Army – despite the law of war which says "when you attack, you must win," what kind of person could fire B-40s, B-41s or 75mm artillery from high points at Xuan Lam, Truong Phuoc, Truong Tho, onto a disorderly "objective" – masses of fleeing people? Where is the victory when those painful figures fell? Pity the soldiers in Medical Company 3 who trusted in their white flag with a red cross and displayed the meaningless piece of rag to cross that death. Northern soldier – it seems that you have no human feelings, that your emotions have died out. Who do you liberate when you kill like that?

I wanted to ask, to let the question resound, to shout it until my throat cracked and my veins burst. I wanted to ask why Man killed Man so blatantly and ruthlessly. From where your gun rested to the "objective" the distance was no more than one kilometer, the closest point being less than 50 meters. Did you not hear their cries when you killed?

I wanted to ask the Northern soldiers with all the hatred inside me. What kind of hatred do you have for a dissheveled woman carrying her child amidst a flow of shattered people? I wanted to ask – a thousand times, ten thousand times, the soldier who said he was from the "People's Army." Who were the "people"? I wanted to ask a million times with the invisible shout exploding in my head as I sat on that empty field.

I wanted to claw my face, pound my chest and smash my skin until the blood poured out, to see myself feel the pain and share it, too.

It troubled me that I seemed to feel nothing when I cast my eyes on a skull with touseled hair. Yes, I wanted to curse myself, too, really . . . I, too, was guilty! Oh, God, I was guilty!

(Ed. - The following comes from a letter written by a North Vietnamese woman to her soldier husband, sent to fight in the South. The woman was a schoolteacher from Nghe An province. This letter was retrieved from the soldier's body at the battle of An Loc. The reader may notice that the woman's words reflect none of the fervent nationalism that the PBS series claims inspired the people of North Vietnam. In fact, the letter could have been written by any wife to any soldier husband in any war. Taken from *Mua He Do Lua*, by Phan Nhat Nam. Translation.)

Dear Huu,

Do you miss much the two Sundays that have gone by? I can say that since the time you and I were married, these last two Sundays have been the heaviest and most difficult to get through. Oh, I know so well – during those moments you want to shout so loud, what can I do to embrace your words, to talk to you? I also know that with every step you take you march on like a man without his sense, who does not know those steps or remember them, for your mind keeps thinking and those things called memories will appear again and play like a drama before your eyes. I can guess exactly what you are feeling then – how can I be so clever? Because I lie inside your heart, your blood courses to the rhythm of my breaths so that whatever, no matter where you are I can guess your heart.

Well then, are your legs swollen from marching yet? Has the skin peeled from your shoulders where you've carried your gun? Does it hurt much, Dear? Do you ask them for herbs to massage it – oh, it's so painful. My Huu, I know it's so bad out there. As you eat dried food, can you buy anything to supplement it? Have you gotten sick along the way? When I think of that I get cold all over and I worry about you and miss you even more. Could I develop a boil that would hurt me more? And this is the season for boils, is it not, "leader"? I just call you that for fun, it's not that I dream of such a thing. Actually, in my heart my only wish is that after your three years in the service are through you will come back to me safely. I want to close my eyes and make time go by faster so that you and I can live in a little house and together we can overcome all difficulties and enjoy the beautiful, happy things. Those beautiful joys I cherish in my dreams, a wonderful dream in my mind and heart filled with fidelity of a husband and wife that budded forth from the beginning. Oh, my Dear, so far from you, I miss you so, I love you so! The way you talk and laugh and give me affection – how can I forget? Who can really understand my feelings when I look at the remnants of your life here, your handwriting in the letters you have sent me and your book .. Oh, I would cling to them and gaze at them, on and on and never get weary. My Huu, I could talk more and never stop missing you . . .

PART 11: HOMEFRONT USA

The American people express their feelings about the war through demonstrations, speeches, teach-ins, violence and votes. Opinion polls and public demonstrations indicate a growing number of Americans oppose the war. Young people resist the draft. Vietnam becomes an election issue as Eugene McCarthy and Bobby Kennedy enter the race. Rioting disrupts the 1968 Chicago Democratic convention. Nixon is elected and his administration attacks protestors and the media. The population of heartland America generally supports the war. Vietnam veterans returning from the war are disenchanted by the conflict and join the protestors.

The Best of Times, The Worst of Times

War has horrified people all through history and the war in Southeast Asia was certainly no exception. Modern wars have spawned pacifist sentiments, and again the war in Indochina was no different. It is a tribute to human nature that people prefer peace to war and no democratic nation would be fair to its citizens if it did not allow for the expression of the desire for peace, justice and sensible government. This is part of recognizing that war is not the only way differences can be resolved and that the survival of humanity demands that all reasonable means be pursued before war is undertaken.

America's involvement in Southeast Asia aroused a great deal of public disapproval in this country and without. Some persons agreed with the government's goals of fighting to contain Communism, but disagreed with the methods being used, such as the bombing of North Vietnam or the incursion into Cambodia. Others questioned whether America could win the war, or, if it could, at what price? These persons did not ask, "Is America's involvement justified?" but rather, "Is it worth the cost?"

Still other persons held that the U.S. had no right to be in the war in the first place. Some went so far as to say that America's involvement was "evil" and "immoral" and they demanded that the U.S. leave Vietnam, the sooner the better.

The 1960s and early 1970s were a difficult time in America's history. The Great Society found the nation affluent and restless. Changes were being forged through new social programs and greater personal freedom. The proportion of young people in the country was greater than at any other time in history. The youth "revolution" was shaking the way of life in the U.S. and much of the world. Old ways were being challenged and respect for traditional authority waned. Blacks and other minorities rose in search of their rights. The average individual's level of education increased, and higher expectations accompanied this change. Advances in communication aided the spread of youth culture. Travel was easy and young people began to see new opportunities for their lives as they shared new experiences. The older generation came under attack. The war and the draft were criticized.

As debate raged over the war, the best and worst aspects of America's national character became apparent. On all sides there were ideals, deeply held values, sensitivities and aspirations that inspired and motivated people to act as they did. On the other hand, there were many weaknesses as well, including ignorance, narrow-mindedness, bigotry, resentment, and sometimes just plain foolishness.

One hour of the PBS series cannot possibly deal with all the social changes that affected America's sentiments towards the war. But the *Television History* is impressive in its own way as it declines to deal with virtually all of the factors that influenced those times (or as Peter, Paul and Mary sing it, "a time to try the souls of men, . . . a terrible time.") In fact, if it were not for a few references to civil rights, one would never know there were other troubles in the country.

Rather than dive deeply into the issues, the PBS series skirts by most of the essential parts of the "Homefront," bringing up themes and suggesting balance only enough to keep the viewers from getting too upset. The problem is that there are good reasons to look hard at those times, even if it means getting upset – upset about the war, the war's supporters and detractors, and, too, about those who claim to educate us about it all. When there is so much to say, what is the use of saying so little?

Despite Part 11's all-inclusive title, the chief topic of this episode is the antiwar movement. Being former members of that movement, the producers are careful about what they show. Like wistful daydreamers recollecting some bygone days, they seem to have memories only of the best or most impressive events, while blocking out the bad times or questionable characters. Their reminiscences come out distorted and one-sided, telling only half the story and conveniently forgetting the rest. History then becomes the victim of myopic memory.

To put the audience at ease, a few scenes are included in the beginning of the episode to give the show an appearance of balance and wisdom. Two Christian ministers, one anti-war and one pro-war, are permitted to speak on their respective sides of the war issue in a segment taken from a 1967 news report. A scene from a teach-in includes an ambiguous exchange between two professors with different opinions about Communism. However, once these scenes are presented and then disposed of, Part 11 gets into its story and one finds that some very notable commentaries are being expressed through self-serving words of antiwar speakers and in curious editing procedures.

Judgment becomes clouded. For example, there is the issue of social polarization. During the great debates going on in this country about society, war and life in general, it appeared to many that the country was being polarized, thrust into two opposite zones pitted against each other with little chance for reconciliation. The cause was clearly two-sided. Conservatives stood at one end, barking about the way things 'used to be' and complaining about the kids and too much freedom. Their heroes were folks like Spiro Agnew, whose grandiloquence may have captured the hearts of some classes, but was completely out of touch with the youth, who were looking for something more down to earth and less condescending. Meanwhile, the liberal youths fixed themselves in the other corner, adorned themselves in the costumes of their generation, and went around acting as if they had invented fun, sex and freedom. Their long hair and deliberately exotic dress were intended to turn off their elders, as if drawing a line between "them" and "us." Each side took the other too seriously and, instead of working out an understanding, they retreated further into sophisms and insults. Labels and denunciations that were intended for a specific group could easily be generalized to include far more than the speaker intended. Thus, when Pres. Nixon referred to violent student activists as "bums," the label came to be associated with all demonstrators, and even all students.

The PBS series interviews Henry Kissinger about Nixon and elicits the response that the president tended to act from the gut and so "never found the language of respect and compassion which might have . . . created a bridge at least to the more reasonable elements of the antiwar movement." Says Kissinger, Nixon's attitude contributed to the polarization of American society and the creation of "civil war" conditions in the country. There the matter is dropped.

Granted, Nixon's gibes at "bums" blowing up campuses and burning books probably did not help smooth out relations between his administration and college students, but neither did the actions of those who blew up school buildings and destroyed books. The latter group, however, is not commented about while only Nixon is singled out and given complete responsibility for driving the country to social strife.

(The *Television History* only adds to the confusion by placing Nixon's May 1, 1970 statement about "bums" *after* the Kent State incident [May 4, 1970], calling it a "reaction" to later protests.)

Likewise, the battle on the "homefront" was fed by the actions of the news media and the way it presented the war. As the Nixon administration bewailed what it considered the abuses of the media, the people in the pressrooms were not interested in listening to criticisms about the way they did their job. In November 1969, Spiro Agnew gave his famous speech against the television networks (the speech being fully approved by Agnew's boss). The news media spokespersons responded by lashing back at Nixon's team, bellowing that Nixon was suggesting "repression" and making a "call to prejudice" by such nasty remarks. It was a field day for observers of the "homefront" battle.

The *Television History* brings in Agnew's speech and follows this up with an interview with John Chancellor, of NBC News. Chancellor has already appeared in this episode, commenting on how the media helped explain the importance of Vietnam to the country in 1964 and 1965. The viewers might expect this remark to be accompanied by a segment from a newscast, exemplifying what Chancellor has just claimed. However, it appears the PBS producers could not find such a scene, and so they put on an official Marine newsreel instead. Interesting. In any event, all the way back in 1964, John Chancellor (so he says) was already worried that perhaps the country was getting into something it could not handle.

Now, the NBC anchorman describes with innocence his reaction to the Agnew tirade in 1969. He tells us that he could only say that, "Well, a good journalist, when he gets into a serious subject, always thinks twice before using certain words, and... that we were thinking thrice."

Chancellor does not say if the news editors were thinking thrice when they charged Nixon with "repression," which is what they did after the Agnew speech. Curiously, these charges would return in 1983 when Pres. Reagan banned the media from covering the Grenada invasion. At that time, the calm and thrice-thoughtful Mr. Chancellor would lose his cool and protest Reagan's refusal to allow the "representatives of the people" into the forefront of the operation. Ironically, Chancellor's outrage would be expressed at almost the same time as his appearance on the *Television History*.

The media was strongly criticized for its portrayal of the war. Critics claim the media was becoming decidedly antiwar, presenting the war as an immoral or unjust conflict. While American soldiers were shown amid scenes of destruction and death, the atrocities of the Communists were being ignored. When news of the My Lai massacre finally broke, many Americans were ready to believe that atrocities by GIs were a common occurrence in Vietnam.

The media lavished its attention on Lt. Calley and Capt. Medina.

Journalists researched the story and wrote books about it. Antiwar
activists used My Lai as a symbol of America's immorality,
supported by the great public attention drawn to the incident by the
media. The fact that only shortly before My Lai the Communists
had systematically murdered thousands of people in Hue became
meaningless. It was all America's war and America's crime.
American soldiers became the world's criminals. That is still the
way television presents them. (Scene from a popular weekly series
shown in 1984: Two kidnappers are about to make their getaway.
One drops down in a helicopter to pick up his buddy. As he lands, he
remarks, "Just like in Nam, isn't it?")

Sixteen years after My Lai, the *Television History* adds nothing to
the story but only tosses up vague questions: "Only Calley was
convicted, in a swirl of controversy: Was he a scapegoat or war
criminal? Was the massacre an isolated case or a common occurrence? Had draft inequities hurt the morale of the army?" The
producers dare say no more, to keep their noses clean of the
controversy. However, in the remainder of the series they make it
clear that burning hootches and dropping hand grenades into holes
is just part of the procedure and that everywhere Americans went
they left death and destruction. No one saw any VC being killed,
only civilians.

Weak Around the Edges

Among the weaknesses of "Homefront USA" is its failure to deal
adequately with the radical elements of the antiwar movement. Of
course, the series presents some scenes of violent protest: demonstrators moving in on the Pentagon, the Chicago convention riot,
Kent State. Protests took on an illegal character: organizer
David Harris describes at considerable length an anti-draft
demonstration in San Francisco where draft cards were collected in
a basket and then dropped at the feet of the federal attorney.

But the philosophies and attitudes that justified violent action
and civil disobedience are not presented, as if simply recalling the
experience will explain everything to the viewers. It is noteworthy
that the most radical statement quoted in Part 11 is Jerry Rubin's
remark about the "menopausal men" running the government.

The producers might argue that the radicals comprised only a small portion of the antiwar movement and that their violence and other antics should not be portrayed as representing the movement as a whole. There is some reason to this argument, of course. However, the producers of this series did not show such a sense of responsibility and fairness when they described the people of South Vietnam as pimps, prostitutes and pushers.

By declining to present the extremist segment of the antiwar movement, the *Television History* denies that segment's significant role in the direction of the movement. For, as one observer wrote, "it was the radicals who gave the antiwar movement its dynamism, its energy, and, most of all, its visibility." (1)

Whether or not the extremists helped organize the numerous demonstrations, protest marches, and other activities designed to express disapproval of the war, they were quite often there to take advantage of these events to display their own opinions in whatever manner they deemed appropriate. More responsible opponents of the war may not have liked those who stomped on American flags or shouted obscenities, but there was little they could do to stop them, short of using the "Gestapo tactics" they denounced.

The violent and offensive behavior exhibited by extremists may have given the movement a bad name, but it did not necessarily dissuade war critics from pursuing their course. Radicals played an important part in some demonstrations. Even in the worst times, moderate protestors were able to rally their supporters against extremists and around the notion that protests must be peaceful and controlled in order to prove to the country that responsible people could, and did, oppose the war.

Protestors were in search of a moral cause. As a result, they accepted new standards of behavior, which probably would have been rejected in other, more peaceful, times. The burning of draft cards took the place of dropping them in baskets. Heckling, haranguing and name-calling were often adopted as proper reactions to the movement's villain figures. Moderate and controlled actions lacked the drama or potency to force attention to the war issue and effect policy changes at high levels. For those who held that America's role in the war was immoral, almost any action against the war was okay, as long as nobody got hurt. Ransacking government offices, spilling red paint on flags, wearing hoods and denouncing the U.S. as a Nazi state became justified as acts of conscience. While most people would not go as far as the SDS, they might still find heroes in Philip and Daniel Berrigan.

The radicals performed wonders in bringing publicity to the movement. Their abnormal dress and abnormal actions attracted both crowds and reporters while quieter demonstrations gained less attention. The radicals made the country stand up and take notice of the antiwar movement. For better or worse, the noise they made impressed Americans and challenged the general public to deal with ideas other than those being proposed by supporters of the war. At times, the movement would be identified with the radicals, despite their limited actual appeal. After the Chicago demonstrations, for instance, the name of Abbie Hoffman became a household word, although there are many who would argue that he did not deserve the celebrity.

Although called the "antiwar movement", the people who protested the war did not make up a single united faction with shared goals and values. In many cases, the real object of protest was not the war, but America. This was especially true among the radicals.

Numerous times during the war, the protestors were accused of being led by Communists. Part 11 includes the accusation, but shies away from admitting that Communists were involved in the antiwar movement. They came from different groups: Leninists, Trotsky-ites, Maoists, Socialists, and others. When in 1966 the House Un-American Activities Committee conducted a hearing to investigate the aims of certain groups sending material aid to North Vietnam, the finding was that the "key leadership" of these groups was "made up of revolutionary, hard-core Communists." The determination was not whimsical; several of those being investigated proudly admitted to being Communists. (2)

As well there were the radical leftists who, while falling short of calling themselves Communists, shared the same goals as the Communists. These factions were often violent and made it clear that their support was for the "revolution," not peace.

It is quite likely that the war protests would not have gained the support they did without the willing assistance of various intellectuals and educators of the cause. These were the writers, commentators, professors and others whose contribution to the movement could almost be measured by the volume of materials they produced to "explain" to the public what the war was all about. Quite often these intellectuals lacked any serious knowledge of Vietnam, history, world politics, warfare, military matters, Asian culture or even Communism. Some were allowed to visit Hanoi to hear the "truth" about the terrible war America was waging against the people of Vietnam; many expressed their gratitude to their official tour guides for giving them brief outlines of Vietnamese history, a subject which they should have been well acquainted with before they even departed for the trip. Nonetheless, these so-called "educators" considered themselves fully qualified to condemn U.S. "interference" in Vietnam's "popular revolution" and described in glowing terms the "patriotism" of those resisting American aggression. Because these individuals tended to avoid the monotonous rhetoric of the Communists, they were able to persuade a good many of their readers and listeners that Communism was okay and Communism in Vietnam was even better.

The success of the antiwar movement was further aided by two attitudes that became popular in the 1960s and persist in some strength even to this day. One was a reaction against American patriotism, which its critics held to be irrelevant to the war and twentieth century global politics. The other attitude was a reaction against anti-Communism, which was considered to be a backward and unenlightened concept, also out of touch with modern-day realities.

Both of these attitudes resulted from changing social values which promoted individual freedom, distrust of the "Establishment," and non-interference in world affairs. Both led to the spurious conclusion that everything America did was based on greed and arrogance, while the Communists represented the right of small nations to determine their own future – through revolution, if need be. Neither attitude was essentially "antiwar," except when applied to the case of America's waging an allegedly "immoral" war in a country in which it had no business. In effect, if not actually stated aloud, persons who adopted these attitudes during the wartime agreed with the pro-Hanoi and pro-NLF stance taken by extreme leftists and not a few antiwar protestors were very glad to see Saigon finally lose the war, even after the Americans had already pulled out.

The rejection of American patriotism and anti-Communism was especially embraced by young people who had come to question their country's basic social institutions in their quest for freedom. The affluence of the Great Society had given them the leisure to think about the world in terms that were not always relevant to the underdeveloped world of Southeast Asia. The social revolution happening in America spurred a new wave of ideas, many of them contradicting the supposed infallibility of the Establishment. Youths became disenchanted by racial discrimination and other social ills. Educated in liberal attitudes, they developed into a generation which "knew everything about the evils, real as well as imagined, of American society and nothing about the evils of Communism or why the spread of Communism was both bad in itself and represented a danger to the United States." (3)

To these young people, the arguments denouncing the war and the U.S. "made sense," while the arguments supporting the war stood in opposition to the ideals they hoped to dedicate their lives to. This was especially true in relation to the draft, which personally threatened them by proposing to make them a part of that distant and alien war they felt had no relevance to their lives. In fact, it may have been the apparent irrevelance of the war, rather than its alleged immorality, that turned more young people against America's involvement in Vietnam. The protest was very much personal, although it was couched in terms of politics.

Many of America's youth abandoned their respect for parents, government and other representatives of the "Establishment" and replaced it with respect for the liberal intellectuals who shared their values and aims. These mentors promoted the ideas of radicals and encouraged their students to invent variations of radical themes. This resulted in an informal cycle of interdependence between radicals and moderates in the antiwar movement that led to the great misunderstanding which clouded the war years: the radicals provided the arguments against the war and the moderates gave these arguments respectibility.

The theories and concepts about the war that emanated from the radical movement became the basis for the intellectual and popular condemnation of the war and of U.S. policy in the late 1960s and early 1970s. The radicals defined the war in simplistic and specious jargon that satisfied the needs of the protestors who knew little about the event they were protesting. Moderates and idealists would borrow slogans from the radicals. Polemics, data and personal accounts recorded by extremists would be borrowed by moderates seeking to support their opinions. Supporters of the war often found themselves forced to answer charges of awesome scope originating from the radical camp. Claims of the popularity of the NLF, allegations of war crimes committed by insensitive U.S. soldiers, charges of senseless destruction of civilian areas by pilots, questions about the morality of fighting Communism, and many other points of dispute all started ultimately with the radicals. They were later picked up by moderates, who accepted certain contentions and assertions as fact without carefully studying the background of the war and the people of Southeast Asia. Because the moderates seemed more open to the radicals than to the U.S. government or military, the radicals were able to affect the ideological direction of the antiwar movement in a most serious way.

In the *Television History* the radicals do not appear very radical at all. In the 1960s, Tom Hayden inveighed against the dispassionate greed of American society and the immoral war in Vietnam. He visited Hanoi, explaining to one American POW that he just "thought it would be a gas." (4) Hayden's lovemate and future wife was Jane Fonda, who remarked at Duke University in 1970: "I am a socialist, therefore I think we should strive for a socialist society, all the way to communism. I would think that if you understood what communism was, you would hope and pray on your knees that we would someday become communist. Members of the political left should take every penny you can get from wealthy liberals. . . . As long as the Movement needs money, I will rip off all I can from Hollywood." (5) With Fonda's help, Hayden has been elected to the California State Legislature.

In "Homefront USA," all Hayden says is "We expect to march. We expect trouble all the time." No kidding, Tom.

David Dellinger was another interesting character in the antiwar

movement. In 1967 he was a "representative" from the U.S. in
Bertrand Russell's "War Crimes Tribunal," an unabashed attempt
to denounce the U.S. in pseudo-Nuremberg fashion with evidence
coming primarily from North Vietnam and its Communist allies. The
"tribunal," whose impartial and disinterested executive president
was French Leftist Jean-Paul Sartre, was considered so radical that
even some radicals refused to take part. In the end, the U.S. was
condemned for carrying out "genocide" and aggression in Southeast Asia, along with various and sundry individual crimes.
Needless to say, the democratic court had no one to speak for the
defense.

In the *Television History*, Dellinger talks about non-violent
resistance and how the 1968 Chicago riots "weakened the antiwar
movement around the edges at least, and that became, the edges
became what Richard Nixon played on." Thus spake David
Dellinger, Middle-of-the-Roader.

The radicals had a profound influence on persons whose respectability in other matters placed them in the limelight in the war
protests. Rev. Martin Luther King, Jr., is one example. Rev. King's
significant contribution to the civil rights movement in America
does not erase the fact that his knowledge of the war in Southeast
Asia was limited. The PBS series quotes his famous speeches and
brings up the question of race and the war. The series might have
quoted Rev. King when he called the U.S. "the greatest purveyor of
violence in the world" (6) or charged that the war was an attempt
to "perpetuate white colonialism," while the U.S. had killed "a
million" Vietnamese, "mostly children." King also compared the
Americans to the Nazis. (7) Statements such as these must have
gladdened the hearts of the extremists. (It is curious to note that
the PBS series links Bobby Kennedy with Martin Luther King's war
stance, and not the black minister's civil rights position!)

Bayard Rustin, too, joins in the suggestion of racial inequality
and the war when he says that "the very fact that there were a
disproportionate number of blacks in Vietnam meant that, very
early, a disproportionate number of caskets began to come back to
the black community." As indicated earlier in this book, the charge
of racial discrimination in the war was made by civil rights activists
at the time, but was not entirely accurate. The PBS series does

nothing to place Rustin's remarks in perspective, but allows them to serve as a reliable critique of the war.

Protest singers and entertainers helped popularize the antiwar movement and spread discontent among the young people. Their considerable talents provided strong support to those participating in demonstrations or protesting the war on campuses. To represent this segment of the antiwar movement, the PBS series might have looked at some of the popular figures of the time. There was Pete Seeger, whose song "Last Train to Nuremberg" brought a moratorium to condemn American soldiers. Even after the war, Seeger liked to talk about all the "wonderful things" happening in Indochina under the Communists. And there was Joan Baez, who was active in promoting resistance to the draft and nonpayment of taxes. Ms. Baez has now changed her opinion of the Communists, especially in light of the Cambodian tragedy and Vietnamese concentration camps. And Bob Dylan, who inspired a generation with songs like "Blowing in the Wind" and "Masters of War." Or Country Joe and the Fish with the "Vietnam Rag." ("Well, it's a-one, two, three, what are we fighting for? Don't ask me, I don't give a damn. Next stop is Viet-nam.") These and countless other performers popularized antiwar sentiment and gave it legitimate artistic expression, connecting it with other anti-establishment themes. In its "Music for Peace" performance, the PBS series can find nothing but Peter, Paul and Mellow singing about what a "terrible time" it was.

Besides their timid presentation of the antiwar movement, the producers give other indications of being supporters of that movement and admirers of the cause. David Harris speaks proudly of the draft resistance and the challenge made to young men to "'Put up or shut up,' no more of this screaming against the war and then coming home and making sure you have your student deferment in your pocket." William Sloan Coffin, Jr. recalls his speech before the Pentagon in October 1967, "which was simply to say that we are here to support these young people in their hour of conscience, and if they are arrested for violating a law which violates their consciences, then we, too, must be arrested." James Fallows beat the draft by working out a medical deferment; however, he movingly notes that "while nine out of ten of my comrades from Harvard and

MIT were getting out with their doctors' excuses," white boys from Boston's working class were preparing to go to war. "Nobody could avoid recognizing what that meant then." And should the viewers still doubt the warmth and sensitivity of the peace people, there is a scene of Eugene McCarthy's campaign workers on the verge of tears as they listen to reports of Bobby Kennedy's assassination; the scene lingers on the screen for a considerable time as if allowing viewers to savor the passionate feelings of the young liberals, who presumably are the only people in the world who share grief when a tragedy occurs.

Meanwhile, the other side of the issue is represented by an obviously agitated Martha Raye who stopped paying any attention to demonstrators because "we got too many good Americans." Chicago Police spokesperson Frank Sullivan spurts, "Gentlemen, the hardcore leadership of (the demonstrators) are Communist." A pro-war demonstrator parachutes into a park because "well, the American people" asked him to do it. Richard Nixon talks about "these bums, you know, blowin' up the campuses" as Henry Kissinger suggests that Nixon's behavior "contributed to the polarization" of American society.

This is how the folks at PBS recall it – the antiwar movement was endowed with morality, reason and human sensitivity, while the "other side" was nasal-voiced, emotional, stumbling, and insensitive. It was the tendency of the latter group to overreact which brought about the disruption of society.

Can the reader guess which side the PBS producers were on?

Welcome Guests

If the American POWs were uninvited guests to Hanoi during the war, the Communists were eager to invite other, friendlier visitors to their socialist paradise. Called "traitors" by some and "heroes" by others, these visitors contributed to the collection of false and misleading information about the war by relying on their Marxist hosts as gems of honesty and decency. No matter how inaccurate their testimony proved to be, their trips to Hanoi gave them publicity, which in turn added to their credibility. These "witnesses" boasted that they "had been there" and had "seen with their own eyes" the havoc that was being wrought in North Vietnam by American bombing as well as the lenient manner in which POWs were being treated.

Hanoi's visitors included "peace" activists, politicians, entertainers, women's groups and others interested in hearing the "other side" of the story. Some, like Jane Fonda, had limited political influence in the U.S. Fonda visited Hanoi in the summer of 1972, posing for pictures and recording propaganda statements for the North Vietnamese. So certain was she that American pilots were willfully and cruelly murdering civilians that, upon hearing the POWs' tales of torture and mistreatment at the hands of their captors, she would later label the released prisoners "hypocrites and liars." (8)

More important were individuals such as Ramsey Clark, the former U.S. Attorney General who visited Hanoi shortly after Ms. Fonda. Clark spoke with a few POWs and brought the word back to America that the prisoners were being well treated, adding their health was "better than mine and I am a healthy man." (9) Notes one observer, "His remarks would have been interesting to men who had spent years in vermin-infested dungeons and who had been starved, tortured, and shackled to their bunks for long periods and forced to live in their own wastes." (10)

New York *Times* Associate Editor Harrison Salisbury nearly won a Pulitzer Prize for his accounts of destructive American bombing in North Vietnam, published in the *Times* after his visit to Hanoi. Salisbury charged that the U.S. was bombing "purely civilian targets" in order to intimidate the North Vietnamese. He cited Nam Dinh, the third largest city in North Vietnam, as an example, declaring, "No American communique has asserted that Namdinh contains some facility that the United States regards as a military objective," adding that "Namdinh is far from being exceptional." As Guenter Lewy points out, "Nam Dinh happened to be a major transshipment point for supplies and soldiers moving south who were coming into and through the city by river and the north-south railroad. On at least three prior occasions, American communiques had referred to the bombing of military targets in Nam Dinh – a large railroad yard, a huge storage depot, a POL storage area, and a thermal power unit." The Pentagon would also disclose that "the city was ringed by antiaircraft gun batteries and by surface-to-air missile sites." It seems Salisbury had made his observations with testimony from the mayor of Nam Dinh and a Communist propaganda pamphlet entitled "Report on U.S. War Crimes in Nam-Dinh City" published in 1966. Salisbury neglected to cite the latter source in his dispatches. (11)

In their search for the historical truth about the war, the producers on the *Television History* fail to discuss Hanoi's welcome guests or consider their influence on the antiwar movement. But these visitors, including Daniel Berrigan, Rennie Davis, Tom Hayden (who promised to deliver a tape to the family of one POW, although they never received it), Women Strike for Peace, Mary McCarthy, Susan Sontag (who changed her mind about the Communists after the Polish crisis of the early 1980s), Joan Baez and other members of the antiwar movement, played a significant role in convincing the world of America's "crimes" in opposing Vietnam's "popular" revolution. The distorted viewpoints of these "eye-witnesses" gave no little boost to the antiwar drive and caused many Americans to question the morality of the war.

PBS' neglect of this issue and its own visit to Vietnam in the production of this series shows no greater enlightenment. It is as if nothing has been learned in all these years.

Vote for Peace

As told by the *Television History*, the 1968 presidential election campaign starts with a peace drive in the New Hampshire primary. After this, Bobby Kennedy battles with Eugene McCarthy for the Democratic nomination until Kennedy's assassination in June. Mysteriously, Hubert Humphrey receives the Democratic Party's endorsement as candidate, and, even more mysteriously, Richard Nixon wins the election.

Actually, the first two competitors for the White House post were none of the above. Southern Democrat George Wallace began his campaign early while his wife was the official governor of Alabama. Wallace toned down his racist rhetoric and made his appeal to low-income whites who were worried about blacks, taxes, bureaucracy and a government full of "pointy heads" that did not respond to their needs. Wallace's independent campaign had its ups and downs over the months (one of the downs was when his running mate, Curtis LeMay, displayed a willingness to use nuclear weapons in Vietnam), but the Wallace vote remained influential until the end.

The first Republican candidate was George Romney, who jumped into the race early, but was unable to clarify his stance on several issues, including the war. Romney gave up just before the New Hampshire primary.

Meanwhile, some liberal Democrats felt that the war issue was more important than Pres. Johnson's social programs, which they generally supported. They combed the country for a candidate to oppose Johnson. Bobby Kennedy, George McGovern and others declined the invitation, but Eugene McCarthy was interested. McCarthy raised a squad of clean-cut college students to carry his campaign to the doors of the voters and he made a surprisingly strong showing in New Hampshire against the write-in Johnson.

Kennedy entered the race a few days later and the contest between McCarthy and RFK over the next few months was characterized by mixed feelings of mutual support and bitterness as their rivalry gained more publicity. Relations between the two were not necessarily smooth when Johnson unexpectedly pulled out of the race at the end of March.

The Republican campaign offered fewer thrills. Nelson Rockefeller and late-comer Ronald Reagan were not able to mount forceful challenges to Richard Nixon, who was seeking a comeback from political retirement. The Republicans wanted to avoid the appearance of divisiveness and carefully staged their convention in Miami Beach, even as race riots shook the city a few miles away. Nixon picked Spiro Agnew as his running mate, and the Maryland governor soon distinguished himself for his rather colorful oratory. The Nixon-Agnew team appealed to conservatives, businesspeople, Protestants, and older persons. However, their style and rhetoric disconcerted, and often offended, younger people, ethnic groups, and some political factions.

Hubert Humphrey arrived in the campaign too late to engage in the primaries, and that may actually have helped him win the nomination. Working behind the scenes, the vice-president collected delegate votes from the party faithful in non-primary states and in time the local contests being waged by McCarthy and Kennedy lost their significance. After the death of Kennedy, McCarthy's campaign faltered and he never stood a chance of beating Humphrey. With riots outside and disruptions inside the convention hall in Chicago, Humphrey went through the voting ritual and took the nomination on the first ballot. (There was a pseudo-charge at the end by supporters of Edward Kennedy, called the "Ted Offensive," but that came to nothing.) Humphrey collected over 1700 delegate votes while McCarthy received only 601.

The election contest was close and unpredictable. In the end, Nixon beat out Humphrey in popular votes, each collecting more than 31 million. George Wallace got less than ten million votes. Eugene McCarthy was no longer in the running, but gained 25,552 votes. Between Wallace and McCarthy were four other candidates, coming from the Socialist Labor, Socialist Worker and Peace and Freedom Parties. (12) Nixon's victory in electoral votes was clearer. The "peace vote" had been split and Wallace's vote appeared to have hurt Humphrey in some places.

The *Television History* reports on the 1968 election with less reality than wishful thinking. The Democratic candidates, who all lost, are covered with more airtime and much greater energy than the Republican candidate, who won. Eugene McCarthy, whose dignified manner of liberal politics brought him a relatively limited following, seems to have impressed the producers more than anti-intellectual showman George Wallace, although the latter's tally of votes outnumbered the former by more than 350 to 1. (Wallace does not even appear in Part 11.) By all appearances, Hubert Humphrey came out of nowhere to steal the Democratic nomination from . . . whom? McCarthy? In fact, McCarthy never had the widespread support needed to push Humphrey aside, despite the vice president's identification with Johnson's policies. No matter how sincerely McCarthy's supporters grieved at the death of Bobby Kennedy, Kennedy's votes did not automatically accrue to the rival peace candidate, but scattered in different directions to boost everyone from George Wallace to Dick Gregory to Richard Nixon.

And while the producers have suggested earlier in the program that there was something nasty about Nixon and Kissinger forcing a peace agreement through the Saigon government in 1972, there is no investigation of McCarthy's proposal for a coalition government in South Vietnam. Hanoi might have jumped at the idea, but would Saigon have approved? Obviously not. What would Pres. McCarthy have done at that point? Forced it on Thieu? The question is intriguing, but the PBS series is afraid to touch it and possibly shake the viewer's respect for McCarthy, who seems to be their boy in the race.

Perhaps the most curious thing about the episode's depiction of the politics of peace is that it stops abruptly in 1971. Had it gone just one year further, it would have had to deal with another important peace candidate, George McGovern.

The omission is striking. Eugene McCarthy is credited with sparking the challenge to the Johnson administration's war policy. He gained some degree of notoriety, won a few primaries, then lost momentum and slipped into virtual oblivion. On the other hand, Sen. McGovern increased his support within the Democratic Party, won the presidential nomination, and campaigned against Nixon and the war until November 1972. By most standards, his political career is of greater historical value than McCarthy's. Yet not once does George McGovern appear in the *Television History*, nor is his name mentioned even in passing connection to the antiwar movement or the Nixon victory in 1972.

Is this because McGovern's radical "peace proposal" (which included a complete, unilateral withdrawal of U.S. troops from Vietnam, the cessation of all military and economic aid to Saigon, and no guarantees for the release of American POWs) was assailed by many observers as being even worse than what Hanoi was proposing at the time? Is it because McGovern's sloppy election campaign embarrassed liberals and others within the antiwar movement? Might it be because Nixon trounced McGovern at the polls?

One can only speculate. The fact remains that the series scrupulously avoids George McGovern and his presidential campaign as if the senator bears no relation to the history of the "Homefront."

Taking stock of the peace movement's political record, one finds a mixed bag. Some members of the movement claim credit for removing one president from office and influencing the Johnson administration toward the end of his term. No peace candidate was elected president, and, ironically, the antiwar movement may have helped elect Richard Nixon by criticizing Humphrey, persuading conservatives to vote, and moving behind George Wallace. War protests apparently influenced the Congress, which began to reflect the popular antiwar attitudes. Eventually, Congress would cut aid to South Vietnam and take such measures as would ensure that Saigon could not defend itself against the Communists. The last achievement is not one that the antiwar movement tends to boast about.

Vietnam Veterans Against the War

If one is to believe the *Television History* (a risky business at this point), all Vietnam veterans returning from the war became pacifists, participated in demonstrations, made antiwar speeches before crowds, and threw their war medals on the Capitol steps. These are the only veterans shown on the "Homefront," the only ones to act as spokespersons for the vets, the only ones whose faces appear on the screen, "official" representatives of the veteran community.

The truth is quite the opposite. Vietnam veterans as a whole did not become radical activists or participate in protests against the war or the government. Many veterans, in fact, were the victims of antiwar demonstrators who abused them and charged them with multitudes of war crimes. Veterans who felt they had done their duty and served their country were taken aback by the cold reception they received when they got home, a situation which owed a lot to the degrading image veterans were given by the members of the antiwar movement, whom the PBS series claims they embraced as comrades.

One of the antiwar organizations that did form among the veterans was a group called Vietnam Veterans Against the War (VVAW). According to veteran Richard Kolb in his review of the PBS series, the "VVAW attracted the active support of one-fourth of one percent of all actual war vets." (13) The organization boasted only 600 members by 1970 and had to its credit a war crimes conference (sponsored by Jane Fonda) whose transcripts included the names and "testimony" of veterans who had in fact never attended the meeting. The organization consistently refused to cooperate with official investigations by giving details of alleged war crimes and atrocities. (14)

On Part 11, antiwar veterans are shown being nice to little old ladies who scowl and tell them to go get a job.

In criticizing the PBS program, Richard Kolb states, "Attention to such groups (as the VVAW) reflects the attitudes of the producers far more than the events featured demonstrated the feelings of the vast majority of vets. Absolutely no opposing views to those voiced by VVAW spokesmen in the 'Homefront' episode were aired by PBS.

"Unfortunately, prideful veterans – that is, 91 percent of all Vietnam vets – appear as tokens. South Boston, for example, suffered a casualty rate three times higher than the national average. And yet its sons remained proud of their service. Insight into the motives and values of 'Southie's' vets – a microcosm of the 75 percent of Viet vets from a lower middle/working class background – would have told viewers far more than interviews with elitist, self-professed leftists." (15)

Instead of South Boston vets, the series approached Boston draft evader James Fallows. Let the viewers make some sense out of that.

Looking Back

Many members of the antiwar movement criticized America's involvement in Vietnam (and at the same time defended their opposition to it) by theorizing that the war was a civil war, a colonial conflict, and/or an agrarian revolution in which the U.S. had no business interfering. These people claimed that Communism would be good for Vietnam – perhaps even necessary – that the Communist leaders were heroes, and that the Vietnamese people as a whole supported the Communist movement and wanted the U.S. out of their country. They predicted peace and prosperity for post-war Vietnam.

Events have shown that they were wrong. Communism is none of the wonderful things they had predicted it would be and Southeast

Asia has been thrown into a state worse than what it knew during the war.

The producers of the PBS series would have done well to ask their friends in the antiwar movement what they thought of Communism and the situation in Southeast Asia now. They might also have asked how these activists view their earlier support for the Communists and probed to find if the antiwar leaders (who tended to think of themselves as morally superior to LBJ and Richard Nixon) felt any sense of responsibility for the fate of Vietnam, Cambodia and Laos. Of course, the producers would not risk embarrassing their friends (and themselves) by such questions.

Still, the answers might have been interesting.

Footnotes

1. Norman Podhoretz, *Why We Were In Vietnam*, p. 88
2. Facts on File, *South Vietnam: U.S.-Communist Confrontation in Southeast Asia, 1966-67*, p. 196
3. Norman Podhoretz, Note 1 above, p. 107
4. John Hubbell, *P.O.W.*, p. 355
5. Quoted in Southeast Asia Review, No. 4, March 1984
6. Facts on File, Note 2 above, p. 405
7. Ibid., p. 407
8. John Hubbell, Note 4 above, p. 585 (and footnote)
9. Quoted in Richard Nixon, *RN: The Memoirs of Richard Nixon*, p. 688
10. John Hubbell, Note 4 above, p. 585
11. Guenter Lewy, *America in Vietnam*, pp. 401-2
12. Richard Scammons, Ed., *America Votes 1968*, Governmental Affairs Institute, Congressional Quarterly, 1970
13. Richard Kolb, "A Viet Vet Looks at 'Vietnam: A Television History'" *Human Events*, June 16, 1984
14. Guenter Lewy, Note 11 above, pp. 316-7
15. Richard Kolb, Note 13 above

Supplements

(Ed - One official visitor to Hanoi was war critic Mary McCarthy, who came to North Vietnam in 1967. During her stay, Ms. McCarthy was allowed to see two American POWs, including Col. Robinson Risner. McCarthy and Risner perceived their meeting in different ways, as their subsequent accounts would show. The reader may find it interesting to see how two people on opposite sides of a conflict interpret such an event.)

Based on Mary McCarthy, *Hanoi*, Harcourt, Brace and World, Inc., 1968: Mary McCarthy had already written critically about South Vietnam before her invitation to Hanoi and so the Communists welcomed her warmly. While in the North Vietnamese capital, she was "allowed to see two captured pilots in the living room of a Hanoi villa (I am not sure whether this was their actual place of confinement)" with an officer present to follow the conversation. She had submitted in advance the questions she was going to ask the prisoners. She noted her discomfort at being seated on a sofa while the other party sat on a stool.

McCarthy had expected that the prisoners had learned something from their captors, but was disappointed. The first pilot had read a lot about Vietnamese history, he said, but "seemed wholly unmodified by his experience and the sole question he put to me was, 'Can you tell me how the Chicago Cubs are doing?' "

The second prisoner she visited was a "gaunt, squirrel-faced" older man who "had not changed his cultural spots either, except in one respect; he claimed to like Vietnamese candy." McCarthy did not recall the names of either of the two men she met.

The Vietnamese captors, she said, were "taken aback by the low mental attainments of the pilots." For her part, Ms. McCarthy was "taken aback by (their) stiffness of phraseology and naive, rote-thinking, childish" like the big round handwriting they used in their letters. "If these men had been robotized, I felt, it had been an insensible process starting in grade school and finished off by the Army," leaving them "somewhat pathetic cases of mental malnutrition."

Ms. McCarthy felt a "cultural distance" between herself and the pilots "so wide that I could see myself reflected in their puzzled, somewhat frightened eyes as a foreigner." This distance, writes Ms. McCarthy, "was a crime against humanity, a reason for protests, for revolutions." If the pilots looked at her as a tool for the Communists "shaped by Eastern education, money, advantages, ... they were right in a sense, for to be against the Vietnamese war was an economic privilege enjoyed chiefly by the middle and professional classes." That is why McCarthy felt more at home with Dr. Ton That Tung than with "those wary cagey pilots."

Based on Robinson Risner, *The Passing of the Night*, Random House, 1973: For Col. Risner, meeting foreign delegations while a POW was the "indignity" he resented the most. "There was something basically inhuman about appearing before delegations and being asked how your food was and having to say it was excellent when it was not. Or to questions of your treatment, to lie in front of cameras and say it was great, when they had literally tortured the stuffings out of you to make you appear." The worst part was being forced to make statements critical of his country.

Before Risner would agree to meet with anyone he was tortured and mistreated. The guards made him stand in one corner with his hands above his head; if the hands dropped, they beat him. He was also threatened with the ropes. The captors told him how to answer the questions that would be put to him. As a reward, they gave him a photograph of his family, which he gazed at for hours. He later had to tear up the picture to prevent its being used for propaganda purposes; for this act, he was tortured again. The guards tied him with his feet up to his throat and stuffed his mouth with rags. He was beaten and placed in heavy leg irons.

On his way to meet Mary McCarthy, Risner was advised to "maintain control of the conversation." The Vietnamese explained, "We do not know her too well and do not want her asking leading questions. Do not say anything – regardless of what she asks you – do not say anything to disgrace or slander our country."

Risner was taken to the Plantation, the prison staff headquarters, a "nice looking" place. He had been permitted to sew the buttons back on his shirt. He sat with Ms. McCarthy near a coffee table. She talked of her husband in Paris and Eugene McCarthy. When she asked if he wanted anything, he said he would like a Bible. Ms. McCarthy barked to the guards, asking if she could send the prisoners Bibles. The guard put her off. Risner also said he missed having sweets and she offered to send him a cake. The guard told her that the prisoners received plenty of food and turned to Risner for confirmation of this. The prisoner nodded, yes, it was true.

As the meeting wound up, "she looked at me and said, 'You know, I don't think they understand me.' I raised my eyebrows and said, 'I think they do.' " Ms. McCarthy knocked on wood, hoping for an early end to the war.

"I was in interrogation for three hours trying to convince (the guard) that raising eyebrows and knocking on wood were not secret signals."

PART 12: THE END OF THE TUNNEL (1973-1975)

The 1973 Paris cease-fire breaks down. The Saigon regime grabs more territory and Thieu announces the beginning of the Third Indochina War. America's troops are withdrawn and the POWs return to the States. Pres. Nixon encounters trouble with Watergate and resigns. Congress acts to end the war and reduces military aid to Saigon. The North Vietnamese launch a new offensive. The ARVN collapses under the attack as soldiers and refugees flee in panic. Thieu resigns and a new government surrenders to the North Vietnamese. The war comes to an end.

Goodbye, Ugly American

The PBS historical record of the war is finally wrapped up in Part 12. So far we have seen the roots of America's mistake, America's complicity in France's colonial war, America's anti-Communist fanaticism leading to a second war, the fumbling of three administrations, death and destruction caused by Americans, America's decadent influence on South Vietnamese society, and the replacing of American deaths with South Vietnamese deaths in America's war as the Americans pull out. Now, at the end of the tunnel, the conclusion: America's shame.

The end of the war (and the manner in which it ended) was a triumph for those who opposed U.S. involvement in Southeast Asia. The confusion and turmoil, the swift victory of the Communist army, and America's humiliating retreat seemed to justify their animosity toward America, as if everything had been "arranged in advance" (to borrow the words of Gen. Phan Phung Tien) and there was nothing more to say about it. America's disgraceful defeat was, so they say, inevitable.

And thus the *Television History* files its report for the books, marking the alleged inevitability of the fall of South Vietnam with the betrayal of Saigon by the United States and the glorified victory for the Communists.

Many persons, American and Vietnamese, share the feeling that the United States set up South Vietnam and then turned its back in Saigon's hour of need. The series adequately points out how Pres. Thieu and his officials trusted until the end that America would never abandon its commitment to South Vietnam. Nixon promised forceful reaction to Communist violations of the cease-fire. Ambassador Bui Diem describes how Thieu's Cabinet was reassured by Pres. Ford's renewal of the pledge. The viewers may recall how in Part 8 the former ambassador is quoted (not once, but twice) to say the Vietnamese "couldn't think that the Americans – once having committed their troops in Vietnam and having spent so much money in Vietnam – could one of these days leave everything and call it quits." Optimistic Graham Martin nurtured this confidence and, relates "CIA Analyst" Frank Snepp, Thieu believed him until it was "much too late."

Indeed, says Col. William LeGro, the U.S., "particularly the Congress because they were making policy," betrayed South Vietnam in the end and "when things got really tough, we really just cut and ran."

The series astutely points out that opposition to the war was coming less from the antiwar movement (which had "dwindled to a dedicated few"), and more from Congress. However, as described by the series, this opposition was to Congress' credit, for it, and not the administration, truly understood the situation and was prepared to put an end to what Sen. Mansfield earlier called "a tragic mistake."

A bombing halt goes into effect on August 15, 1973 as Congress takes "the first decisive step" toward ending the war. The administration argues for more aid to South Vietnam, but the Congress is not listening. As told by the "CIA Analyst," the "U.S. establishment in Saigon" refused to deal with the corruption issue because "if the South Vietnamese looked anything but pristine pure, the U.S. Congress would not vote any additional aid to Saigon."

But the ruse does not work. Congressman Pete McCloskey

visits Vietnam in the last months of the war, but finds Ambassador Martin "so emotionally wrapped up in the desire to save South Vietnam" that he is "incapable of giving a fair appraisal" to the delegation. The narrator informs us: "The delegation concluded that South Vietnam had received enough American aid. It would have to fight alone." Pres. Ford's last ditch request for assistance is identified by Congress as "a maneuver to blame them for the impending disaster." They turn him down. Rep. Millicent Fenwick sums it up neatly: We sent battleships, bombers and billions to help South Vietnam; if that couldn't do it, nothing can.

For the antiwar producers of the *Television History* the scene is priceless. Throughout its lengthy course, the series has attacked the premise behind the war, U.S. involvement in the war, the bombing campaigns, the "invasions" into Laos and Cambodia, secret wars, the policies of individual presidents, and the alleged atrocities of U.S. soldiers... Now the producers can enjoy the best of two worlds. On one hand, they can justify the decisions of an antiwar Congress to bring the war to an end by crippling South Vietnam in its most desperate moment. At the same time, they can mark the disgrace of the U.S., which just cut and ran when things got tough.

The hypocrisy is almost tangible. Antiwar elements both inside the Congress and out were not only predicting Saigon's defeat, they were willing to make that prediction come true. They would argue against Ambassador Martin's positive outlook on South Vietnam's condition, but they themselves were monumentally eager to see only the positive side to the possibility of a Communist takeover. When Congress decided to cut aid to South Vietnam, this was not simply because they thought Saigon ought to go it alone, but because they expected that Saigon could not go it and would quickly lose the war. Their action was based on the intensifying belief that the people of South Vietnam would be better off under Communism than they would with Nguyen Van Thieu and war. By April 1975, many Americans were ready to accept the New York *Times* headline that ran: "Indochina Without the Americans: For Most, a Better Life." (1) Some would soon be echoing the sentiments of George McGovern, who was to remark, "90 percent of the Vietnamese refugees would be better off going back to their own land." (2)

But life did not improve when the Communists took over and thousands more refugees were to flee in years to come. The antiwar crowd has conveniently forgotten their own misguided optimism concerning the war's end and, as the *Television History* shows, they still throw the blame for Saigon's fall on everybody but themselves.

Welcome, Liberators!

South Vietnam fell to the Communists after years of bitter fighting. The end came in a torrent of disgrace and tragedy as the South Vietnamese watched their government and army collapse in just a few weeks as the North Vietnamese army pressed on in its big offensive.

Those Vietnamese who viewed Part 12 of the *Television History* could relive some of their shame and grief as they again witnessed scenes of their country's downfall and the tragic flight of thousands of people from the advancing Communist soldiers. The series includes scenes that touch their memories deeply: Thieu's secrecy, leading to distrust of the president by his officers. The disintegration of half of South Vietnam's army. Officers ordering their men to fight and then fleeing the country. Soldiers leaving their positions and contributing to the panic, fighting civilians for seats on boats and planes. Pandemonium, death, the breakdown of order. The final, emotional evacuation from the capital with thousands of people struggling to find a way out of the country before Saigon fell.

And finally, there is the image of the victorious Communist army smashing through the gates of Independence Palace to take the surrender of Duong Van Minh.

The shame felt by the Vietnamese is heightened by the awareness that their own people share some of the responsibility for the country's swift collapse. With justification, they may criticize the U.S. for its part in the tragedy (the Paris agreement left the South Vietnamese in a weakened military position and allowed Northern troops to remain in the South; military aid was drastically reduced, undermining the country's defense capability; the Americans did not respond to the Communists with force, as promised by two presidents; etc.). At the same time, intelligent Vietnamese will openly admit that problems and weaknesses within their own country contributed to its fall. The government had failed to instill confidence in the people, so that by late 1974 many Vietnamese were convinced that the end was near. In the last months of the war, frustration with Pres. Thieu was being openly expressed, further exemplifying a lack of respect for his leadership. Several high-ranking military leaders performed badly at critical points, inviting a series of errors and losses that helped demoralize the general populace. In Part 12, Phan Phung Tien acknowledges that "those of us who had been in responsible positions felt kind of ashamed and dishonored... and there was nothing that the Vietnamese officers at the lower echelons could do to prevent the situation from coming apart."

The ARVN did not fall completely apart. At Xuan Loc, the 18th Division, considered to be one of the worst units in the South Vietnamese army, held off and also counterattacked the much bigger and better equipped North Vietnamese soldiers of Gen. Van Tien Dung. Although the battle was eventually lost, it stands as a tribute to the determination of Gen. Le Minh Dao and his men who defended their capital.

And not all the Vietnamese officers escaped from the country in those days. Some, like Gen. Dao, fought to their last round of ammunition and were honored by the Communists with indeterminate prison sentences in concentration camps. Others committed suicide rather than surrender to their liberators. The fate of these men is not likely to appear on any documentary like this one.

Nothing was going to stop the Communists on their resolute drive to conquer the South. Hanoi had promised victory in 1963, in 1965, again in 1968, and then in 1972. Each time the Communists failed, each time at a cost of countless lives. When they finally liberated the South, the offensive took 55 days instead of the anticipated one-two years. But by that time, one might well have asked: Was it worth the cost? The *Television History* does not allow for such questions, however.

Still, there is something singular about the PBS version of the war's end. In this one-hour episode, the story is twisted in a curious way so that the South Vietnamese, who were defending their country against aggressive action by the North, become themselves the aggressors, while the Communists, who spent 20 years manipulating the war in the South, slaughtering thousands and terrorizing thousands more, come off looking like angels of liberation! It is very strange indeed.

According to PBS, Saigon was the sole belligerent following the signing of the Paris cease-fire. South Vietnam "greeted" the accords "with a defiant display of flags" as the Saigon regime, equipped with new American weapons, "ordered its troops to seize more territory." A South Vietnamese farmer laments the loss of two of his sons in the war, and fears that his third boy might be forced to go fight, too. Unmoved, the heartless Pres. Thieu continues the battle, counting on "American airpower to save him." Late in 1973, he announces "the start of the 'Third Indochina War,' launching an air and ground offensive against the Communists."

While all this is going on, the Viet Cong and North Vietnamese sit on their hands, never moving out of the "zones they controlled in the South," patiently "awaiting a political compromise." Says Bui Tin, "We were not invading any country, and we were determined to prevent any country from invading us and trampling on the land of our ancestors." (The series does not clarify who the "invaders" are at this point, when the Americans have already left!) The Communists "focused first on politics" with their "legitimized" Provisional Revolutionary Government. Apparently their army lay dormant militarily between 1973 and their final offensive in 1975, suffering no casualties worth mentioning, although through some mysterious and inexplicable means the South Vietnamese lost 31,000 men in 1974.

In this way, the *Television History* makes it infinitely clear that – just as with the Geneva Agreements in 1954 – South Vietnam alone was responsible for violating the letter and spirit of the 1973 Paris Accords. Needless to say, that was not quite the way it happened.

After the cease-fire was signed, both South Vietnam and the Communists violated the agreement. As much as the series' producers refuse to accept it, the Communists wanted to impose a military solution on the South and Saigon wanted to prevent that from happening. Politically the Communists were weak, having disenchanted the Southern population since the Tet Offensive, and they, like the South Vietnamese, fought for territory before the Joint Military Commission (provided for in the Paris agreement to mark out territorial jurisdiction) came to determine who controlled what.

At the same time, keeping in tune with their long-range drive for conquest, the Communists maneuvered to withdraw from more than 90 of their more secure hamlets and about 300 seized quickly during January 1973. Their purpose for this move was tactical. As the South Vietnamese rushed to capture control of the abandoned hamlets, they appeared to be the aggressors and that image may have lost them support in the U.S. Militarily, the South was hurt as well as the ARVN forces overextended themselves to cover the additional ground. (3)

Meanwhile, the Communists took advantage of the lull in the war to consolidate their support in the South and increase the flow of men and equipment down the roads to their bases in the Central Highlands and the Mekong Delta – actions clearly prohibited by the Paris Accords. Without U.S. bombing to stop them, the Communists built a four-lane, all-weather highway from the DMZ deep into the South. To protect their supply lines, the Communists attacked strategic South Vietnamese military bases and captured several of them by the end of the first half of 1974.

Aid from "sister" socialist countries continued pouring in. A U.S. intelligence report, backed up by the State Department, declared that: "Total Communist military and economic aid to North Vietnam in 1974 was higher (in current dollars) than in any previous year; in 1974 the delivery of ammunition to Hanoi markedly increased over 1973 and reached a level as high as that of 1972; North Vietnamese forces in South Vietnam, supported by record stockpiles of military supplies, are stronger today than they have ever been." (4)

In the fall of 1974, Communist troop strength had risen to at least 285,000 men, more than half of whom were in regular infantry divisions in the Central Highlands and on north toward the DMZ. Their fire power had grown so that "Communist artillery and armor equalled that of the (South Vietnames) in number, while more than 10 percent of this inventory included weapons that could be fired completely out of range of the ARVN's field guns. Enough ordnance had been stockpiled by the (North Vietnamese Army) to sustain an offensive at the 1972 level for a year." (5) The majority of South Vietnam's units were in defensive positions, and so Hanoi's illegal build-up in the South successfully tipped the balance of strength to the Communists.

From the beginning, the Communists refused to cooperate with the inspection forces created by the Paris agreements. The activities of these groups came to a halt when an American member of the Joint Military Commission was killed by a sniper while investigating the site of an air crash. (6) Polish and Hungarian delegates to the International Commission for Control and Supervision ignored Hanoi's violations of the agreements and purchased gold, jewelry and other items from the Communists. They also supported Hanoi by acting as agents and by preparing maps for the North Vietnamese. (7)

The possibility of a political solution to the question of South Vietnam's future was virtually nil. The Paris Accords had provided for a National Council of Reconciliation and Concord to deal with South Vietnam's internal affairs. Not without good reason, Pres. Thieu never trusted the Communists and the stipulation that the Council's decisions be unanimous prevented the Communists from putting any serious hope in subverting that organization. Negotiations between the two sides were stalled, boycotted and effectively terminated with Saigon demanding that Northern troops leave the South and Hanoi demanding that Thieu resign (the same basic arguments that had held up negotiations for the past several years). The real conclusion to the war was to come on the battlefield and the Communists knew that, even if certain television producers could not see it eight years later.

Finally there came the last big offensive. The Communists had taken the military advantage. They were encouraged by severe reductions in American aid to South Vietnam and limitations imposed on the U.S. president by the Congress. Many Southerners were demoralized and anticipated an eventual Communist victory. By late 1974, Thieu had accepted the possibility that parts of the country might have to be given up, including the Central Highlands and substantial portions of the northern and central coastal regions. In that event, the more populous areas would have to hold, especially the region south of a line extending from Tay Ninh, near the Cambodian border, to Nha Trang, on the coast.

In January 1975, the Communists attacked and captured Phuoc Long province as a test to measure America's reaction to their aggression. Thieu withdrew his forces, deciding not to waste them on the sparsely-populated area. At the time, the ARVN was thinly spread out and ammunition was being rationed. To fight against the well supplied North Vietnamese, the ARVN had: "one hand grenade per man per month, 85 rifle bullets per man per month, four rounds of 105mm artillery ammunition per howitzer per day and two rounds for 155s." (8) A lack of spare parts and fuel had drastically reduced helicopter and aircraft missions. The South Vietnamese had expected "vigorous" reaction by the U.S. in the face of the Phuoc Long attack. They were stunned when the Americans failed to come to their aid.

In March 1975 Gen. Dung moved on the Central Highlands and overwhelmed ARVN defenders at Ban Me Thuot in a surprise attack. The ARVN moved to counterattack when Gen. Pham Van Phu, Commander of Military Region II, suddenly ordered the evacuation of Pleiku. Soldiers and their dependents living in the area were joined by tens of thousands of civilians as they pulled out of the city.

They traveled on Route 7, a dirt road heading southeast to Tuy Hoa on the coast, some 150 kilometers away. (See Fig. 1) The road had been abandoned and had to be cleared and rebuilt in places to permit movement of the soldiers and refugees. The evacuation was ill-conceived and proved disasterous for the thousands who fled their liberators by foot, bicycle, cart, car, truck, bus or military vehicle.

Gen. Dung blocked the road and chased the fleeing masses with an army division. Guerrillas sniped at the refugees and Dung's courageous warriors attacked defenseless crowds with artillery, mortars and recoilless rifles. Miles of corpses lined the rugged road in a scene reminiscent of the Highway of Terror. Women, children, elderly people, and poor civilians were among the victims. At one point, 15 Russian Molotova trucks drove into the refugees at high speed, killing dozens. (9) The exodus was dubbed the "Convoy of Tears."

Figure 1: Approximate route of refugees fleeing Pleiku –
"The Convoy of Tears," March 1975

Figure 2: Flight from Pleiku as depicted on
4.5 million dollar PBS series

In its version of this tragic event, the PBS series blatantly omits the Communist slaughter of panic-stricken people escaping Pleiku and even shows the South Vietnamese running in the wrong direction. According to a map indicating the route of the flight, the people left Pleiku and headed for Danang, about 230 kilometers due north of the mountain city. Another line traces the route of apparently other refugees fleeing the southern areas for Danang at the same time. (See Fig. 2)

In the period following the debacle in the Highlands, the South Vietnamese forces withdrew from the northern parts of the country. They were accompanied by hundreds of thousands of refugees, who obviously were not eager to be liberated by Gen. Dung's gallant troops. The people fled Quang Tri and Hue, where in the past the Communists had massacred their relatives and neighbors, and went to Danang. Although their path was blocked, they continued to flee by sea and many died. Danang's population doubled in a few weeks, but the city lacked the facilities to care for the refugees. The ARVN command collapsed there. Security broke down and panic struck the crowd. In the chaos that ensued, perhaps 50,000 people died.

Still, in Danang as elsewhere, there was no general uprising to greet the liberation army. With a stunning absence of logic that characterizes the entire series, Part 12 not only fails to explain why people fled from, rather than rallied to, the Communists, but it also portrays the Communists in such a pretty light that one can conclude that those who fled the liberation were fools to do so. According to this episode, the Communists were simply courageous, strong, and brotherly human beings whose arrival was a welcome relief to the people of South Vietnam.

We see Miss Thu Van, a member of Gen Dung's propaganda film crew, meeting her mother for the first time in twenty years. Says the narrator: "Many Vietnamese families had members fighting on both sides. Now, some were reunited for the first time in decades." Happy reunion in Danang, is it not? The series might have mentioned one liberation soldier who did not run into the welcome arms of his mother in Danang. This was Premier Pham Van Dong, whose mother reportedly died trying to escape her son's joyous embrace. (10)

Likewise, the series does not explain the fate of persons like Thu Van, who had nephews fighting in the "puppet" Saigon army. Subsequent events would show that these families were discriminated against by the new government, which distrusted anyone with connections to the old regime. Many persons were sent to New Economic Zones to "help rebuild the country." Some were executed as traitors by the ideologically "pure" Northerners. However, details of this nature are irrelevant to the PBS history.

How did the liberation army treat the defeated ARVN soldiers who surrendered to them? Early in Part 12, the viewers were taken to the South Vietnamese military cemetery near Bien Hoa to witness the graves of those soldiers who had died fighting as mercenaries in "America's war." Miss Thu Van's movies contain a scene of ARVN soldiers being treated nicely by North Vietnamese troops – all looks well. At the end of the program, Col. Bui Tin tells all patriots to have no fear, it is a great day for all Vietnam!

But the series says nothing about Hanoi's munificent policy of reconciliation carried out after the war, which would include bulldozing the ARVN military cemetery, crushing the graves of "puppets" and "traitors" who did not deserve to rest in peace. Instead of showing propaganda films, the series might have alluded to prisons and concentration camps that would become the new homes for soldiers guilty of the crime of resisting the Communists. What warmer treatment could cousins give cousins?

It seems the heroes of fairy tales cannot be ugly princes or brutal "liberators," so these trivial matters are generously omitted by the balanced and objective producers from PBS.

Mother, Where is Saigon?

As Part 12 goes on, the heroic liberation forces reach "the gates of Saigon" on April 28, 1975. Xuan Loc has fallen. Thieu has resigned and been replaced by Tran Van Huong. The aged and stubborn Huong is replaced in turn by Duong Van Minh, "regarded as a figure the Communists might accept."

"As Minh spoke, a thunderstorm erupted. The Communists had beat (sic) the rainy season to the capital. General Dung had met his deadline."

Americans and Vietnamese evacuate the city in terror. One

American begins to weep as he searches for a friend whom he fears will become the victim of reprisals. Embassy Aide Kenneth Moorefield describes the scene in Saigon as "almost total chaos" and "virtual anarchy," with soldiers in half uniform looting and causing disturbances. (The vicious looter who appears on the screen is, however, not a soldier in half uniform, but a tiny child in shorts scurrying away with a huge mattress on his head.) But if the viewers should ask: Why the fear? Why the chaos and panic? – the PBS series does not provide an answer.

The North Vietnamese army crosses the bridge and enters the city. One soldier, Nguyen Cong Thanh, is confused by the streets and asks an old woman, "Mother, where is Saigon?" She responds, "You're in Saigon!"

Military newspaper editor Bui Tin arrives at the presidential palace and strides to General Minh to accept the surrender of the new government. "When I saw fear in the faces of Minh and the others present, I said: 'The war has ended today, and all Vietnamese are victors. Only the American imperialists are vanquished. If you still have any feelings for the nation and the people, consider today a happy day'."

That night, he lay on the palace lawn ("ecstatic," says Stanley Karnow), agreeing with his crew that "it was the happiest day of our lives because it was a day of complete victory for the nation."

The show might also have added that, in the command post at Ben Cat, Le Duc Tho celebrated his joy by embracing Pham Hung, the Southern Communist leader.

Alas, it was not a happy day for all Vietnamese, be they patriots, cowards, or even Communists. However, the viewers would never know this by watching the smiling, courageous North Vietnamese soldiers and hearing the gentle reassurances of propagandist Bui Tin.

As hinted at by Steven Cohen's *Anthology and Guide*, which accompanies the series, the image of a friendly post-war transition seems to be based in part on a book called *Reaching the Other Side*, by Earl S. Martin (Crown Publishers, Inc., 1978). The author is not an ordinary observer of the war, but a member of the Pennsylvania Mennonites, who, like the Quakers, sent volunteers to Vietnam to work with the people. (The Mennonites continue to send workers to

Vietnam and Cambodia with the approval of the Communist government.) Earl Martin lived in Quang Ngai province in Central Vietnam for several years and was in the unique position of being one of the few foreigners to follow the North Vietnamese troops to Saigon in the final weeks of the offensive in 1975.

Ostensibly, Martin did not take sides on the war, as his religious faith prescribes. However, by his own admission his sympathies lay more with the Viet Cong than with the Americans or South Vietnamese (the latter he portrays as puppets without a sense of identity or purpose). His values were shaped by antiwar professors in the U.S. who opened his eyes to see that the "official rationales" for American policy "had become but a whitened sepulcher full of dead men's bones." While conceding that "enormous suffering had been caused by the guns of the revolutionaries," he nonetheless describes his meeting with a representative of the PRG with child-like awe and excitement. The VC, he contends, taught him virtue and idealism.

On the other hand, Martin is unable to conceal his disgust with the ARVN, whom he depicts as beasts of the lowest level that humans can sink to. Sitting in an ARVN outpost near the end of the war, Martin suddenly became fearful that the site might be the target in a Viet Cong attack. He mused: "A ghastly thought: to die by accident, by an anonymous piece of mortar shrapnel *in an ARVN outpost* – what an inglorious end!" (Author's emphasis)

The pacifist Mennonite seems totally oblivious to memories of the massacres at Hue in 1968 and Quang Tri in 1972 as the refugees flood by him. He remained in Saigon for three months after the war, painting a most optimistic picture of Vietnam's future. No reprisals. Peace and independence. He even compares the Communists favorably to young America after this country's revolutionary war! It is based on testimony such as this that the PBS series makes its extraordinary claims of a happy day for all Vietnamese.

One can only wonder what Earl Martin's Viet Cong friends are thinking now, nine years after "liberation." They had fought for local rule, but were kicked out and replaced by Northerners. They had wanted religious freedom, but instead were persecuted, Buddhist and Christian alike. They had hoped for clean, responsive government, but have encountered greater corruption than ever before. Families that were reunited after 20 years have again been split apart by prison camps and new economic zones. Instead of growth and prosperity, their country has found only poverty and fear.

Likewise, officials of the National Liberation Front had believed that they would be given a role in the new government after their cousins from the North helped them overthrow the "tyrant" Thieu. Among these was Truong Nhu Tang, who joined the Front in 1960 and became the Minister of Justice for the new Communist government. But he and many others like him were displaced by Hanoi's favorites and left powerless and disappointed. Many, like Tang, have fled their country and "liberation."

Betrayed as well were the soldiers from the North. The proud troops who marched into Saigon on April 30, 1975 were not all 50- or 60-year-old veterans of the war against the French, and later the "imperialist" Americans. They were young boys, some 13 and 14 years old, the remnants of a society that had sacrificed hundreds of thousands of its finest young men for the dubious honor of making Pham Van Dong the premier of a unified Vietnam.

Like Nguyen Cong Thanh, these soldiers were lost when they arrived in Saigon because the city was not what they had expected. Their superiors had told them of a squalid, poverty-stricken slum whose population was being exploited and enslaved by rich foreign capitalists and corrupt South Vietnamese officials. The Northern troops came bearing crude wooden bowls and chopsticks as gifts for the poor people of Saigon who supposedly could not even afford these basic eating utensils. The soldiers were shocked to find a modern city where the people were more prosperous than their liberators. And some, then, began to doubt their great leaders in Hanoi.

The families of the liberation troops had been relieved to hear of the war's end. Now their sons and brothers would be returning home after several years in the field fighting for their country. But many families still would not be united with their loved ones as hundreds of thousands of soldiers remained to occupy the South, and soon 200,000 troops would be sent to conquer Cambodia. There was no end to the warring.

All of these people were deceived and betrayed – not by Henry Kissinger and Richard Nixon, nor by Gen. Westmoreland, Pres. Thieu, the American soldiers or the "puppet" army of Saigon. They were betrayed by the followers of Ho Chi Minh, whose motive was not the welfare of the people, but a thirst for power.

But Col. Bui Tin's "happy day" retains its glitter – at least for the PBS camera.

Yet the truth is that even as thousands of people evacuated Saigon in its last hours before surrender, the Communists were charging the U.S. with creating a "forced evacuation," just as they had done in 1954 when 900,000 people chose freedom over the Viet Minh. But the Communists could not halt the wave of refugees. One person who escaped was the daughter of Nguyen Huu Tho, Chairman of the National Liberation Front. (11)

And in case anyone had any doubts, the true face of liberation was to be exposed in a particularly striking manner just a few months after the Communist victory. On November 2, 1975, twelve monks and nuns, members of the Unified Buddhist Church (which earlier had protested religious repression under the Saigon government), burned themselves in protest against oppression by their new Communist masters. Where was David Halberstam then?

Drawing Conclusions

The fall of South Vietnam was not a foregone conclusion. It was not a statement on "neocolonialism," which the PBS series accuses the United States of promoting. Defeat was not proof that the Saigon army was a mercenary force ("paid for by American aid, armed with American weapons"). Nor was the event a victory for Communism, which was then and still is more unpopular than anything the anti-Communists had to offer. The Hanoi clique won their absurd "victory" by force of arms, not the will of the people. Writes Norman Podhoretz: "Indeed, the Communists had lost the 'people's war', and the war they finally won was a straightforward conventional war fought by regular uniformed troops equipped with tanks and planes and missiles, not an insurgency fought by primitively armed guerillas in black pajamas. To have lost such a conventional war to a stronger invading army no more proves that South Vietnam was an unviable or illegitimate state than the fall of

France in 1940 to the Nazis proved that France was unviable or illegitimate." (12)

America was not replacing colonialist France in Indochina, but fighting Communism, however unsuccessfully it did so. The cause of the war was not America's arrogance but the drive of Communist powers to overthrow a weak nation through a phony "revolution" that made a mockery of the ideals that true revolutions stand for.

The ultimate issue in the fall of South Vietnam is not America's so-called "policeman role" in world affairs, or the matter of how imperfectly the South Vietnamese responded to the challenge posed by their enemy. The issue is that the Communist challenge was, of itself, so unique and complex that even "sophisticated" Western nations – with all their military might and democratic principles – were unable to deal with it effectively. The fact is that even if the Saigon government had been "pristine pure" and the Vietnamese had been better prepared for the war, the Communists would not have given up their pathetic quest for power, no matter how many people had to suffer for it.

As well, the Communists "won" in South Vietnam because their objective was primarily destructive in nature: the disruption of a government and society so as to bring about that country's down-fall. Communism has nothing constructive to offer in economics, politics or society. As an ideology, Communism is bankrupt. Consequently, the Communists have no foundation on which to build a nation or society. They can only continue to pursue their destructive path, since to stand still is to invite failure. That is why only a few years after Saigon's surrender the Vietnamese Communists were already pounding at the gates of Phnom Penh. Now, they are reaching Thailand.

When will come the end of the tunnel?

(For Stanley Karnow, of course, the war's conclusion was due solely to the Communists' "will to win." The Communists were inspired by an "absolute cause," the popularity of which is exemplified by the 600,000 soldiers who "willingly sacrificed" themselves for victory. To the Vietnamese, "there is no substitute for victory." Perhaps it is better said that "there is no substance to victory." Karnow likes to tell the story of the meeting between an

American colonel and a Communist colonel after the war. The American asserts, "We never lost a battle," to which the Vietnamese responds, "That may be true, but it is also irrelevant." Once again, Karnow's critical sense has failed to catch the irony of this tale, for although the Communists "won" the war, what have they done with their victory?)

Footnotes

1. New York *Times*, April 13, 1975, quoted in Norman Podhoretz, *Why We Were In Vietnam*
2. TIME, May 19, 1975, quoted in William Liu, *Transition to Nowhere*
3. Allan Goodman, *The Lost Peace*, 167-171
4. Denis Warner *Certain Victory*, p. 20
5. Allan Goodman, Note 3 above, p. 171
6. Ibid., p. 173
7. Denis Warner, Note 4 above, p. 55
8. William Westmoreland, *A Soldier Reports*, p. 484
9. Denis Warner, Note 4 above, pp. 60-63
10. Ibid., p. 75
11. Alan Dawson, *55 Days*, p. 337
12. Norman Podhoretz, *Why We Were In Vietnam*, pp. 172-3

Supplements

(Ed. - The Communists did not stop their war of liberation despite the cease-fire agreement signed in Paris by Le Duc Tho. Their efforts included dropping mortars and rockets into civilian areas and murdering unarmed people. In June 1974 they hit a school in the town of Cai Lay, killing and wounding scores of children. The following day, a rocket fell into a hamlet near Bien Hoa, killing a pregnant woman and her two small children in their sleep. The woman's brother, writer Le Tat Dieu, wrote about his feelings in his book *The 492nd Day of the Cease-fire*, printed in the U.S. in 1977. Translation.)

The echoes of the brutal rocket explosion now are probably heard only in a few brief official denunciations full of stock phrases played on the radio. In a few days there will be nothing more. On the other side, behind the man who fired the rocket, the explosion still resounds, with the echo of "glory" and "victory." In such a case, the Communists will never tell what really happened in this attack. Instead, the gunner will be proclaimed a hero and courageous soldier. The point of explosion will be labeled an "enemy base," and all those who were murdered, young and old alike, will become the "enemy." The liberation does not want anyone to know about the little children sleeping peacefully in their own beds in the house beside the green field. And while the wretched are burying their loved ones in the cemetery already filled with other victims, in the jungles of the liberation zone the revolutionaries are organizing a ceremony to honor their hero who killed the enemy.

It suddenly struck me that today is one day in the cease-fire. The cease-fire agreement has already been signed a long time ago. Today is how many days since then?

I feel no ill will towards the judges who awarded a Nobel Peace Prize to Henry Kissinger and Le Duc Tho. How could they know what was happening in this country? How could anyone interfere with their early joy in believing that they had caught a glimpse of that rare dove? They granted the award in good faith, because of their longing for peace, because they wanted to wish happiness on my country. No one can really blame them for being the victims of a clever con job.

It is only too bad that such honor and faith in a false peace agreement has made that part of humanity living outside the suffering of my country more blind and deaf.

During this time, and for some years, we have been mute defendants standing day after day before the court of the people's conscience.

We cannot speak up for our righteousness. We cannot plead our case. All the world turns to the Communists with their clever speech, an extremely sharp defendant supported by a brilliant lawyer. The entire court is moved, pained, each time he recounts a fine achievement. Meanwhile, the mute defendant, clumsy, stammering as he tries to speak, is met only by the judge's scowls and hate-filled looks. He is worried, afraid, and finally conceives of himself as being guilty. He turns himself into a defendant deserving of curses. And, before the blind, slanted conscience of the world, those who deserve curses and punishment are we . . .

(When the rocketing of the Cai Lay Elementary School occurred) the Communists said nothing. As for the Free World – the part of the world that calls itself civilized, humanistic – it just ignored the incident and turned its back on this new atrocity. People raised their voices ever so softly, making it appear that the children of Cai Lay were not children at all. And to say the Free World reacted in this way is being generous. Really, the only reaction, shown in the press, exposed its peculiar character.

Looking through a stack of old newspapers, one can see it plainly. When the My Lai incident occurred, they made a storm with their outcry. Their feelings were intense and they made a thorough investigation. They acted as if they could sympathize with the children and innocent villagers even more than the Vietnamese themselves could. Yet when another group of children were blown apart by rockets in a schoolyard, the big newspapers of the world barely whimpered, because the authors of that event were the Communists.

Anyone who truly loves people and cares for children will find it hard to forgive the American lieutenant for what he did. Even more, that person cannot accept the artilleryman who was so degenerate that he could attack and kill only children. But the newspaper editors and great intellectuals guiding the public opinion of the Free World have decided to show humanity only when it will not perturb the Communists. They do not even hide this fact. That is the strange thing . . .

Since then, as if crossing a watershed, the rocket attacks on schools, markets, and residential areas have become greater in number and more brutal. The tragic deaths disappear, helping none and eliciting no response or bit of concern about those who dropped a rocket on my sister and her kids.

Surely all the deaths that occurred one morning in a little hamlet beside the Vac Bridge will stir no sentiments among the part of humanity living outside of poor Vietnam. The blind judge sees nothing, hears nothing, not even the quiet moans of the victims.

(Ed. - For the many thousands of refugees who fled their country in April 1975, the departure marked a painful and dramatic change in their lives. The PBS series gives no hint of the gravity of the event, but instead looks only at the victors, who promise a bright future. Following is a brief personal account of one refugee recalling the final moments before departure. Translation.)

I will never forget that night. It happened that the last days of South Vietnam fell on the middle days of the third lunar month. The moon was bright and clear. Around noon on April 27th, we had heard that the South was preparing to surrender. So, although we were on a remote island, we could not put off leaving any longer. We were about to go away . . . forever. We were uneasy and restless – one seperated from his children, one from his parents.

It was quite late that night. We sat on a skirt of land by the edge of the jungle, talking to each other and looking out to sea. There on the water were fishing boats with their lamps shimmering. It occurred to us that the number of boats out there seemed greater than usual, all of them heading in the same direction, south.

What kinds of boats were they? Fish or shrimp boats of the local people going about their business? Boats of our frightened countrymen fanning out as they sought a way to escape on the ocean when they heard the fatal news? Was it really true that tonight there were more boats out than on previous nights? Nothing was certain. But at that time all of us felt we were witnessing something strange and unusual. And from that point, we kept our eyes glued to the dancing lights far out on the horizon.

From one hour to the next, boat after boat sailed out. The spectacle caused each of us to begin thinking about our personal situations. D-- and his wife exchanged a few words in a low voice; then they cried together.

We were leaving without all our families. As for D--, when he and his wife left Phu Quoc island with us, his parents, brothers and sisters had to organize their own escape by a small boat leaving Vung Tau. D-- thought of his relatives out there in the flickering lights of the sea. Perhaps his parents were there on one of those boats heading out yonder. They all entrusted their fate to one fragile boat, one point of light among the countless tiny meaningless lights far out. Could they make it? Would they ever meet again? Still, when they had parted, they had had no chance to say good-bye.

As the hour grew late, the moon became brighter, lighting up the surface of the sea and the wide jungle. We no longer said anything, but split up, not wanting to see each other's tears. That night D-- and his wife wept and wept.

PART 13: LEGACIES

A review of the legacies of the war, including life in Vietnam, boat people refugees, relations between Vietnam and the United States, genocide in Cambodia, American foreign policy, veterans' issues, MIAs, lessons and questions.

The Great Equalizer

Part 12 concluded with the North Vietnamese army celebrating the "happiest day of their lives," a day of "complete victory for the whole nation." They have just reunited their country and brought families back together for the first time in twenty years. South Vietnamese soldiers have surrendered and the people have been reassured about the future. The Communists never considered themselves aggressors, just good patriots who wanted to keep foreigners from trampling on the graves of their ancestors. Only the American imperialists have been vanquished. If some people were trying to flee the country, well, that is simply because they did not understand.

The *Television History* might have ended at that point, and, indeed it did for those who viewed the program before its public airing in the U.S. The last episode, "Legacies," was not even completed until sometime during the PBS broadcast in late 1983. As an integrated whole, the program would not have suffered if Part 13 had been omitted. By this time, the lessons have already been drawn out for the viewers. It would seem that there is nothing left to be said.

However, the PBS series promotes itself as an educational experience and in this day and age "educational" means leaving "open questions" so that the students can "make up their own minds" and teachers preserve the veneer of "impartiality."

357

In the case of the *Television History* this means adding one more episode to deal with the questions and concerns that have arisen after the war. Many faces appear on the screen, the so-called "talking heads" that prattle on without coherence in a confused jumble of thought fragments that do little to clarify post-war issues, but satisfy the producers' simple requirements for "balance."

For the first time in the entire series, we hear from veterans who do not belong to the antiwar movement, talk about war crimes, praise the enemy or impress upon the viewers how easy it was to buy dope in Vietnam. Still, their appearance comes too far late and is too brief to have much significance at this juncture. The antiwar veterans continue to get the final word.

Similarly, the Vietnamese refugees finally make a responsible appearance to discuss concentration camps, oppression and the difficult escape from their country. Their testimony even begins to look credible. Refugee Nguyen Muoi tells how he escaped from Vietnam with his family despite the knowledge that the trip would be "very dangerous." "But we had no choice," Muoi goes on, "There is only one choice – the choice between freedom or death." Although resettled in the U.S., Muoi hopes to return to Vietnam some day . . . but only if "my country is not Communist anymore."

Before Muoi there is Mary Truong, whose father bribed a North Vietnamese soldier so his family could escape. And young Nguyen Minh, who had been willing to give the Communists a chance, but later came to "realize a lot of terrible things," such as how the Communists tried to make people like "robots" to serve the Party.

A former teacher left Vietnam because the situation was getting "worse and worse." Two former South Vietnamese pilots relate their experiences in "re-education" camps. One had been stuffed into a small box for a week as a punishment for trying to catch a frog to eat. Once out of prison, the pilots knew they had to flee their homeland "at all price."

The price was great, as evidenced by the dazed and feeble boat people refugees interviewed as they reached land and safety. They had been at sea for 15 days, most of the time without food or water, and had survived attacks by pirates.

The narrator hums: "Life in post-war Vietnam was grim." He adds, too, that the people of Indochina were left "poverty-stricken, oppressed, and almost entirely dependent on the Soviet Union."

Before this information can sink in, however, the scene switches back to the patriotic followers of Ho Chi Minh. The viewers know them already. For twelve hours the audience has been fed hearty portions of their "nationalism" and heroic zeal. Officials and low-ranking cadres from the North and South have entertained us with their choreographed speeches about their love of country and desire to be free and independent of the imperialist aggressors. Generals and soldiers have serenaded us with patriotic lullabies. Films depicting the unanimous determination of the people have dazzled our eyes. Even Americans have told us of the super-nationalists who would toss off centuries of tradition in order to become village heroes. Now, their enthusiasm has been turned into action to rebuild their beloved homeland!

Old Nguyen Chi Thanh speaks from Lang Son on the Chinese border: "I want to remain forever in Lang Son. After me, my children; and after my children, my grandchildren . . . No matter how many times the foreign invaders come and destroy this place, I will continue to rebuild to remain here forever."

Capt. Cao Xuan Nghia, hero of the battle at Dien Bien Phu, wants to build a socialist nation and keep Vietnam unified for his children, grandchildren and their children after them.

Dr. Ton That Tung trolls, "My whole life and that which is most beautiful of my ideal are so closely connected with Vietnam. I can never leave her."

At this point the viewers might find themselves cross-eyed, for there are two contradictory pictures of the Communists being presented. With one eye, we behold straightforward, sincere and almost tender patriots who have graced our television screens throughtout this history of the war. But with the other eye we glimpse a different side of the Communists – corrupt, cruel, promising paradise but bringing hell. How does the PBS series reconcile these schizophrenic images?

It doesn't.

However, the series' producers do believe that Part 13 will prove their overall balance and show that the producers were not "duped"

(to use Stanley Karnow's term) by insidious Communist propaganda. They felt that by describing life in Communist Vietnam and
Cambodia they could placate those who might otherwise criticize
them as being pro-Communist or anti-American. They did, after all,
advise us to wait until the end of the program before making a
judgment.

[But the few moments given to the mention of re-education camps
and New Economic Zones are simply far too little far too late. After
watching for hours as the South Vietnamese people have been
insulted and the Americans treated with disdain while their enemy
calls them puppets and imperialists on public television, the viewers
can hardly be expected to fall on their knees in respectful homage
just because Richard Ellison had the good sense to interview boat
people.]

Even the little that is told is hardly adequate. The narrator:

"Tough Northern officials, determined to build a Communist
society, took over from their former Viet Cong comrades."

This begs for an explanation. For 12 hours all the viewers have
seen are scenes of perfect harmony and bliss between the revolutionaries of the North and South. Why the difference now? There is
no answer from PBS.

(Stanley Karnow attributes the change in this situation to
traditional conflicts between the two regions and suggests the U.S.
should have exploited these differences to seek a "sophisticated
diplomatic solution" to the war. (p. 37) The reader may note the
contradiction in Karnow's thinking. First, he told us that the U.S.
should have gone along with Ho Chi Minh and his followers; now he
says we should have helped the Southern revolutionaries *against* Ho
Chi Minh and his followers. In any case, the Chief Political Analyst
forgets his history. After assuming power in the North in 1953-54,
the Viet Minh proceeded to eliminate many of their former
supporters there for ideological reasons. The possibility that the
purge in the South 20 years later might have had something to do
with fanatical Communism is something Karnow refuses to
contemplate.)

["The bloodbath predicted by many – mass executions of political
opponents – did not take place in Vietnam."

Many thousands of Vietnamese disappeared after the fall of the

South and nobody knows what happened to them. According to Communist officials who have left the country, thousands of people were executed in the countryside, far from the probing eyes of foreign reporters. Likewise, Cambodians tell of mass executions of their people by the Vietnamese invaders in the provinces and villages. The Communists do not have a habit of publicizing their atrocities, but the PBS producers were satisfied to take their word.⌉

Still, what are the producers trying to prove by making such a statement in the first place? "The bloodbath predicted by many did not take place in Vietnam." One sees here an attempt – a rather weak one, at that – to make antiwar forecasters look good (they always said there would be no bloodbath, you know) and anti-Communist forecasters look bad. The last two words, "in Vietnam," are included as the producers avoid linking the horrors of Cambodia to the whole situation. The Vietnamese Communists retain their glossy image as moderates who never meant any harm, but were set upon by vicious America making nonsensical claims about blood-baths.

"One and a half million Southerners were forced to resettle in New Economic Zones."

⌈Even.this statement (with the admission that "the zones were remote and the land was often poor") has the edge taken off it by the remark that some people left these areas because they "found the work too hard and the diversions too few." There is no mention of malnutrition, disease, poor living conditions, the extent of forced labor that finds people digging canals or clearing bad land all day. We only hear that there were "too few diversions."⌉

As well, the series neglects to talk about the possibily half a million Vietnamese sent to Siberia and Eastern Europe as "hired" laborers to help Hanoi pay off its war debt to the Soviet Union. That, presumably, is inessential.

"(The new government) interned more than 200,000 political suspects in so-called 're-education camps' in the first 12 months of peace."

Again, the Communists are not boasting of their accomplishments in this field, although Pham Van Dong is said to have announced in 1978 that he had released one million prisoners from these camps, that number being 20 times more than his government admitted to having arrested. The series might have noted that among the "political suspects" arrested were Buddhist monks, Catholic priests, Christian ministers, teachers, intellectuals, former government officials, soldiers, former opponents of the Saigon regime, former Viet Cong, and many people with no particular ideological or political affiliation, but who just happened to be in the way. If these people do not perish from malnutrition, torture, or other forms of abuse, they are often driven to the depths of despair by their cruel masters. The producers who admire so much the "will power" of the Communists might stop and consider what prison guards tell their inmates in these camps: "If you work hard and have the will, you can make the stones turn into rice." (Karnow puts the number of prisoners in camps at 50,000 to 100,000, the lower of the commonly heard estimates. (p. 29) He discusses only camps in the South, as if no such thing ever existed in the North. Although he notes the abuses within the prisons, he still looks on the cheery side— the camps are "less savage than the methods of Stalin and Mao Zedong." Long live Ho Chi Minh!)

And the series says nothing about religious persecution, the outlawing of political parties, the closing down of newspapers and radio stations, the reorganization of the school system, the banning and confiscation of· "reactionary" books, a war crimes museum opened up in Saigon, the creation of neighborhood security groups, the absolute economic disaster that has befallen the country under the enlightened socialist leaders in their "agrarian revolution," the starvation that is a part of life in Vietnam... All of this escapes the PBS producers, who think only in terms of Nguyen Chi Thanh who swears he will never leave Vietnam. (One note of irony: During his trip to Vietnam, Karnow interviewed "a leathery old peasant by the name of Duong Van Khang" who told the Chief Correspondent that in the worst days under the Japanese in 1945 "so many of his fellow villagers died that 'we didn't have enough wood for coffins and buried them in bamboo mats'." (p. 144) The truth is that today in Vietnam people are "re-cycling" coffins, using them for one funeral and then saving them for another. See how life has progressed under Communism?)

By now, hundreds of thousands of people have fled Vietnam by sea and land to escape their liberators, just as their compatriots did in 1954 when the Communists took over the North. PBS might have found it interesting that these people have fled without the aid or encouragement of the CIA.

The series goes into the Khmer Rouge atrocities in Cambodia: mass executions, torture chambers, starvation – all of which took place despite the protests of consultant Gareth Porter. Hard-core antiwar activists shrug off the Communist brutality here by saying the whole thing would not have happened if it hadn't been for the Nixon Doctrine. PBS takes the same stance.

Meanwhile, the series all but ignores the murderous Vietnamese invasion of the country in 1978-79 when countless people died in the fighting or from starvation induced by the invasion. Since taking over the country, the Vietnamese have executed thousands of people, confiscated land, forced intermarriage with their soldiers and new "settlers," brought their language into the school system, transferred children to Vietnam and Moscow and completely taken over the Cambodian culture and traditions, replacing these with concepts of the "New Socialist Man," which allegedly have been so "successful" in Vietnam. By any measure, this might be called assimilation. The *Television History* says it is nothing more than an act of fervent "nationalism." Stanley Karnow explains: The Vietnamese "have never portrayed their invasion as a humanitarian venture designed to rescue the Cambodian people from almost certain genocide (under Pol Pot). Indeed, they privately admit, despite their knowledge of the holocaust, they refrained from acting. The real motive, they explain, was their concern that Pol Pot's forces, underwritten by China, intended to embark on a campaign to invade the Mekong Delta and other parts of Vietnam that had formerly belonged to the Cambodian empire. 'When we look at Cambodia,' a Vietnamese official in Hanoi told me, 'we see China, China, China'." (p. 45)

This is certainly not what the Vietnamese told the Cambodians. According to Khmer refugees, the Vietnamese claimed they were saving the people from the evil Pol Pot. In at least one case, a large group of people were expecting to be executed (the graves had already been dug) when just a few days before the fatal deadline the Vietnamese came to "save" them from that gruesome ordeal. The

Khmers claim the Vietnamese established a "contract" with the Heng Samrin government by which the Vietnamese would remain in Cambodia only until the Khmer could protect themselves, ie., until the Khmer Rouge were destroyed. This contract was soon modified to say that the Vietnamese would remain for one to five years until the situation improved. And later again, the "contract" was extended to 10-25 years.

One might take into account, too, the situation Cambodia found itself in just prior to the invasion. With a numerically smaller army, a starving population, and murderous internal divisions within the Party, Cambodia was hardly in a position to risk such a major military venture as an assault on Vietnam. If the Vietnamese refrained from halting the Pol Pot massacres earlier. that was because it was to Vietnam's advantage that as many Khmer as possible died before the invasion took place.

The Vietnamese "liberators" are clearly in Cambodia to stay. They do not hesitate to kill their enemies with chemical weapons, and tests for new weapons are being conducted on Cambodian children in the Hospital Sovietique in Phnom Penh, as well as on islands in the Mekong. The Vietnamese have robbed cities and towns of valuables, taking with them even a large gold statue of Pol Pot.

All this is overlooked by Stanley Karnow, whose journalistic nose failed to "sniff" deep changes in Cambodia, as it did in Vietnam. Likewise, the PBS producers could not "sniff" beyond the horror exhibits created by the Vietnamese to discover that the massacres have not stopped, but are now being carried out in the name of Ho Chi Minh.

And again, Laos totally escapes recognition as it suffers persecution and genocide at the hands of the heroic Vietnamese liberators. Dr. Ton That Tung appears on the series self-righteously denouncing the use of Agent Orange on his people without uttering a word of regret about his government's use of yellow rain on the Hmong. No excuse (not even "nationalism") is given for the Vietnamese conquest of Laos, which presumably did not happen. Once more, the bloodbath that accompanied the Communist takeover is disregarded, along with the realization that given the right technology, the Communists will do anything and commit any war crime to achieve their goals.

On the television series, the Communist atrocities are soon forgotten as the Vietnamese "patriots" appear once more to reassure us of their gentleness and sincerity. Col. Bui Tin has the final word, as he expresses a sentiment shared by Stanley Karnow: "If the French government and the various American administrations had been more reasonable, more understanding and more intelligent, then the war could have been avoided ... We never wanted to have a war."

The tragedy of post-war Indochina is thus conveniently blamed on the Americans. It was America's responsibility, America's stupidity, and now – the last message of the program – it is time for America's reconciliation with Vietnam.

Back in the U.S.A.

The post-war issues that arose in the U.S. are presented hastily in this last hour of the series. Pres. Carter gives a blanket pardon to draft evaders. Returnees are represented by Anthony Rodriguez, who sings the theme song of PBS' "legacies," namely "reconciliation." He is countered by POW Donald Rander, who is firm, but not too interested in reconciliation.

Carter sends delegates to Hanoi to seek an accounting of MIAs. Says Richard Holbrooke, Asst. Secty. of State at the time, the MIA issue was a "powerful, emotional issue which grabbed the souls of many Americans." This is followed by a scene of emotional Ann Griffiths, from the National League of Families, crying, "We want an accounting!" The critical issue of Hanoi's stubborn insistence on treating the victims of war as political pawns is brushed aside. The fact that France was still negotiating with Hanoi for its MIAs fully two decades after the First Indochina War ought to say something about the alleged sincerity of the Communists – at least the series portrays them as sincere for 12 hours.

Pham Van Dong comes to France to discuss establishing diplomatic relations with the U.S. He is met by hooting mobs of Vietnamese as he punctuates his optimism with a diabolical laugh – perhaps the only sincere noise uttered from his mouth in the entire series. Even this scene is included as a gimmick; Prod. Ellison wants to show his viewers that he knows what Pham Van Dong is really like and isn't letting himself be taken in by the old premier! Reader, are you impressed?

Richard Holbrooke returns on behalf of Stanley Karnow to say that Hanoi took "an idiotic position, in my view, a self-defeating position which the American public understandably and instantaneously rejected," namely that of tying diplomatic recognition to war reparations. By the time Hanoi wised up and dropped the demand, there were other complications. Not content to speak only for the American people (which he has done twice already), Holbrooke now speaks for the whole world (and Stanley Karnow in particular): "The boat people were pouring out in the Southeast Asian waters . . . and there was a world-wide uproar."

This writer does not recall any world-wide uproars about the boat people. In fact, there was a nasty stink in 1979 when Malaysia threatened to tow refugee boats out to sea if no one would accept any more refugees for resettlement. Even in 1984, the nations of the world are reluctant to take more refugees from the camps in Southeast Asia, and few governments (or media editorialists) are in an uproar over Hanoi's inhumane policies that have driven thousands of people away from their homeland. But Karnow and PBS are not interested in such mundane realities.

The narrator tells us that Hanoi viewed America's China initiative as "ironic," given past animosity between the two countries. Yet Hanoi's policies over the years have been loaded with ironies that are not singled out for amused attention by the narrator. Like crying about "imperialist aggression" and then invading two countries. Ironic? Not to Karnow and Ellison.

There follows a quick succession of opinions about the war.

Former Ambassador Elbridge Dubrow appears as a token to link the fall of South Vietnam to later U.S. setbacks in Angola, Yemen, Afghanistan and Iran. You can be sure he won't be heard from again.

Gen. Maxwell Taylor and Adm. Thomas Moorer are cleverly quoted out of context. Gen. Taylor is given wry ambiguity as he suggests the U.S. should know its allies, its enemies, and itself or else "keep out of this dirty business." Adm. Moorer comes off advocating the overthrow of governments.

Daniel Ellsberg concludes by remarking that the U.S. should

think "ten times before we arrogate to ourselves the right to kill anybody in a foreign country in order to determine the government of that country as we see fit." Presumably this caution does not extend to the Soviet Union or the Communist Vietnamese.

Next come the Vietnam vets, who return home to "indifference, hostility, or silence." In the context of the PBS series, the cold reception is related to the terrible war fought on behalf of America's erroneous policy, and to the shameful things the vets were supposed to have done in Vietnam.

Viewers are reminded of the "continuing spectacle of American impotence" and the "humiliation" in Iran as Vietnam veterans demand recognition for their sacrifices. Grave questions about Iran (America's commitment to support an ally, the issue of how a rational government deals with a fanatic revolutionary government that refuses to respect international laws) are ignored, although they bear directly on the "Vietnam experience."

Veterans describe symptoms of delayed stress, presumably brought about by the immoral actions they committed during the war. (One testimony comes from Jack Hill, who has been accused of gross atrocities at Thuy Bo; atrocities were, you may recall, just part of the procedure.)

Even war hero David Christian can do nothing but complain about the government. (The viewers may be suprised to see that the war did have heroes. It should be noted that Part 13 is one of television's forlorn attempts to "make up" for the industry's historical animosity toward the vets.) Christian touches on the matter of Agent Orange, typically used by antiwar stalwarts as a symbol of America's criminal war policy, now a symbol of the government's betrayal of the veterans.

The issue of Agent Orange and other chemical defoliants used in the war is a serious one and ought to be given responsible attention. In the PBS series, however, it is marred by the appearance of North Vietnamese "doctor" Ton That Tung, who supposedly represents the Vietnamese people, victims of America's imperialist war policy in general and America's criminal chemical war in particular. The absolute hypocrisy of Tung's testimony is completely lost on the crusading producers who see only their self-assigned moral obligation to expose the ills of American government and defend the

Vietnamese people without recognizing the dubious qualifications
of their spokesperson.

But there is more. The inevitable analogy between Vietnam and
Latin America is finally brought up with Pres. Reagan on one hand
declaring that Central America will not be another Vietnam,
although he refuses to commit himself on this; on the other hand
there are two members of Congress deploring the administration's
policy of "naivete" and "ignorance" (the latter side supported by
Stanley Karnow, who believes strongly in the theories of indigenous
revolution and America's arrogant "exceptionalism").

After a peculiar balancing act between statements by antiwar
activists and Vietnam veterans (suggesting that the two sides are
somehow reconciled at this time) the story shifts to veteran Robert
Muller, who visited Vietnam after the war. Although Muller's
attempts to achieve personal "closure" in relation to the war seem
sincere, one cannot help but be flabbergasted by the ludicrous scene
in which he has placed himself. Here he is moving through the
streets in the capital city of his former enemy. All around are gawky
North Vietnamese soldiers dressed in helmets and dust-colored
uniforms (in fact, there seem to be an unusual number of soldiers
present in this country supposedly at peace). Once boasting of how
many Americans they could kill with their bayonets, now they are
armed with balloons (yes, balloons!) as the "mingle" with the crowd.
Citizens who not so long ago were shaking their fists and insulting
the American pilots while cursing the "imperialist aggressors" who
were "trampling on the graves of their ancestors" are suddenly
stopping cordially and shaking hands with imperialist Muller in
what is supposed to be a spontaneous outburst of human warmth.
Through simple observation one can tell that the scene was set up
and Mr. Muller's good intentions were being taken advantage of by
the Communists in their never-ending campaign to portray themselves as poor, misunderstood revolutionaries in an unfriendly
world. Despite the disingenious nature of this film, the PBS
producers not only take it at face value, but promise the viewers that
this is what lies in store for Americans if we should just open up our
arms and embrace the followers of Ho Chi Minh!

As might be expected, the war and the series end with veterans
marching to the Vietnam memorial in Washington, D.C., leaving an

"open question" about the war. Although the problems and issues of the veterans deserve a good documentary series in themselves, they are buried here with the memorial, which is supposed to cure all ills and resolve all differences. As far as the producers are concerned, the open questions have already been answered.

The Legacy

But what, after all, has the war taught us? And what great lesson has been learned by watching the 13-hour PBS series, which cost four and a half million dollars and is allegedly the greatest documentary movie ever made?

As this writer sees it, the legacy is this: That the Communists can kill thousands of their people, lie to their own followers, cheat their friends, torture their enemies, invade their neighbors, exterminate at will, exploit the ideals and aspirations of their people, teach children to be killers and old people to prevaricate, cause parents to fear their offspring and children to denounce those who raised them, wipe out culture and faith, utilize every atrocity known to humanity and invent some of their own, slander, corrupt and subvert . . . and while they are doing these things, they can twist us around so that we call them heroes and make ourselves out to be criminals!

As Stanley Karnow and Richard Ellison will gladly attest, the Communists are very good psychologists.

Supplements

(Ed. – Former Navy lieutenant Ha Thuc Sinh spent five years in concentration camps after the fall of South Vietnam. He has written a number of songs dealing with life in the camps and in the South after the Communists gained control. Below is a translation of one of his songs, describing the loss of dignity a prisoner suffers in the camps. The author says that the Communists have turned evolution backwards, bringing people back to the existence of animals. Translation.)

Camp of Metamorphosis

Last night a young man of thirty years awoke
Suddenly and looked at his friends around him
Lying together like a heap of dried firewood.
As he lay there, he felt the earth cry out
    for the stink of flesh, bones and blood.
As he lay there, he felt a man's life
    was worth no more than rotten fruit.
    An insane power,
    Absurd crime,
    In the deep abyss within his soul
    The wind whirled and whirled.

Last night a young man of thirty years awoke
Suddenly and looked at his friends all around
Lying together like a heap of dried wood.
As he lay there, he felt all those of talent
    reduced to simple grains of rice.
As he lay there, he felt all human dreams
    preferring boiled manioc to spring.
    Dawn stirring,
    The twilight spreading,
    The hero of yesteryear curled
    Up in grim sleep.

The world grows narrow in this place,
    clouds pause and birds can go no further.
Civilization heads for the twilight of obscurity.
In this place, too, God is grieved, having placed
    Man above all other creatures.
The fire of Sodom is aflame somewhere.

Last night, a young man of thirty years awoke
Suddenly and looked at his friends all around
And he broke out in strange sobs.
As he lay there, from his lips
came unfamiliar sounds
As he lay there, upon his frame
new skin replaced the old.
The moon shone in
Where wild animals lay.
He was nowhere to be seen.
Only a mass of fresh animal fur.

(Ed. – Following is a story written by a refugee, Luu Thi Ky Nam, a former teacher who lived in Vietnam after the fall of her country. This article, which she wrote in English, tells of some of the changes that took place once the South was "liberated." Reprinted by permission of the author.)

As a student, I had never thought that someday I would be a teacher. I could say that I hated teaching because I had heard that students were easily forgetful. Teachers would not receive any gratitude, affection, or love from them. They just came and went thoughtlessly. But this was not true for me when I became a teacher. The time I lived close to my students was a happy time. I loved them like my little sisters. I treated them as my dear friends. They became a deeply important part of my life.

Time passed very fast. My school fell into the hands of the Communists. The yellow flower trees in the school yard were cut down and dug up. The new principal told us that we needed the space to grow sweet potatoes. I did not have time to watch my students walking, playing, or fooling around in the school yard. I did not even have time to talk with them any more. In the morning I had to teach classes. In the afternoon, I had to make banners, slogans for the school. Meetings occurred many times a week. We had to learn about the new doctrines, the new educational system.

In the evenings, besides doing lesson plans, sometimes we had to stay late at school to attend emergency meetings to welcome high ranking officers, who would come to visit our school the next morning. All of the teachers were exhausted from working too hard. I noticed some of my friends whose hair was turning grey after only half a year of working for the Communists. Now I had to believe that worry makes people's hair turn grey and makes people grow old faster. All of the teachers looked so wretched, worried, and frustrated. If we were not careful in what we said, we would lose our job and our families would be in danger.

The students now had to have physical exercises during break-time in the school yard. All of the class teachers were responsible for watching them to see whether they obeyed the school regulations or not. One day I saw one of my students still staying in the class. I asked her why she had not gone out for exercises. She told me she was too hungry to do it. She said that she had no breakfast. Every morning she had to save her own breakfast for her younger brothers. Exercises during breaktime did not build up any strength for the students since most of them had no breakfast before school. With living costs rising, their parents hardly made enough money to support the whole family in the worst economic situation Vietnam had ever known. Sometimes some of the students fainted during the exhausting exercises. Exercises, after all, help only when people have enough food for their bodies and at a proper time. The school leaders knew it, the Communists knew it, but they ignored it. They wanted the students to have no free time to talk with one another. They were afraid the students would be up to something against the government.

Every week the students had to do labor in the school – raising pigs, growing plants or vegetables, or knitting bamboo strips. Once a month, all students and teachers had to do labor far away from school such as digging canals or ditches in the countryside

In the educational system of the Communists, every lesson should go along with an ideological education. Once in one of my classes, after I taught my students about the Taj Mahal, I began to "indoctrinate": "In the old time of Feudalism, kings were inhuman; they exploited the labors of their people by forcing their people to build up such a luxurious tomb." Unexpectedly, one of my students raised her hand, "Teacher, what about the tomb of Uncle Ho Chi Minh?" I held my breath looking down at a Northern student sitting in the back of the class. I knew she was assigned here to follow up all the activities in my class in order to report them to the school principal. Her eyes were staring at me waiting. I was so frightened but I tried to keep my head. I said hesitantly, "Well, Uncle Ho's tomb was built by our people's volunteers. Our people were delighted to do it." After saying these disgusting words, I felt my ears and then, my two cheeks burning. Before, I had believed that teachers taught their students only the truth; now I heard myself lying to them cynically. I knew for sure that my students were looking at me with their mocking, resentful and displeased eyes. They did not dare burst out laughing, but in their eyes I felt their knowing smiles. I did not deserve to be their teacher any more! Unwillingly, we – teachers – became the symbols of the Communist regime. We had to say what they wanted us to say, teach what they wanted us to teach, and appear to think what they wanted us to think. Painfully we became our students' enemies! In some sense, I knew that they understood my terrible situation, but it was hard for them to control their emotions or reactions when they heard such untrue words. They and I would never sit together and talk openly as before. We did not dare to tell the truth to each other. We were losing each other. Everyone would become a lonely, small island to live with her own thoughts and feelings.

I happened to remember some sentences in the song "Sayonara" that one of my students sang for me, "No more we stopped to see pretty cherry blossoms! No more we're beneath the trees looking at the sky!" The cherry flowers were not the yellow flowers in our school yard but we meant it. I opened my eyes. The purple flowers were beautiful as ever above my head.

My eyes blurred.

(Ed. – Dr. Dang Kim Anh was born in 1941 in Hanh Thien village, Nam Dinh Province in Vietnam. In 1965 she graduated from Hanoi University and ten years later was sent to the South to serve as Secretary of the Party Committee for Cho Ray Hospital. Dr. Anh went to New Zealand in 1982 for training and in 1983 she led a delegation from Vietnam to receive further training in Holland.

That year she defected, asking political asylum. Earlier, her elder sister, Dang Kim Thu, also defected from Communist Vietnam. What makes this story particularly interesting is that Dr. Anh and her sister are nieces of Dang Xuan Khu, better known as Truong Chinh, First Party Secretary of the Socialist Republic of Vietnam. Dr. Anh was interviewed by the Western press. Below are excerpts from material provided by the European Free Youth Forces, Holland Section, and the Vietnamese Students and Compatriots Association in Liege. Translated from an article in *Doc Lap* magazine, October 1983, West Germany.)

Question: Could you please tell us what encouraged you to leave the Communists when you held a position of a privileged cadre with the Party and Government?
Answer: The reason was . . . to find Freedom! In the true meaning of the word. Yes, we were the privileged ones of the system. But like all other people, I cannot live in an atmosphere of oppression and fear where I do not have the freedom I would like. Furthermore, under the Communist system any Party element, even the exceptional, is looked at with suspicion and jealousy and given no real opportunity to contribute to the building of the nation. Everyone has the same concern . . . I have harbored such thoughts of the Communist system for some time. But the idea to dissociate myself from the system only began in 1975 when I was sent to work in the South as Party Committee Secretary for Cho Ray Hospital. The lives of the people all over the South, the advancement of the Southern people in technology, thought and culture forced me to think, to wonder . . . and this opened my eyes and my heart.

Q: What is the general idea of the Communist cadres in your group? And based on what factors and opportunities did you come to the decision to dissociate yourself from the Communists?
A: The majority of us have, as I said before, opened our eyes. Everyone hates the system. Everyone wants to break away from it. But no one dares open his mouth to express this. This shows the success of the Communists in managing the people to the point of terrorism so that it paralyzes all thoughts of opposition and breaking away. In the groups, everyone is suspicious and afraid of

the others, even within the same family.

Additionally, all still have families stuck in the country or they are concerned about the future once they decide to become political refugees in a country that is foreign to them . . . An appeal letter (from the Youth Forces) gave me faith and the attitude of choosing freedom.

Q. The Hanoi Communists like to propagandize about their strength. In your opinion, what actually are the Communists' most important weaknesses?
A: The strength of the Communists lies in their management of the people. (Intensive checks of ration papers help the Communists easily control and direct their stern machine.) The main weakness of the Communists today is the loss of confidence among the Party and government cadres. The majority of the cadres are painfully disappointed in the system and have come to the conclusion that their years of sacrifice and struggle have become meaningless. The loss of confidence is the most serious fear of the Vietnamese Communists. (The taking of the South was not a total victory for the North. On the contrary, it created for them a tense and difficult reaction.) Meanwhile, the resentment of the Northerners toward the system has a chance to explode. Especially among the families whose children were given to the war and now that "peace has returned" their boys are still fighting in the army. I firmly believe that if a resistance force won a few victories then all the people would rise up strongly to overthrow the inhuman, unfair and oppressive system.

Q: Please tell us about the present situation of the Communist Party in Vietnam. Are there power struggles and internal contradictions?
A: The Communists believe in dialectical materialism. How can they avoid conflicts and contradictions? Currently, there are five clear factions competing for power. These are: 1) the Le Duan faction with the internal Party mechanism; 2) the Truong Chinh faction with the military (with Van Tien Dung), the youth (Dang Quoc Bao) and culture (Vu Khien, or Dang Vu Khien); 3) the Le Duc Tho faction, leading the purging mechanism of the Party (apparently just purged); 4) the Pham Van Dong faction, with the

government organ; and 5) the Pham Hung faction of the South . . .
The strongest factions are those of Le Duan and Truong Chinh.
The weakest is Pham Hung's. But because of the psychological
influence of the masses and the world, none of the other four dares
eliminate the Pham Hung group.

*Q: If the Party has such clear contradictions and divisions . . . why
haven't the Communists been overthrown?*
A: Their collapse is just a matter of time. Although they have
contradictions and power struggles, at this time they all are aware
that they have many enemies, internal and external, so they must
accommodate in order to survive. As I said before, because their
system for managing the people is very sophisticated, the Vietnamese Communists for the time being have not been overthrown.
They will be toppled once there is strong resistance in a number
of cities.

CONCLUSION: LOSERS ARE PIRATES

As this book was going to print, PBS began airing the Vietnam documentary series for a second time. According to new reports, a few "minor corrections" have been made since the first showing, but essentially the program remains the same piece of "balanced" journalism viewers saw the first time around. In a June 26, 1984 memo from WGBH to PBS affiliate stations, the program's producers indicated that there were only five changes that needed to be made to "clarify meaning, eliminate ambiguity, and in one case, to correct an error of fact." Placed in the context of the series as a whole, these changes are indeed "minor," being, as they are, smothered by 13 hours of inaccurate and biased reportage. Even still, there is finality in the words of Richard Ellison who concluded his report by saying, "No further changes... have been made or are being contemplated."

It will take more than minor corrections to salvage the *Television History* and make it an acceptable documentary or worthwhile educational material. From the word "Go" the producers set off on the wrong track and they never got things together even at the very end. The errors in the program are not simply small, isolated mistakes that can easily be amended by changing a word or two or by selecting a different picture. They are fundamental distortions resulting from the attitudes of the producers which interfere with their judgment and sense of common decency. They are, as well, the consequence of careless research and reporting, symptoms of greater weaknesses in the journalistic profession.

The failures of the *Television History* are many and sometimes astonishing in their scope.

The program insults the people of Southeast Asia and makes a mockery of the suffering and grief they have endured as a result of war. The cultures and societies of these people have been defamed

377

through shallow generalizations that reflect negatively on them and reveal the inadequacies of the producers as historical chroniclers. The armies of the anti-Communist governments are deliberately maligned by means of degrading comments, faulty generalizations, and clever editing that add outrage to the already deep injury they have suffered in losing the war and their homelands to brutal aggressors. The victims of the war are further victimized by the condescending sympathy of the producers, who allow them to be used as puppets of propaganda, approved and supported by the Communist government of Vietnam which they know denies its citizens the right to express freely their true thoughts and feelings.

Likewise, the series treats the American soldiers with condescension bordering on contempt. The producers have deliberately selected scenes and images to coincide with specific themes they believe are representative of the U.S. armed forces. The soldiers are reduced to stereotypes, figures without personalities or individual qualities, no longer people, but "subjects" for superficial television research. As perpetrators of America's "immoral" war, the GIs are portrayed at first as vicious killers, then as victims of an indiscriminate war policy – the greater evil. They are the "villains" in a high technology war, yet at the same time naive stumblebums who were just doing what they were told. Only the "mature" theme of reconciliation saves them from complete condemnation.

The war policies, actions and atrocities of the Communists are played down to a minimum – almost to nonexistence. The viewer is never made aware of the countless instances of senseless brutality carried out by the Communists in their quest for power. Instead, the war is presented as an American atrocity where every action taken by the Americans or South Vietnamese contributes to the wicked quality of the conflict. For their part, the Communists were simply conducting an honorable revolution while fighting against the foreign aggressors. In the PBS series, the Allies can do no right; the Communists can do no wrong. The defeat of the Allies is now written in stone as the inevitable consequence of a tragic mistake.

In making this presentation, the producers of the series have made free use of inaccurate information, which originates from questionable sources, Communist propaganda films, interviews with "witnesses" who were rehearsed by their government officials, and the advice of consultants whose views have long been discredited. They have chosen to disregard the advice and suggestions of several of their own consultants while they persist in reporting the war through the distorted viewpoint of those who feel that the Communists truly liberated Southeast Asia from the evils of American foreign aggression.

At the same time, the producers have blatantly disregarded scores of responsible persons and heaps of recorded information for the simple reason that these people and this data contradict their preconceived notions about the war. While boasting of balance and objectivity, the producers have applied some of the most bizarre techniques to achieve their goals, including the comparison of an unverified account of U.S. Marines massacring 145 villagers near Danang with the known systematic executions of thousands of people by the Communists in Hue. Propaganda material has been placed on the same level as scholarly resources and Communist informants have been given greater credence than individuals who risked their lives fleeing the Communists.

Research for the program was narrowly confined to the space provided by the prejudices of the producers. Interviewees were abused through contrived editing. The concept of "theme" takes precedence over truth and impartiality. The effort to provide a supposedly "enlightened" moral message interferes with the recording of reality. The series evolves, then, not into a history, but a pictorial summary of the myths of the war, as related by an antiwar media that wishes to share its special insight with the world. So enchanted are these producers by their vision of the war that they cannot see beyond it to realize the truth is a much different story and the stars in their eyes are caused by the artificial lights created by their own fantasies.

All of this makes *Vietnam: A Television History* one of the most shameful products to come out of television broadcasting. The disgrace is compounded by the fact that the series was supported by public funds and advertised as an educational tool. In the end, the public is the victim of the legacy of post-war television journalism.

As for Stanley Karnow's companion book, little can be said. With all the author's political reverie, rambling monologue and buzzing quotations from personages great and small, some readers might be fooled into thinking the Chief Correspondent is actually saying something. However, when looking deeper, one finds only the erratic wandering of an aimless mind – sort of a journalistic James Joyce.

The bulky nature of Karnow's book should not imply there is worthwhile content. A saying goes: "A head, like a house, crammed full without order is only littered, not furnished." This might well describe Karnow's effort. As a history of the war, the volume leaves much to be desired. By this writer's observation, it has been utterly rejected by the Vietnamese refugees, who feel it is no true history of their people. For students of the war, the book has little value unless the reader is willing to spend hours checking the author's information, correcting inaccuracies and searching for more objective data. Still, the book is not completely worthless –the 700-page tome does make an impressive bookend.

Some critics have suggested that the *Television History* is an attempt to rewrite history, to revise the recording of events to fit the viewpoints of the producers. In a very broad sense this can be said of all historical accounts, which, quite naturally, reflect the perspective of each historian. This is true of white Americans who have their version of the Indian Wars in this nation's history. It is also true of the Vietnamese, who see the Trung Sisters as heroines while the Chinese call them barbarian renegades. The Vietnamese have a saying borrowed from the Chinese that expresses how perspective colors the historical record: "Winners are called kings; losers are pirates."

The PBS series is unique in that here the losers voluntarily castigate themselves, call themselves criminals and praise their enemy. The producers assign their own interpretation of the war to all Americans, making us all share guilt for the atrocity they allege the war really was. The fight for freedom against Communism is thus stripped of its nobility and America's mistakes in judgment are made to be worse than the Communists' brazen immorality.

This attitude stems from a moralistic pseudo-psychology that demands people constantly beat themselves over the head as a reminder of how evil they are while all the rest of the world is OK. In a curious way, the series resembles a Communist-style criticism session: Right in our own homes we are forced to watch helplessly as, one after one, accusers are presented, shaking their fists and calling us "murderers," "imperialists" and "pirates." Moving pictures drawn from all over the world have been carefully selected to substantiate these charges and heighten the drama. We are given a half-hearted opportunity to defend ourselves, but our testimony is edited and disposed of quickly as we are made to endure another barrage of incriminating evidence and more irate witnesses. Finally we break down, overcome with guilt and horror, obsessed with our wickedness. Yet even as our eyes are opened and we recognize the truth, a way out is offered us – confess and be reconciled! The burden is lifted as we embrace our enemy, pausing once in a while to beat ourselves on the head again so that we do not lose sight of our inherent wretchedness.

It is said that Lenin once remarked: "The capitalists will sell us the rope with which we will hang them."

The *Television History* is evidence that the capitalists will provide the money and the rope and then go out and hang themselves.

What, then, has PBS wrought? The 13-hour historical documentary on Vietnam is a failure as a history and a disaster as a documentary. It may arguably be described as an abuse of free speech. It does serve to show how much Americans still need to understand the war and how any understanding can become muddled by sloppy, opinionated journalism.

There are those who would ask if any journalist can produce an objective, knowledgeable and fair documentary about the war. This writer concedes that there is probably considerable plausibility to the suggestion that somewhere there is a journalist up to the task, just as there might be a Bigfoot or life on other planets. But this writer is not holding his breath in anticipation of that individual's emergence.

We may only hope that in the future, when the Indochina story is reviewed by scholars, historians, humanists and other interested parties, that it will be kept in mind that the war was not fought by ideologies and slogans, bombs and booby traps, or dollars and rubles. The war was fought by human beings, a fact that seems to get lost when one slogs through the morass of analyses, critiques, propaganda, denunciations and counter-denunciations. It is only when the war is returned to humanity that it will come into perspective and become, at long last, an educational experience rather than a flare of temper or soreness in the heart. Perhaps at that time we will be able to see that people do make errors in pursuit of noble goals, that there are both good and bad among us, that we are both wise and foolish, and that life cannot be adequately described in simple expressions and generalizations. When we finally bring the war back to humanity, then we may begin to understand it and ourselves. We may cease being pirates and begin being human.

APPENDIX

(Ed. - The Vietnamese refugees reacted against the PBS television series about the war in their country with anger and frustration. Below are some samples of Vietnamese reaction to the series. The Vietnamese Communist Army newspaper *Quan Doi Nhan Dan* reviewed the series in an article by Le Tien, of the Vietnamese Broadcasting Committee. That article is translated below. First there is an editorial commentary from the refugee magazine *Dan Toc*, printed in San Jose, which carried Le Tien's review in the fall of 1983. Translation.)

Special from *Dan Toc*:

> Those who call themselves "Anti-Communist Nationalists" and side with the "impartiality" of the series *Vietnam: A Television History,* please read this article.

Vietnam: A Television History
in the eyes of the Hanoi Communists

The Vietnamese refugees in America have only been able to see this documentary series since October, but it has already been shown by BBC in London in the middle of April and in Cannes (France) in early May this year.

In August 1983, *Quan Doi Nhan Dan* in Hanoi announced this series shown on the Vietnam TV station and the writer, Le Tien, of the VN Broadcasting Committee, praised the series as "the big event of 1983."

As we know, the series called a Vietnam history only shows a part of the truth and surely not all the truth, so once again it has created a bias about the VN war.

As evidence of this, we publish below an article by the Hanoi Communists where they see the series as a golden opportunity to propagandize for their system.

Before reading the enemy's material, with the spirit of anti-Communist nationalism, we wish to note a few primary ideas about the series:

1) The producers tried to appear fair, with no prejudice, but in fact they have, deliberately or by accident, upheld the inhuman government in Hanoi.

2) All the images of the Communist side were chosen by Hanoi, from materials to the characters and words spoken. The producers had only to select from the samples given them. This is history in the hands of the victors.

3) The images of the free world were taken from one huge store of all the European and American media, but in 30 years of war this material has been drowned in a defeatist and anti-war spirit.

4) The series sees the two wars against France and the U.S. as a Communist victory bringing independence to the country. The important thing is the result of each stage. After the French defeat in 1954, over one million Vietnamese left the Communists in the North with its murders, denunciations and purges to find freedom. After the South was taken, over one million crossed the sea for freedom, leaving a country free and independent in name, but actually enslaved. The slave system run by Vietnamese dragged our people into 20 years of war. In the past, in our worst days under the French, the farmers pulled plows behind buffalo and produced the second most rice in Southeast Asia (after Burma). Forty years later, under Communism, reunified and independent VN has become the poorest nation in the world, the whole country a prison with many concentration camps. They eat ersatz rice, sorghum, and pull the plows themselves. That is the price of the "heroic and sacred" war praised by the inhuman Communists and polished up by cinema philosophers in the U.S. and Europe in this film costing four and a half million dollars.

Following is the article from *Quan Doi Nhan Dan* (People's Army) August 1983.

DOCUMENTARY TV SERIES: VIETNAM
(Produced by Americans, English and French)

Coming up on the central television network and to be shown daily for half a month is a film series entitled: *Vietnam*, produced by major television organizations in the U.S., England and France. One might call this a pictorial summary of a stage of historical significance for the Vietnamese revolution, 30 years fighting to liberate our people (1945-1975).

The Big Event Of 1983

At 9:00 PM on April 11, 1983, Channel 4, BBC in London began airing the first part of the series entitled "The Vietnam Project," officially called "Vietnam: A Television History." On the days to follow, the series will be brought to the people of the U.S. and France. The press in Western Europe, North America, Canada, and Japan have commented on it in succession. By the close of April and the beginning of May in Cannes, France, a city which traditionally hosts an annual television fair and film festival, with representation by 125 countries interested in purchasing movies or making competition, everyone sought out the film *Vietnam* with acclaim. Since June, the series has been distributed widely with its screen time of 13 and a half hours divided into 12 parts. This is the greatest undertaking of a proper journalist documentary about Vietnam ever, a cooperative effort of three major television stations: BBC (England) (sic), Boston (U.S.), Antenne 2 (France). At first, production costs came to $10 million (U.S.) and the task had to be completed in two years in Boston, U.S.

The viewer is dazzled by facts of Vietnam recorded on priceless film footage gathered from 60 countries (among these were materials we provided from the archives in England, France, America, Japan, Sweden and Canada). A multitude of things we have heard or read about but never seen before follow one after the other, mixed with discussions, interviews with over 100 characters, including national leaders, generals, soldiers, farmers, scientists, victims . . . of the sides taking part in the war.

An outline of this series had been prepared since 1977. At that time, executive producer Richard Ellison, an American, was director and editor of major current events topics for CBS. He read and viewed films about Vietnam and in 1979 agreed to go to Europe to act as supervisor for current events programs. There he had the conditions to realize his plan. Richard invited Martin Smith – an Englishman – to be primary director, along with 50 scientific and historical researchers to work with the writers. A producer of documentaries, Mr. Smith is also a well-known newspaperman concerning the major topics of the world war and the foreign policies of different nations. The facts in Chile, Cuba, Nicaragua, the role of the U.S. intelligence agency in the overthrow (of governments), have been reproduced very "cleverly" (sic) by Smith in the film *Camera*, or *Secret Revealed*.

In 1981, as he began making this film, Smith went to Vietnam for two months gathering materials.

Recently, we contacted the heads of the Boston (U.S.) station, which holds distribution rights to the historical series on Vietnam, and they told us they had already informed the American people that the film was 810 minutes long and that such length was necessary because this is a problem of Vietnam, a problem of our age, the longest war of this century. Dir. Smith wrote: "... Because this was the most talked about and filmed war ever." The Boston station also said that up to that time, in a short period, besides television stations of different countries, many research institutes on foreign policy, defense, economics, science, military studies, and large universities in various countries were waiting to buy copies of the film. According to our agencies with responsibility in these matters, many of our foreign affairs cadres and compatriots abroad have inquired, "Do you know about this series back home?" It is a natural feeling, a proud feeling we share at this time.

Shining Heroic Epic Of Vietnam

It all begins with a picture of a youthful Ho Chi Minh leaving his country to look for a way to save the nation. He wrote newspapers, struggled and brought together the revolutionary organizations of the colonized people under France and composed *Judgment on Colonialism*. From there we see shots of contemporaries describing the suffering of a people who have lost their country, but who are also a people with a tradition of independence. The historical facts of the time before the uprising, the August 8th General Uprising, especially the bubbling revolutionary spectacle in Ho Chi Minh City (called Saigon at the time), the important processes as the Japanese surrendered and the allied army arrived, the rising up of the ones who sold out our country, harassing and destroying . . . these rare film footages are shown in Part 1, called *Roots of War.*

Part 2, *The War With France,* has scenes we have never seen before, such as the fighting of the National Defense Troops of the Hanoi self-defense force, Saigon at the end of 1946 and the beginning of 1947. We are moved to see Uncle Ho, humble, confident, in the midst of difficult negotiations with France. During those turbulent hours, Uncle talked to and mobilized our compatriots abroad. There are scenes we have never seen, as when Uncle rested in midsummer in Boulogne in Paris. He lay resting on a carpet of grass surrounded by the children of Vietnam far from their home. His brow is high and clear, but anyone watching can tell that he has a hundred matters on his mind, preparing the whole country for the upcoming resistance.

Part 3 is called *America's Mandarin,* with material concerning the interference of the U.S. in Vietnam. It tells of the disruption of peace and reunification of the country. Diem brutally repressed and failed.

America jumping into Vietnam is described in Part 4, *Johnson Steps In.* Parts 5, *America Takes Over Responsibility,* and 6, *Fragments of War,* make the viewer hate the atrocities of the Americans and the results of the war caused by the Americans. Our heroic battles and the terror of the enemy along with attractive scenes of the strategic Tet Mau Than attack are seen in Part 7, *Tet.*

The harsh pacification campaigns and the collapse of Vietnamization of the war are described in Part 8. And rare materials concerning Laos and Cambodia appear in Part 9, called *The Secret Wars.* The devil alliance between the U.S. and China and the treachery of the U.S. in negotiations with the Vietnamese come out in Part 10, *Peace is at Hand.* The viewer gets swept up with the crowds of American protestors, whirling around shouting against the war and the American leaders. That is Part 11, *The Front in the*

Heart of the U.S.. The conclusion of the war, the total victory and the reunification of the country make up Part 12, *End of the Tunnel.*

It is during the scene of the happy day of our great victory with firecrackers going off all around that the narrator concludes: "America will need many more years to bear the results of this war."

A Series For Our Time

It is not an accident that the world should view this as a series of major proportions. Through proper journalism, radical use of television symbols (carefully leading up to the facts through reports and accounts by the characters), the writers have created a series in the manner of a chronological history in pictures. The historical material leads us through the facts, flowing through each fact and opening up a huge space with depth from all sides related to the war. Professionally, they say this is the way to build up "depth of space" to raise high the stature of the facts. Techniques joining to create scenes parallel and symmetrical, the connecting of the front lines with the rear, leaders and ordinary people – these are used widely. We recognize in all twelve parts the image of Uncle Ho placed high with the greatest respect along with the victorious army: the heroic Vietnamese army and the heroic Vietnamese people.

Naturally, because of a passion for the facts, at times the series goes astray and takes a slump; to show objectively the producers used information sources of different sides, even to the point that in a number of instances its analysis is simplistic and incorrect. And although it is twelve parts long and 13 hours, the series cannot mention all the problems the 30 years of revolution brought to the people of Vietnam, and to the U.S. and all people.

Aside from these limitations, overall, this is a scientific artistic labor, a serious effort providing the world with a meaningful evaluation and understanding of Vietnam, to learn of the lessons of Vietnam. We see more clearly the topic of our "ten thousand day struggle, night and day never resting," very significantly brought out at this time, especially when people are still talking about "teaching Vietnam a second lesson!" The precious materials and convincing pictures of this television series have hot value for this age.

– Le Tien
Vietnam Broadcasting Committee

(Ed. - The following is an excerpt from an article by Nguyen Quoc Bao Anh, in *Vietnam Ngay Nay*, No. 21, Nov. 3, 1983, printed in Santa Ana, California. Translation.)

The PBS series *Vietnam: A Television History* shown the past few weeks is stirring up the indignation of the Vietnamese community in the United States, even though at the time of this writing only four of the thirteen parts in the series have been aired as PBS tries to introduce to the American viewers its look at the process of modern Vietnamese history.

This is their goal, but after only four parts the Vietnamese can already see clearly the intentions of the producers who have deliberately distorted the historical facts, brutally and brazenly trampling on the suffering and grief of millions of Vietnamese who have endured Communism, while utilizing the most forceful and effective communications medium to bring to the American public a totally false view of Vietnamese history and of the deepest ideas and aspirations of our people for more than half a century. To put it simply: the series plays a propaganda role benefitting the Vietnamese Communists, thereby indirectly, but insolently, trampling on the righteous cause of millions of people – the Vietnamese who for freedom must live in exile all around the world.

(Ed. - The following comments concerning the PBS series are made by composer Pham Duy, who was interviewed for the show and quoted in Part 2, *The First Vietnam War*. Translation.)

OPINION
by Pham Duy

This series is not simply the co-production of American, English and French television stations. The Communist government in Hanoi is also a co-producer, since it provided much of the material about Vietnam used in the series. It is common knowledge that the Communists use literature, poetry, music, theater, television and photography only to propagandize. We may then conclude that this series is a propaganda film for the Communists. The producers have deliberately deceived the American, British and French people. Thus, the credits should have included the Vietnamese Communists as co-producers. The note that Ngo Vinh Long is a private individual is a deception as if the American, English and French people are stupid and blind! Not one Vietnamese is deceived by this, because all know full well the propaganda game being played!

The series wants to be seen as a historical documentary, but, alas, it is no more than a distortion of history. World history after World War II has been a conflict between the U.S. and the U.S.S.R. and the war in Vietnam was a war on behalf of those two countries. The Vietnamese (and Cambodians and Lao) killed each other with American and Soviet weapons. On one side was the advance post in opposition to the Communists; on the other side the thrust of Socialism. Still, it was called the "Vietnam War"! It should be called by its true name: "Vietnam – a War on Behalf of the Capitalist and Communist Blocs." Furthermore, the capitalist world is losing to the Communists because it is cowardly, lazy, eager for life and fearful of death, and especially because there are individuals in the Free World who – through naivete or deliberation – demonstrate, write, and produce films beneficial to the Communists.

(Ed. – One commentator, Kieu Phong, wrote several critical reviews of the series. Below is one of them, published in various Vietnamese newspapers in October and November 1983. Translation.)

THE WAR IN SOUTHEAST ASIA ON TELEVISION:
AN EDUCATION OR ... ?

by Kieu Phong

The Vietnamese living in the United States are expressing their outrage and frustration over the documentary series currently being shown on PBS, namely *Vietnam: A Television History.*

This anger, brought out in letters and activities expressing opposition to the content of the series, echoes the protest made against another series, *Vietnam: The Ten Thousand Day War,* which has already been aired on some local stations in the country. At first, the Vietnamese had planned to wait patiently until the last of the 13 parts is broadcast before making public comment.

At the time of this writing, five parts have so far been shown and already Vietnamese are writing to their television stations and speaking to local newspapers to inform them of their feelings about the program.

Perhaps you are asking: Are they not being too hasty in making any judgments about the series.

The answer is No. The focus of this wave of protest from the Vietnamese rests on the method used by the producer in developing the series. One might even say that the problem could be seen even before the *Television History* reached the homes of the American public.

In making this series, the producers relied on a translator with a notorious reputation among the Vietnamese in the United States. Not only has this individual served as translator for the series, but he has also been used as a consultant in the gathering of resources. This in itself tells us something about the inclinations of the producers.

Furthermore, the production crew was permitted to make a visit to Vietnam to "collect historical data," as if one might expect to find the truth about the war hidden somewhere in a country run by brutal dictators who have a long history of covering up their atrocities from public view.

After several requests and some time of waiting, in 1981 the
producers of the *Television History* were permitted to enter
Vietnam. It was not until the following year that Hanoi allowed the
cameramen in to take their shots in various places around the
country. It is not foolish to presume that in the interim Hanoi had
finished setting the stage for everything the producers were to see
and prepared all the "historical data" that was to be presented.

Thus far in the program, we have seen interviews with Premier
Pham Van Dong and high military officials. We have also seen a few
people who appear to be peasants coming right out and condemning
the U.S. There has been quite a bit of film produced by Hanoi
brought in to complement this "historical data" for the documentary.

There are some Americans who live with the illusion that if you
don't give the Communists a hard time, but are nice to them, they
will be nice to you in return. They tell us, for instance, that if we aim
for peace and freeze deployment of nuclear weapons then the
Soviets would never dare threaten us with these destructive arms. I
doubt these people can sympathize with the Vietnamese and share
their anger over this film.

On the other hand, there are Americans who, while sometimes
forgetting the lessons of the past, nonetheless recall vaguely that
the Communists use deception as the basis for their foreign policies.
Perhaps these Americans will not find it hard to understand why the
refugees are furious about this program.

Fortunately for us, there was an incident not too long ago which
helped refresh our memories about the type of "historical docu-
menting" performed by the Soviets in describing events connected
to them. I'm speaking of the "truth" that the Kremlin hoped we
would swallow regarding the downing of the Korean passenger
plane, KAL 007, last September.

Let us imagine that Executive Producer Richard Ellison had been
hired by PBS to develop a documentary concerning this incident.
They handed him $4.6 million and asked him to do the same type of
job on it that he did with the war in Southeast Asia.

First, he would dig up a member of the KGB to act as translator
and resource consultant for the program. Then he would secure
permission from the Soviets to enter their country and interview

several high-ups in the Kremlin to get the "historical truth." To make the story more down-to-earth and realistic, Ellison would go out and interview a number of "Russian peasants," who might describe how the skies are always filled with American spy planes buzzing overhead. The producers would not stop to note that perhaps some of these "peasants" were undercover agents placed on-the-spot just for the interview while the real farmers who were there could only echo the "truths" that had been drilled into them beforehand by the government.

As a special going-away present, the Kremlin would give Producer Ellison a file of "historical movies" made by Moscow itself to facilitate presentation of his program. He would be happy to accept these films along with his other resource material.

Thus, one day we should see on TV a new production from PBS: *KAL 007: A Television History!*

The viewers at home, curious about this historical occurrence, would sit riveted to their chairs gaping at super-close-ups of Comrade Andropov railing at the American president and the CIA, crying out in indignation how they are the true culprits in the terrible accident, how the Soviet pilot assumed the jetliner was a spyplane because it had the number "007" on the side, and so on ... Then a Soviet general would appear, telling the "truth" about how the plane flew around and around in circles over Soviet territory on its cunning spy mission. A parade of Russian "peasants" would follow one after another with their testimony to teach the American people a "historical lesson": that the U.S. government sacrificed the lives of 269 innocent people in carrying out a clandestine mission over the Soviet Union.

Of course, the producers would reserve a few minutes to show selected American politicians with divergent viewpoints about the affair in order to "balance out" the presentation.

But when it came time to show the "historical films" provided by Moscow, the narrator would have nothing to say regarding the truth or deception in that sort of film and thus the Kremlin's propaganda, rejecting any guilt and denouncing the U.S., would be treated with the same respect as more serious research data.

I cannot predict how the American public would react to such a presentation. But I do know that more than 60 American families would be irate – namely, the families of the victims of this atrocity. It is difficult to sit still when you see murderers appearing before you on television denying any wrongdoing on their part, while throwing the blame on the U.S. president and government, thereby slandering the victims as spies who deserved to be executed. I would guess that they would be angry, too, at those who created the opportunity for the murderers to stand before the public with their insulting remarks. Meanwhile, all of this would be seen as a "historical documentary," a lesson for the American people.

Those who would be upset with such a production are those who will sympathize with the Vietnamese living in this country. *Vietnam: A Television History* has given the murderers in Hanoi a marvelous opportunity to give a good impression of themselves while offending their victims. Like the 60 families of the American victims of the Korean airliner, the Vietnamese living in the U.S. have relatives who were murdered by the Communists. Some of them have died in the war, in concentration camps and prisons, by execution and starvation, and so on. Hundreds of thousands of others have perished while trying to escape their country and the brutal regime in power there; these share a grave with the 269 victims of the Korean plane downing – the bottom of the sea.

(Ed. – On December 9, 1983, a group of Vietnamese refugees in San Diego staged a demonstration with three purposes: first, to mark the anniversary of the signing of the Declaration of Human Rights and call for an accounting of human rights violations in Vietnam; second, to honor the American veterans who served in Vietnam, especially those who gave their lives in the war; and third, to protest the PBS television series. Following is an address presented at this demonstration by Ha Thuc Sinh, a writer and former naval lieutenant who spent five years in the Communist prison system. Translation.)

*Address by Ha Thuc Sinh on the 35th Anniversary of the
Signing of the International Declaration of Human Rights*

Ladies and Gentlemen:

Today, December 9, 1983, is the day before the 35th Anniversary of the International Declaration of Human Rights. We Vietnamese refugees of Communism living in San Diego gather here today to make our contribution to the statement of the great authors of that declaration. At the same time, we solemnly commemorate all those soldiers around the world who have sacrificed their lives fighting the dictatorships that murder, limit and oppress the bodies and dignity of people, as we try to bring ourselves back to that status where we might live as true human beings based on freedom and equality.

Today also marks a special time in the year when we, the Vietnamese people, not accustomed to being ungrateful, can meet together to thank our American friends who have actively supported our people with men and material in the war for freedom. More especially, we wish to express our deepest thanks to the families of the more than 50,000 American young men who followed the sacred call to defend freedom and human rights by going to Vietnam, fighting side-by-side with our people and sacrificing their lives for noble goals in that land. Finally, we cannot forget to thank the government, the Congress, and the people of the United States who have opened their arms to accept us from the refugee camps in Southeast Asia and helped us secure and establish our new lives since April 1975.

Ladies and Gentlemen:

As political refugees, we are always extremely aware of our duty to our new society in which we enjoy freedom. Today, as well based on that freedom and equality which have been established by the Constitution to be enjoyed by all citizens and immigrants, the Vietnamese community in San Diego publicly announces a political stance in opposition to the television series called *Vietnam: A Television History*. The film is largely based on propaganda material from the international communists aimed at slandering the cause of the struggle for freedom of the Vietnamese people and the Allied forces, especially the United States. By this, the blood shed by the Vietnamese on the advance guard of the Free World is equated with the blood of mercenaries, while the U.S. armed forces are described as invaders and pirates! Ironically, this film is being presented on National Public Television and funded by the tax money of the American people, including relatives of the 50,000 Americans who gave their lives for the Vietnamese nation and the Vietnamese living in the United States.

Disguised as popular education regarding the history of the Vietnam war, National Public Television has publicly joined hands with the "false historians" in propagandizing for the Communists through the U.S. communications media!

Today, at this demonstration, we, the Vietnamese community in San Diego, after meetings, research and discussion, by common consent make the following decisions. We categorically protest support for Communist propaganda by the producers and broadcasters of the series *Vietnam: A Television History* on National Public Television; the slander and distortion of the cause and stance opposing the Communists taken by the Vietnamese people and the Allied forces; National Television's use of tax money from the people for noneducational purposes.

We earnestly appeal to the government, Congress and the American people to review the position and methods of responsible officials in the Public Broadcasting System; to the American people, political, cultural, social and religious groups, especially the Vietnam veterans associations, on behalf of the conscience and honor of the American people and the nation, to support us in protesting this series; to officials in charge of National Public Television to use the media at their disposal to publicly express their regret to the anti-communist Vietnamese community living in the United States as refugees and apologize to the families whose sons have sacrificed themselves for the cause of freedom in Vietnam (should those families agree to accept an apology).

Ladies and Gentlemen:

The war against the Communists is fought not only in Vietnam, but all over the world to the point of a life-or-death struggle. With experience not limited to books, but costing us our own blood in over twenty years of struggle against the Communists, our people are very aware of the fact that in this war military weapons are not the key to victory. Rather, the key involves making clear the cause of freedom to achieve the active support of the people. Victory is not assured in the end if one continues to denigrate the value of propaganda while respecting too much the freedom of our internal enemies as well as those who are less aware in the propaganda war.

Ladies and Gentlemen:
The Vietnamese people have a tradition respecting the truth and honoring those who have died for truth. Today, the Vietnamese refugee community hopes that the people of the United States who clearly understand the ideal of fighting the Communists to defend freedom and human rights for our people for the past two decades will raise their voices with ours to defend the truth, to demand human rights for those people now being oppressed by a dictatorial system and to bring honor and peace to all peoples of the world.

(Ed. – Also present at this demonstration was this writer, who gave a brief speech criticizing the PBS series. The main portion of that speech is given below.)

At this time, Public Television stations across the country are broadcasting a 13-part series about the war in Southeast Asia entitled *Vietnam: A Television History.* So far, the program has run through eleven of the thirteen parts, but even from the beginning it has been clear to many viewers that the information presented on the show is not accurate or a true reflection of the war and the entire situation of Southeast Asia over the past half century.

Although the program makes pretense of balance and impartiality, in fact it is quite the opposite. The series presents information that is sometimes partly true, other times distorted, and quite often completely erroneous. It is an attempt not to review history, but instead to rewrite it, to resculpture it according to the views and interpretations of the producers. The viewers are not being given the facts. They are being given bias.

Among its many failings, the series strives to paint a very pretty picture of the Communist movement in Vietnam. It portrays the Communist leaders as heroes and victims of American policy. It ignores the countless atrocities and violations of human rights that have occurred in Vietnam, Cambodia and Laos over the past fifty years. It downplays the Communists' use of terrorism and deception in order to achieve their ends. And it denies the people who have lived under Communism the opportunity to describe the reality of that brutal and oppressive system.

At the same time, the television program takes a condescending look at the people of Vietnam, Cambodia and Laos. When it does not ignore them completely, it tends to present them in an unfavorable light or in any such way as will promote the theories and assumptions of the producers. And, most tragic of all, the series insults the millions who have died or are now suffering imprisonment, torture and persecution because they have opposed Communism.

America, too, has been insulted by a narrow and superficial portrayal of the war and America's part in it. Our soldiers have been offended and our nation as a whole has suffered the abuse of shallow criticism and judgmentalism. Now, we endure one more abuse as we are asked to accept as truth information which is incomplete and inaccurate in the form of a so-called "educational" program. Through the use of distorted, biased and selective information, this series tramples on the dignity of the victims of the war and Communism in Southeast Asia. Those who now lie in their graves or suffer in concentration camps or prisons cannot express their feelings to the world concerning the reality of life in a Communist land. We who enjoy freedom must then stand up on their behalf and declare to the world the truth which cannot be erased by distortion and propaganda. For this truth, we protest the Vietnam television series being presented by Public Television and make clear our dissatisfaction with the program and its producers. We ask only for truth and fairness to preserve the dignity of the ideal of freedom.

Freedom and I

Freedom is like a song sung
From the most exalted love.
It is the tears needed for
A man to live his life.
It is proof to me
That there is a heart in man.

Freedom is like salt.
It is like drinking water,
The nutrient substance of the world,
From the time we are but dust
And a mother shares her body
That we might taste life for ourselves.

Though it is a life filled with changes
          and bitterness,
Of hard labor or exile,
Though the night is black
And I walk the line over the abyss,
Still the words I sing echo only freedom!

And one day when my hair is a cloud of white
And the earth calls out to me
And when my heartbeats become lazy,
Then will freedom leave me
          with a rosy smile on my lips.

— Ha Thuc Sinh

BIBLIOGRAPHY

*Following is a list of some of the principal books
and materials used in this study:*

Braestrup, Peter, *Big Story: How the American Press & Television Reported and Interpreted the Crisis of Tet 1968 in Vietnam and Washington* (Abridged Edition), Yale U. Press, 1983

Dawson, Alan, *55 Days: The Fall of South Vietnam*, Prentice-Hall, Inc., 1977

Denton, Jeremiah A., Jr., *When Hell Was in Session*, Reader's Digest Press, 1976

Dooley, Dr. Tom, *Deliver Us From Evil*, Farrar, Staus & Giroux, 1956

Elegant, Robert, "How to Lose a War", *Encounter*, August 1981, London

Fall, Bernard B., *Anatomy of a Crisis: The Story of the Laotian Crisis of 1960-1961*, Doubleday and Co., 1969

–, *The Two Vietnams: A Political and Military Analysis*, Frederick A. Praeger, 1967

Fishel, Wesley, Ed., *Vietnam: Anatomy of a Conflict*, F. E. Peacock Inc., 1968

Foreign Area Studies, *Area Handbook for Laos*, American U. Press, Washington, D.C., 1972

–, *Area Handbook for the Khmer Republic (Cambodia)*, American University Press, Washington, D.C., 1972

Goodman, Allan, *The Lost Peace*, Hoover Institute Press, 1978

Hoang Van Chi, *From Colonialism to Communism: A Case History of North Vietnam*, Frederick A. Praeger, 1964

Hosmer, Stephen T., *Viet Cong Repression and Its Implications for the Future*, Rand Corp., Heath Lexington Books, 1970

Hubbell, John G., *P.O.W.: A Definitive History of the American P.O.W. Experience in Vietnam 1964-1973*, Reader's Digest Press, 1976

Kosut, Hal, Ed., *Cambodia and the Vietnam War*, Facts on File, 1971

Lewy, Guenter, *America in Vietnam*, Oxford U. Press, 1978

Nixon, Richard, *RN: The Memoirs of Richard Nixon*, Grosset and Dunlap, 1978

Pike, Douglas, *History of Vietnamese Communism 1925-1976*, Hoover Institute Press, 1978

–, *Viet Cong*, M.I.T. Press, 1966

Podhoretz, Norman, *Why We Were In Vietnam*, Simon and Schuster, 1982

Ponchaud, Francois, *Cambodia: Year Zero*, (tr. Nancy Amphoux), Holt, Rinehart and Winston, 1977

Radvanyi, Janos, *Delusion and Reality: Gambits, Hoaxes and Diplomatic One-Upmanship in Vietnam*, Gateway Ed., Ltd., 1978

Risner, Robinson, *The Passing of the Night*, Random House, 1973

Santoli, Al, *Everything We Had: An Oral History of the Vietnam War By 33 American Soldiers Who Fought It*, Random House, 1981

Sobel, Lester, Ed., *South Vietnam: U.S.-Communist Confrontation in Southeast Asia*, Facts on File, 1961-1973

Stanton, Shelby, *Vietnam: Order of Battle*, U.S. News Books, 1981

Strauz-Hupe, Robert; Kintner, William R.; Dougherty, James E.; Cottrell, Alvin J.; *Protracted Conflict*, Harper and Rowe Publ., 1963

Thee, Marik, *Notes of a Witness: Laos and the Second Indochinese War*, Random House, 1973

Thompson, Sir Robert, *Defeating Communist Insurgency: The Lessons of Malaya and Vietnam*, Praeger Publ., 1966

Toyle, Hugh, *Laos: Buffer State or Battleground*, Oxford University Press, 1968

Warner, Denis, *Certain Victory: How Hanoi Won the War*, Sheed Andrews and McMeel, Inc., 1977

West, F. J., *The Village*, Harper and Rowe, 1972

Westmoreland, William C., *A Soldier Reports*, Doubleday and Co., Inc., 1976

Woodrow Wilson International Center for Scholars, *Some Lessons and Non-Lessons of Vietnam: Conference Report*, 1983